Regulating reproduction

MANCHESTER
UNIVERSITY PRESS

To Greg for his love, consideration, support and advice

Regulating reproduction

A century of conflict in Britain and France

MELANIE LATHAM

MANCHESTER UNIVERSITY PRESS
Manchester and New York

distributed exclusively in the USA by Palgrave

Published by Manchester University Press
Oxford Road, Manchester M13 9NR, UK
and Room 400, 175 Fifth Avenue, New York, NY 10010, USA
www.manchesteruniversitypress.co.uk

Distributed exclusively in the USA by
Palgrave, Inc., 175 Fifth Avenue, New York, NY 10010, USA

Distributed exclusively in Canada by
UBC Press, University of British Columbia, 2029 West Mall,
Vancouver, BC, Canada V6T 1Z2

British Library Cataloguing-in-Publication Data
A catalogue record for this book is available from the British Library

Library of Congress Cataloging-in-Publication Data applied for

ISBN   0 7190 5699 3   *hardback*

First published 2002

10 09 08 07 06 05 04 03 02   10 9 8 7 6 5 4 3 2 1

Typeset by Carnegie Publishing, Lancaster
Printed in Great Britain by
Biddles Ltd, Guildford and King's Lynn

Contents

Preface and acknowledgements

This book grew out of doctoral research conducted at the University of Manchester between 1989 and 1993 under the supervision of Margot Brazier and Jill Lovecy. I am extremely grateful for their enthusiasm and support.

The book also owes much to the personal interviews I was able to undertake both in France and Britain. Those who kindly agreed to be interviewed were extremely informative and their insights genuinely helpful. It is therefore a pleasure to record my thanks to Janine-Mossuz Lavau, Mariette Sineau, Simone Novaes-Bateman, Françoise Laborie, Michèle Fellous, Maître Michel Grimaldi, Guy Braibant (Conseiller d'Etat), Cécile Dauphin, Odile Dhavernas, Frédérique Dreifuss-Netter, Phillipe Granet, Pierre Jouannet and Naomi Pfeffer. In addition, numerous groups and individuals were generous enough to provide informative answers to written questions, namely the Abortion Law Reform Association, Amy Mazur, Anne Fagot-Largeault, Arlette Farge, the British Pregnancy Advisory Service, Carol Smart, CNIDF, Co-ord, the Family Planning Association, Françoise Laborie, Geneviève Fraise, Jane Jenson, John Bell, Joni Lovenduski, Labour Abortion Rights Campaign, LIFE, the National Abortion Campaign, PROGRESS, Roy Cunningham, Socialist International WOMEN, Women In Medicine, and Yvette Roudy (Ancienne Ministre Députée-Maire de Lisieux).

I would also like to thank some of my friends and colleagues who share my enthusiasm for the subject of women's healthcare rights and who have been both helpful and inspirational: Jo Bridgeman, Tammy Hervey, Kirsty Keywood, Maxine Lattimer, Ellie Lee, Siobhan Leonard, Jean McHale, Sue Millns, Derek Morgan, Katharine O'Donovan, Aurora Plomer and Sally Sheldon.

Special thanks must go to Marie Fox who has spent much time reading, commenting on and encouraging me to complete the book in its final stages. Any omissions or errors are of course mine. To the best of my ability I have referred to the law as in force in September 2001.

Melanie Latham

List of abbreviations

AI	artificial insemination
AID	artificial insemination by donor
AIH	artificial insemination by husband
ALRA	Abortion Law Reform Association
ANCIC	Association Nationale des Centres d'IVG
ANEA	Association Nationale pour l'Etude de l'Avortement
ANESV	Association Nationale pour l'Etude de la Stérilisation Volontaire
ANM	Académie Nationale de Médecine
ART	assisted reproductive technique
BAAF	British Agencies for Adoption and Fostering
BCC	Birth Control Campaign
BCT	Birth Control Trust
BMA	British Medical Association
BPAS	British Pregnancy Advisory Service
CA	Court of Appeal
CAC	Campaign Against the Corrie Bill
CADI	Campaign for Access to Donor Insemination
Cass.	Cour de cassation
Cass. civ.	Chambre civile de la Cour de cassation
CCNE	Comité Consultatif National d'Ethique pour les sciences de la vie et de la santé
C.E.	Conseil d'Etat
CECOS	Centre d'Etude et de Conservation de la Sperme
CERES	Campaign for Ethics in Research
CFDT	Confédération Française Démocratique du Travail
CFTC	Confédération Française des Travailleurs Chrétiens
CGT	Confédération Générale du Travail
Ch.	Chambre (Court)
CHU	Centre Hospitalier Unitaire
CNMBR	Commission Nationale de Médecine et de Biologie de la Reproduction

CNMBRDP   Conseil National de Médecine et de Biologie de la
             Reproduction et du Diagnostic Prénatal
CNRS   Centre national de recherche scientifique
Cons. const Conseil constitutionnel
Coord   Coordinating Committee for the Defence of the 1967 Act
COTS   Childlessness Overcome Through Surrogacy
Crim.   French Criminal Court
D.   Recueil Dalloz
D and C   Dilatation and Curettage
DHA   district health authority
DHSS   Department of Health and Social Security
DI   donor insemination
ECHR   European Convention on Human Rights
FACT   Fertility Action and Campaign for Treatment
FINRRAGE   Feminist International Network on Reproductive Rights and
             Genetic Engineering
FPA   Family Planning Association
GEFV   Groupe d'Etude de la Fécondation in vitro
GIFT   gamete intra-fallopian transfer
GIS   Groupe Information Santé
GMC   General Medical Council
GP   general practitioner
GP/Gaz. Pal Gazette du Palais
HFEA/HUFEA   Human Fertilisation and Embryology Authority
HL   House of Lords
ICSI   intra-cytoplasmic sperm injection
ILA   Interim Licensing Authorit
INSERM   Institut National de la Santé et de la Recherche Scientifique
IPPF   International Planned Parenthood Federation
IUD   intra-uterine device
IVF   *in vitro* fertilisation
IVG   intérruption volontaire de grossesse
J.   Justice
JCP   Semaine Juridique (Jurisclasseur périodique)
L.J.   Lord Justice
LARC   Labour Abortion Rights Campaign
LCR   Ligue Communiste Révolutionnaire
LHA   local health authority
MFPF   Mouvement Français pour le Planning Familial
MLAC   Mouvement pour la Libéralisation de l'Avortement et de la
             Contraception

MLF	Mouvement de Libération des Femmes
MOH	Ministry of Health
MP	Member of Parliament
MRC	Medical Research Council
NAC	National Abortion Campaign
NBCC	National Birth Control Council
NHS	National Health Service
NRT	new reproductive technology
NSM	new social movement
OPECST	Office Parlementaire d'Evaluation des Choix Scientifiques et Technologiques
OTC	over the counter
PAS	Pregnancy Advisory Service
PCF	Parti Communiste Français
PID	Pre-implantation genetic diagnosis
PMA	Procréation Médicalement Assistée
POS	Political opportunity structure
PS	Parti Socialiste
PSU	Parti Socialiste Unifié
RCN	Royal College of Nursing
RCOG	Royal College of Obstetricians and Gynaecologists
RHA	regional health authority
RMP	registered medical practitioner
RM-PA	Royal Medico-Psychological Association
SLA	Statutory Licensing Authority
Somm.	Sommaire
SPUC	Society for the Protection of the Unborn Child
TGI	Tribunal de Grande Instance
UDF	Union pour Démocratie Française
UDR	Union des Démocrates pour la République
VLA	Voluntary Licensing Authority
WGNRR	Women's Global Network on Reproductive Rights
WHRRIC	Women's Health and Reproductive Rights Information Centre
WIM	Women in Medicine

Table of English cases and statutes

Cases

Statutes

Table of French cases and statutes

Cases

Statutes

I

Introduction: reproductive rights and the policy process

Reproductive medicine has posed formidable challenges to society, judges and law-makers across the developed world. Governments across Western Europe have sought to assert a degree of control over the provision of fertility treatment. People seeking such treatment have asserted their right to reproduce. The medical professionals who have taken part in developments seek a role in its provision. Religious groups for their part have sought to ensure that their own values and beliefs are respected in any legislation passed. Moreover, women form a section of society for whom reproduction has been a significantly important issue, and who have put forward their own evolving and increasingly significant perspectives.

The UK and France have both had to grapple with fundamental medical and social issues central to reproduction, such as the opposing rights of women and the foetus. Gradually over the twentieth century they provided statutory responses to these problems. However, comparisons between the legal provision and heated political debates of each country demonstrate forcibly their very different cultural and social heritage. This heritage continues to determine debate on reproductive and medical issues to this day.

During the twentieth century there were many changes of a political, legal and social nature in both countries. The position of women in society and attitudes toward their reproductive rights have shifted dramatically. The most important laws on the liberalisation of reproduction, *inter alia*, were also passed. This book examines how the three main reproductive issues of contraception, abortion and assisted conception have been dealt with legally and politically over this period of social change.[1] It attempts to do this by observing the power struggles that have gone on between women's rights campaigners, religious groups, French pronatalists and the medical profession, by ascertaining who is in control of reproduction, and by uncovering the histories behind the legislation that is now in place in the UK and France. These two countries began the century with extremely contrasting attitudes toward women's reproductive freedom. The British looked at such issues from a pragmatic viewpoint, while attitudes in France were heavily influenced not only by the Roman Catholic Church, but also by the existence of the highly regarded group promoting the French birth rate, previously referred to: 'pro-natalists'.[2] Legislation relating to reproductive rights was passed in 1967 on contraception in both Britain[3] and France, laws were enacted on abortion, in 1967 and 1975, respectively and laws on assisted conception were passed in 1990 in the UK, and in 1994 in France. By the end of the twentieth century, then, 'reproductive rights' existed to a greater degree in both countries than they had at its inception.

In this book I attempt to chart the development of that legislation. The overriding questions this book seeks to address are these: what different types of reproductive rights legislation were passed in the UK and France? Why did they take so long to come about? Which groups in these societies could be said to have been instrumental in bringing about such pivotal legislation? Moreover, in legislation that was crucial to women's liberation, what role in this was played by those groups who campaigned above all for women's rights?

Methodologically, this necessitates an interdisciplinary approach. The book therefore draws on the tools and methods of both legal analysis and political science. In addition, the study is comparative in the sense of being cross-national. Together these methodologies can provide deeper insights into the genesis of policy and law. Their combination in such a study can also offer insights to those coming from the different perspectives of law and politics.

These features of the study are reflected in the structure of the book, with separate examinations being made of contraception, abortion and assisted conception. Individual chapters are organised on a comparative basis, examining relevant developments in both the UK and France. The analysis of changing legal provisions on each issue is provided initially in Chapters 2, 4 and 6 on contraception, abortion and the new reproductive technologies (NRTs), followed by separate chapters which assess the role and influence of the main interest groups involved (in Chapters 3, 5 and 7).

The legal and policy sector contexts

This book looks at reproductive law and policy within the theoretical paradigm of the political theory of interest group behaviour known as policy community theory. It attempts to discover the situating of power in the reproductive policy arena. Thus it examines the interplay between medical, women's rights and religious interest groups and their representatives in government. All these groups operate within the same policy area. Whose discourse was legitimised by the government and given the force of law? Feminist perspectives are examined. .

However, ideas of legal deconstruction or critical legal theory are seen as an issue separate from feminism. (That is not to say that the construction of the subject of women is not also evident in the situating of women under medical and state control, and in opposition to foetal autonomy, in laws passed during this time.)

As briefly alluded to above, observations from two different though related and complementary perspectives are made here: those of law and those of politics. A legal analysis offers insights into the law itself, whether statute or case law. A political perspective reveals more about the processes behind the policy-making which leads up to that legislation.

Critical legal scholars now argue that law and politics are very closely related and that one cannot validly differentiate between them. (Indeed, the practice of law itself demonstrates the closeness of the two subjects, with parliamentarians debating law, and judges going on to interpret and apply it.) Despite their efforts, the majority of writers in these areas deal with law and politics separately. This book attempts to fill that gap. It traces, *inter alia*, the unfolding history behind the development of both the law and policy on reproduction. The book is also 'political' in the sense that it sets out to apply a political theory to the way in which legislation on reproductive issues was the subject of lobbying.

It goes on to offer further insights through comparison between France and the UK and over time. These two countries are Western European liberal democracies with very similar economies and shared histories. Yet comparison reveals not only their different political and legal processes, but also offers insights into the various types of policy processes and debates that can lead up to legislation. In the final analysis, this is also an in-depth study of just two countries rather than what could be a more cursory study of many. It is hoped that this will provide a greater insight.

It is increasingly acknowledged how multidimensional subjects are. Any examination of the major reproductive laws in two countries spanning a century, alongside a detailed examination of the political debates behind those laws necessarily involves much research. The usual pressures of time and space have therefore not permitted the inclusion here of a wider cultural or historical examination than was strictly necessary. Nor does the book look in detail at ethical arguments, political philosophy or theories of culture. To those for whom this apparent lack of a wider analysis may disappoint, I can only recommend that they satisfy their curiosity by turning to other texts alongside this one. That said, a thorough analysis from both perspectives has been attempted.

The adoption of both a comparative and an interdisciplinary approach has shaped the choice of the three main themes of the book.

The first and second themes concern exogenous factors shaping the influence of campaigners. Here we are concerned with the ways in which differences between women's rights movements in these two countries are largely explicable by reference to the contrasting environments in which they have operated. One crucial part of that environment is constituted by the existing legal provisions on contraception, abortion and other reproductive technologies.

Thus the first theme that this book explores is: in what ways have the objectives that campaigners, particularly feminists, have developed on these three issues and their capacity to develop unified action on these, been shaped by the existence of significantly different legal provisions in each country? This in turn requires analysis of the ways in which such existing provisions themselves reflect different patterns of organised interests and dominant values regarding these issues, and thus entail differences in the potential for alliance-building and for opposition to feminist claims in each country.

Such differences in established policy provisions are, in any case, further reinforced by their insertion into two quite distinct kinds of legal system. Law in the UK and France is a combination of common law and statute (in addition to being subject to European Union law). The French have a civil law system consisting of Codes. The approximate equivalents to the High Court, Court of Appeal and House of Lords, are the departmental 'tribunaux de grande instance', regional 'cours d'appel', and 'Cour de Cassation' for civil and criminal law, and the 'Conseil d'Etat' for administrative law, this latter, amongst its other differences from English administrative law, having a separate court system. Case-law judgments, or 'jurisprudence', have less influence in France, and the French system is less adversarial than its English equivalent. Moreover, French magistrates in superior courts can only interpret the letter of the law and send the case back for reconsideration by the inferior court. However, in both countries sources of medical law and reproductive rights for women have been contract law, tort, family law, European law, administrative law and criminal law.

The French legal system is additionally endowed with human rights provision through the Fifth Republic Constitution of 1958, and its 1946 Preamble, which records the central place of the Declaration of the Rights of Man of 1789. The European Convention on Human Rights (ECHR) was also ratified by France on 3 May 1974. Interested parties within France have been able to attempt to use the rights afforded by the Constitution and the ECHR, which are overseen by the French Constitutional Court, to gain a declaration of incompatibility with legislation. In 1974 seventy-seven Deputies thus sought the opinion of the Constitutional Court on the compatibility of the Abortion Bill, then going through Parliament, with Article 2 of the Declaration of the Rights of Man (right to freedom and safety) and with Article 2 of the ECHR (right to life, except in cases of capital punishment). They were unsuccessful. The Court declared itself incompetent on the issue of compatibility with the ECHR, but that the Abortion Bill was not incompatible with the French Constitution as it provided for *women*'s freedom and safety in seeking a termination for reasons of distress and medical need (*see* Chapter 5).[4]

By contrast, British parties have not enjoyed such legal possibilities. With the ratification of the ECHR through the Human Rights Act 1998, in force from 2 October 2000, this may yet change, however. A plethora of cases citing the Human Rights Act began to appear in late 2000. A male homosexual couple, for example, did not enjoy pension rights following the death of one partner equivalent to those of a married couple and were seeking legal advice. They cited the Convention rights of property and peaceful enjoyment of possessions (First Protocol, Article 1) as protected by the 1998 Act. The incompatibility of legislation with the Act is a question which English courts may consider, but they may not strike down any particular legislation. In relation to an issue such as abortion, then, the Abortion Act 1967 may be declared incompatible with the right to life (Article 2), such as in the case of a late abortion, but it is for the government to decide whether or not to act on this declaration. The question of standing also remains an issue for debate. The extent to which human rights case law involving reproduction rights may be seen in the UK to the same extent as constitutional law in France remains, then, at present, a subject for speculation.[5]

Legal provisions are only a part of the environment in which groups such as feminists operate. Alongside this we need to consider other features such as the party system, organised interests, the parliamentary process and 'policy-style norms' regarding the scope and status of consultation procedures. Of no less importance are legal or constitutional rules concerning the scope of primary as opposed to secondary legislation in the UK and the 'domaine du loi' as against the 'domaine réglementaire' in France.

The second theme the book explores is therefore: how far can variations in feminist influence be accounted for by differences in the institutional and political environments in each country for making policy in this sector? Whilst this second theme seeks to focus on broader political and institutional features, it also overlaps into more specifically legal features that have been referred to above, such as the relationship between enacted statute and case law in the UK, and the exigencies of codified law and the limited scope of court judgments in France.

Moreover, if the legal environment is largely determined by the legal provisions and legal systems of each country, then the political environment is shaped by those factors which determine the number and range of potentially relevant actors and organised interests which may be incorporated into the different phases of the policy-making process in any given policy sector. A range of concepts and models have been developed in the literature on the policy process which could be applied to the field of women's reproductive rights and to the issue of assessing influence over policy outcomes. Relevant literature extends across the four broad frameworks provided by pluralist, elitist, corporatist and 'the new institutionalism' theories. Also relevant are the three literatures which focus on the concepts of policy styles, political opportunity structures and policy communities and networks. In practice, these concepts can be employed to draw on a variety of insights offered by the four theoretical approaches noted above.[6] However, it is these three concepts which are of particular interest here. In differing ways each helps to clarify the distinctiveness of the different phases in the policy process in which campaigners might aspire to intervene.

Policy styles

Writings on policy styles have been concerned with establishing general cross-national contrasts between national political systems, their institutions and dominant political cultures. Jordan and Richardson writing in 1987 identified the established British policy style as reactive and consensual and characterised by 'the logic of negotiation'.[7] In a similar fashion, Harrison, writing in 1980, has described the British governmental system as consensual and therefore ideal for forms of sectoral corporatist practice. Despite the adversarial logic of party political competition, parties in government adjust, 'in a piecemeal fashion to problems as they arise and after organised pressure groups have been formally consulted'.[8]

However, in the period since Jordan and Richardson undertook their research, a notable shift in policy style was evident in the UK during Margaret Thatcher's period as Prime Minister and after. Under Thatcherite governments 'negotiated order' largely became the norm. Extensive change was initiated during this period, including the reorganisation of the National Health Service (NHS), though it is questionable how far this affected the policy sector concerned with *reproduction*. Reproduction is a social or conscience issue that does not receive the highest priority even within the health policy sector itself. Negotiated order may not have had as much of an effect on this conscience issue therefore.

The 'heroic leadership'[9] element of French policy style largely derives from the constitutional settlement of 1958 and the introduction of direct universal suffrage in presidential elections from 1962. This paved the way for the consolidation of a 'presidentialist' regime in France, with the presidency dominant within the governmental arena. The more routine and reactive policy style that was already established was in turn transformed by the increased powers that were now accorded to government at the expense of Parliament in relation to parliamentary debate, the parliamentary agenda and select committee examination.[10] Suleiman [11] also underlined the importance of administrators as opposed to that of parliamentarians at the actual drafting and committee stages, especially if the policy involved the public sector. Pierre Grémion [12] examined consultation in France between interest groups and the administration and divided French policy style into several constituent parts. He offered a more nuanced analysis, showing how the administration absorbed the values of the interest group it consulted with on a regular basis, eventually defending it, anticipating its needs and acting in its interest as policy was made. Jack Hayward has also argued that the Fifth Republic from 1958 was authoritarian with its emphasis on executive power, rhetoric and heroic leadership. Until there are substantial amendments to the Fifth Republic's Constitution, this is unlikely to change, despite attempts at decentralisation in administration from Paris, or the enforced cohabitations of President and Prime Minister which have occurred more recently.

Political opportunity structures

Writing which has focused on the concept of political opportunity structures (POSs) has also been employed primarily to identify and account for overall contrasts between national political systems. These are of particular interest because they have been developed precisely to account for cross-national contrasts in the activities, and success, of a number of 'new social movements' such as environmentalists which, like radical feminists, can be characterised as being outsiders in the mainstream policy process.

According to the POS of a regime, new social movements' strategies are usually assimilative, if the system is open or weak, 'where movements attempt to work through established institutions because POS offer multiple points of access' (lobbying, petitioning, electioneering). However, they may be confrontational if the system is closed and strong, with 'disruptive strategies orchestrated outside established policy channels' [13] (public demonstrations, civil disobedience).

The literature on the application of the POS approach to the UK and France would seem to emphasise for the UK (like the policy styles literature) the possibilities even for outsiders like feminists to gain some forms of access through consultation procedures, and through forming alliances with some 'insider' actors (either in the party system or in other sympathetic organised interests, for example, in relation to women's reproductive rights, among doctors), although in both cases this may require first gaining visibility and acquiring some agenda-setting influence by public mobilisation and campaigning that demonstrate broader public opinion support on women's reproductive rights issues.

In the case of France, while (as with Hayward's routine normative patterns) studies of France in the contemporary period suggest the importance of regular contacts and dialogue for established and recognised interests, writers such as Kitschelt emphasise the extent to which outsider interests and organisations are excluded and need to resort to direct action (and often to violent confrontations with the French state) to ensure that their most important demands are indeed taken into account by those making policy. However, this will still leave them excluded from formal or routine access to the policy-making process.

The policy community model

The policy community and policy networks literature that has appeared since the late 1980s is more concerned with exploring and accounting for the variations that are found between different policy sectors in any one state, than with exploring the differences or similarities that may be found cross-nationally in any one policy sector.[14] It provides the most useful framework for an analysis of reproductive rights campaigns and the involvement of policy community groups, which took place in one, at most two, policy sectors: those of health policy and perhaps of legal policy (see below).

In 1987, Jordan and Richardson talked about the network within the community or 'inner core' being created in order to reduce the number of actors and issues to 'a manageable polity'. These bring in specialised knowledge and legitimise policy. In their view, such networks especially took the form of Quangos, and of standing and ad hoc advisory committees.

The distinction developed by Wright in 1988, building on previous work by Rhodes (1988), between policy communities and policy networks, is important since the former embraces all those affected by a particular sectoral issue area and which in the context of liberal democratic institutional arrangements and norms might potentially organise themselves to gain access to, and seek to influence, the making of policy. In contrast, the policy network designates those actors and organisations which 'interact in a structure of dependent relationships'; they may be drawn from one or more 'policy communities'.

Network members exchange resources with each other in order to balance and optimise their mutual relationships, with government actors at the head of the network. These actors, according to Wright, are more concerned with relationship management than policy-making.

Because management of the relationships of the actors within the closed network within each community is paramount, the outcomes and behaviour of policy makers may become inconsistent with the general norms associated with them. It leads to a difference existing between what the government says policy is and why (government rhetoric or dual policy style) or what is expected of the government, and actual policy in practice as determined by the norms of the network and their 'rules of the game'. There is also much intersectoral conflict at all levels of the policy area in both the UK and France. The needs of the members of the network, according to function, strategy, resources and objectives outweigh the general needs of the area (the Department) or government.

Membership of the network is controlled by the government agency. They are selected from the policy community involved in the subject area, such as health and from others if the issue is a combination of subject areas. Membership is determined by similar characteristics to membership of corporatist consultation and 'insider' status – a common identity or interest (size, politics, strategy, interest, members), stability, professionalisation. 'They possess resources of authority, money, information, expertise, and organisation.'[15] However, the members are limited by the accepted rules of the game. These have included, in the UK, mutuality, consultation and informality, acceptable mode and language, the avoidance of legal remedy by the government actor. These Wright has inferred from the behaviour of members.

In the health policy community, groups that might network would include civil servants, interested Members of Parliament (MPs), ministers, backbenchers, committee members, Lords on the governmental side, and medical, social, religious, legal interest groups, professionals and academics on the non-governmental side.

Mény, looking specifically at the French case, has argued that the policy community concept, 'has provided a stimulating analytical framework for research on the development and implementation of public policies'.[16] In France, according to Mény, much more than in the UK, the strong, centralised state has created the organisation of members of the policy network, by supporting them financially to create a manageable polity. How far the French state is obliged to work with entrenched professions, such as the medical professions, is unclear. In the French case, the strength and legitimacy of the bureaucracy and technocrats ensures 'their unchallenged control of policy making'. Ministers and civil servants 'are concerned to avoid being subjected to the rival claims of social pluralism or market competition between interest groups'. This creates a situation however where groups excluded from the network – 'outsiders' – will try and force their way in. Such groups are then incorporated by being included on a consultative committee (of which there are thousands), only to be ignored and thereby weakened. 'The most optimistic assumption is that these committees can provide information or exercise pressure on the administration. More frequently, they serve only as a forum for the ritual sword-play of adversaries ...' [17]

The French State has often laid claim to being republican, Codified and democratic – the guarantor of equality, the representative of the people. This 'French exceptionalism' – the claim to difference – has legitimised an activist role for the state.[18] The British government, by contrast, has never claimed this and hence British policy responses have been pragmatic and flexible. Wright and others have pointed out that the UK has been permeated with what it sees as acceptable forms of policy communities and policy network consultation in the policy process. Both pragmatism and policy networks would be something that France would see as non-egalitarian and non-republican. But is this merely government rhetoric on the part of France? Are policy networks in operation and is consultation carried out by the State with selected groups, which in turn leads to the relations of dependency referred to by Mény and Hayward. Who is controlling who here? Dominique Colas wrote in 1988 of a state-dominated policy community with the state acting as gatekeeper. When the state soon became reliant on those 'appropriate' members it had accorded membership, this caused a shift in the balance of power within that community and led to the entrenchment of certain groups in particular sectors.[19] This leads to pointers to what to expect in the reproductive rights field.

Of the established policy sectors with their own established policy communities and networks, the policy areas of contraception, abortion and assisted conception could not readily be assigned to the health sector. Here, however, given the entrenched position of the medical professions and their commitment to exercising clinical judgement, such issues are liable to be 'medicalised' at the expense of developing any clear definition of individual women's rights (see below for a discussion of 'medicalisation').

Feminists have been particularly concerned that the medical professions should not have authority over women's reproductive rights, but rather women themselves should control the 'right to choose'. Radical feminists have argued that women should, wherever possible, be enabled to administer such 'treatment' to themselves. Even doctors have been known to question the medical status of reproductive rights. Moreover, in relation to the recent policy debate on assisted conception in France, initially it was a legal policy network that was as profoundly involved as that on health. This did lead subsequently to the effective vetoing of formulated government policy by the medical professions. However, this question of which particular sector is concerned with reproductive issues is especially significant for reproductive rights campaigners as an outsider group, as uncertainty about policy sectors can make the lobbying process more complicated. The situation has been made all the more difficult as campaigners such as feminists have in any case suffered as an interest group from a lack of agreement and unity on many aspects of women's reproductive rights.

The policy community approach is therefore one that can clarify the particularities of the different stages of policy-making, identify necessary interest group resources, while also emphasising the importance of alliance-building.

On further consideration, this approach might also suggest that what has been distinctive about claims made in the field of women's reproductive rights is that campaigners were seeking to combine three goals. First, to alter the existing pattern of resource distribution in the healthcare sector (either through the introduction of additional resources or the redistribution of existing resources) in order to fund procedures that had hitherto been excluded from official (and professional) definitions of medical care. Second, and more specifically, to challenge an entrenched principle in both countries' patterns of healthcare delivery: the primacy of clinical judgement. Third, and intrinsic to both of these goals, to challenge the composition of existing healthcare policy networks, from which any organised representation of women as having special and distinctive healthcare needs and interests had hitherto been excluded.

Such claims, however, would seem to ensure that such campaigners would not be invited to be members of the policy network. Rather the policy community literature points to the probability of reproductive policy being medicalised. Whilst the policy community may include campaigners who are prepared to lobby along with their allies, the actual policy network will centre principally on the medical professions, legal specialists and, in the case of assisted conception, other biomedical researchers, as well as relevant pharmaceutical industry representatives, and from time to time in each country religious groups and pronatalists.[20]

Medicalisation

It is pertinent at this juncture to offer a definition of the term 'medicalisation'. Kohler Riessman[21] refers to two processes of medicalisation. It serves both to ensure that deviance is the focus of medical control in order to secure adherence to social norms, and also to define behaviours or conditions as health or illness. It is the latter definition that largely concerns us here, particularly as it relates to reproduction.

Kohler Riessman posits her own suggestions as to how medicalisation comes about:

Physicians seek to medicalize experience because of their specific beliefs and economic interests ... Women collaborate in the medicalization process because of their own needs and motives, which in turn grow out of the class-specific nature of their subordination. In addition, other groups bring economic interests to which both physicians and women are responsive. Thus a consensus develops that a particular human problem will be understood in clinical terms. This consensus is tenuous because it is fraught with contradictions for women, since, as stated before, they stand to gain and to lose from this redefinition.[22]

She also notes, however, the disagreement about how medicalisation occurs between those arguing from an economic, political or sociological viewpoint.[23] The medicalisation of health care over the twentieth century has been in evidence, particularly, in relation to women's healthcare and their reproduction. Why should this be the case? Kohler Riessman[24] argues that this may well be due to the correspondence between women's biology and medicine's biomedical orientation. In particular, biological processes in women such as menstruation and birth can be easily understood medically as visible 'external markers', whereas these are hidden in men. In addition, women's social roles make them available for medical scrutiny as they are more likely to accompany children to the doctor. Once in the surgery, women's own health, particularly their reproductive health, is subject to a great degree of medical scrutiny. Finally, 'Social relations in the surgery replicate patriarchal relations in the larger culture under the guise of science ... Dominant social interests and patriarchal institutions are reinforced'.[25]

Why is the medicalisation of health and health care of importance? In terms of language used to define health and illness, medical definitions often ensure that a medical solution will be more readily approved of. In turn this increases the risk of iatrogenic disease,[26] and lessens the chance of a more holistic environmental solution being found to women's reproductive concerns.

Looking at the specific example of abortion, Sally Sheldon (1997)[27] has also referred to the extent to which medicalisation may have improved access to abortion services (in terms of safety). She adds, however, that, '[a]t the parliamentary level and, to a large extent, also within the rhetoric of the campaigning groups, the rights discourse is being superseded by the use of medical discourse and a deployment of medical knowledges'. This ensured that political debate has concentrated on finding a solution to the needs of the individual and shied away from any discussion of social factors.

Sheldon argues

Whilst medicalisation has helped to extend access to abortion, such access remains tightly grasped in the deadlock of medical control. Medicalisation has been the greatest strength of British abortion law and its greatest weakness. It has simultaneously depoliticised the extension of women's access to abortion services, defused political conflict and left women dependent on the vagaries of medical discretion and good will.[28]

Medicalisation also has important links with power, both at the level of the surgery and at the level of government and society. Foucault argued extensively, for example, that the body was becoming a new site of power in society. The State controlled society through surveillance, and the body was subject to the discipline and punishment meted out. Clinicians were the handmaidens of the government in this process. It can be seen that this idea can be extended to view the position of clinicians in the government's health policy network as offering both a contract or partnership which enables the medical professions to have a monopoly over health care and the State to have concomitant control over the population.

Kohler Riessman[29] considers that 'the political dimension inherent in medicalisation is underscored when we note that structurally dependent populations – children, old people, racial minorities, and women – are subject disproportionately to medical labelling ... Of course, physicians act on behalf of the larger society, thus further reinforcing existing power relations'. The existence of policy networks featuring clinicians, which play an important role in the health policy sector, underlines the nature of the power and status of the medical professions. Such status is reinforced and institutionalised by the extent to which clinicians have been given responsibility for the resources behind national health services, particularly the NHS in the UK, and for ensuring that health care is administered to the population. The wider the umbrella of medical definitions of health and illness, the greater the responsibility given to these professionals.

It would appear that the medical professions have status and power over social as well as medical definitions, to the extent that whether something becomes labelled as an illness – something needing medical involvement – depends on what they see as 'good' or 'bad' for society. Thus, the control of women's reproductive freedom is seen by clinicians to be necessary for the good of society – to ensure that the generation of human society is controlled by doctors, as it is too important to be left in women's hands alone. But men's aggressiveness outside the home ensures the workings of the capitalist system, so is deemed to be 'good' or 'normal' and therefore not in need of control and limitation by the medical professions. Clinicians thus act as social arbiters in partnership with the government. Sheldon[30] reflects that who controls abortion 'remains a deeply and inherently political matter. It is political because it concerns how as women we are able to live our lives and control our own fertility. This is a matter of fundamental importance for men and women alike in deciding how we wish to order our society.'

Sheldon here refers to men and women. Many have argued, however, that medicalisation affects women in particular. Both Sheldon[31] and Kohler Riessman[32] argue that medicalisation has eroded women's autonomy. It has been cast in technical medical terms and has been removed from the purview of (lay)women themselves.

Sheldon[33] applies this to the case of abortion. She distinguishes between four different levels of medical control: 'technical control of the actual performance of abortion operations, decisional control over which women should be permitted to terminate their pregnancies, and paternalistic and normalising control which may be exercised over women who request termination (regardless of whether they are granted access to it)'. This takes the decision about abortion out of the hands of the very woman whose body lies at the centre of the decision-making process.

Ideas of power – such as Foucault's 'bio-power'[34] – resonate particularly with any work which concentrates on politics and law. This book seeks to examine questions of power among those making policy and law in the health sector. It seeks to confirm whether or not policy network status accorded power and influence to those interest groups who made up its members. Since it has a premise accepting medicalisation, it seeks particularly to examine the extent to which the medical professions have displayed power in this way and what effect this has had on women's health provision and law in the area of reproduction.

Membership of any policy network considering reproductive issues was subject to change over the course of the century. Sheldon[35] extends Foucault's arguments about clinicians being 'priests of the body', and underlines the change in the latter half of the twentieth century in the UK whereby the importance of moralist discourse was replaced by that of medical discourse.

> The 1967 Act marked a landmark victory for the medical discourse or paradigm, constructing abortion as falling primarily within the sphere of medical, rather than moral or religious authority ... This victory was consolidated in 1990 debates and reform where the 24 week limit was predicated on the medical construction of 'viability' – which was when medical machines could save the life of a premature baby, rather than on women's social considerations or needs.

It is noteworthy that Marie Fox in 1998 posited that one of the few benefits of medicalisation (and thus the position of clinicians in the policy network) for women may have been that it has lessened the possibility of interference into women's health by other groups such as religious groups or pronatalists.

Here I look to confirm such conclusions in relation to discourse on all three reproductive issues in both the UK and France as reflected in the importance of interest groups in the policy community.

Feminism and reproduction

In contrast to the legal and policy sector contexts described above, the third theme the book explores is concerned with the endogenous sources of the influence of reproductive rights campaigners, particularly feminists. At its simplest, the assessment of interest group influence in relation to any set of policies or policy sector involves identifying the objectives of that group (and how far they are internally united or not as regards those objectives), the resources they are able to bring into play, the availability or not of allies or allied interests, including the salience of that issue more broadly for public opinion and the presence or absence of other significant actors and organised interests committed to different or opposing objectives.

The main aim of the book is to assess the importance of reproductive rights campaigners. The focus is therefore on a succession of 'outsider' groups: sets of actors who have not been (or sought to be) significantly integrated with major political parties, and who do not enjoy consultative or other similar status with relevant ministries. The study also focuses on a set of issues not previously clearly allocated to an established policy sector, precisely because they concern acts that either had been actually unlawful or were not positively provided for in law by legislators with other priorities.

However, all three issues of contraception, abortion and assisted conception have clear if somewhat variable linkages into medical practice and the health-care provision available in the two countries and thus the health policy sector. We should note that both countries have what are effectively national health services, the French system differing in that it is based on a combination of private insurance and state reimbursement.[36] For each of these three issues, moreover, the technologies available in the two countries have been similar, and changes in these technologies in the recent period have taken place in both countries more-or-less contemporaneously. Thus one would expect to find new legal provision being enacted in both countries on these issues. As will be seen, such provision has been largely dependent on the concerns and priorities of government and those actors with an established role in govern-mental consultation procedures, namely the medical professions, religious groups and, in France, pronatalists.

The third theme considered in the book is therefore: given these environ-ments, how did feminists in particular conduct their campaigns on reproductive rights as an outsider interest group? What effect on their status as consultation partners did their conflict with governments and other interest groups have? Moreover, this leads on to the question of what difference to the success of their campaigns was made by the alliance-building capacity of first-wave liberal feminism before 1968, and by the influx of second-wave radical feminism after

1968 with its refusal to build political alliances and its extensive internal disunity? This involves analysing the different strands within feminism in the two countries and changes in each country over time. As will become evident, conflict between the different strands that went to make up women's rights organisations at this time also weakened their ability to influence policy makers.

Campaigns for reproductive rights have been made up of important individuals and various liberal-minded associations. They deserve their place in the history of reproductive rights liberalisation. A central place must go, however, to 'feminist' groups. Such groups were made up mostly of women whose main priority as an organisation was the liberalisation of women's condition. Such a liberalisation as was seen to be necessary at that time, though with hindsight may be criticised for setting limited goals for the liberation of all women. As part of that, the liberalisation of women's reproduction was crucial.

Within this introductory chapter, I examine the evolution of feminism and feminist thought in relation to women's reproductive rights. In the book as a whole, emphasis is laid upon the role played by feminists or women's rights campaigners. The subject-matter of the book is reproduction. We should not forget that either reproduction does indeed concern women more than it does men, or that women merely concern themselves more with it. Either way, a special place must go to the actions of feminist groups in this area. More than that, as a political study of interest group behaviour the actions of feminist groups serve as an example of the political power games behind policy-making in the UK and France.

The importance of political organisation and campaigns for rights can be traced as far back as Mary Wollstonecroft's *Vindication of the Rights of Woman with Strictures on Political and Moral Subjects* (1792). As Hilaire Barnett,[37] among others, has acknowledged:

> From a feminist perspective ... the gaining of legal rights has played a central role in the quest for the elimination of discrimination on the basis of gender ... While it may be acknowledged that law alone cannot produce social change ... rights have played and continue to play an essential role for women in the movement for equality.

Feminist thought on reproductive rights underwent dramatic changes during the period covered by this book. The criticism by many first-wave feminists in the nineteenth and early twentieth centuries, especially those in the UK, of the restrictiveness of marital law, the prevailing domestic ideology and the double standard of husbands, was used as a rallying cry against motherhood alongside other important mobilising issues such as education, work, politics and religion. In the UK, this led to campaigns against laws on prostitution such as the contagious diseases legislation of 1867 and in France against laws on illegitimacy set up by the Napoleonic Code of 1804, namely articles 340 and 341 of the Civil Code.

Early in the twentieth century, 'reproduction' was by and large a biological term. Women did not claim 'reproductive rights' as such. They accepted motherhood as a natural part of life and for this reason, in so far as they did campaign, this was for it to be improved for the sake of women's health, if necessary through medicalisation. First-wave feminists from the nineteenth century to the late 1960s were not however in a position to campaign on such issues as 'abortion' and 'contraception'. Before more effective contraception and medically safe abortion became feasible, reproductive issues were in a sense non-issues.[38] It was issues such as suffrage, education, employment and marital rights which were of particular importance to those campaigning for women's rights at that time. It was not until after the First World War that feminists turned their energies to first contraception and then abortion in the UK, and not until after the Second World War that this happened in France.

Feminists who organised themselves into groups or who questioned women's condition in the first half of the twentieth century were essentially middle-class women. Although they raised discussion about women and even initiated legislation, when compared with the later women's liberation movement they were moderate groups who fought for change outside parliament in 'reformist' associations, and diverse women's groups working together temporarily. They participated in political parties, and in interest groups, as well as more traditional 'women's' activities – voluntary work and charities. However, an outspoken feminist movement was not seen in either country until the 1960s. Any growth in feminism that there might have been appears to have been interrupted by the conservative social aftermath of two World Wars and appeared to be suspended until such time as technological progress played its part in enabling women to demand such things as the contraceptive pill, or non-surgical abortion. Moreover, in France, women still suffered from a culture where the Roman Catholic religion was strong, pronatalist views were widely held, strict laws criminalised such issues as contraception and abortion and basic family and civil rights were not won until many years after they were awarded in the UK- suffrage in 1944, and equality in marriage, financial arrangements and parental rights in the late 1960s.[39]

The last thirty years have seen the development of new forms of feminist organisation and mobilisation – often referred to as 'second-wave' feminism. At the forefront of their concerns and campaigns in this period have been a set of issues that have come to be defined as collectively constituting women's reproductive rights. If motherhood 'is at the heart of women's "condition" (and therefore) central to feminist analysis',[40] feminist analysis in this period has come to centre on the claim that public policies should be reshaped in order to prioritise support for individual women's right to self-determination in respect of their child-bearing capacity. A minimum requirement for autonomy is control over what happens to one's own body and this extends necessarily to fertility. Unfortunately, however, women's physical autonomy has suffered as a result of medicalisation. As Kohler Riessman[41] has noted

> Women's lives have undergone a more total transformation as a result of medical scrutiny. Medicalization has resulted in the construction of medical meanings of normal functions in women – experiences the typical woman goes through, such as menstruation, reproduction, childbirth and menopause. By contrast routine experiences that are uniquely male remain largely unstudied by medical science.

The concept of women's reproductive rights has thus centred on the three distinct sets of issues noted above, concerning, respectively, contraception, abortion and assisted reproduction. None of these issues were new in themselves in this period.[42] But in the course of this period they were greatly transformed by the advent of new technologies – the contraceptive pill, the Karman method, *in vitro* fertilisation (IVF). More recently the abortion pill RU 486 has moreover blurred the boundaries between contraception and abortion.

Whilst those writing on French feminism have necessarily examined its origins due to the fragmentation and disunity in France, conversely literature on British feminism has focused on the different and evolving ideas present in the feminism of the 1970s, 1980s and 1990s. As with most commentators on feminism, Bouchier, Lovenduski and Diana Coole, for example, divided the types of feminism that emerged from 1968 generally into liberal, socialist and radical feminism and these three can be applied to both countries though these authors, particularly the first two, have written mainly on the UK and the United States. Claire Duchen, writing on France, divided the French feminist movement Mouvement de Libération des Femmes (MLF) into three categories: liberal feminists who were single-issue organisations who lobbied for women's laws and rights, socialist feminists, 'luttes des classes' and two types of radical feminist groupings, 'Psychanalyse et Politique' and 'non-aligned feminists'.

As with any typology, there are dangers inherent in reductionism and over-simplistic interpretation or classification. This applies equally to the typology of feminism as being liberal/socialist/ radical/postmodernist. Postmodernist deconstruction in particular has criticised the use of such schemas. But deconstruction may have been a luxury that those without basic freedoms could ill afford. Postmodernist feminism has also criticised the reliance on 'woman' as a universalising term, as this excludes the voices of women of colour, lesbian woman and women in the developing world. This definition of 'woman' has been seen as critical, particularly in relation to the health services which women utilise or are given access to. This can differ according to their social definition as a good or bad woman. A woman of colour presumed by her physician to already have too many children may be persuaded to submit to sterilisation. A white woman may be refused her request for abortion.[43] Sheldon has illustrated compellingly the often derogatory and invariably controlling definitions given to women using abortion services by MPs in the UK Parliament during debates on the Abortion Bill in 1966. Her arguments echo those put forward by Carol Smart about the control of women's reproduction in the nineteenth century.[44]

Earlier definitions of woman and women can be seen with hindsight, then, to have been exclusive and shortsighted. But as regards the law and policy which early campaigners were trying to influence at the time that this took place, a more simplistic typology of groups and of women may have seemed appropriate to organisation around patriarchy and inequality.

'Second-wave' feminists who were involved in campaigns on reproduction from the late 1960s not only chose to campaign on issues related to motherhood and reproduction, they also chose tactics which were much more radical than first-wave feminists. However, the new second-wave type of group were more likely to be politically radical as feminists, whereas other feminists, such as liberals and socialists, continued to behave like interest groups who lobbied the government as part of their campaigns. The 'third-wave' or 'postmodern' feminist movement from approximately the 1990s has shown itself to be much less concerned with campaigns on reproduction than with more cultural and theoretical issues.

The Policy Community Model posits certain resources as being essential to membership of the policy network and to being a party to consultation and law-making. How far did feminists enjoy such resources? Three factors will be considered here which have been identified in the Policy Community literature as being critical to determining effectiveness, to see whether feminists managed to place issues onto the political agenda and influence the content of laws. First, distinctive forms of organisation and mobilising capacities derived from the particular strengths of the different strands of feminism, though feminists' capacity to be insiders themselves was negligible. Second, therefore in order to have influence, interaction with existing allies and political movements was an instrumental interest group resource to feminists as they were outsiders. This was only acceptable to liberal feminists, however (whose campaigns were often joined by socialist feminists), as only they were prepared to seek and accept alliances which may involve compromising their aims or methods.

This leads on to the third factor of how far feminists had the capacity to unite different strands in common campaigns and to be a strong, united force, as this was an important factor in their alliance-building capacity. All three strands differed not only in ideology – their differing theories on women's oppression and women's most important needs determined their ideas about which particular issues should be campaigned on and how to go about it. This led to serious disunity and had a detrimental effect on feminist lobbying power, especially in France due to the greater strength of radicalism there. Also, when looking at the relative strengths and forms in France and the UK, differences can be related to timing, at least in part (and to the limited liberal movement present in late first-wave feminism, especially in France), and to a balance between the three strands with their relative socialism and radicalism, and thus their capacity for relatively united action.

The capacity to be insiders

Feminist theory has invariably determined the structure of the groups who adopted it. As Lovenduski has advanced,[45] it was essentially radical by its assertion of women's equality and its questioning of current assumptions of femaleness. Thus by adopting feminism groups were often transformed from pressure groups into alternative lifestyle movements. Radicals were more 'feminist' than the other groups, but each practised separatism to a certain extent and eschewed hierarchical organisation within their own groups and within the movement as a whole, and no one group claimed to speak for their country's feminism. The lack of leaders and role specialisation led to debate about structure. Freeman, for example, argued in 1979 that attempts at structurelessness did not eliminate the formation of élites and that, without organisation, goals and continuity could not be achieved and tasks and staff were duplicated. She also argued that groups could suffer from a 'tyranny of structurelessness' where any display of useful skills was regarded as competitive and anti-feminist. Such structurelessness would mean that feminist groups were not following the rules of the game advanced by Policy Community theory. It would be more likely therefore that they would be outsiders.

Christine Delphy, a French radical feminist, wrote in 1981 that well-structured and organised groups, such as the abortion campaigners 'Choisir' and 'Psych et Po', fed off the movement for their own gain thus strengthening themselves and weakening the rest of the MLF. She blamed the structured groups therefore for weakening the rest of the movement; if they had been unstructured too, all would have been well. By contrast, she argued that the radicals and socialists complemented each other, with these radicals providing the ideas and the socialists putting them into action (see Chapter 5).

The capacity to work with insiders

This structurelessness determines the alliance-building capacity and concomitant desire of outsider groups to ally. The methods that liberal feminists, and to a large extent socialist feminists, subscribed to achieve their aims were mostly legislative and political. They supported legal actions on issues and worked for political parties (mainly on the left-wing). Combined with the deep links between the Left and feminists from early times, this meant that during periods of left-wing government liberal feminists attempted to increase their alliances and thereby improve their lobbying. Thus when the Socialists were swept to power in 1981 in France, feminist priorities were reshuffled.[46] The Socialist government created a department with full ministerial status with a socialist feminist Yvette Roudy, at its head. Under her leadership, the Ministry managed to provide an increased amount of information about contraception, the reimbursement of abortion, professional equality legislation and the spreading of the feminist movement to the provinces. However, the pre-election promises of the Socialist party in 1981 led many feminists to abandon their struggle in the (false) hope that the new government would do all of their work for them.[47] Thus many feminists complained that established political parties 'co-opted' ideas from the MLF on women's liberation, and diluted them. However, in both countries it is under left-wing governments that the most important reproductive freedoms have been won, and under right-wing governments that these freedoms have been threatened.

Liberal feminists also attempted to ally with insider groups such as trade unions and the medical professions, hoping to have their demands incorporated by these established bodies. Bouchier argued therefore that a liberal feminist was one who had faith in the democratic system, the legal system and fellow citizens, '(t)hey ask for and expect concessions which involve real costs for other groups, on grounds of fairness and equity. Socialists and radicals alike view this as a strategy which ignores the true realities of power'.[48] However, both liberal and socialist feminists have been prepared to form alliances with each other in both countries in order to further their cause.

The capacity to be a strong, united force

Alliance-building and the effectiveness of outsiders is also determined by disunity, and there has unfortunately been disunity between feminists in both countries, and not only on the fundamental issue of separatism. In the UK, for example, there was also disagreement between socialist and radical feminists on the issues of separatism and lesbianism and of creating a 'female' culture.

Though individual radicals in both countries may well have contributed to reformist campaigns such as abortion, anti-pornography and gay rights, they essentially disagreed with the other strands about strategy. Fundamentally they believed in organising in small non-hierarchical groups to encourage women to join and to avoid the male conflictual structure, thus creating a counter-culture of cooperative, leaderless women and spontaneous radical actions to raise consciousness generally. Their main difference from liberals and socialists was their aim to organise and act separately from men. Socialists criticised radicals when they blamed men for women's oppression, as capitalism could then divide and rule the working class. In the late 1970s, socialists began to accept that women suffered from a double oppression from men (patriarchy) and capitalism, something which radicals had also accepted, so there was a convergence between the two. Thus the only major difference in the 1980s was a criticism of liberalism for benefiting only middle-class women and being limited in its aims.

In France, even greater disunity was created because of the existence there of the radical group 'Psych et Po',[49] who not only differed on strategy but also fundamentally on certain issues, thus weakening French feminism as a united force even more than its British counterpart. They believed that changes in concepts, language, writing and relations with other women were also essential to upsetting patriarchy. Belief in their project as the only valid revolution for women meant that they denied all other feminist approaches any value. For them, all other feminist groups were insufficiently committed to the exploration of the women's unconscious and the radical subversion of society. They often refused to participate in feminist *manifestations* because they viewed them as imitations of male power within the male establishment.[50] This had a more concretely damaging effect on the movement as a whole, culminating in the 'Psych et Po' group legally adopting the name MLF as their own from 1979.[51]

The initial impetus of the MLF was provided by its diversity, but the lack of leadership strategy, or of agreement on issues, compounded to weaken the structure of the movement, with the result that its factions became smaller and weaker. It was for this reason that they were then more easily absorbed into larger, more general movements of the left such as the Socialist and Communist parties who co-opted the original demands and watered them down to fit in with their own manifestos. In addition, the public image of the MLF was tarnished due to the obvious disagreement within the movement. This weakened their support among women outside the movement, which in turn reduced their ability to change the system they were fighting against.

However, second-wave radical feminist structurelessness did arguably have some beneficial effects on campaigns after 1968. Lovenduski has argued that 'goals of self-realisation may require an organisation ill-suited to the goals of political change', especially 'when the movement is under threat or when it wants to bring about a concrete and immediate change'.[52] One benefit of radicalism was that through its small consciousness-raising groups women could be more easily persuaded to become feminists and then often went on to join more liberal groups to gain political power and influence. 'An implicit division of labour was possible whereby issues could be raised by the radical branch of the movement, formulated into effective demands by socialist feminists and followed through the political system by liberal feminists.'[53] The extent to which feminist influence over reproductive policy was affected by their ability to act as a successful interest group will be the subject of the ensuing chapters.

2

Contraception and the law: from obscenity to consumerism

Statutes liberalising contraception were passed in the UK and France in the same year – 1967. Before this time, however, their official attitudes toward it were very different. The law on contraception was governed by case law in the UK, which concerned itself with ideas of the extent to which contraceptive information could be considered obscene or immoral. In direct contrast, statute criminalised contraception in France.

When comparing the two countries, a pattern emerges of both congruence and divergence. In the nineteenth century, prosecutions for the supplying of contraceptive information or methods were rare in both countries. However, divergence appeared from 1920, when the law in France was much stricter in content and implementation. It is therefore significant that liberalisation came in both countries in 1967, though in content the French law at this time remained less liberal than its counterpart in the UK.

The analysis of contraceptive law also raises questions about the demo-graphic debates behind liberalisation. In France, mothers were almost compelled into bearing more children; in the UK, women were encouraged to improve their own health and that of their existing children. Nevertheless, for women of both nationalities the end results were that the government restricted access to contraception, which was to women's disadvantage. Voluntary provision was tolerated and largely ignored by governments who preferred that responsibility, both economic and social, should lie with the medical professions. This responsibility was not shouldered by clinicians, however. Indeed, in France the official regulatory body for the medical profession publicly advocated legal restriction of contraception. This contributed to the prevalent French endorsement of pronatalism (the pursuit of reversing the declining birth rate).

The relative rights of spouses and minors in relation to contraception and the issue of sterilisation were not dealt with by the 1967 statutes on contra-ception, but were dealt with later by separate legislation. Nevertheless, they are an integral part of contraceptive law affecting women. Sterilisation legislation itself is a particularly interesting example of the differences between the strategies of the two countries, as in France voluntary and non-therapeutic sterilisation has been chiefly unauthorised and on this issue the influence of pronatalists and the Roman Catholic Church is apparent. More recently, access to contraception has begun to be widened on both sides of the Channel with emergency contraception being made available over the counter (OTC).

Contraception in the UK: 'immoral' and 'obscene'

Contraception in the UK was never formally illegal. When the first voluntary contraceptive clinics opened in 1921, there was no law that could prevent them. There were no legal restrictions on the use or manufacture of contraceptives, nor was there any absolute ban on their sale or availability. However, there were legal mechanisms that could limit the availability of contraception to women and thus limit women's ability to control their own reproduction.

The advertising of contraceptives and the distribution of literature on the subject fell within the ambit of the Metropolitan Police Act 1839, the Town Police Clauses Act 1847 and the Vagrancy Acts of 1824 and 1838, which made it unlawful to sell, distribute or to expose to public view any profane, indecent or obscene book, drawing or print. In addition there were restrictions on the selling in public places of contraceptives, through vending machines, made by local authorities under the Local Government Act of 1933 Section 249 (for the suppression of nuisances) and byelaws adopted in 1949.[1] The publication of information on contraceptives was not prohibited unless it could be considered 'obscene' under the Obscene Publications Act of 1857. In the Bradlaugh and Besant trial of 1877, Charles Bradlaugh was convicted of publishing an 'obscene libel', Knowlton's *The Fruits of Philosophy*, which advocated and explained methods of birth control.[2]

By 1922 the Home Secretary, Mr Shortt, was saying, 'the Government had no intention of introducing legislation (to prevent the publication of literature on contraception), since a court would not hold a book to be obscene merely because it dealt with contraception'.[3] However, despite the fact that there was no specific legislation against contraception in the UK, there were cases in the 1920s against information on contraception to the detriment of women's rights.

In January 1923, for example, a couple were convicted for publishing obscene literature, a common law crime, namely Margaret Sanger's pamphlet *Family Limitation*. The magistrate of the West London Police Court found the pamphlet obscene and ordered copies to be destroyed.[4]

In the famous case of *Sutherland* v. *Stopes* (1925),[5] Marie Stopes sued Dr Halliday Sutherland for libel. In *Birth Control: A Statement of Christian Doctrine against the Neo-Malthusians* (1922), he had accused Stopes of experimenting on the poor, and instructing working women in a method of contraception (the check pessary) that an eminent professor of gynaecology had called the most *harmful* of which she had experience. He called the birth control campaign *monstrous* and more serious than that for which Bradlaugh had been jailed. In the House of Lords Sutherland won by a majority of 3:1. Here it was decided that fact and opinion could not be separated and if the jury believed the words to be true in fact and substance they must be fair comment. There was also a general acceptance by the media at this time that many aspects of contraception were distasteful and the jury did believe that the use of the check pessary was an experiment on the poor. Moreover, reactionary forces in the UK opposed contraception as much as in France. In this particular case, Viscount Finlay[6] expressed the opinion that 'it appears to me that it is impossible to hold that the bounds of fair comment are exceeded by the expression of an opinion honestly held that such practices are revolting to the healthy instincts of human nature. There is an old and widespread aversion to such methods on this ground'. He also found the campaign monstrous and described the effect of the literature on young people as deplorable.

Pronatalism in France from the 1920s

In contrast to the UK, in France at this time contraception was outlawed altogether.

In the nineteenth century, attitudes toward contraception in France were similar to those in the UK. Though abortion was outlawed by the rarely applied Article 317 of the Penal Code, contraception *per se* was not illegal.[7] The law on pornography of 16 March 1898 outlawed the giving of information on pornography so that publications did not have to be obscene to be prosecuted, they only had to be immoral,[8] and contraceptives were added to the list of 'unlawful products' ('ventes illicites'). However, those involved at this time in informing the public and supplying contraceptives, such as the neo-Malthusians, were very rarely charged under the law.[9]

That is not to say that contraception was accepted but, for the first twenty years of the twentieth century, governments were not sympathetic to those bills presented by religious groups and later by pronatalists or doctors which proposed to restrict contraceptive information. The Republicans in power were determined to underline the new separation between the Church and State and run a 'République des Libertés'. On 17 March 1910, for example, the Barthou Bill was rejected and on 7 February 1913, the Lannelongue Bill was adopted only by the Senate. The latter's stated intention was to combat the activities of the neo-Malthusian groups by forbidding public meetings on contraception, private or public sale and public showing of contraceptive materials or their distribution by any means, postal or otherwise, if these led to attempted abortion or (as amended by the Senate) to the use of contraceptives.[10]

The turning point came in 1920 when, for the first time, the giving of information on contraception became a criminal offence.[11] The ideology of pronatalism had been popular even in the nineteenth century, as evidenced by anti-abortion legislation and medical practice. It was reinforced by studies evidencing a decline in the French birth rate, especially after the losses of the First World War. Moreover, radicals were replaced in 1919 by more conservative politicians. Pronatalist and medical ideas of banning contraception and thereby increasing the population received increasing support from parliamentarians in debates.

Nevertheless, the rapidity with which the 1920 law was passed is surprising. It was based on the Barthou Bill and proposed in the Chamber of Deputies by a left-wing Republican Edouard Ignace at the end of the session on 23 July, thus indicating that pronatalism was supported by both left and right. The Justice Minister supported the idea of debating the law that day, and in only a few hours the law of '31 juillet 1920' was proposed, debated and voted in by a large majority of 500 votes to 51.[12]

The legal restrictions on abortion and contraception in France were connected. The stated aim of the 1920 law was to suppress resort to abortion and propaganda against procreation. The giving of information and the practice of contraception (called 'propagande anticonceptionnelle', but mentioned separately from abortion in the Lannelongue Bill therefore probably referring to contraception) was punishable by imprisonment of between one and six months and a fine of between 100 and 5,000 francs under Article 463 of the Penal Code (art. 6). The information the Act referred to was specifically that which would encourage people to limit their family size ('propagande anticonceptionnelle') by certain means (articles 1 and 2), such as instruction or the offer of instruction on methods of how to tell if a woman were pregnant ('prévenir la grossesse') and the supplying of such methods (art. 3). The means in Article 1 were namely by public meeting, private and public sale, public showing, private or public distribution of any material, advertising in surgeries and, in Article 2, by selling or distributing. Also it was illegal to sell medications that were claimed to prevent pregnancy (presumably pre- and post-conception), even if these claims were false (art. 4).[13] The main aim of the 1920 law was to prevent abortion (articles 1, 2 and 5); contraception was secondary to that (articles 3, 4 and 6). Indeed, it is unclear why the provision of contraceptives and information thereon were included. It would appear that either the Deputies placed contraceptives under the heading of abortifacients (which their mentioning of the use of contraceptives to indicate pregnancy or to make menstruation resume would indicate), and/or that they were included so as to eradicate all actions that could have a negative effect on the birth rate.[14] Certainly, no distinction appears to have been made between abortifacient and non-abortifacient means of contraception, and exemptions on grounds of health were not permitted.

Male contraceptives – condoms – were not included in the 1920 law as they were considered to be a method of preventing venereal disease; these were available in pharmacies, though whether they were manufactured in France is unclear. Men were not affected by the 1920 law as regards self-protection. This raises questions about whether it was the birth rate the French were attempting to resurrect or women's abilities to control their own reproduction without interference from male or State.

The Ogino (used to calculate fertility) and temperature methods were advocated by the Roman Catholic Church from the 1930s as natural and therefore acceptable methods of contraception; their publicity and distribution from this time were in fact illegal, but were not subject to prosecution.[15] This demonstrates the power and influence of the Roman Catholic Church in France, certainly at this time.

The 1920 law was rigorously applied. There were increasing numbers of convictions under it, five cases in 1930, ten cases in 1938, eighteen cases in 1946, twenty-six cases in 1950, and a case even as late as 1960.[16] In one case the judge, M. F. Gollety, criticised the lack of clarity of the law and the confusion it led to 'On a trop souvent tendance à confondre la provocation à l'avortement d'une part, et la propagande anticonceptionnelle', thus indicating that the law was a catch-all in its application and very restrictive of the availability of contraceptives to women. For example, in 1927 a feminist schoolteacher Henriette Alquier published an article in the *Bulletin des groupes féministes de l'enseignement laïque* describing a system of feminist lay education whereby young people would be taught that family size should depend on means, the mother's health and her free consent. She was accused under the 1920 law and appeared before a tribunal at Saumur, but acquitted.[17]

The pronatalist policy behind the law of 1920 failed to increase the birth rate which was in 1930 equivalent to that of 1914. The only reason it had failed to drop was due to the influx of two million immigrants during these years.[18]

However, this did not curb the pronatalism of the French State. In 1939, a wide-ranging pronatalist family policy was introduced to bolster the existing laws encouraging women to give birth – the 'décret-loi de 29 juillet 1939 rélatif à la famille et à la natalité française'. Article 91, according to Trifirino, emphasised the illegality of providing patients with 'objets' favourable to abortion.[19] The main body of the decree included child benefit for the first born, increased family allowances, reorganisation of child protection, including orphans and illegitimate children, the suppression of 'stupéfiants' including alcohol, compulsory teaching of the problems of demography in France and stricter control on nursing homes where women gave birth with the creation of 'maisons maternelles départementales'.[20] During the Occupation, Nazi ideology exacerbated the situation for women, who were forced to leave work and exhorted to give birth.[21] Between 1942 and 1944 there were hundreds of cases where people were sentenced for 'propagande anticonceptionnelle', against Article 317 of the Penal Code, including a M. Humbert who sent a book describing methods to a farmer at the farmer's request. He was sentenced to eighteen months' imprisonment and fined 6,000 francs.[22] Interestingly, Humbert was charged with aiding and abetting an abortion, 'complicité de tentative d'avortement', so the two were clearly linked with, for example, spermicides being seen as abortifacient, though this distinction was probably unnecessary in such a wide-ranging law.

Maternal health in the UK

While all supplying of contraceptives was prohibited in France from 1920 to 1967, gradually by contrast, in the UK, from the 1920s the government began to allow for contraceptive advice and eventually provision. It could be said that any pronatalist tendency in the UK focused on ensuring that more healthy babies were born as opposed to more babies *per se*, which was the case in France. There is no evidence of a specifically pronatalist movement in the UK, indeed, the idea of women's emancipation coming from the freedom to choose not to bear children gained support increasingly among Labour and Liberal party women. However, in the face of opposition to contraception from trade unions[23] and religious bodies and medical indifference, the government concentrated on the issue of improving maternal health throughout the 1920s and 1930s.[24]

This is underlined by the fact that no publicly funded British health service existed in the 1920s, but government interest in the welfare of children and maternal mortality, following the publication of numerous reports up to the Second World War, did ensure that maternity and child welfare centres were set up by local authorities from the 1920s. This was an improvement for women's reproductive health. These centres did not offer contraceptive advice to mothers however; they were designed to improve the health of mothers and children, but that did not include advising women to have fewer children or on how to avoid having children at a time of relative ignorance on sexual matters. In 1922, Edmonton Council dismissed a health visitor who had distributed contraceptive advice. Welfare centres were also threatened with the withdrawal of government funding if they attempted to provide actual contraceptives, despite the fact that this would not be illegal.[25]

However in the late 1920s there began to be indications of public support for contraception.[26] In July 1930, the Ministry of Health (MOH), issued Memorandum 153/MCW, whereby local authorities could give instruction on birth control to mothers whose health would be affected by further pregnancy. Really this amounted to the lifting of Circular 517 on Maternal Health, issued in 1924 where the Minister of Health banned welfare centres from providing information to mothers under any circumstances. Initially this Memorandum was not issued to the press or local authorities. Its meaning was also obscure. 'While local authorities had "no general power to establish birth control clinics", they could do so under the Notifications of Births (Extension) Act 1915, which enabled local authorities to exercise the powers of the Public Health Acts, for a) expectant and nursing mothers and b) "sick" women suffering from gynaecological conditions.'[27] Medical advice could be given to married women at centres only if 'further pregnancy would be detrimental to health' and if given separately from other advice. The Minister of Health added that it was in the interests of health that he was allowing contraceptive advice to be given, but without parliamentary approval he could not permit public money to be spent on giving contraception to any woman who asked for it. However, this was the first 'official' sanction of contraception.

The clinics set up by local authorities in the 1920s and 1930s, and the advisory aspects of welfare centres, were administered mainly by the women volunteers of the National Birth Control Council (NBCC).

The issue of maternal mortality rates encouraged the government to permit contraceptive provision by the NBCC through government reports on the issue, publicity and lobbying by women's birth control groups. Therefore the 1930 Memorandum was extended in 1934 by Circular 1408 so that advice could be given to patients with illnesses that could be treated with birth control, for example gynaecological disorders or any illness that could render pregnancy dangerous to health. Provisions for maternal health were also provided in the Midwives Act of July 1936 and Circular 1622 in May 1937, which advised local authorities to set up post-natal clinics where mothers could have birth control advice on medical grounds.[28] R. v. Bourne (1938)[29] reaffirmed the precedence given to maternal health, as after this case abortion was permitted to safeguard the life and the mental and physical health of women. Such a test could arguably be extended to other forms of contraception and voluntary sterilisation.

Voluntary provision in the UK

From the 1920s, the British family-planning movement set up clinics, providing advice (and supplies) nationally and ostensibly being sanctioned by the government. Such provision was not available in France until the 1950s, and even then it certainly did not enjoy government approval.

When the British health services were reorganised into a National Health Service in 1946, the voluntary clinics set up since the 1920s still continued to provide contraception to the public, as family planning had not been mentioned in the Act. Before 1946, the clinics had been autonomous, but under the authority of local authorities who funded them and provided premises. This continued after 1946.

Pre-war directives still therefore applied to local authority responsibilities. Local Health Authorities (LHAs) had the power under the NHS Act 1946 to contribute to any voluntary organisation formed for the purpose of the care of expectant and nursing mothers (Section 22) and for the prevention of illness, care and aftercare (Section 28). The guidelines set by Memorandum 153/MCW were also still applicable. These guidelines were interpreted in varying forms throughout the country; some authorities (more than a third) did not assist the Family Planning Association (FPA) in the setting up of clinics, though others provided grants and premises to them.

Despite the voluntary provision of contraceptives in the UK this was only tolerated if provided on medical grounds, illustrating once more the growing medicalisation of contraception during this period. Doctors were not obliged to give contraceptive advice unless they considered it medically necessary. This meant that they did not have to give free provision if it were on social grounds, which led to disputes between general practitioners and the Ministry as to the dividing line between social and medical grounds. In 1952, the Ministry felt it necessary to rule that if a doctor charged a fee for 'non-medical' provision, he may have to justify his reasons to the local medical committee. This does not mean to say that doctors provided contraception on non-medical grounds on a wide scale. In 1961 oral contraceptives were permitted to be prescribed for therapeutic purposes on the NHS; it was up to the individual doctor to decide whether there were sufficient medical grounds and whether or not he could justify charging a fee otherwise. In 1964, fees were set for the issuing (on non-medical grounds) of private (non-NHS) prescriptions for oral contraceptives and for the prescription and fitting of contraceptive appliances and intrauterine devices (IUDs). Surveys in the late 1960s showed increased surgery attendance by women and a tendency for doctors to restrict advice to that on oral contraception.

Hospitals 'could provide contraceptive advice for "sick" women (but) many gynaecologists lacked time in their already overcrowded departments'.[30] Some doctors did set up hospital clinics, usually run by the FPA, but this depended on the cooperation of the gynaecologists and the hospital board. In 1954, the Minister of Health decided that hospitals could let premises for FPA clinics where contraceptive advice could be given to patients referred for medical reasons by hospitals, their general practitioners (GPs) or by LHAs as nursing mothers.

The NHS could not at this time therefore provide contraceptives to minors, single women or on non-medical grounds. Up until the late 1960s, establishment attitudes were still resistant to birth control. This created countless difficulties for women attempting to limit pregnancies and have control over their own sexual health.

Voluntary provision in France

Voluntary family planning clinics in France were also set up, though not until 1956, by the French family planning movement, Mouvement Français pour le Planning Familial (MFPF). The only common contraceptive practices in France at this time were the use of condoms or of 'coitus interruptus'. Diaphragms were available up until the 1920s through neo-Malthusians, but after that time, to the detriment of the majority of French women, modern methods were only available to middle-class women who travelled secretly to the UK, the Low Countries and Switzerland.

However, family planning began to be tolerated and cracks did begin to appear in the French legal armour. In 'l'affaire Bac', for example, ostensibly a case on infanticide but relevant to the issue of contraception, a young couple were sentenced to seven years' imprisonment for unintentional manslaughter of their fifth newly born child. The first judgment of June 1954 at the assizes court of the Seine was thrown out for 'vice de forme' in March 1955. The second trial at the assizes court of Seine-et-Oise on 6 June 1955 presented another opportunity for debate. This was especially the case when the accused couple were freed, having been in custody for two years. Their defence rested on the fact that the woman had been through five pregnancies in as many years, since the age of 20, without any material, familial, social or medical support. Therefore, at the time of the death of the infant the mother was no longer physically or mentally capable of looking after her children and this had led to the death of the last born. In addition, all the witnesses and experts defended the accused, including the French family planner Dr Weill-Hallé, who emphasised that such cases were unheard of in Anglo-Saxon countries where contraceptives were legally available.[31]

The French family planning movement (MFPF) by the 1950s had started to set up centres, publish on contraception and inform patients on methods and the procuring of supplies; they did so completely illegally due to the 1920 law, but with impunity. Though it was not the aim of the founders to inform only middle-class women, they were never as successful in attracting working-class women members. In the 1960s doctors prescribed the oral contraceptive pill ostensibly for therapeutic reasons. It was therefore mainly working-class women who bore the brunt of the law, as they were affected by the successful policy of not informing the public on contraception. Those already in the know were less affected as the law was ineffectual on contraception and tended to concentrate on abortion.

Rights of spouses

Most of the cases that discussed contraception and sterilisation early in the twentieth century were heard in the divorce courts, and can be seen as a barometer not only of attitudes at the time but of spouses' rights around the issue of parenting. This raises the important issue of how far the law allowed a woman to control her own body and fertility.

In *Baxter* v. *Baxter* (1948) a husband had been forced by his wife since their wedding to use contraceptives during intercourse, despite his objections. The House of Lords judged this not to be non-consummation as intercourse had been physically possible under the Matrimonial Causes Act 1937 and was therefore not grounds for annulment of the marriage. However Viscount Jowitt, with whom all the other justices concurred, stated that 'the proper occasion for considering the subjects raised by this appeal is when the sexual life of the spouses, and the responsibility of either or both for a childless home, form the background to some other claim for relief'.[32]

In other words, that grounds for divorce could be found in such a case as this one, namely that of cruelty (replaced in the Matrimonial and Family Proceedings Act 1984 by the test of unreasonable behaviour).[33]

Arguably, women's reproductive rights have been continually curtailed by the law. A husband has a right to the consortium of his wife and the law has expected a wife to have a maternal instinct, which could be injured should the husband use contraceptives.[34] Between 1948 and 1954 there were several cases where husbands were found at fault for denying their wives' wish to have children. However, in *Forbes* v. *Forbes* (1956) a husband was given leave to divorce his wife when she denied him children because she simply did not want children, and also made intercourse 'unpleasant' for him through her use of contraceptives.

In France, the law regarding spouses rights and contraception at this time was similar to that in the UK due to the provisions of the Civil Code. Case law also granted equal rights to both partners to determine whether contraception should be used. In the nineteenth century there were cases where grounds for divorce were found after male contraceptives had been used (which was more likely at this time).[35] Between 1899 (after the Naquet law allowing divorce) and 1959, tribunals allowed divorce on the grounds that it was contrary to the duties of marriage to take contraceptives for a long period of time thus preventing conception.[36]

Since 1975, in France women have been allowed to use contraceptives of their own accord and without the consent of their husbands, but an unjustified and obstinate refusal to have children can be cited as injurious and therefore grounds for divorce, 'une 'injure' à l'égard de l'autre conjoint'.[37] Thus it is not the fact of using contraceptives themselves that constitutes a fault, but the refusal to satisfy the legitimate desire of a spouse to have children. Judges will distinguish between cases of young women refusing to have a first child after several years of marriage, and a multiparous mother who could be endangered by further pregnancy. However, marriage is legally consummated if contraceptives are used.[38] The obligation to have children is arguably implicit in the Civil Code itself, whereby spouses must live together (art. 215) and feed and raise their children. The liberalisation of contraception and abortion in no way detracted from this marital duty.[39]

Statutory reform in the UK

By the 1960s, the British government was forced to come to terms with public usage of contraception. The Pill was available to married women on therapeutic grounds on the NHS from 1961 and on social grounds privately from 1964, along with contraceptive appliances. It was not available for minors, single women or on the NHS on social grounds. It was popular with doctors as it did not necessitate insertion of appliances or detailed questioning of the patient on sexual behaviour, both of which were time-consuming and potentially embarrassing. This acceptance of the Pill may go someway to explain the new prominence given to doctors in the new legislation, as the Pill had inherent side effects, unlike previous methods. Provision of the Pill through doctor's surgeries, and the inclusion of this practice in the Act, also indicate a significant extension of the influence of the medical professions over contraception at this time by the professions themselves to the detriment of women, as women's voluntary groups had been providing freedom of choice to women for decades.

The National Health Service (Family Planning) Act 1967 cleared up many of the anomalies of birth control provision. LHA contraceptive services were extended to include social as well as medical criteria, with no restriction of provision on grounds of age or marital status (largely due to the involvement of Kenneth Robinson, the Health Minister). Section 1 empowered LHAs in the UK and Wales, with the approval of the Minister of Health, to make arrangements for the giving of advice on contraception, for medical examination of persons seeking such advice (again indicating medical influence) and for the supply of contraceptive substances and appliances.

Unfortunately the drafting of the Act had not dealt with certain problems. Contraceptive provision was still permissive, not mandatory, to the detriment of women's rights. Hospital services were to remain under ministerial guidance through memoranda. Nor did the 1967 Act refer to wider aspects of birth control such as sterilisation, which were 'not considered appropriate for local authority community services',[40] or the question of minors and their consent to treatment. Finally, it was not stated in the Act that contraceptives in all cases would be free. Instead a ministerial circular to local authorities would stipulate that advice only would be free. Moreover, the Treasury would have the final say on the granting of funds to LHAs, not the Minister. The National Health Service Reorganisation Act 1973 repealed the 1967 Act and in Section 4 replaced the power of LHAs with a duty on the Secretary of State, with contraceptives provided on prescription with the usual exemptions. This was superseded in the National Health Service Act 1977, which imposed a duty on the Secretary of State in Section 5(1)(b) in place of Section 1 of the 1967 Act.[41]

Women's rights were enhanced from April 1974, following the election of a Labour government, as contraceptives were provided free, though there were still GP prescription charges and the service was not completely free in hospitals. In May 1974, the Department of Health and Social Security (DHSS) issued Circular H. S. C. (I. S.)32 outlining the arrangements of a comprehensive family planning service within the NHS. It was accompanied by a Memorandum of Guidance that dealt *inter alia* with family planning clinics. Finally, in July 1975 the Government promised that there would be no prescription charge, but GPs refused to provide free condoms for men as doctors viewed these devices as being non-medical. Again this illustrates the freedom enjoyed by the medical professions to restrict women's rights, and arguably men's rights too. 'The outcome represented the first completely free, universally available, birth control service in Western Europe.'[42] There does not appear to have been much regulation of testing, sales and usage, however.[43]

Contraception has now become largely accepted in the UK as being as much a medical treatment as any other. It has therefore to be administered following the same guidelines, whether statutory or professional. Thus a GP must offer learned and prudent advice, must examine his patient competently and gain her consent for such examination or treatment. Family planning clinics must do so too and bear in mind the general health of the patient, not necessarily pertaining to contraception.[44] That is not to say that threats to the provision of contraceptives have not been seen nor that women's rights campaigners have not had to demonstrate a keen awareness and vigilance during campaigns on contraception (*see* Chapter 3).

In two cases, women sought compensation after the contraceptive Depo-Provera was administered to them without their necessary informed consent. Mrs Potts[45] thought she was being vaccinated against rubella. She did not know she was being given Depo-Provera and thus could not give her informed consent nor make a choice about treatment before the contraception was administered. Her claim for assault therefore succeeded. Compulsory contraception would not be allowed. In *Blyth* v. *Bloomsbury AHA*,[46] it was held that in order to consent, a woman must have the advantages and disadvantages of a drug explained to her, even if she initially consented, for it to be a fully informed consent. However, in the Appeal Court this decision was overruled, as the *Sidaway*[47] professional standard was said to apply. Mrs Blyth was therefore considered not to be entitled to any more information about contraceptive treatment than any other medical treatment. Arguably, this was yet another step on the road to the medicalisation of contraception. Doctors are held to be entitled to decide what women are entitled to know, rather than women themselves. Women patients need information as well as access, but unfortunately their rights have been restricted.[48]

Statutory reform in France

France also enacted a statute liberalising contraception in 1967 (which was also amended in 1973 and 1974), though this was not as extensive as the English Act.

Throughout the post-war period, parliamentary debate on contraception was periodically initiated. Between 1948 and 1956 three bills were introduced on the liberalisation of contraception; between 1957 and 1967 eleven bills were proposed, mostly by the left wing, but ignored by the government. In 1965 Socialist Deputy, François Mitterrand made the issue part of his manifesto during his unsuccessful presidential election campaign.[49]

Finally, Lucien Neuwirth, a Gaullist deputy and masonic ally of members of the MFPF, put forward a backbench bill on birth control that would modify Articles 3 and 4 of the 1920 law relating to contraception rather than abortion. Debates in committee, the Assembly and Senate mirrored those of 1920, with emphasis being laid by opponents on the birth rate and immorality.[50] As in the UK, there was also a new emphasis on the need for medical safeguards with the introduction of the contraceptive pill, and on the social and economic need for contraception due to the new support of ideas promoted by the MFPF. In contrast to the animation surrounding the 1920 debate, the law of 1967 was finally passed in the Assembly on the last day of the session, 19 December 1967, in the presence of only sixty deputies. It became the law of 28 December 1967, the 'loi Neuwirth'.[51]

Under the 1967 law, contraceptive medications and appliances were now available, but the law was still restrictive on the actions of women patients, which were closely monitored by the State. Under Article 2, contraceptives could in theory be manufactured and imported, subject to administrative guidelines. But not until 1969 were guidelines issued on the actual legal position of the sale and manufacture of contraceptives in France, which deterred those organisations involved in this side of things and restricted the availability of contraceptives.[52] It remains questionable how far the manufacture of contraceptives can be monitored by the State. Contraceptive medications were added to the official list of 'stupéfiants', or drugs, by the Minister of Social Affairs. Abortifacients were still outlawed under Article 3. Prescriptions were limited in time and number, with receipts, 'carnets à souches', to be made out for each patient every time contraceptives were prescribed.[53] Prescriptions for minors had to contain the consent of one parent.[54] This was at a time when the age of majority was 21 (until 1969).[55]

Contraceptives could only be supplied by pharmacists and IUDs had to be inserted by a medical practitioner in a hospital (or clinic – 'milieu hospitalier') (art. 3), subject to ministerial and administrative guidelines, respectively. (This became significant in the late 1990s when emergency contraception began to be more freely available.) Contraceptives were not free. Publicity was no longer directly prohibited but 'antinataliste' propaganda was, and commercial publicity on contraceptives and pregnancy test kits, 'objets de nature à prévenir la grossesse', was restricted to medical journals (art. 5). Information could only be provided by 'les établissements d'information, de consultation et de conseil familial' and 'les centres de planification et d'éducation familiales' and these non-profit-making, private or public, family centres only provided information, not contraceptives themselves (art 4). Doctors were not obliged to give advice on or supply contraceptives and thus many refused.[56] Reflecting the widespread fears among politicians of the effect of contraception on the declining birth rate, under Article 8 the Social Affairs Minister was instructed to present an annual report on demography and how far the law was being applied. Under the law, the unlawful import, manufacture and sale of contraceptives, the unlawful giving of information or patients not filling out 'carnet à souches' and the treatment of minors were punished with increased severity.

Even this rather inadequate law was not fully operational until April 1972, as the Government delayed the publication of the necessary 'décrets d'application'. This attitude was typical of the early 1970s and outsiders continually campaigned for improvements in the law. For example, Deputy Lucien Neuwirth expanded the provision of information and publicity on contraception through the setting up of a group to promote sex education, the 'Conseil supérieur de l'information sexuelle, de la régulation des naissances, et de l'éducation nationale' in the 'Loi du 11 juillet 1973'.

The law of 4 December 1974,[57] initiated once more by Neuwirth, amended the 1967 law by replacing Articles 3, 5 and 6, and thus eradicating the necessity for records, or 'carnet à souches', and parental consent for minors, and introducing reimbursement by the State of the cost of contraception. Abortifacients were no longer outlawed, thus indicating that the morning-after pill could now be made available. To the detriment of French women, the government attempted to ensure that women could be monitored through medical examinations by maintaining prescriptions. These had to be exchanged at chemists (apart from for spermicides and condoms, which had to be paid for by the patient (art. 1)) and under a decree of 5 May 1975 (75–317), the Public Health Code was altered to further restrict the supply of contraceptives on a single prescription to three months, with repeat prescriptions only up to one year.[58] Moreover, in a case in 1981 it was found that chemists were not obliged to make contraceptives available.[59] For minors who did not want their parents to be informed, or those who were without medical assurance and whose costs would not be reimbursed by the Social Security, designated centres would receive grants from the State to give contraceptives free of charge (art. 2). Medical examinations would also take place at these centres.

The influence of pronatalism was still apparent as 'anti-nataliste' propaganda was still illegal and commercial publicity on contraceptives restricted to medical journals, while information on pregnancy testing was not (art. 3). The law also advocated a publicity campaign on contraception, but this was only put into practice by the Socialist government under the aegis of its Ministry for Women from 1981. However, information on contraception became obligatory under the abortion law of 17 January 1975, whereby the establishment carrying out the abortion was obliged to inform the patient of contraceptive methods. There were penalties for ignoring this rule by Article L. 178 of Code de la Santé ('retrait de l'habilitation' – withdrawal of approval) and the decree of 27 September 1983, whereby abortion clinics had to have family planning facilities. Despite this, the rule is not always followed.[60] Naturally this is an improvement for women, but appears to underscore the prevalence of pronatalism within Parliament and government, in that widespread contraceptive information only became available to prevent abortion, and was thus seen as a lesser evil. This also indicates the strength of the moralist lobby at this time.

When comparing statutory provision in the two countries three points emerge. First, neither country supplied contraceptives free of charge until 1974. In the UK, only advice was free from 1967 and from 1974 limits were still set. Second, the limited character of governmental support for this policy is indicated by the fact that only after 1973 in the UK was a duty imposed on the Secretary of State to provide contraceptives, and in France even the 1967 law was not implemented until 1972, with guidelines on manufacture not being introduced until 1969. Finally, in France pronatalism ensured that an annual report on contraceptive usage was introduced in 1967 and restrictions on information and 'propagande' kept each time the law was amended.

Provision for minors after 1967

In the 1967 Statutes of both countries the position of minors remained relatively unclear. In the UK after 1967 there was no restriction on provision on grounds of age, but the law on parental consent was unclear. In France, by contrast, from 1967 it was stipulated that prescriptions for minors had to contain the consent of one parent, although paradoxically from 1974 free contraceptives were available in designated clinics for minors who did not want their parents to be informed.

In the UK, the NHS Acts on family planning failed to put an end to heated debate about its provisions and during the 1970s and 1980s, through statute and case law, rights on contraception were amended and clarified, for example, as regards minors, as well as on sterilisation, consent to treatment and women patients' rights.

The Family Law Reform Act 1969 clarified the legal position of age limitation and parental consent by establishing the medical age of majority at sixteen – two years lower than the general majority age of eighteen. Provision for minors under the age of 16 created legal problems of parental consent when contraceptive advice began to be given in Brook Advisory Centres and FPA centres to under 16s from 1969. Brook Advisory Centres were established primarily to cater for the under 16s, and they continue to do so. On LHA premises, FPA clinics followed MOH guidelines and gave treatment to over 16s without proxy consent. Under 16s would need consent however. By 1972, 161 out of 232 LHAs used the FPA to provide contraceptive services, with eight LHAs restricting services for the unmarried.[61]

In *GMC* v. *Browne* in 1971[62] a Brook Advisory Centre provided a 16-year old with the Pill and informed her family doctor in confidence. He then decided to inform the girl's parents. The Centre took the case to the General Medical Council (GMC) who found the doctor not guilty of serious professional misconduct for breach of confidentiality as he had thought he was acting in the patient's best interests. The GMC subsequently advised their members not to disclose confidential information concerning their patients.[63] The FPA left the decision to doctors on whether to provide contraception and advised them to seek consent from the patient to inform her parents. This provided legal problems of parental consent and patient confidentiality.

Section G of the 1974 Circular (H.S.C.(I.S.)32) accompanying the Memorandum of Guidance dealt with regulations for family planning clinics and 'The Young'. This section was revised in the December 1980 Circular (H.N.(80)46) in the light of the Lane Report (Cmnd. 5579) and the wording of the Circular was changed so that the risk of pregnancy and of sexually transmitted diseases and the threat to family life of the refusing of contraception to minors, replaced the risk of abortion. With these risks in mind, it was considered that in exceptional circumstances where parents 'were unconcerned, entirely unresponsive, or grossly disturbed' or if girls had left home, then the doctor should decide whether or not to provide contraceptives to a minor without involving the parent and should respect the girl's confidentiality, so as not to deter her from seeking advice and supplies. However, the medical professional whose advice was sought must try and involve the parent immediately and only proceed after they had failed to persuade the girl to involve her parents.

Victoria Gillick attempted to gain declarations against the Area Health Authority and the DHSS that the notice was unlawful and wrong in *Gillick* v. *West Norfolk and Wisbech Area Health Authority* (1984) (1985).[64] In the High Court, Justice (J.) Woolf saw her argument as being twofold – that any doctor following the guidance would be causing or encouraging unlawful sexual intercourse with a girl under 16 (Sexual Offences Act 1956) and that it was inconsistent with the rights of parents not to be consulted. He found against Mrs Gillick, first, because a doctor would prescribe contraception in exceptional circumstances, having advised against it; his action would not produce intercourse and the contraceptives are not an instrument for the crime he would not therefore be abetting, counselling, procuring or aiding the crime, respectively. Second, because parents had duties to their children, not rights over them and in the absence of binding authority, a minor could consent to treatment if she showed 'maturity and understanding'.[65] She 'must be capable of making a reasonable assessment of the advantages and disadvantages of the treatment proposed'. This would depend on the treatment – a minor could not consent to sterilisation, for example.

Woolf, J. believed that the law should take into account the change in social attitudes since the Victorian era.[66] The Court of Appeal did not however.[67] In the leading judgment, Lord Justice (L.J.) Parker stated that only courts or parents could consent to medical treatment for minors except in emergencies according to several cases from the last century and the Family Law Reform Act 1969 s.8(3), which preserved the common law power of parents to consent on behalf of their children despite s.8(1) which allowed 16-year olds to consent. In the House of Lords, Victoria Gillick finally lost as the majority disagreed with this interpretation of nineteenth-century cases and s.8(3), finding that at common law parental rights were contingent on parental duties to the child and the child's best interests; that parental rights were now dwindling and ended when the child had sufficient intelligence and understanding to consent; and that it was public policy that if girls under 16 were going to have sex, though this was illegal and regrettable, pregnancy was an additional evil to be avoided and this should be taken into account when assessing such a girl's best interests.[68] Lord Templeman dissented, as he believed that although the criterion for capacity to consent in minors for normal medical treatment could be their age and understanding, where contraception was concerned parental rights of control should remain as this might prevent them from having sexual intercourse.[69]

However, Lord Fraser provided five considerations that the doctor must take into account before deciding whether or not to treat the girl and keep the information confidential,[70]

(1) that the girl (although under sixteen years of age) will understand his advice; (2) that he cannot persuade her to inform her parents or to allow him to inform the parents that she is seeking contraceptive advice; (3) that she is very likely to begin or to continue having sexual intercourse with or without contraceptive treatment; (4) that unless she receives contraceptive advice or treatment her physical or mental health or both are likely to suffer; (5) that her best interests require him to give her contraceptive advice, treatment or both without the parental consent.

Thus only treatment of benefit to the girl could be authorised and if a doctor provided contraception to an immature child he could be prosecuted for assault.

Moreover, if the child did not have the capacity to consent, she was less likely to be owed any duty of confidentiality by the doctor.[71] At the same time the test for assessing whether the child has understood is unclear from the judgments. In addition, it appears that Lord Fraser had merely transferred the power of the parent to decide on behalf of the child to the doctor without providing a review procedure for this discretion, whereas Lord Scarman let the child decide for herself.

Both countries now place the child's interests above the interests of her parents. However, the Gillick case has meant that English law now poses potential restrictions on younger women's rights, as the assessment of whether or not a girl under sixteen is mature enough to consent to contraceptive treatment is in the hands of doctors.[72] Contraceptive law for minors in France is much more favourable and straightforward than English law due to codified assurances. From 1974 in France there has been no minimum age for the supply of contraceptives or advice without parental consent. The law balances individual freedom with physical risk posed by a particular medical treatment.[73] In normal medical treatment of minors in France, the interests of the child are considered to be paramount in deciding between parent and child, with magistrates coming down in favour of treatment. For example, religious withholding of consent is not allowed as it could endanger health or life, which is unlawful if it can be considered to be 'non-assistance à personne en peril' (non-assistance to a person in danger) and 'défaut de soins à enfant de moins de 15 ans, de nature à compromettre sa santé' (behaviour which could endanger the health of a minor).[74] Ideas of pronatalism do not extend therefore to forcing minors to bear children, as their future reproductive health is more important. This would again indicate that pronatalist ideology is more prevalent than Roman Catholicism. The strength of moralism or Roman Catholicism in the UK is open to debate.

Sterilisation

Sterilisation, though an essential part of contraception for many women, has been treated as a separate question in both the UK and France, and also left unclear in legislation. Moreover, each country has dealt with the issue legally in a very different fashion. In the UK, sterilisation became an accepted part of medical contraceptive treatment that could be voluntary and non-therapeutic much earlier than in France, where there is evidence of pronatalist and Roman Catholic influence. Indeed, even up to the present day there is much less acceptance of sterilisation as voluntary and non-therapeutic in France, and medical discretion over sterilisation is the order of the day, to the detriment of women's rights.

In the UK there was moral and legal criticism of sterilisation up until the 1960s. According to the *Report of the Departmental Committee on Sterilisation* in 1934,[75] voluntary sterilisation in the UK in the 1930s was illegal or doubtfully legal. Interest groups campaigning for contraceptive liberalisation at this time did not feel that sterilisation was a safe topic. The NBCC never associated itself with the issue of sterilisation at this time but confined its campaigns to family planning or the spacing of children, rather than never having children. The Eugenics Society had a bill introduced in July 1931 to allow sterilisation of the mentally unfit. The bill was defeated and the issue abandoned by its supporters in the wake of publicity about the misuse of sterilisation in Nazi Germany.

The test for cruelty in divorce cases involving birth control was established in a case involving sterilisation, *Bravery* v. *Bravery* (1954), as that which was damaging to health, here alluding to the mental health of the wife as it prevented her from having children.[76]

Most notably the Law Lords also pointed out that they disagreed with the dissenting judge, Denning, L.J., who found for the wife and moreover claimed that when sterilisation was done 'with the man's consent for a just cause, it is quite lawful, as for instance when it is done to prevent the transmission of an hereditary disease; but when it is done without just cause or excuse, it is unlawful, even though the man consents to it'.[77] Denning, L.J. believed that sterilisation was a criminal assault and could not be excused therefore by the consent of the patient, and such operations would cause 'licentiousness' which was against the public interest.

His assessment has been criticised: acts that are contrary to the public interest or that encourage promiscuity 'are not criminal in themselves, and sterilisation cannot therefore be a criminal act in se simply because it may lead to either of these results'.[78] Other forms of contraception that were lawful could have the same results 'aside from its relative irreversibility',[79] and 'the common law has not chosen to treat surgical operations as illegal in and of themselves'.[80]

In *Sullivan* v. *Sullivan* (1970),[81] it was found that divorce would only be granted when the sterilisation had taken place during the marriage and not before. The majority of members of the court found that the wife did not suffer damage to her health as a result of a vasectomy undergone by her husband before the marriage, there had been no post-marital 'misconduct' and she could not therefore divorce him on the grounds of cruelty. They did point out that, in their opinion, sterilisation had 'grave potentialities' for marriage.[82]

However, the fact that sterilisations have been part of normal medical treatment in the UK since the 1950s rendered this debate largely unnecessary. As early as 1960 the Medical and Dental Defence Union was advising members that voluntary consent to sterilisation carried out for substantial reasons that were 'not obviously immoral by present day standards' would probably not be unlawful.[83] Doctors have only ever been under a duty to take reasonable care for the health and safety of their patients, not to provide treatment they did not wish to provide. Unfortunately, in essence this now means that a husband's right over reproduction has been transferred to the doctor who will have the final say over whether or not to allow sterilisation.[84]

Rights to sterilisation were therefore actually curtailed by the 1967 Act as British local authorities had no powers to finance vasectomy operations. The FPA opened clinics for vasectomy in 1968 and 1970 and members of the public showed increasing interest. Private clinics undertook approximately 30,000 operations in 1972.[85] A Private Member's Bill in 1971/72 to amend the 1967 Act became the NHS (Family Planning) Amendment Act 1972 and vasectomy was now provided free by LHAs. Throughout the passage of the bill opposition came from Roman Catholics and those worried about the alleged psychiatric problems associated with vasectomy. This was met, however, with intense lobbying by interest groups, and backbenchers in support of the bill.

There have been occasions when female sterilisation has been carried out concurrently with other operations without the consent of the woman concerned. It has now been held that it is unlawful to do so, and that women patients must be given the opportunity to consent.[86] A doctor must also fully explain the operation to a patient to gain an informed consent in a manner consistent with good medical practice. Initially, in *Udale v. Bloomsbury AHA* (1983) the law refused to compensate for unplanned births after failed sterilisations, but the Court of Appeal in *Emeh v. Kensington, Chelsea and Fulham AHA* (1983) overruled this policy judgement.[87] In *Allen v. Bloomsbury AHA* (1993) Brooke J. held that a woman could recover damages for a failed sterilisation in relation to some discomfort during pregnancy, financial loss and stress were the child handicapped.[88] After *Fish v. Wilcox* (1993), damages for loss of earnings or the cost of care of a handicapped child will not be recoverable.[89]

Voluntary sterilisation is now generally available in France, since the law of 4 July 2001 on abortion and contraception, whose Article 2123 authorised sterilisation. Before then it was a criminal offence, unless it could be clearly shown that the operation was performed in order to preserve the health or life of the patient and was therefore therapeutic.[90] It was a criminal offence in so far as it was a battery 'incompatible with human dignity'. Consent could not excuse it, as it cannot excuse criminal conduct of any kind. Therefore, though the French State reimbursed therapeutic sterilisation and male sterilisations in the case of genetic disorder, non-therapeutic operations were not reimbursed and not commonly covered by professional insurers (though some insurers would cover such operations along with abortions).[91] Until July 2001, no legal text dealt with the issue specifically; it was left entirely in the hands of medical practitioners who were able to operate on the grounds that their function was to cure and prevent illness.[92] The effect on women's rights and the inherent medical influence of this situation is clear.

The various bodies that make up the medical profession in France drafted their own set of rules that apply to therapeutic sterilisation. Firm positions were taken against non-therapeutic sterilisation in the 1950s.[93] These were reiterated as late as the 1970s.[94]

Non-therapeutic sterilisation of non-consenting men and women has been outlawed since the case of the 'stérilisateurs de Bordeaux'. On 1 July 1937 the criminal chamber of the Cour de Cassation confirmed the judgment of the Cour d'Appel at Bordeaux and convicted a Mr Bartosek under Article 309 of the Penal Code under 'coups et blessures volontaires' (battery and wounding) for the performance of a vasectomy. An experienced performer of sterilisations, though not a doctor, he, with two assistants, had carried out around fifteen such operations on consenting patients. Initially they were accused under Article 316 of castration and violence of a permanently incapacitating nature. The defence argued that vasectomy was not permanent, as it could be reversed and was not therefore an act of castration and the case was withdrawn. The accusation was therefore changed to one of premeditated battery and wounding under Articles 309, 310 and 311 of the Penal Code. The defendants pleaded not guilty as, though they agreed with the fact that operations had taken place, they had not acted with criminal intent and their actions were excused by the consent of the patients. They made analogies with other operations that were non-therapeutic but legal, such as plastic surgery, circumcision and ear-piercing.[95]

However, they were found guilty firstly by the Tribunal correctionnel, then the Cour d'Appel at Bordeaux. Finally, the Cour de Cassation found that the Cour d'Appel had applied the texts in a fair manner and that it was the law that physical damage to oneself with one's consent was only allowed by the necessity of legitimate defence or where it was therapeutic in some way, because it was against the public interest. Consent did not mean that 'pré-méditation' did not apply. Nor was it relevant if the operation was performed by a doctor. Consent would not excuse an operation that was against the public interest, which, in other words, led to an inability to procreate, as this endangered the future of society. The only sterilisation that was legal was a therapeutic one, and that must be carried out by a doctor. Eugenic or contraceptive sterilisation is, therefore, doubtfully legal.[96] More specifically, it appeared from the case that on consent the law was surprisingly still covered by nineteenth-century case law, which ruled against duels and suicides.[97]

Some members of the medical professions have spoken in favour of non-therapeutic sterilisation. For example, a more progressive medical body was set up in December 1975, L'Association Nationale pour l'Etude de la Stérilisation Volontaire (ANESV).[98] An obstetrician, Professeur Merger, also argued in 1979 that female non-therapeutic sterilisation was now more successful and more acceptable socially with the rise of feminism and the law on abortion which promoted the idea of women making such a decision, and that judges would no longer follow the decision of the 1937 case.[99] At the same time, more liberal doctors stated that male sterilisation did not lead to psychological problems and was now reversible, and could be a form of contraception for men within couples.

It would appear that the Code de Déontologie itself compelled doctors to perform voluntary sterilisation. A decree of 28 June 1979 did not mention sterilisation but Article 22 stated that mutilation could only be carried out in extremely serious medical cases and, unless it were impossible or an emergency, with the consent of the patient and 'intéressés'. However, 'mutilation' could not apply to non-therapeutic sterilisation for several reasons. First, this would contradict the Resolution of the Council of Europe of 14 November 1975, which France voted for, which recognised voluntary sterilisation as a medical act and one method by which couples and individuals could exercise their right to limit their family number. Second, Article 7 of the Code de Déontologie and more general rules on consent could be seen to place the choice of having the operation in the hands of the patient, advised and informed by the doctor; it would be up to the patient therefore to have a non-therapeutic sterilisation, not the doctor, though as with all medical treatment in France it has not been usual to obtain formal consent in practice.[100]

Moreover, in reference to voluntary and non-therapeutic sterilisation, it is unlikely that a prosecution would ever have been launched if the patient were competent to consent. It is arguable whether it would ever really be found to be a public order offence, and moreover, the 1937 judgment itself could be considered as a violation of personal liberty.[101] However, as with contraception, the use of which constituted grounds for divorce in cases at least up to 1959, sterilisation could be seen as a lack of devotion and duty in marriage. Judges would appear to prefer that the couple consent together to the operation, to prevent it being used later as a ground for divorce.[102]

Furthermore, in practice, voluntary sterilisation on men has been carried out and doctors have been advised to perform a reversible operation, with the written consent of a well-informed patient. The sperm storage organisation, Centre d'Etude et de Conservation de la Sperme (CECOS), carried out vasectomies from the late 1970s. But their rules are strict. The patient must see a psychologist before the doctor,[103] they may leave a deposit of sperm for their own use and the couple must have at least one child. However, the questionable legal status of non-therapeutic sterilisation has meant that in civil cases in the early 1980s, women who claimed damages for the failure of the operation were unsuccessful. This seriously impairs women's rights, though these cases have at least extended the legal grounds for therapeutic sterilisation. In October 1981 at the Cour d'Appel at Nîmes a woman had became pregnant for the seventh time after a failed sterilisation. It was decided that there were no therapeutic grounds for carrying out the sterilisation, it was therefore illegal and the woman had no case for the doctor to answer. However, the doctor was charged with carrying out an illegal operation.[104] In the case of 9 mai 1983, a woman of 28 who could not take any form of contraception fell pregnant for the sixth time after a failed sterilisation. Her claim for damages against the doctor was rejected for non-suit at the Cour d'Appel in Rouen in 1982, but the Chambre civile de la Cour de Cassation ruled that the operation *was* therapeutic and took into account the health and social aspects of the woman, thus extending the grounds for such an operation. The doctor had to pay damages to the woman (20,000 francs) on the grounds that he failed to inform the woman of the possibility of failure of the operation, but not, in contrast to English case law, for the unplanned birth of the child that the failed operation had incurred.[105] There do not appear to have been any cases brought by people claiming to have changed their minds or not consented.

Emergency contraception

The provision of contraceptives to women is currently undergoing change, perhaps even revolution, in both the UK and France in relation to emergency contraception. Emergency contraception, or the morning-after pill, acts either on the ovum before fertilisation or before implantation has taken place and a pregnancy begun. It consists of two pills, one to be taken as soon as possible after sexual intercourse, the second twelve hours later, both within seventy-two hours of unprotected sex. It differs from the abortion pill RU486 or Mifegyne, which acts to expel the embryo once it has established itself in the wall of the womb and can be taken up to eight weeks after conception. This has repercussions in relation to the law in this area. RU486 is, naturally, governed by abortion law in both countries and is therefore subject to much stricter surveillance, medical and political, than emergency contraception.

In May 2000, the Department of Health began a six-week consultation exercise on an application by Schering Health Care to reclassify under the Medicines Act 1968 the status of the emergency hormonal contraceptive containing levonorgestrel 0.75mg (Levonelle 2). This reclassification would change the contraceptive from a prescription-only medicine to one available without prescription to women aged sixteen or above by amendment to the Prescription Only Medicines (Human Use) Order 1997 ('The POM Order') which sets out what may be supplied by a registered pharmacist. Only medicines not classified as being a risk to human health may be supplied without the supervision of a doctor under Directive 92/26/EEC and the Medicines Act 1968, Section 58A. The Medicines Act 1968 governs the retail sale and supply of medicines.

Organisations such as the Birth Control Trust and the British Pregnancy Advisory Service (BPAS) have argued that women's needs would be best met by having a variety of providers and OTC emergency contraception would lessen the stigma attached to requesting such a medicine from a doctor.[106]

More importantly, however, they have been joined by the providers of emergency contraception in Britain, Schering Health Care, who manufacture the principal product used, PC4. In a press release on 12 June 1998, Schering stated their support for the idea of group protocols being used to enable a wider group of prescribers than GPs to be involved in the supply of emergency contraception. A number of MPs also published an Early Day Motion in June 1998 advocating pharmacy prescription of emergency contraception.[107]

In France, Norlevo (called Norvelon, Levonelle 2, or levenorgestrel in the UK), a form of emergency contraception, has been available without a medical prescription from pharmacies since June 1999, though not reimbursed by the national health service, in contrast to other contraceptive provision. Segolene Royal, the French Minister of State for Schools, went further and announced on 6 January 2000 that emergency contraception would be available from nurses in secondary schools as well as from doctors in order to reduce the teenage pregnancy rate of 10,000 pregnancies and 6,000 abortions annually. These nurses would be instructed to gain medical information about their patient. A nurse would also be under an obligation to inform parents where the girl was a minor. If there were no parental consent, the nurse was advised to refer the patient for treatment at a Family Planning Centre, unless in an emergency. Despite the misgivings of conservative and religious members of French society, an opinion poll showed two-thirds of the French population to be in favour of school-nurse providers.[108] A furore ensued during the summer of 2000. On 30 June, the Conseil d'Etat ruled that the provision of emergency contraception must under Article 3 of the 1967 law be limited to pharmacists and could not be administered by school nurses. A government bill was published in turn on 27 July 2000, which sought to liberalise statute law on contraception and abortion (see Chapters 3 and 5). This became law on 4 July 2001, officially sanctioning provision.[109]

Reaction from across the Channel to the pharmacy provision available in France came in the form of another Early Day Motion published by cross-party British MPs in November 1999.[110] The sixteen MPs, three women, and thirteen men, congratulated the French, criticised the restrictive availability of emergency contraception in the UK and called for its swift reform. It was made available OTC from January 2001.

This new form of contraceptive provision raises a series of questions. Will there be sufficient safeguards to protect women's health? What issues are raised by girls under sixteen seeking contraception? Will pharmacists ever agree to supply contraception OTC on practical grounds or on moral grounds?

Despite the freedoms that the deregulation of emergency contraception offers, it raises concerns in many people's minds of the dangers of self-medication. Hormonal contraceptives do carry a small risk of causing medical complications. These include thrombosis, ectopic pregnancy and strokes. Oral emergency contraception contains a higher dose of hormones than standard hormonal contraceptives and if used other than in moderation can increase the risk of deep vein thrombosis.[111]

It should be borne in mind, however, that drugs which are potentially more dangerous than contraceptives are already available OTC and have been for a number of years. Aspirin and paracetamol, for example, are available in supermarkets as well as pharmacies though they carry with them high risks of stomach bleeds, liver failure and death from overdose. Indeed their dangers were highlighted when the Department of Health in the UK instituted changes to packaging reducing their number to sixteen per packet and introducing new health warnings in late 1996.[112]

The risks of contraception should also be compared with the risks associated with not having contraception. A woman is at a higher risk of thrombosis from pregnancy than the Pill. An unwanted and unplanned pregnancy has serious and long-term consequences for a woman's mental and physical health. Contraceptives are less of a risk to health than abortion, pregnancy or childbirth. It does not follow, therefore, that contraceptives are too medically dangerous to be available OTC.

Indeed, the concept of patient autonomy has already had some recognition in the medical law of both Britain and France. In Britain, *Chatterton v. Gerson*[113] underlined that patients have the right to be given adequate information in broad terms about a medical treatment in order for their consent to that treatment to be valid. Following *Whitehouse v. Jordan*,[114] they have a right not to be harmed by a medical treatment as doctors have a duty of care, and patients the right to refuse any form of treatment. In relation to side effects arising from the self-medication of oral contraception, under the Consumer Protection Act 1987, a contraceptive manufacturer would be subject to strict liability for injury arising from a defect in its product if there were evidence that the manufacturer failed to act on evidence of risk to health not justified by the product's contraceptive benefit.

Certain legal issues in relation to OTC emergency contraception remain unresolved, however. In relation to informed consent, in the *Sidaway*[115] case it was held that a doctor who conforms to a responsible body of medical opinion when deciding what to tell a patient about the side effects of a proposed treatment discharges his duty of disclosure to that patient. Any opinion a defendant is claiming he or she conformed to must have a logical basis however, and cannot be excused merely because it is a medical opinion of what service or information should be provided to a reasonable patient.[116] It is unclear how far this applies to pharmacists and remains to be resolved due to the lack of case law involving pharmacists. It is unclear, for example, whether the pharmacist needs to ensure that information relating to a medicine is read, heard and understood for a truly informed consent.

In France, the provision of emergency contraception by pharmacists has been deemed by the French Government to be acceptable under the present law. The French statute of 28 December 1967, 'loi Neuwirth', provides that contraception shall only be available on prescription.[117] Emergency contraception, however, is not a contraceptive drug, as it does not prevent 'conception' but acts to prevent the implantation of the egg in the womb. Moreover, the European Directive 92/26/EEC requires levonorgestrol to be available without a doctor's prescription and this takes precedence over French law, though a European Directive requires implementation by a member state of the European Union.[118]

In relation to English law on minors, there is also the problem of pharmacists supplying contraceptives to girls under the age of sixteen. Unfortunately for minors in the UK, it appears that the application by Schering Health Care to reclassify the status of the emergency contraception only makes this available, at least officially, to women aged sixteen or above. Women under 16 will still have to apply to their GP for emergency contraception on prescription. Here the *Gillick* ruling would therefore apply that a girl would have to appear to be mature enough to understand any advice she was given, and that the GP felt it was in the girl's best interests to be given contraceptive advice and treatment.

There are pharmacists who are reticent. Some see emergency contraception from a moral standpoint as an abortifacient and do not want to be involved in the supply of the drug. Such pharmacists can use their right to conscientious objection.[119] The Committee on Safety of Medicines has, however, given its approval and considered that a pharmacy would be able to complete all the necessary steps for the safe supply of emergency contraception. Such steps would include the referral to a doctor of any woman asking for emergency contraception if she were found to be taking other contraindicated medicines, the encouragement of women to see a doctor for advice and that such recommendations should form part of the information leaflet which accompanied the medication. Such advice does seem unnecessarily paternalistic, but, given that this is one step toward liberalisation, may have to be accepted, albeit with reservations. The Royal Pharmaceutical Society of Great Britain also developed its own guidelines for pharmacists to ensure the safe supply of emergency contraception OTC from January 2001.

There is a need for safeguards to protect women's health. These might be provided by pharmacists acting in women's best interests and keeping themselves and their customers informed of the potential dangers of such products as emergency contraception. Further safeguards might also include keeping a record of personal details of a transaction and liaising with local GPs, though bearing issues of confidentiality in mind. In addition, pharmacists might offer to carry out pregnancy tests before supplying contraceptives. Indeed, pregnancy testing is a service which pharmacists already provide.

Conclusions

The contraceptive issue neatly illustrates the legal differences between two countries, where one country's law is mainly written into case law and another's law as statute or code. Case law is more susceptible to be challenged and can evolve more easily to keep pace with social change. Contraceptive law in the twentieth century has therefore been more liberal in the UK than in France. Bearing this in mind however, the 1967 statute law in France was relatively more progressive, due to the restrictiveness of the 1920 law which it was replacing. There are also similarities between the contraceptive law of the two countries. For example, spouses have enjoyed equal contraceptive rights, and the 1967 statutes had to be amended in the early 1970s in order to make contraception free and available to minors. Sterilisation was also largely treated separately from other forms of contraception in both countries.

Contraception is also an issue which neatly illustrates the main differences between France and the UK in relation to medicalisation, pronatalism and women's rights.

In France, voluntary sterilisation remained illegal until July 2001, to the extent that women were not compensated for unplanned births following illegal failed non-therapeutic sterilisations. The fact that non-therapeutic sterilisation remained illegal in France is therefore a striking example of medicalisation in this area, and is testament to the fact that the medical professions are in agreement with pronatalist arguments. Medicalisation has also been evident in the English case law that has transferred reproductive rights in relation to sterilisation from husbands to doctors rather than to women themselves. In both countries, medical power was also officially recognised by the 1967 statutes, due to the influence of the Pill and the need when prescribing it for medical safeguards, though such power could only be officially sanctioned in the UK before 1967, as contraception in France was explicitly illegal.

Both countries' contraceptive ideology was also influenced by demography, though this was especially the case in France. In the UK, government funding of contraception was prevented due to a lack of parliamentary support, which also ensured that government support for birth control was only on the grounds of maternal health and medical backing. Nevertheless, lobbying by family planners did secure the extension of both the supply of information and of contraceptives themselves. This situation was better than in France where there

was very little legal access before the 1967 law, and this had to be further
amended in 1974 to finally ensure equitable supplies. However, to the benefit
of women's rights, pronatalism in France may have ensured that minors have
specific legal access to contraception. Here is another example of how in recent
years Roman Catholics may have lost out in France, in contrast to the UK
where it was religious groups which sustained the *Gillick* case, albeit with
qualified success.

In relation to women's rights various legal impediments remain; in the UK
minors' access to contraception is unclear. However, in the UK, women's
access to contraception was endorsed by the government decades before
women's rights in France were given even a semblance of recognition, even
after the granting of statutory provision. More recently, the availability of
emergency contraception across the counter has been instigated on both sides
of the Channel. Another positive step on the road to the liberalisation of
women's reproductive rights.

The factors determining the legal differences and similarities between the
UK and France, and the relative influence of those interest groups who
campaigned around the issue of contraception in both countries, will be more
thoroughly analysed in the next Chapter.

3

The creation of contraceptive policy

Despite the fact that in both the UK and France there was statutory provision for contraception for the first time in 1967, the laws themselves were quite different. These differences were a result of the nature of the legal environment that campaigners were working within in each country, in other words the laws themselves. It was also a consequence of the *political* environment and the effect this had on the interest groups involved in the policy process.

An assessment of that political environment and policy process assists in an analysis of the impact of reproductive campaigners on potential allies and on legislators. This entails an examination of groups campaigning for contraceptive provision and of opposition groups, their membership, structure, aims, methods and resources. As detailed in Chapter 1, interest group theory predicts how far these will limit and in turn also determine the place that group will take or be offered by the government in the policy-making arena. In turn this will determine their relative influence on any resulting policy and legislation.

Birth control campaigns took place in the UK from the 1920s and in France from the 1950s. An important role in these campaigns was played by women's rights groups. Early, liberal feminists had an alliance-building capacity and enjoyed the support of numerous allies, particularly on the left wing. They faced vigorous opposition to their ideas from certain quarters – particularly from the Roman Catholic Church and certain medical professionals.

It was in the face of these opponents that family planners in both countries unavoidably contributed to the medicalisation of policy on contraception.

Campaigns in Britain: contraceptive provision and medicalisation

It was not until after the First World War, when women were granted suffrage, that women's rights campaigners had the time to devote to other matters concerning female emancipation, such as birth control. These campaigns were made up of 'suffragettes', women members of the Labour movement, and individual Liberal and Conservative women. They were essentially middle-class women working voluntarily, and their activities followed the model set in the late nineteenth century by such bodies as the British Women's Temperance Association.

The first two, unrelated, clinics providing contraceptive services were opened in 1921 by Marie Stopes in March and the Malthusian League (the Walworth Women's Welfare Centre) in November.[1] Both intended that the government should be encouraged to imitate their example by extending State involvement in maternal health to include the provision of publicly funded contraception in maternity and child welfare clinics.[2]

Unfortunately there were differences of opinion between Stopes and the League in the early 1920s. Stopes set up the Society for Constructive Birth Control and Racial Progress in August 1921 to carry out propaganda and 'recognise the sacredness of motherhood'[3] and was jealous of others being involved separately in contraception. She disagreed with their methods and economic arguments.[4] It is noteworthy, however, that these early clinic pioneers shared a belief in the link between contraception, Malthusianism and eugenics.[5] These disagreements among women's rights campaigners did not hamper campaigns however, as later radical feminism had an unfortunate tendency to do, and the clinic idea spread nationally. Marie Stopes' publications led to widespread publicity, as did the libel case in which she was involved in 1924,[6] though the derogatory descriptions of the methods used by Stopes in this case indicate that contraception at this time was not yet widely accepted in society.

In July 1930, a coordinating body was set up – the National Birth Control Council (NBCC) – with vocal support coming from politicians and doctors. Its members came from different walks of life ranging from aristocrats to radicals. Some supported contraception on social grounds, some on eugenic grounds. Initially they aimed to continue their role as a pressure group promoting the cause of family planning and persuading established groups to support State provision. When local and central government showed reluctance in the face of economic difficulties, Roman Catholic opposition and medical indifference, the NBCC had to assume the short-term task themselves of expanding clinic provision further, to meet married women's demands, until such time, they assumed, as the State took on this role.[7]

In 1939 the role and name of the NBCC was changed to the Family Planning Association (FPA) due to the negative connotations of their former name following fears of a population decline. From this time the FPA would have broader commitments to women's health, and marital difficulties with medical provision for involuntary sterility and minor gynaecological ailments.[8] Throughout the 1950s, the FPA had financial problems, but was able to use the media to promote itself. It thus benefited from the respectability afforded by visits from Health Ministers to its clinics. In the 1960s, the FPA found its resources even more stretched as it began to supply the IUD, cervical smears and domiciliary advice.

Unfortunately the campaign to persuade conservative parliamentary and public opinion of the need for contraception was such that those feminists involved had themselves to lean towards conservatism and medicalisation. Leathard argues that because the family planners needed to set up efficient clinics with a view to government takeover, its members' time was taken up with clinic work and it relied on its charitable status and donations for funding, '[t]his shift in policy directly affected and weakened [their] role as a pressure group'.[9]

Commentators have criticised the FPA for not being a campaigning feminist group, but rather offering a limited service that provided much-needed jobs to women doctors who could not easily find employment and who wished to combine medical practice with raising a family [10] and for allowing the medicalisation of a non-medical issue. In 1965 the BPAS complained that the FPA did not extend clinic provision beyond medical needs to include the social. 'Although anxious to relieve ill-health and poverty [they] never regarded birth control as a "kind of patent medicine" for economic distress, as did the neo-Malthusians at the turn of the century'.[11] By providing contraception mainly to women, they also encouraged research into women's contraception and not men's.

This led to medicalisation for a number of reasons. Medicine during the twentieth century with the onset of technology was seen as progressive. The law itself ensured that contraception was seen in terms of maternal health from the 1920s. The FPA had to conduct medical research itself. (They produced the first spermicide, 'Volpar', and drew up a list of tried and tested spermicides in 1934.) They were the only ones providing medical training in the 1950s. Finally, in the 1960s it was decided by the management of the organisation that it would be necessary to work more closely with the medical profession within the NHS and to start treating couples rather than women on their own, although no services for the unmarried were envisaged. In addition, medical leadership was felt necessary to cope with the demands of modern birth control, to be better respected by the professions and to eradicate the 'Women's Institute' image the FPA felt it had. It would therefore become a national society with local branches. The local branches were disappointed with the reorganisation, but it received praise from the media as they believed that medicalisation signified safety.[12] The medicalisation of the FPA continued when the contraceptive pill was introduced in the UK. They conducted the trials in this country and carried out training courses on the subject under strict medical supervision.[13]

Campaigns in France: 'natalisme' and Roman Catholicism

After the passing of the 1920 law, it was not until the 1950s that debate opened again on the subject of contraceptive provision in France, as a result of Roman Catholic and 'nataliste' pressure.

French family planners from this time until the legislation of 1967 were first-wave liberal feminists as in the UK. The founder of the French Family Planning Movement, Dr Marie-Andrée Lagroua-Weill-Hallé, was converted to the idea of family planning through her personal experiences as a medical student of the suffering of women who had undergone clandestine abortions. This contradicted the moralistic and spiritual teachings on love and marriage given to students in the 1930s. It was common practice at the time for women who had had incomplete abortions to be given a scornful reception at the hospital and then given a curettage without anaesthetic so that they would never want to have to go back,[14] as punishment for their illegal and 'immoral' act. The patients concerned dared not complain, as they had indeed broken the law. This illustrates the pervasiveness of 'nataliste' and Roman Catholic influences throughout society as well as on the medical professions.

Dr Weill-Hallé was further persuaded of the benefits of widespread distribution of contraceptives and information after a visit to the Margaret Sanger Birth Control clinic in New York in 1947. The birth control provision and attitude there were completely different to those in France. Initially she was shocked at the idea that the American doctors were offering their female patients a means to reject motherhood[15] and space their births according to their own wishes, as a means to avoid abortion. Gradually, faced with cases of abortion and the serious medical, financial and emotional problems associated with large families in her own medical practice, Weill-Hallé began to see contraception as a means of family limitation. Due to the fact that she herself was a doctor, Weill-Hallé believed that contraception should be administered via GPs who had personal contact with local families.

At first she attempted to spread the word among her medical colleagues. She published an article in 1953 in *La Semaine des Hôpitaux* criticising medical treatment of women who had had abortions and the lack of help given to women about contraception. She went on to speak on the subject at the Congress on Moral Medicine in March 1955, citing a case where a young woman, who refused a therapeutic abortion in her third pregnancy despite a heart problem, died in the fourth month of gestation. Among the French Roman Catholic doctors there, the reaction to her was very critical, although international doctors supported her sentiments. Before the Academy of Moral and Political Sciences in the same month, she cited another case *L'Affaire Bac*. Here Dr Weill-Hallé, at her own request to the defence, had been called as a witness. She used the opportunity to promote the case for contraceptive provision and denounce the 1920 law citing the example of Anglo-Saxon countries where such cases were unheard of as a result of family planning. She believed that the only answer was a national network of family planning clinics where young couples could be given advice on moral and psychological problems as well as on contraception. For the first time ever, passionate debates in favour of birth control were held in the newspaper columns. The witnesses and experts were unanimous in defending the accused woman. For several weeks articles on birth control appeared in the press and readers showed real interest in a subject that had been taboo for thirty-five years.[16]

Along with a more left-wing orientation to the French political climate of the mid-1950s under the left-wing government, individuals on the Left in various organisations and professions began to discuss birth control and initiate a network of non-conformist contacts (Protestants, Jews, Freemasons) centred on Dr Weill-Hallé. Jacques Derogy researched a series of in-depth articles on birth control for *Libération* in October 1955, which attracted much public interest, especially from couples and women who were in favour of the idea.[17]

Dr Weill-Hallé received letters of support from women all over France, many of whom would become important to the Women's Movement later, and to the Family Planning Movement at the time.[18] Evelyne Sullerot, for example, who was to be the first Minister for Women in the 1980s, played an important part in the setting up in March 1956 of a national (though low-key) association for family planning headed by Dr Weill-Hallé called, euphemistically, 'La Maternité Heureuse' or Happy Motherhood. In 1958, it became affiliated to the International Planned Parenthood Federation and in 1960 became the fully-fledged French Family Planning Movement, 'Mouvement Français pour le Planning Familial' (MFPF).

From the beginning, the MFPF was deliberately woman-led and woman-centred. It was a first-wave feminist liberal movement, much like its British counterpart. Its organisation was centralised and hierarchical. The MFPF 'challenged neither the discourse which claimed all reproductive capacities for state use, nor that which confined French women to an essentialist maternity. Instead [it] remained a movement for couples to gain control over their fertility and thus plan for their family needs.'[19]

It also demarcated itself from neo-Malthusianism. Birth control would not be used to reject motherhood. Instead it was necessary for medical and social reasons to enhance the sexual relations of women and couples. Its overriding objective was for women to have the children they wanted, when they wanted them, a revolutionary idea at that time in France.[20]

Its three aims were therefore to reform the 1920 law as regards the use and teaching of contraception, to survey public opinion on the subject to assess

people's knowledge of it and to set up family planning centres. The task of
the MFPF generally would be to be informed by the public and to inform
them in turn. This would reduce the number of abortions, but not necessarily
lead to a drop in the birthrate. The MFPF also aimed to be legally accepted
and for the State to take on the provision of contraception, abortion and sex
education due to their deleterious social and medical effects, much like its
British counterparts, the FPA.[21]

How did such an association provide contraceptives to the public in the
face of such a restrictive law? Staring prosecution in the face, the MFPF felt
the need to actively court public opinion and support and continuing government inertia too. It was determined to open up the necessary family planning
centres. This differs from the British family planners' reasons for setting up
clinics and is perhaps related to the fact that in France the 1920 law on
contraception was extremely restrictive, whereas English law on contraception
was much less so. Such legal restrictions made the more militant Grenoble
branch of the MFPF, for example, decided to give the public access to
contraception despite the law. However, to avoid prosecution and the dissolution of the MFPF, this idea necessitated the Centre being the entire
responsibility of the MFPF Grenoble group, who within the privacy of the
Centre would encourage women to use contraceptives. They did benefit from
medical and legal resources. A separate *medical* group, 'Le Centre d'études
médicales pour l'orthogénie', providing prescriptions to women patients was
established. Their *legal* adviser and member, Maître Eynard, also informed
them that only propaganda was unlawful, not the use, prescription or sale to
individuals at their request. In addition, under the 1901 law on associations,
information could be given to members of an association without constituting
propaganda.[22]

Prosecution for their actions would have been possible. They were merely
fortunate that though the authorities were not prepared to support family
planning, they chose not to seek prosecution of the MFPF at this time.[23] When
the Grenoble Centre opened, it was supported by local bodies such as the
local council, teachers, professionals and the national press. There were no
Roman Catholic demonstrations, as had been feared, and the representative
of the 'Conseil de l'Ordre' declined his invitation, thus though these groups
disapproved they did not prevent the Centre opening. The Centre was immediately swamped with members – mainly working women who were informed
through their professional journals – in search of contraception. Another centre
soon opened in Paris when no legal reaction was forthcoming, which was
itself swamped with applicants from all over northern France. By 1965, there
were centres in fifty-nine Departments.

Despite their popularity with the public who used their facilities, this does not mean to say the MFPF did not face difficulties at this time. The contraceptives themselves – diaphragms – had to be imported illegally and secretly from Switzerland and the UK, which often led to confiscation by the central authorities. It proved more difficult to conceal the large quantities of spermicidal cream needed, with the result that the MFPF developed its own at Grenoble and manufactured it secretly. The haphazard nature of the supply of contraceptives in turn deterred many women from keeping up their membership of the association. Finally, the prescribing doctors faced a barrage of insults from others in the profession, including the 'Conseil de l'Ordre' itself. The doctors had attempted to evade the possibility of their work being banned by the 'Conseil' by forming themselves into a separate body in 1962, the 'Collège médical'.

As in the UK, medical power was also firmly entrenched in the MFPF. In 1965 the MFPF voted as honorary presidents the Nobel prize winners in medicine, Lwoff, Monod and Jacob. The more modern methods that the MFPF was advocating, such as the IUD (which had to be inserted by a doctor) and the Pill (which was available on prescription for infertility from chemists), were by necessity transferring control of birth control away from the MFPF and into the hands of the medical profession. Moreover, the expansion of the MFPF from 1961 saw the opening of new centres and an influx of male professionals, doctors and Freemasons who assumed leadership roles and held paid posts, with the approval of the President Weill-Hallé, a doctor herself. Commissions parallel to the movement formulated ideas for it, but their members were usually professionals; some of them were not even members of the MFPF.

As noted before, the law itself dictated the form taken by organisations campaigning for contraception. From 1962, the MFPF became more formalised and centralised. The criminality of contraceptive provision there ensured that the ruling council felt that the strategy of the MFPF must be strictly controlled and centralised to become legitimate in the eyes of the government.

Several similarities thus emerge between the feminist campaigns for contraception in each country. In each parallel campaign women volunteers played a major part in the provision of contraceptives, the setting up and staffing of centres and the education of those who came to seek their advice.

The birth control movement in the UK began at an earlier time, which may go some way to explain its own conservativeness in relation to its members and methods. The aims and methods of the MFPF were relatively more radical, as they were illegal and used by the movement to court public attention. Both were joined in the main by middle-class women volunteers based in Paris and London, who were usually from Protestant, non-conformist or non-religious backgrounds.

The services of the FPA went further than those in France to reach other aspects of women's health that were not met at the time, such as infertility and psycho-sexual counselling. Both suffered financial hardship and relied on funding from supporters, a factor which encouraged their development in medical research and led to medicalisation. This led to conservatism for both, from the 1960s in the MFPF and the 1930s in the FPA, in order to gain support from established groups and local and national government. They exploited any publicity they could, as they did not have the financial resources for advertising in the UK or the legal ability in France. Without the time, commitment and voluntary work given by their members, their success would have been diminished.

In both countries, the family planning organisations had an agenda-setting role, publicised the plight of women and their own relatively radical aims, held national public meetings and demonstrations and made networks with useful insider contacts for lobbying and changing legislation. They were also consulted by the government though they were never taken as seriously by the Establishment as more entrenched groups, such as the medical profession. Nevertheless, the parliamentary environment was such that family planners were able to set up clinics, even though this was a potentially illegal action in France.

Both countries' campaigners also experienced medicalisation of its aims, women doctors working in the clinics were a central part of the organisation from the beginning and in France the Collège Médical was mostly male and autonomous. Both began as women-led and women-centred small organisations, subject to structural reorganisation ordered by a hierarchical leadership who began to emphasise health rather than women's rights in order to be accepted into the health policy community. Both aimed to change the law, though on a more far-reaching scale in France, provide education and information and provide clinical services.

Contraceptive campaigners and their allies

The alliances feminist activists and groups were able to build in the political climate is pertinent to this study. The birth controllers enjoyed the support of many important allies in the policy community throughout their campaigns, most of whom were non-conformist and left wing, and in France particularly Freemasons and teachers who have a history of supporting radical and anti-Catholic movements. In the UK, birth control was accepted earlier by society and thus was a safer issue to support for the national church than in France. It is therefore noteworthy that there was some medical support in France outside the MFPF, despite the disapproval of the medical authorities, perhaps because the 1920 law was so restrictive, whereas the constraints of the English law were more nebulous.

In the 1930s, the British clinics attempted to profit from the contemporary economic and social climate and gain left-wing support by emphasising that birth control could reduce unemployment, abortion rates and maternal mortality rates. A study by the clinic also proved that they had encouraged increasing working-class usage among their patients. By the 1940s however, middle-class women were the prime users of the service.[24]

Left-wing allies were important as the issue took a long time to gather pace throughout society. The majority of political support did not come from political parties, but rather from left and liberal individuals and organisations such as the women's sections of the Labour and Liberal parties, and individual Tory women. However, most left-wing organisations in both countries, which were at the time male dominated, were divided on the issue, with some seeing it as a vote loser, 'at best a diversion from the struggle for social change and at worst a technique that could be used for outright oppression'.[25] The Labour Women's Conference in 1927 voted in favour of birth control information to be given to the poor, but this was defeated by the full conference due to the Roman Catholic influence in the Labour movement.[26]

France was much less unionised than the UK, especially among women and especially before the 1970s, thus French trade unions played a less important part in campaigns there. The Communist union, the Confédération Générale du Travail (CGT), followed the party line. The other main union, the Socialist Confédération Française Démocratique (CFDT), did not exist until 1964. Before that time, as the Confédération Française des Travailleurs Chrétiens (CFTC), it had links with the Roman Catholic Church, thus adopting their stance on contraception. From 1964 after splitting with the Church, the new union did come out in favour of contraception.

In the UK, Victorian prudish attitudes prevented birth control being talked about openly and precluded any sanction being given by the Church (the Lambeth Conference came out against contraception in 1908) or by the medical profession (whose ignorance due to contraception's absence from the medical syllabus exacerbated their hostility). There were individual churchmen and doctors who were less hostile, however.

By 1930, the ideas of family planners in the UK were taken up by members of Establishment organisations such as the Anglican Church, the medical profession and the MOH. Field points to the support given by State institutions in the UK, such as the judiciary and the House of Lords, as they did not have to be representative of any particular group's opinion.[27] Such elements supported the actions of the FPA rather than joining it.

The support of the Anglican Church in the UK was instrumental in helping to get contraception onto the agenda of the health policy community. In October 1921 the King's physician, Lord Dawson of Penn, gave his support to birth control at the Church Congress. The Church of England's Lambeth report of 1930 declared that birth control could no longer be ignored and that if there were a moral reason to limit parenthood and not to practise abstinence, contraception could be used. They were persuaded by the dangers of incessant pregnancies to women's health.[28] Anglican bishops went further in 1958 and spoke out in favour of birth control due to problems of world overpopulation, the increasing knowledge of birth control and the change in the meaning of marriage to emphasise the importance within it of love rather than procreation. This endorsement received much media attention and was used by the FPA to gain more support for their cause.[29]

In France support grew among medical organisations in the 1960s. In 1962, the 'Société Française de Gynécologie' organised a study day on the 'régulation de la conception'. In 1963, the 'Société Nationale pour l'Etude de la Sterilité et de la Fécondation' held the first scientific symposium on contraception in France, and stated that the law was now absurd, when so many couples practised birth control (which methods the organisation was referring to is unclear – most of the reliable methods were not available at this time).[30] Pharmaceutical firms also discreetly aided the MFPF in their search for contraceptive supplies.[31]

In addition the 'Collège médical' offered courses on contraception to doctors. The 'Collège' took the opportunity to proselytise on contraception and recruit members – by 1967 there were 500.[32] It is noteworthy that the position of the 'Collège' differed from that of the MFPF and was very medical in nature, which could explain their greater acceptance by doctors. The 'Collège' argued that state prohibitions on the prescribing of contraception and its non-reimbursement by the health service constituted an attack on clinical discretion as well as patient rights. This group was important to the MFPF's campaign for a change in the law, as they were instrumental in persuading other doctors of the values of contraception and their lending of some respectability to the MFPF.

The opposition

The strength of the opposition – the extent to which there is opposition to an interest group, their strengths and their legitimacy in the eyes of the government – is important to a study of interest group debate as it determines in turn the strength of campaigners and their allies. The most vociferous opposition to contraceptive campaigns at the time – from 1920 in the UK and 1956 in France – came from the majority of the medical professions and the

Roman Catholic Church. In France, these bodies also formed part of the predominant pronatalist lobby. The legal profession in the UK restricted its pronouncements on the law to court judgments. Even this was not possible in France, as this could have constituted illegal propaganda [33] whether favourable or not, and, moreover, the codified legal system in that country lessens the importance of judicial opinion.

The Roman Catholic Church

A most significant pressure group which did not support the aims of the family planning movement in the UK was the Roman Catholic Church. However, as a religious group they were not represented in any policy network close to the British government, and certainly enjoyed less leverage than the other Churches of Protestant origin. Indeed, some question whether Roman Catholics have ever been formally consulted by the British State. There is evidence that they have been excluded from those groups consulted by Government Commissions, or the remit of a Commission has been limited in order to facilitate their exclusion, such as that on Population in the 1930s. [34] Their role has been more influential on individual's opinions, especially on conscience issues. This has repercussions on voting behaviour in Parliament.

In 1926 Dr Halliday Sutherland, who had successfully sued Marie Stopes for libel in 1924, set up the League of National Life, a largely Roman Catholic body, which argued that birth control was murder, led to sterility and would destroy the family. It criticised the lack of reaction from the government, the Anglican Church and the medical profession, but found some support in the Labour Party. 'The general climate of opinion, however, was against this group.' [35]

From the 1940s, Roman Catholics were concerned at the growing use of birth control and its support from society. They did enjoy influence on attitudes at the local policy community level. In the 1950s the government, local authorities and medical professions were all influenced by the opposition of the Roman Catholic Church, indeed around 22 per cent of doctors were Roman Catholic when only 8 per cent of the population were. This was despite their being relatively few in number. Indeed, Francome attributes their strong reaction to birth control to a desire to increase the size of their flock. [36]

Individual Roman Catholics were beginning to accept modern methods of birth control by the early 1960s. This included Roman Catholic doctors of whom 80 per cent prescribed modern methods, such as the IUD, to Roman Catholic patients and 50 per cent criticised the 'rhythm method', a large majority favouring modern methods. [37]

The Pill served to create a wider gulf between the Roman Catholic Church and other groups who formed an opinion on birth control. Papal Commissions were set up to discuss the matter of whether the Pill was natural enough to be approved. It took several years before these Commissions finally came out in favour of leaving the matter of contraception to the individual conscience. It was left to the Pope to have the final say on the matter and he decided to retain the traditional stance on all contraception apart from the rhythm method. 'Humanae Vitae' was not an 'infallible statement', however, and it became clear following it that Roman Catholics in the UK would continue to use contraception – a 1968 Gallup poll showed that 54 per cent disapproved of the ban. Bishops also accepted that they would leave the matter up to the conscience of the individual.[38]

The Roman Catholic Church in France is an important interest group, despite its separation from the State (in contrast to the Anglican Church), as most French people are Roman Catholics, and certainly until the late 1960s many attended church. The structure of the Church is very hierarchical and gives most weight to the views expressed at the top. From April 1956, the hierarchy of the Roman Catholic Church reiterated its uncompromising stance against contraception through popular Roman Catholic newspapers such as *La Croix*, with articles written by male priests and theologians who upheld 'sexual dignity' against 'contraceptive madness'.[39] In 1958, an encyclical 'Casti Connubi' was published by Pope Pius XII, reiterating the Roman Catholic stance, condemning 'deliberate intention and positive action taken by any means to deprive sexual union of its procreative potentiality'.[40] Only the Ogino method, whereby body temperatures indicate fertility levels, perfected by a French Roman Catholic doctor during the 1950s, was permitted to be used.

In addition, national Roman Catholic associations, which were extremely numerous at this time, were instructed to take part in any useful action necessary to combat birth control campaigns. However, from the early 1950s, further down the ranks of the Church, some clerics and lay workers, especially those working with the young, were beginning to change in their attitude to contraception and began to promote the idea that contraception was acceptable for medical and social reasons, and ultimately therefore a matter for the individual conscience.[41]

The medical professions – the official position

In the UK throughout the twentieth century, medical views on contraception ranged from disinterest in a 'non-medical' act to outright hostility toward an immoral act. This played a large part in the FPA having to take on the medical aspects of family planning itself and delayed the success of the FPA's agenda-setting role within the policy community as the medical professions were such important members of it; indeed of the policy network itself.

In 1930 at the British Medical Association's (BMA) annual representative meeting, it was decided that doctors should only have to give contraceptive advice at their own discretion, as opposed to on demand from their patients or from the local authority.[42] For the rest of the decade, both male and female physicians were prepared to accept the encroachment of family planners rather than reorganise their own curricula because they did not believe that birth control was the task of the doctor – in their view it was not a cure as such and clashed with the doctor's role in obstetrics.

Contraceptive methods did not change until the late 1950s. The lack of research in this area is illustrative of medical attitudes of the time. For example, Walsh ascribes this not only to the Second World War which took scientists away from this work, but also to religious and social prejudices against such research and the moral attitude of the profession (despite their own use of contraception from the late nineteenth century, and the demands of women and women's groups). This attitude prevented the provision of contraception through surgeries and in chemists and its teaching in medical schools.[43] Ironically, the lack of research justified the medical accusations of contraception being non-medical until well after the Second World War. At the time medicine did not include preventive health care or economic or social considerations. Only if the life or health of the mother were in danger – when it was a definite medical case – would contraception be considered.

Panic about underpopulation from 1936, in which many doctors participated, jeopardised contraceptive provision. It is ironic, then, that in the 1950s it was the fear of overpopulation in the Third World by the government and the public, especially in the United States, which finally legitimated research into birth control and facilitated the development of the contraceptive pill.[44]

Though not the only reason for the increasing control of contraception by clinicians, with its danger of thrombosis and other side effects, the Pill was the catalyst for the medical profession to become increasingly involved in birth control, as it had to be prescribed by a doctor. Their involvement did not extend to making the Pill widely available, however, as medical squabbles with the government over the cost of prescribing contraceptives on social grounds prevented the Pill from being widely available.[45]

The 'Conseil National de l'Ordre des Médecins', the statutory body for the medical profession and therefore an influential member of the health policy network in France, initially took a stand against the involvement of doctors. Doctors who were members of the MFPF were rarely present at their conferences in fear of reprimands from their medical bodies, knowing the official stance of the 'Conseil'. The 'Conseil' argued that it did not believe that doctors had a role to play in family planning, as contraception was not a medical matter – their only role was to treat patients who had fallen ill from using contraceptives. It also argued that it was unethical to circulate lists of doctors prescribing contraception as this constituted the formation of a private clientele (French patients being free to choose and change their doctor). Any doctor flouting these rules would be subject to disciplinary action.[46]

By 1965 the 'Conseil de l'Ordre' was beginning to be at odds with the sentiments of its regional members. At their request for redefinition of the official medical stance on contraception, the 'Conseil' merely reiterated that it was a non-medical problem. This was at a time when doctors were now not only faced with requests for contraception and abortion from women in desperate situations, but were also able to prescribe the contraceptive pill to women with menstrual or fertility problems – a pretext some women used to take the Pill as a contraceptive, though certainly not on a large scale.

Contraception came to be widely discussed by the French media. In 1966, the 'Conseil de l'Ordre' was asked by the right-wing paper *Le Figaro* why they had not debated the question at their International Congress on Moral Medicine. In reply the 'Conseil' did not come down for or against contraception, but only said ambiguously that it was 'studying the issue'. A few days later on 4 June 1966 they went further and announced that the matter was of interest to doctors who wanted to ensure healthy patients and happy families. Doctors were free to give advice, although they should dissuade patients who were using contraceptives for convenience only. They were also against publicity and believed that information should only be supplied to fiancés and married couples by qualified medical staff, rather than MFPF clinics. Though fainthearted, this was the first time that the 'Conseil' had publicly supported contraception, coming at a time when it was still criminalised. Whether or not public opinion, the government, other physicians or the MFPF (perhaps at best their 'Collège médical') played a part in persuading the 'Conseil' is unclear.[47] Within networks, relationship management is an overriding factor however and disputes within the medical profession would be disliked by the 'Conseil' and by the government.

In both France and the UK, the Roman Catholic Church and the medical professions were major opponents of contraception. The medical professions were members of the health policy network in both countries and shared the resources detailed by Wright and others (as discussed in Chapter 1). Both organisations argued that contraception was a moral, non-medical issue and did not support the liberalisation or provision of contraceptives. Not until the 1960s did the main body of medical professionals come to accept the need for change, due to demands by women for the contraceptive pill to be supplied by doctors, and the agenda-setting techniques and demands for medical involvement by family planners and other members of the policy community, including some doctors in France and the government in the UK. The profession retained its power during implementation however by sometimes refusing to prescribe or, as in the UK, disputing payment. It is interesting to observe the way in which clinicians' views on contraception developed during this time. They changed from outright opposition to wanting control of whatever provision there was. Women's bodies thus remained under medical control.

Roman Catholics opposed contraceptive liberalisation in both countries, but had more influence in France than the UK, as they, along with pronatalists, enjoyed the power brought by membership of the policy network. On the issue of contraception, the government thus appears weak in France: its actions appear to have been designed more to accommodate the opinions of the members of a network, which included pronatalists and religious groups. The eventual law was thus inadequate. In contrast, UK physicians continually demanded more recompense for their services and had a two-way relationship with the government. Up to the late 1960s in the UK, Roman Catholics may have had an influence on local Labour party representatives, and the kite-flying process used for the eventual bill does illustrate governmental fears of the Roman Catholic influence. However, 'relationship management' is more obvious with physicians, especially after 1967 when free contraceptives were brought in by the Labour Government.

Parliamentary debate and the response of the government

The political environment in any campaign is determined by government and parliamentary attitudes and their receptiveness to an issue. Of almost equal importance is how far individual parliamentarians might be prepared to ally with campaigners and lobby on their behalf. The British government was receptive to contraceptive campaigners from the 1930s, whereas its French counterpart was still reticent about the issue up until the 1960s, due to the continuous opposition of important members of the policy network and the 'nataliste' ideology of the French State.

In the UK from the turn of the twentieth century, the State showed increasing interest in the health of the nation.[48] The lack of fit and able conscripts led to government concern about the health of working-class children and infant and maternal mortality. Venereal disease was also a problem that led to research on its treatment and medical and government involvement with gynaecological disorders and the use of sheaths to prevent them. Thus maternity and child welfare clinics were provided by local authorities. But this set a precedent for services only being provided for mothers, and limited provision for single women.

The issue of maternal mortality, 'a safe public health topic',[49] was very important to the relative success of the NBCC as regards its inclusion in the health policy community at this time, though it remained excluded from the health policy network, as did the contraceptive issue itself. Thus the government conceded merely to safeguard the health of mothers, though the demands of the NBCC itself went no further than this. Indeed, the association felt so close to the MOH at this time that they decided against a debate in Parliament on the subject in 1937, for fear that a vote against might jeopardise this relationship.

In the UK, birth controllers attempted to encourage local authorities to extend the maternity services already provided to include the provision of birth control. They were hampered by the fact that, although this would not be unlawful if given on medical grounds, the government threatened local authorities with the withdrawal of central funding if they did so. However, the networks established among women birth controllers and their left-wing allies did eventually prove fruitful in 1930 when, after a national conference which was covered by the press and radio, and constant lobbying by Labour sympathisers, the MOH partially conceded to their demands and published Memorandum 153/MCW, whereby instruction on birth control could be given to mothers whose health would be endangered by a further pregnancy. However, without parliamentary debate the Health Minister felt he could not sanction public money funding the provision of contraceptives to all women.[50]

Despite this government response, local authorities remained reluctant to provide birth control more generally, due to the cost of such a service. The NBCC also faced the strong opposition of Roman Catholics in the local policy community. In 1932, Janet Campbell produced a second report on maternal mortality for the Government, which, along with lobbying by the NBCC, led to the extension of facilities (Circular 1408) in 1934.[51] The largely eugenic and nationalistic population scare from 1936 prevented the British government from extending provision for contraception any further.

When the NHS was formed in 1945, the FPA and its clinical provision were not included. Women's health rights might well have been extended with health rights generally, but the FPA President, Lord Horder, had ideological misgivings about the NHS, and it was felt by the FPA that there was something to be said for retaining autonomy from State interference and reorganisation. This sits somewhat strangely with the FPA's long-term aim of State funding and provision. Moreover, at this time, there was a distinct lack of support from the State and the medical professions for State provision of contraception, or for the birth rate to be maintained at a low level.[52]

Under the National Health Service Act 1946 birth control provision came under the aegis of LHAs. This was important for the FPA as the NHS could contribute to voluntary organisations which dealt with the health of pre- and post-natal mothers. This was interpreted widely, and two-thirds of LHAs in the 1950s gave grants and premises to the FPA. From 1954, clinics could also be set up within hospitals to provide contraceptives to women on health grounds, referred by their doctor.[53]

It was not until a Royal Commission on Population in 1949 reported that the population was not in decline that government attitudes were finally won over and only Roman Catholic interest groups remained in opposition to birth control as a means of family limitation. Moreover, the report underlined the social reasons behind the use of contraception. It praised the work of the FPA and criticised the restrictions on local authority provision – NHS family doctors should be trained to give advice in this area.[54]

From the mid-1960s, in line with the changing climate of opinion in British society, the Labour government came out in support of contraception and included it in their social programme of reform. This was also a result of pressure from their women's sections, who were therefore acting in the capacity of allies of the British family planning movement. The Minister of Health from 1964, Mr Kenneth Robinson, 'played an important part in opening up the field'.[55] Despite civil servant advice to the contrary, Robinson felt that the political dangers of the contraception issue were more 'myth than political time bomb' and reflected, 'politicians must lead; we were not leading'.[56] In February 1966, he therefore dispatched the first MOH circular for thirty years on 'Family Planning' to local authorities, instructing them to implement government regulations. His aim was to force the hand of those who ignored him. Again, during the passage of the Family Planning Bill in 1967, a major role was played by sympathetic Ministers and the new Labour majority who were now younger, professionally qualified and articulate, as well as disillusioned with the old economic ideas of socialism. Labour members were also becoming depressed by the Government's 'general lacklustre' in managing the economy and therefore the bills provided something for which they could fight.[57]

The introduction of the Family Planning Bill itself was only indirectly the work of the FPA or other birth control groups. Leo Abse (Labour MP) was concerned to improve sexual equality, advised Dr Edwin Brooks (Labour MP) who took an interest in his women constituents' difficulties with unwanted pregnancies, to make use of his seventh place in the Private Members' Ballot to 'widen the legal criteria governing local authority family planning assistance'.[58]

The bill received an extremely warm reception, despite government apprehension. It enjoyed the support of all parties, Mr Robinson and the government. Its Second Reading was practically unopposed; 'that advice might be available to the unmarried, and even to teenagers, caused scarcely a raised eyebrow'.[59] In Committee, the National Health Service (Family Planning) Act

1967 passed unamended in a single sitting. It was debated in the Lords in seventy-seven minutes without opposition.

Leathard has argued that, for several reasons, it was the simultaneous passage of the Abortion Bill that facilitated that of family planning. The time and energy of the only opposition, the Roman Catholic Church, was consumed by the abortion battle, against which their arguments were more clear-cut. The expansion of family planning was felt to reduce the need for abortion, thus opposers could only condemn the former with difficulty. Within the Roman Catholic Church, before the publication of the Papal Encyclical 'Humanae Vitae', views had changed among the clergy and the laity, who were by this time, in the 1960s, more educated and liberal-minded than before, which weakened their stance against contraception in contrast to abortion (Edwin Brooks received hundreds of letters condemning abortion, but only seventeen against contraception).[60] The medical profession also seemed prepared to accept provision as long as payment was organised and in the hope of preventing abortion. In turn this forced the hand of MPs.

In France, state interest in increasing the number of live births, 'natalisme' was exacerbated by the losses of the First World War, which startled the French establishment as it had the British one. However, in France this led to the strict laws against contraception and abortion in 1920 and 1923. By the time of the MFPF this attitude had not changed. For example, in 1956 the government demographical institute 'INED' published in its journal *Population* an article entitled 'The limitation of births in France'. The article concluded that contraceptive liberalisation would lead to a reduction in the numbers of unwanted births and a desire for less children generally. They also concluded that liberalisation would contradict and cast doubt on their family policies. Only small incremental steps should be taken and these closely observed.

However, alliances that feminists had built upon on the left wing began to produce results as, in the same year, four opposition bills were put forward by deputies from each left-wing faction in Parliament in early 1956. The Communist proposition in May reaffirmed its anti-birth control stance, but demanded the reform of the 1920 law and more leniency as regards therapeutic abortion.[61] Three other Socialist bills, in February, March and May, would have enabled contraceptive products to be sold. Despite the fact that in the mid-1950s power was held by a left-wing coalition of Socialists and Radicals under Guy Mollet, not one proposition was permitted to be debated. This may have been due to one or more factors: perhaps a reticence to be associated with a subject it was believed the public did not favour, an unwillingness to alienate valuable Roman Catholic support in the country, and right-wing and Communist support in Parliament when the government did not have a majority, or merely a lack of urgency when compared with other contemporary matters, such as the increasingly preoccupying uprising in the French colony Algeria.[62]

The French media was in the main hostile to contraception in the 1960s, stressing the dangers of modern methods such as the Pill and IUD. For example, during the presidential elections of 1965, media interest finally led to a political stance having to be taken when Jacques Derogy used his position as a journalist on *Libération* to persuade François Mitterrand, the Socialist candidate, to make birth control part of his campaign. Mitterrand agreed in the knowledge that this issue might attract the support of women, the young and the radical. Of the voters he might alienate, these were on the right and of Roman Catholic persuasion, who probably would not support him anyway. The other candidates were then forced to comment on the same subject. The MFPF used the opportunity to present their own ideas for legal reform: that contraceptives should be available through doctors without any commercial publicity; for sex education in schools and showing the new undercurrent of feminism now present in their discourse, for the wider extension of women's rights.

This agenda-setting meant that between 1964 and 1966 representatives from both sides in the National Assembly had presented bills. With all parliamentary parties taking positions on birth control, the right-wing government was called upon to undertake investigations into the effect of the Pill on women. Though hardly an indication that the government was now in favour of liberalisation, perhaps even a method of discouraging women from taking the Pill by emphasising its dangers, the fact that the government did commission a report in October 1965 showed its acceptance that contraceptives in France were now a reality to be faced. The government's Marcellin Commission reported in December 1965 that the Pill was innocuous, and went so far as to say that women should have control over their own bodies, '[c]e n'est pas à nous à dire aux femmes: tu auras ou tu n'auras pas d'enfant. Nous pouvons simplement leur dire: ton corps est à toi.'[63]

With this fillip, the MFPF propagandised on the issue more extensively than ever with publications and television appearances during 1966 and 1967. More importantly, they took part in every government commission they could, promoting their own prototype of a bill and being consulted in the policy community on medical and legal matters. The association's Masonic members took advantage of their already existing network of influence, at least in Parliament, by lobbying Masons there. Finally, members of the MFPF – the left-wing parliamentarians, Masons and doctors, men and women – persuaded their right-wing but Masonic ally, Lucien Neuwirth, to put forward an opposition bill on birth control. By 1967, public opinion was becoming increasingly conscious that it was the right-wing government that was the stumbling block on the issue while press debate became more progressive, concentrating on contraceptive liberalisation as opposed to moral issues.[64]

However, in contrast to the British government's condoning of contraception since 1930, the French government ostensibly resisted liberalisation right up to the passing of the 1967 law. The government was only prepared initially to set up a Commission to 'study the idea' behind the Neuwirth Bill, which was made up of Deputies representing the various tendencies in the debate, including Mitterrand. Neuwirth's Bill was based around the fact that birth control was already widespread including 300,000 clandestine abortions a year resulting in death and injury. Interest groups who were invited to present their case included 'specialists' on the subject and representatives of the main schools of thought, but only the Roman Catholic Church came out against legal reform. Of the MFPF only representatives of the 'Collège Médical' were invited to present their case, however, and this was essentially medical in nature: that contraceptive advice should be authorised by a medical and paramedical team within a hospital.[65] The Commission adopted Neuwirth's Bill with two members abstaining – M. Dubois (Centre démocratique), who thought the law would be too liberal and M. Mitterrand (Socialist leader), who believed that the law would be too restrictive due to the fact that distribution was limited to medical bodies, no publicity was allowed except in medical journals, women were obliged to register with a pharmacist and have medical authority before being prescribed and minors needed parental authorisation. The Neuwirth Bill was not a radical bill and was more restrictive than the MFPF would have liked judging from their own procedures at clinics.

Before allowing the bill to be debated in Parliament, the government also waited for the publication of a report by the 'Senior Consultative Committee on Population and the Family' in January 1967. Their 'nataliste' opinions as members of the policy network were important to the government and the report was presented by professor Debré who was well known for his 'natalisme'. This report was in favour of permitting the use of contraception, but was against any idea of actually encouraging the French to use it, in fact they were in favour of actively discouraging its use. The Family Planning movement in the early 1980s believed that this was such a successful government policy that it had prevented any reduction in abortions up to that time.[66] Indeed, the Report itself went on to say that through government licensing and funding of centres, it would be able to control contraceptive use which it had been unable to do until then.[67]

After the March 1967 legislative elections, Neuwirth was driven to present a new proposition. It was debated in the National Assembly on 1 July 1967. Again the bill did not receive as much government sanction as its British counterpart as it was debated at the end of the parliamentary session.

Arguments against focused on the threat to the birth rate, the high medical risks involved, accusing the left of a political conspiracy, and the immorality of contraception, with its danger to health and to men's virility by empowering women (similar arguments would be used seven years later during the debates on abortion legislation). The proposition was adopted, however. In the Senate such fears were repeated, but economic and social questions were brought to the fore by every speaker.[68] Although both the 1920 and 1967 laws contain emphasis on 'natalisme', in contrast to the debates in 1920, in 1967 there was less emphasis in both Houses on the abstract idea of obligation to the French birth rate and more mention made of concrete ideas of physiological needs, and technical, medical and social problems associated with contraceptives. It was adopted by raised hands after two readings and a 'Commission Mixte Paritaire' made up of members of the Senate and the National Assembly in order that they could come to agreement about its content.[69] Eventually the 'loi Neuwirth' was passed in the National Assembly on the last day of the session, 19 December 1967, in the presence of only sixty Deputies.

Parliamentary debate and the amendments of 1974

The 1967 laws on contraception of both the UK and France were extended in 1974, by the National Health Service Reorganisation Act 1973 and the French law of 4 December 1974, to allow contraception to be provided free of charge. In the UK this was the result of a combination of factors. It came at a time when the reorganisation of the health service was under review. There were ecological and eugenic fears of overpopulation and dismay at the 'alarmingly high' abortion rates reported in the press. Campaigners played an agenda-setting role and persuaded allies within the policy community. Roman Catholics however believed free contraception would license immorality,[70] but their influence was even less than before on this issue. In France, though Roman Catholics remained in opposition there too, alongside pronatalists radical feminism reformed the feminist campaign on contraception and changed the government agenda on contraception.

The rise of second-wave feminism in the UK was instrumental in forcing the women involved in family planning to take a more radical view. Liberal feminists criticised the double burden faced by working mothers; radicals advocated abandoning motherhood altogether. From June 1972, even the FPA supported new radical ideas. However, they preferred another group to take on this pressurising role, and it was in fact members of the Abortion Law Reform Association (ALRA), instrumental in the passing of the 1967 Abortion Act, who took up the cause of population, the inadequate facilities for contraception, sterilisation and abortion and the cost of unwanted pregnancies to the community. Alastair Service and Vera Houghton set up the Birth Control Campaign (BCC) in April 1971. The BCC benefited from the experience of lobbying, the professional expertise and a grass-roots organisation gained from ALRA and the FPA. They used fears of overpopulation, commissioning surveys to prove these existed, to promote family planning, 'BCC workers were essentially "women's rights" campaigners not "population" people'.[71] Other feminist activities were seen in the lobbying activities of Labour women in 1970, the Women's Liberal Foundation and the National Council of Women in 1971.

In France too, amendments were very much the result of second-wave radical feminist ideas on contraception and their methods of direct action. Radical feminists saw the implementation of the law and liberalising amendments as part of a reproductive rights package along with abortion and sex education. This included important individual members of the MFPF and from 1975 the MFPF itself.

The radicalisation of the MFPF came about in the early 1970s. Although the 'loi Neuwirth' was approved of by the top echelons of the MFPF in Paris (indeed its President Dr Weill-Hallé resigned immediately before its passing), the rank and file were dissatisfied with its content. Many of the unpaid women in the provinces felt exploited and ignored and began to demand more recognition. Even in Paris rifts were beginning to show between the central think tank and the clinic workers. (Interestingly, the FPA members in the UK never demanded payment to the extent of causing a rift, perhaps due to the tradition of voluntary work in the UK from the nineteenth century.)

The left-wing political disturbances of May 1968 in Paris exacerbated the rifts within the MFPF. Two opposing strategies now made themselves felt. Those at the top from 1968 to 1973 wanted the clinics to prepare to apply the law, with a view to becoming an organisation recognised and funded by the State by 'reconnaissance d'utilité publique'.[72] They also did not want to be associated with the new battles for abortion and so approved of the Association Nationale pour l'Etude de l'Avortement (ANEA) being set up separately by MFPF members.

For the women volunteers by contrast, the ideas of sexual freedom, women's liberation, non-specialisation, socialism and democracy seemed to be applicable to their own problems within the MFPF. They criticised the medical hierarchy of the MFPF for setting up a medical journal while women patients with social problems were not being helped by the clinics. This happened to individuals from 1970 and led to the taking over of the MFPF by militants at the Congress of June 1973 and the breaking away of medical members. The structure was then changed to be non-hierarchical and MFPF aims became extended to include a woman's right over her own body, patients' medical rights, no power to specialists and no research on women.[73] This absorption

of feminism reduced the chances of being included in the policy community
that the old leadership had been working towards. Had they been in the policy
community, extension of the law would have been easier, indeed extension
may not have been necessary, but their new ideals prevented them wanting
to be included in it, and their tactics became even more those of an outsider
group.

The new MFPF not only campaigned on contraception and sex education,
but was a prominent member of the struggle for abortion liberalisation. This
led to them not being funded by the State or asked to sit on the 'Conseil
supérieur de l'information sexuelle, de la régulation des naissances et de
l'éducation familiale' set up in 1973. The MFPF protested by setting up an
alternative 'Conseil bis' and sending its unsolicited opinions to the official
'Conseil'.

In the UK, feminist ideas that the 1967 Statute could be improved were
supported by such important allies as doctors. In 1971, a medical pressure
group 'Doctors and Overpopulation', was set up to promote the idea that
unwanted births led to overpopulation and that doctors should use their
influential position in society to exhort the government to extend family
planning services within the NHS. From the government's point of view, this
group received much media coverage and enjoyed the support of 200 doctors,
several established medical journal editorials and certain MPs. The FPA, still
a charity, continued to play a discreet role supporting population stabilisation
and free, comprehensive services.

Those members of the policy network in France who opposed contraception,
namely pronatalists, Roman Catholics and the 'Conseil de l'Ordre', had a
much greater influence than their counterparts in the UK. This can be seen
from the content of the law and its non-implementation. It would appear from
this that French governments, until the advent of the Socialist government in
1981, were either weaker in relation to opponents of contraception or more
or less in agreement with them.

The official Roman Catholic position did not change in France after the
passing of the law. In 1968 the Encyclical 'Humanae Vitae' was published.
Throughout the 1960s the Church had set up working groups to study the
idea of liberalisation of abortion and contraception. At some point there had
been rumours of a new liberal attitude coming from the Vatican, but the Pope
himself ultimately decided that the Church's position would not change –
artificial contraception, abortion and sterilisation were condemned, 'an act of
mutual love which impairs the capacity to transmit life which God the Creator,
through specific laws, has built into it, frustrates his design which constitutes
the norms of marriage, and contradicts the will of the author of life'. The
Pope called on governments to ban contraception by law and warned that its

usage could lead to marital infidelity, immorality among the young and a general lowering of moral standards.[74] Perhaps this was due to the fact that the Church hierarchy found it difficult to make a U-turn in its policy as this might undermine its authority over its members. It led to much confusion and divided opinion in France as well as the UK.

In relation to support for the new regulation, the medical profession remained uncooperative in France, in contrast to their British counterparts. Doctors were not prepared to assume the role assigned to them by the legislation. Medical education on contraception remained inadequate, and many publications by pronatalists emphasised the medical and social dangers of birth control.[75] This limited the access to contraception of French women.[76]

Medical support in the UK did not initially convince the now Conservative British government for an extension of facilities. In 1972, the then Health Minister Keith Joseph, refuted the idea that the government should concern itself with population, nor that contraception should be free, except in special cases, as this might create an anomaly between contraceptives and other drugs on prescription.[77] In reply, the BMA was not in favour of the doctor having to 'make medical decisions on social grounds', and the BCC argued that this would only reduce unwanted pregnancy by 10 per cent, whereas free services could reduce them by up to 75 per cent.[78]

It was in the context of the reorganisation of the whole NHS structure that victory for campaigners finally came about as the free services were pushed as part of the NHS Reorganisation Bill by FPA and BCC supporters in the House of Lords (members of the FPA believed the Peers did this to show they were worth 'preserving' and because they had no constituents to please).[79] Debate on the family planning aspect in Clause 4 outweighed all other aspects of proceedings. The press supported the Lords, as did thirty-one medical, political, church, population and women's organisations and 64 per cent of the public.[80] It was a handful of Conservative MPs who sustained the battle, rather than Labour, the latter believing contraception to be a conscience issue. Leathard believed it was a 'battle' in 1974 rather than 1967 because the issues were more serious – free, comprehensive services rather than providing permissive powers to local authorities.[81]

It was under a new Labour government in 1974 and 1975, when abortion rates and the birth rate had dropped, that Barbara Castle, Secretary of State for Social Services, finally implemented the changes and abolished prescription charges for contraceptives without parliamentary consultation and David Owen, Health Minister, organised fees and contracts with doctors. In 1976 FPA clinics were finally handed over to the NHS.

The government in France showed its reticence in actually formally approving of the widespread use of contraception by delaying until April 1972 the publication of the necessary 'décrets d'application', in order that the law would be finally in place.

It was therefore, in the face of growing demands for abortion liberalisation because of backstreet abortion, that most French politicians, including former opponents, saw contraception as the lesser evil. It is noteworthy that so many amendments to the original law were passed in quick succession between 1972 and 1974 – a time when abortion campaigners were at their strongest.

Lucien Neuwirth, continuing his backbench campaign on contraception, attempted to ensure that the law would be used by women by expanding the provision of information and publicity on contraception. He thus set up the 'Conseil supérieur de l'information sexuelle, de la regulation des naissances, et de l'éducation nationale' ('loi du 11 juillet 1973'). This was despite the obstruction of the Health Minister, Jean Foyer, who wished to ignore the contraceptive issue, 'la contraception, moins on en parlera, mieux cela vaudra' and the Interior Minister, Raymond Marcellin (who refused to fund the MFPF as part of the scheme).[82]

Another important issue to second-wave feminists in relation to contraception was that of minors' access to contraception. In April 1974, Neuwirth attempted to modernise the law and make it more accessible by abolishing the medical record keeping of contraceptive usage, 'carnet à souches', relaxing regulations relating to minors (they no longer needed parental consent), and introducing the reimbursement by the State of the cost of contraception. The bill was discussed and adopted without opposition in the National Assembly in June 1974 and by a more reticent Senate in November 1974. It became the law of 4 December 1974 replacing Articles 3, 5 and 6 of the 1967 law.[83]

Contraception for young and single women in the UK was not catered for until the opening of the voluntarily run first Brook Advisory Centre in 1964. There were ten by 1970. This was separate from the FPA and the Eugenics Society whose members were split on the issue. Some felt it was too radical, not respectable and something that could jeopardise their charitable status, alienate some charitable workers and overstretch their resources. However, the FPA was forced to change its policy by 1967 in line with the change in public and media attitudes to premarital sex in the new 'permissive society'. The *Gillick* affair from 1984 to 1986, over contraceptive provision to minors took place in court and in the media, not in Parliament. It therefore brought out the more extreme viewpoints of, on the one hand, Roman Catholics, who supported Mrs Gillick's stand against contraceptive advice being given to minors without parental consent, and on the other hand, contraceptive campaigners fighting for freedom of choice for the minors in question. Unfortunately for the latter, it also led to a somewhat unsatisfactory legal situation whereby doctors were unsure of the assistance they could give to minors seeking contraception, and I would suggest, a current situation where teenage pregnancy has been seen as a problem by those groups still fighting for better sex education.

In France, by contrast, provision to minors is now legal and free. The lack of apparent opposition to this is due to a large extent by an inability to have the law changed through case law or by initiating debate on the issue in Parliament due to the relative lack of interest there, particularly under the Socialist governments of the 1980s.

Emergency contraception, or the morning-after pill, can be taken up to seventy-two hours after unprotected sex. This offers women the ability to protect themselves against unwanted pregnancy. In the summer of 1999, the debate over whether this should be made freely available to women OTC in pharmacies received new impetus. The BPAS made this available to women in the UK from July. In France, meanwhile, emergency contraception was available from pharmacists, though not reimbursed, from June 1999.[84] The governments of both countries showed themselves to be lagging behind when other organisations such as BPAS in the UK and the MFPF in France were taking the initiative on this issue on behalf of women. It will be interesting to see whether their respective governments follow their lead and finally instigate regulation and financial support. Unfortunately for French minors, the Conseil d'Etat issued a ruling on 30 June 2000 that it was unlawful under the 'loi Neuwirth' for school nurses to be allowed to supply emergency contraception to pupils. Article 3 of the 1967 law stipulates that contraceptives must be supplied by a pharmacist (on medical prescription). Interestingly, this ruling was instigated by a group of French 'pro-life' organisations, which was claiming that the government had acted *ultra vires* by extending contraceptive provision through secondary legislation in this way. The incompatibility of the Neuwirth law and the European Directive of 31 March 1992, outlining the criteria for prescription-only drugs, was already clear to the French state. The reaction to this from the left wing and from the government was that the Neuwirth law itself would be amended accordingly, alongside further liberalisation of the abortion law (*see* Chapter 5).[85] This led ulitmately to the law of 4 July 2001.

In the UK, Prime Minister Tony Blair appeared to be much influenced by the representations of 'pro-life' sympathisers, particularly as they criticised emergency contraception for being an abortifacient rather than a contraceptive. The Medicines Control Agency's Report of 1999 also advocated a provision limited to women over sixteen.[86] Influential support came from the medical profession, however, in the form of the British Medical Association General Practitioners Committee.[87] A number of cross-party MPs also published Early Day Motions in June 1998 and in November 1999 advocating pharmacy prescription of emergency contraception.[88] The involvement of pharmacists and their support was also important when emergency contraception was liberalised in Jamuary 2001.

Conclusions

Contraceptive campaigns in both countries led to statutory provision in 1967. Involved in the often difficult campaigns were newly formed interest groups – contraceptive campaigners and their allies – concerned with the issue alongside, as well as in opposition to, well-established members of the health policy community and policy network. What is important to this study is to see exactly how far those campaigners were influential in relation to that statutory provision. In turn, this indicates whether they were outsiders. If an outsider group, how did they build alliances with members of the policy community or policy network, given the legal and political environments they were campaigning in?

Essentially, in both countries, the most influential groups in the policy community on contraception were the policy network members, namely the medical professions, religious groups and in France pronatalists. Contraceptive campaigners, particularly feminists, were not members or this privileged group. Instead, they were 'outsiders' and thus played a less influential role. Essentially, contraception was classed as a conscience issue, with free voting taking place by parliamentarians in both countries. Despite this, network members still managed to exert large amounts of influence on individual politicians.

The provision of contraception in both the UK and France was delayed by fears of low population growth. These fears took the form of scares from 1936 to 1949 and in the 1970s in the UK. In France, they lasted throughout the twentieth century and formed a basic tenet of health policy on all sides of the political spectrum. As for the comparative influence of demography on contraception provision, in the UK the issues of maternal mortality, women's health and initially immorality, were more important to legislators than that of demography, due to the contrasting religious influence in both countries of Protestants and Roman Catholics, whereby Roman Catholic interest in demography was only of any real influence in France. Indeed, Article 5 of the 1967 law in particular stipulated that all antinatalist 'propaganda' was prohibited. Moreover, it was for pronatalist reasons that the French government itself wanted to control access to contraception. The Social Affairs Minister spoke in favour of the law as it would place power in the hands of government as it could not regulate something that was illegal, but tolerated by all.[89] It was for this reason that the French government attempted to frustrate the provision of contraception, and fundamental amendments were necessary in 1974.

Most importantly, however, it can be concluded that the medical aspects of birth control outweighed any demographic or moralist considerations by the 1960s. This was especially the case in the UK where, for example, contraceptive provision by GPs took precedence over clinic services until the 1970s, to the detriment of women's rights. Medicalisation of the issue was exacerbated in both the UK and France by the necessary alliances with doctors by the family planners themselves.

This contributed to the inadequacy of the 1967 Act in the UK in terms of women's rights and of the aims of family planners for numerous reasons. It was left very much to the FPA to force the implementation of the 1967 Act up to the early 1970s, which proved difficult as many women, especially those with larger families, were hard to contact as they were less likely to attend clinics. Hospital services were inadequate, to the chagrin of the Health Ministers Sir Keith Joseph (Conservative) and Richard Crossman (Labour). GPs, despite readily prescribing the Pill, remained untrained, without time or inclination, and at odds with the government over payment (they were not paid for social treatment in contrast to clinic staff, and they felt underpaid for medical treatment). Unfortunately, the response of the FPA was to implement further medicalisation of the association in order to train more doctors in contraceptive technology.[90] This not only enabled medicalisation to happen, it also meant that a limited, disparate service was passed on that women have become dissatisfied with, and full inclusion in the NHS and the full availability of contraception to all women was delayed through their conservatism.

On the other hand, the FPA can list many achievements. They worked hard to change attitudes on a controversial subject, improved standards, furthered contraceptive technology, pressed for expansion of the medical curriculum, expanded birth control internationally, and provided a public service for women for the first time on contraception, infertility, pregnancy testing, sexual counselling, sterilisation and domiciliary family planning. As late as 1970, 90 per cent of clinics were run by the FPA, and these were then easily taken over by the NHS.[91]

In France the MFPF essentially caused a fundamental shift in public opinion, but their own ideas on legislation were not enacted in 1967 or even implemented before the mid-1970s, due to the inherent Roman Catholicism and 'natalisme' of the French Establishment. Dhavernas, writing in 1978, saw the victory as belonging to the government and the opposers of contraception as by legislating they were once again co-opting and deluding campaigners by appearing to be in favour of women's rights when they were in fact more interested in social stability, '(o)n ne favorise pas celle-ci parce que c'est un droit pour les femmes, mais parce qu'il y va de la stabilité sociale et de l'intérêt général ... la récupération de nos luttes par le pouvoir est en même temps le signe de leur victoire et, pour nos adversaires, le moyen le plus efficace de les dévoyer'.[92] Even so, family planners in France fought successfully to establish that information and contraceptives should be supplied to women by law.

Both contraception laws were inadequately implemented after 1967 and each was amended to provide free contraceptives and improved access by 1974. By this time liberal family planners in the UK were accepted in the policy community and were fuelled by radical feminist demands, but concentrated on the more liberal actions of conducting surveys and lobbying and concentrated on the issue of overpopulation. In France by this time, the influence of Roman Catholics on the issue of contraception had waned and, despite their opposition, the law was further liberalised. Other policy community members now supported change and allied with campaigners such as second-wave liberal lobbying feminists, and this persuaded the government of the need for change. The significance of Parliament should not be ignored, as backbenchers played important roles. Their change of heart was an indirect result of contraceptive campaigns. There were also in the early 1970s radical campaigns by family planners and others on abortion, which at this time was still illegal, and this, perhaps even more than any radical feminist input into contraceptive campaigns, played an important part in persuading the French Establishment and opposition groups to further liberalise contraception.

Essentially then, in both countries the lack of second-wave radical feminist input in contraceptive campaigns ensured that, even when contraception had been put onto the parliamentary agenda by contraceptive campaigners, those groups who enjoyed the most representation in this policy sector – religious groups, pronatalists and particularly the medical professions in later years – were able to shape the content of the laws of 1967 to the detriment of a clearer definition of women's rights.

4

Abortion and the law: from criminalisation to medicalisation

Statutes liberalising abortion were finally enacted in the UK in 1967 and in France in 1975. Amendments to these were passed in France in 1979 and 1982. Abortion legislation in the UK was further amended through statute during the passing of the Human Fertilisation and Embryology Act 1990. This Chapter explores abortion law in Britain and France during the twentieth century leading up to these statutes and their amendments. This involves an examination of the law passed in the nineteenth century and early twentieth century that criminalised abortion. In France this period was dominated by pronatalist orthodoxy that was to have a dramatic effect on women's reproductive laws, more so indeed than the Roman Catholic Church. In addition, in both countries the need for fully trained medical personnel to undertake abortion (given the technology available) meant that the medicalisation of abortion, the control of its provision being secured by the medical professions,[1] was also largely unavoidable.

The comparison of case law and statute law liberalising abortion which follows illustrates the extent to which each country assured women their reproductive rights: in the UK the 1967 Abortion Act only provided abortion on specific grounds, whereas in France after 1975 early abortion was available on request. This statutory difference is arguably due in part to the fact that during the years between the passing of each country's laws a new method of abortion, the Karman method, made abortion much safer in the first three months of pregnancy. Differences between the abortion provision of the two countries are further underlined by an examination of the competing rights and interest of partners, medical professionals and the 'unborn children' themselves. The political debates behind these legal developments will be analysed in Chapter 5.

The criminalisation of abortion

Throughout the nineteenth century in the UK abortion was a criminal offence.

The first English statutory legislation relating to criminal abortion was enacted as early as 1803 and there were convictions during the nineteenth century under common law for abortion post-quickening. Moreover, it cannot be assumed that at common law abortion before quickening would not have been prohibited, as the lack of case law may only be due to the difficulty of detecting abortion pre-quickening.[2]

Lord Ellenborough's Act of 1803 Act formed the basis of the Offences Against the Person Act 1861, which is still in force today. Under Section 58, a pregnant woman must not unlawfully attempt to procure her own miscarriage with any substance or instrument. Likewise, any third party may not unlawfully use any substance or instrument to procure her miscarriage whether or not she is pregnant. Until 1939 this was noticeably more strict than the French law in this respect. Section 59 relates to third parties unlawfully supplying a substance or instrument knowing they are to be used to procure miscarriage, again, whether or not the woman is pregnant. The Act abolished capital punishment for abortion but it was tightened under medical pressure and the distinction between pre- and post-quickening was made clearer.[3] By the Infant Life (Preservation) Act 1929 it was an offence of child destruction to kill a child 'capable of being born alive' unless it was done under s. 1(1) 'in good faith for the purpose only of preserving the life of the mother'.

As in the UK, a nineteenth-century law criminalising abortion in France is still in force today. This is Article 317 of the Penal Code of 1810 (the Penal Code provision outlawing abortion is now Article 223–10 to 223–12). Under this law it is a crime if anyone procures or attempts to procure with food, drink, medication, violence or any other method, the abortion of a pregnant woman, with or without her consent, punishable by between one and five years' imprisonment and a fine, with a punishment of between five and ten years' imprisonment and a fine for professional abortionists.[4] The woman who aborts herself, and any member of the medical profession or pharmacist who assists or carries out the operation, are similarly liable to imprisonment and a fine. Medical practitioners in particular seem to have been targeted by the government as essential to ensuring the enforcement of the law, and any who advised on or assisted with abortion were banned from practising for at least five years,[5] and punished with forced labour if the abortion was successful.[6] In contrast to the law in the UK, women who underwent abortions were not prosecuted, as it was presumed they were innocent victims. Supplying substances does not appear to have been outlawed. The law did not manage to prevent classified advertisements for help with bringing on menstruation, discreet midwifery services[7] or doctors providing abortions in private clinics.[8]

In the twentieth century criminal law against abortion in France was further tightened by extremely restrictive statutes which a conservative Establishment refused to repeal and applied with vigour. (These will be dealt with below.) In this way French law contrasts dramatically with English law in its restrictions of women's rights. French legislation in the twentieth century also closely linked the criminality of abortion with that of contraception, in contrast to English law.[9]

We have seen, when examining contraceptive law, that the first relevant statute of the twentieth century in France came after the First World War when fears had grown about the relative population decline in France in comparison to that of Germany. In addition, many lives had been lost. Women's rights movements and neo-Malthusians were blamed for the decline and it was proposed that contraception, abortion and 'propagande anti-conceptionelle' be outlawed, and that article 317 of the Penal Code was no longer sufficient as it applied only to the operation itself. The ideology of pronatalism in France thus had a powerful impact on abortion law. Perhaps surprisingly, this impact was stronger even than that of the Roman Catholic Church.

The loi du '31 juillet 1920 réprimant la provocation à l'avortement et la propagande anti-conceptionnelle' not only covered contraception, but also prohibited any incitement to abortion, whether by spoken or written word, sale, distribution or offer of abortion or abortive substances, subject to a fine and imprisonment of 6 months to 3 years whether used or not (art. 1); sale, or distribution of abortive substances or instruments in the knowledge they were intended for an abortion whether used or attempted and whether they were effective or not (art. 2). This incurred the same penalty under article 317 of the Penal Code (art. 4). The proposer of the bill, M. Ignace, intended that the law should be once more aimed particularly at the medical profession for using its skills to destroy rather than cure, 'Ils sont en effet plus coupables que la femme même, lorsqu'ils font usage, pour détruire, d'un art qu'ils ne doivent employer qu'à conserver'.[10]

A year later, the government initiated another pronatalist law intended to reinforce that of 1920. This became the loi du 27 mars 1923, 'loi modifiant les dispositions de l'article 317 du Code pénal sur l'avortement, D. P. 23, IV, 200'. The woman herself was to be punished less severely (six months to two years' imprisonment and a fine) than the abortionist (between one and five years' imprisonment and a fine). The list of medical personnel covered by the law was lengthened and these would be punished in addition by being banned from practising temporarily or permanently, and from having any leave for from two to ten years. Abortion was seen by Dr Pinard in Parliament as a crime against the nation ('un crime contre la nation').[11]

In addition, the judges of the 'cours d'assises' were criticised for not punishing abortionists severely enough.[12] It was true that the juries involved appeared to sympathise with women by this time and felt bound by the severity of the punishment to acquit many of them. Between 1831 and 1889, 40 per cent of those accused of abortion (including doctors, chemists and midwives) were acquitted. Between 1906 and 1910 the number increased to 73 per cent – only a dozen were convicted.[13] In 1923, 68 per cent were acquitted.[14] Thus it was decided in 1923 to change the action from a crime to a 'délit', which meant that cases would be heard by magistrates at 'tribunaux correctionnels' whom the government hoped would be stricter and where surrounding publicity would be reduced. When the law came into effect the number of acquittals dropped to 18 per cent and ten times as many people were convicted.[15]

By the late 1930s the birth rate in France had failed to increase. This led the government to try to tackle the problem with a new, wide range of pronatalist family policies, which used a carrot-and-stick approach, but which were ultimately repressive. In 1936 child benefit was introduced. In 1939 the 'décret-loi relatif à la famille et à la natalité française du 29 juillet 1939' was passed. The French had now caught up with the stipulations of the 1861 Act in the UK, as Article 317 of the Penal Code was now altered so that a woman need only be assumed pregnant by the prosecuting authorities. This tightening of the law came at a time when it was difficult to prove that a woman was pregnant and so presumably closed any loophole that could be exploited by medical practitioners or magistrates. Moreover, women who aborted frequently had their sentences increased to between five and ten years.[16] Doctors were also now officially asked to betray the confidence of their patients, thus heralding another step on the road towards the medicalisation of abortion as the medical professionals were increasingly expected by the government to act as partners controlling, with the government, women's reproductive health.[17] This curtailment of women's rights in the 1930s was seen by the state as a necessary sacrifice by women for the sake of the nation and the family. The Second World War caused yet more problems for women in occupied France as the nationalistic Vichy government took this yet further. The law of 17 October 1940 banned married women from working in administration or any similar occupation. The law of 14 September 1941 made abortion a crime against nature, the nation, the state and the French people ('infractions de nature à nuire à l'unité nationale, à l'Etat et au peuple français'). The law of 15 February 1942 made abortion a crime against the State ('contre la sûreté de l'Etat') and allowed the Secretary of State for the Interior and the Departmental Prefect to intern without judgment those who had been accused of serious abortive practices, such as performing abortion, or advising on methods frequently or for profit. The accused appeared before the 'Tribunal d'Etat' – a high court created by the Vichy regime – and their sentences were posted on their front doors and workplace for a fortnight. The penalties ranged from imprisonment to the death penalty.[18] One woman was guillotined on 30 July 1943 for performing twenty-six abortions – the last woman to be guillotined in France.[19] The Vichy regime also increased the power of the medical professions when it created the 'Conseil de l'Ordre des Médecins', one of whose roles was to assist with the repression of abortion and who after the war continued as the extremely influential supreme medical body. The 1942 text was repealed after the liberation. Even this small concession to women met with considerable protest from the Society of Medicine and Law and the Dean of the Parisian Medical Law Faculty.[20] Despite these protests, the number of convicted abortionists was in fact increasing – there were 5,251 in 1946 – more than any under Vichy.[21] In 1950 there were 2,895 convictions; in 1960 289; and even as late as 1964 there were 700.[22]

In the UK, therapeutic abortion was more widespread than in France and the English law much more liberal even from the nineteenth century. Therapeutic abortion was considered to fall within the remit of lawfully procuring a miscarriage as opposed to 'unlawfully' under the 1861 Act if the operation were carried out to save the mother's life and also health, with health being widely interpreted by some as including social and economic circumstances. However, the idea of lawful abortion was still unclear and members of the medical profession differed in their interpretations of the grounds on which they could perform it.[23] The combination of these medical limitations and the criminality of abortion led many women to resort to backstreet abortion.

Throughout this time in France, therapeutic abortion was also lawful. The 'loi du 29 juillet 1939' codified the accepted practice of using abortion with impunity 'par un motif grave et urgent' to save the mother's life,[24] but this had to be certified by three doctors, one of whom should be a medico-legal expert.[25] However, it was not as liberal as English law after the decree of 28 November 1955 whereby, under article 38 of the Code de Déontologie Médicale the three doctors recommending a therapeutic abortion had their names added to a departmental list (presumably to check that individuals were not carrying out too many); the patient had to consent, unless it was an emergency (to allow a woman to sacrifice herself if she so wished); and a doctor could conscientiously object but must find another doctor who would carry out the abortion.[26] Therapeutic abortion was still not practised very often by doctors as there had to be a real danger of death to exempt them from the crime of abortion. Many doctors, therefore as in the UK, found this difficult to interpret with absolute certainty and many preferred to send patients to hospital, if for example the woman was bleeding, rather than be accused of assisting with an abortion. They therefore ignored their legal duty of assisting a person in danger. Indeed they were warned of the dangers of assisting such patients by the new Conseil de l'Ordre.[27] Most were also intimidated into not making use of Article 87 of the Code de la Famille which allowed for the possibility of therapeutic abortion if the mother's health were at stake.[28] This latter law was probably to prevent the rest of the children being deprived of a mother.

Liberalisation of abortion law in the UK

For the abortion issue in the UK, the 1930s was the most important decade in terms of a more widespread reappraisal of the law and its effects on women by judges who took a liberal interpretation of what 'lawful' abortion meant. Such liberalising judicial interpretation through case law was not a possibility in France. In the UK by contrast even pro-abortion interest groups had the ability to initiate test cases in order to clarify the law. Moreover, though there may have been sympathetic judges in both countries, in France this could only be on a random case-by-case basis according to mitigating facts, and no woman could be sure that she would come before a sympathetic judge. In the UK, on the other hand, when judges expressed liberal opinions, they were, in effect, liberalising the law by declaring that no offence had been committed.

For example, in 1931, and then more importantly in 1938, there was great public interest in the liberal critique of the 1861 Act in three cases. In November 1931, in an unreported case, two women pleaded guilty to having aborted themselves and were bound over. McCardie J. called for an amendment of the law, which was 'out of keeping with the conditions that prevail in the world around us'. He appeared to be influenced by the poverty of the defendants and the fact that one at least already had several children. In December 1931, in another unreported case, he refused to sentence a woman accused of carrying out an abortion, saying

> You are charged under an Act that was passed seventy years ago. Since then, the national point of view has been greatly changed. I think these abortion cases will continue so long as the knowledge of birth control is withheld ... In my view, and I say it plainly and publicly, the law of abortion should be amended.[29]

It was members of the women's pro-abortion interest group, the Abortion Law Reform Association (ALRA), who brought the most important abortion case of the period concerning therapeutic abortion, the legal tests for it and therefore its availability to women in 1938: *R v. Bourne*.[30]

In his summing-up to the jury in this case McNaghten, J. referred to the 1861 Act and the Infant Life (Preservation) Act 1929. He concluded that to be guilty of unlawfully procuring a miscarriage under the 1861 Act, the defendant, Dr Aleck Bourne, would have had to have not acted in good faith for the purpose only of preserving the mother's life. He believed that the word 'unlawfully' in the 1861 Act implied that *lawful* cases were those at common law where the doctor acts in good faith to preserve the life of the mother, as under section 1(1) of the 1929 Act.

He concluded that, as he could see no clear line between life and health:

> I think myself that those words ought to be construed in a reasonable sense: if the doctor is of the opinion, on reasonable grounds and based on adequate knowledge, that the probable consequence of the continuation of the pregnancy would indeed make the woman a physical wreck, or a mental wreck, then he operated in that honest belief, for the purpose of preserving the life of the mother. [31]

He also warned doctors that 'if a case arose where the life of the woman could be saved by performing the operation and the doctor refused to perform it because of his religious opinions and the woman died, he would be in grave peril of being brought before this Court on a charge of manslaughter by negligence'. [32] McNaghten, J. distinguished between the criminal professional abortionist and the skilful surgeon who performed a therapeutic abortion on grounds that were charitable and open. [33]

The *Bourne* judgment did not, however, create a satisfactory legal situation as far as doctors were concerned. The grounds for therapeutic abortion had been left to clinical judgment before 1938, but after this judgment McNaghten, J. may have actually reduced their discretion on health grounds as judgments before this time had merely indicated that 'lawful' abortion was permitted without specifying the exact circumstances. (McNaghten, J. in effect did specify the circumstances.) [34] This may have deterred some doctors from carrying out operations. *R v. Bergmann and Ferguson* (1948) clarified the position somewhat in that 'there must be a threat to the woman's life which is related to pregnancy, and is capable of expression in terms of physiology or psychiatry', but abortion is carried out due to a seriously malformed foetus the law does not permit the operation though 'it may refrain from interfering'. [35] Further liberalisation came in *R v. Tate* in 1949, where a husband sentenced to five years' imprisonment for killing his wife when attempting to abort her had his sentence reduced to immediate release on appeal. In the opinion of Goddard, J., the social circumstances of the case were deplorable as the couple had already had two children and were living in one room. [36] Such social circumstances would probably not have saved the defendant in a similar case in France at this time. In *R v. Newton and Stungo* in 1958, Ashworth, J. stated that 'health meant not only physical but mental health as well'. [37] However, for women, the law was still illiberal in the UK, certainly before this last case, as far as grounds for therapeutic abortion were concerned.

Following the lobbying of Parliament by interested campaign groups, Private Members' Bills were introduced throughout the 1950s and 1960s to further clarify and liberalise abortion and embody it in statute, but without success.

Public debate became more favourable towards abortion liberalisation in the early 1960s, and in the changing social climate of the time with a younger post-war generation coming of age, rather than for the sake of 'women's rights' as such. Of importance was the Thalidomide debacle, which saw pregnant women being prescribed the Thalidomide drug and then giving birth to deformed children. The idea of there being a need for abortion on grounds of foetal abnormality thus gained ground. The Medical Termination of Pregnancy Bill introduced by Liberal MP David Steel was debated at Second Reading on 22 July 1966, which was, remarkably, 'the first full debate ever in the House of Commons on the issue'. [38] It passed by a majority of 223 votes to 29. The bill returned to the House for the Report Stage and Third Reading, which lasted from 2 June to 13 July. The bill passed by 163 votes to 83. A week later Lord Silkin introduced the bill in the Lords, where it was passed by 127 votes to 21. The House of Lords made an important, and, in practice, liberalising amendment (introduced by Lord Chief Justice Parker), to prevent problems of the courts defining 'grave' and 'serious' risk, whereby risk to life or injury to health must be greater by continuing the pregnancy than by terminating it – known after this time as the 'statistical argument'.

The bill received the Royal Assent on 27 October 1967 but did not come into force until 27 April 1968. In its final form, the Abortion Act 1967 illustrates the continued government preoccupation with maternal health and medicalisation. It provided in section 1(1) that a pregnancy could be terminated by a registered medical practitioner if two registered doctors (in an emergency, one) were of the opinion, formed in good faith, that, under section 1(1)(a), the continuance of the pregnancy would involve risk to the woman's life or injury to the physical or mental health of herself or any existing children of her family, greater than if the pregnancy were terminated; or, under section 1(1)(b) that there was a substantial risk that if the child were born, it would suffer from such physical or mental abnormalities as to be seriously handicapped.

Minors were not as such catered for by the Act, but when the medical age of majority was lowered to 16 by the Family Law Reform Act of 1969 any woman aged 16 or over could obtain an abortion without parental consent.

The operation had to be carried out, except in an emergency, in an NHS hospital or approved nursing home and the Chief Medical Officer at the DHSS was to be notified within seven days. Doctors' surgeries and small specialised units were therefore not approved after 1967.[39] However, the real problem with minors was not the 16 to 18 group but those under 16. The Act ultimately avoided that problem, leaving the legality of abortion at under 16 years old to the mercies of the *Gillick* litigation,[40] after which a doctor could perform an abortion on a girl provided she had a mature understanding of abortion as a medical treatment.

The original bill, as presented by David Steel, was specific on the grounds for which there was a 'right' to abortion. However, during parliamentary debate, an amendment was added whereby a doctor could conscientiously object to carrying out an abortion, in order to assuage those doctors who had opposed the bill as they feared that their 'professional judgement' would be undermined. The Act, as passed, therefore confirms the medicalisation of abortion – doctors would henceforth officially be able to refuse to carry out abortions and to further prevent women's access to a statutory right.

Section 6 stated that the 1967 law only provided exceptions to sections 58 and 59 of the Offences Against the Person Act 1861, and therefore the latter still applied to abortions performed outside the law. Under section 5 of the 1967 Act, the Infant Life (Preservation) Act 1929 still applied. The 1929 Act had been enacted to fill a lacuna in the 1861 Act and to extend it: before 1929, doctors had been able to escape prosecution if they 'aborted' a woman who was already in labour as they could not then be accused of inducing labour and thereby procuring miscarriage. After 1929, such an act would constitute child destruction. The crime of child destruction was committed whenever a child 'capable of being born alive' was destroyed. The Act further provided that from twenty-eight weeks the presumption was that the child was so capable. Therefore, although abortion was unlawful after a child was capable of being born alive, the law remained unclear throughout this time as the term 'capable of being born alive' was open to interpretation. This led to case law on the issue and amendments to the 1967 Act in 1990.

In 1990, the British government was not expecting to have to reconsider the issue of abortion in depth and the issue was considered to be of minor importance, politically a backbench issue. It was not included in the remit of the Warnock Report in 1984. However, the government extended the title of the Human Fertilisation and Embryology Bill by the words 'and the subsequent development of the embryo'. Section 37 of the Human Fertilisation and Embryology Act 1990 therefore made changes to the Abortion Act 1967. Such an amendment was less likely in France where legislation in 1975 provided non-therapeutic abortion not only on demand but also only before the relatively short time limit of twelve weeks, making it unlikely that the abortion statute of 1975 itself would be brought into question by doctors in relation to the viability of premature babies.

Two factors forced the government to allow amendments to be tabled to the Embryology Bill relating to the upper time limit for lawful abortions. First, 'pro-life' campaigners, led by David Alton MP, sought a further opportunity to reduce that limit to eighteen weeks. Second, medical advances enabled doctors to preserve the lives of increasingly premature and low birthweight infants well below twenty-eight weeks. The definition of the phrase 'capable of being born alive' in the 1929 Act was much disputed.[41] Moreover, doctors and nurses were disconcerted by the fact that in one ward of the hospital they struggled to save a premature baby while in an adjacent operating theatre a foetus of similar gestation was being aborted.

In *C* v. *S* (1987)[42] 'pro-lifers' sought to use the 1929 Act to reduce the effective time limit for abortion. However, the CA ruled that a child of eighteen weeks' gestation could not be capable of being born alive as it was not capable of sustaining an existence independent of its mother – it could not breathe either independently or with the aid of a ventilator. Every child developed at a different rate so there could be no certain time when this would be the case. Section 2 of the 1929 Act was ambiguous and unclear and was clearer if one used the medical term 'viability' which referred to being born alive and then being capable of an independent existence. Therefore the plaintiff could not bring an injunction to prevent his girlfriend aborting her eighteen-week-old foetus, as it would not be criminal under the 1967 Act.

The Court of Appeal ruling in *C* v. *S* moved the 'pro-life' campaign to Parliament but 'pro-life' attempts to persuade Parliament to reduce radically the abortion time limit backfired badly. Section 37(4) of the 1990 Act amended the 1967 Act to this effect so that even if the foetus is, 'capable of being born alive' and is destroyed, no prosecution will lie as long as it is carried out in accordance with section 1 of the 1967 Act.

There are now four grounds for lawful abortion.

1. A twenty-four-week limit applies to abortions where the continuance of pregnancy would involve risk, greater than if the pregnancy were terminated, of injury to the physical or mental health of the woman or any existing children in her family (s. 1(1)(a)).

2. Where there is a risk to life there is no time limit on lawful abortion, which was also the case under the 1929 Act (s. 1(1)(c)).

3. There is no time limit where there is a risk of grave permanent injury to the physical or mental health of the woman (s. 1(1)(b)).

4. There is also no time limit where there is a substantial risk that if the child were born it would suffer from such physical or mental abnormalities as to be seriously handicapped (s. 1(1)(d)).

Subsections 1(1)(b) and 1(1)(d) of the Act in effect radically extend existing abortion law. In relation to the provision of abortion they may well have formalised existing practice. They have given doctors leeway to allow abortion for foetal abnormality after twenty-four weeks, but in practice this has not led to many more post-twenty-four-week abortions, and women can be refused an abortion depending on the abnormality and how seriously an individual consultant takes that particular abnormality. Again, this depends on clinical discretion. In 1997 a total of seventy-four abortions were carried out after twenty-four weeks. This amounted to 1.2 per cent of abortions – a figure unchanged since 1981.[43]

The Abortion Act 1967 was itself amended (s. 5(2)(a) and (b)) at a late stage in debates in order to take into account new reproductive techniques which might be questionably lawful under the old Act. These amendments to allow selective reduction of multiple pregnancy were the result of an acceptance of such treatments as *in vitro* fertilisation. The 1990 Act enables the transfer of up to three embryos into a woman's uterus. Reduction is usually carried out at between eight and fourteen weeks because although some of these foetuses may die spontaneously, if they are all carried to term, there is a strong chance that some may be handicapped at birth, may die at birth or shortly after, and that there may be damage to the woman's health. Thus the reduction may be carried out on the grounds of section 1 of the amended 1967 Act, as above. This reduces any potential rights of the unborn healthy child, destroyed because it forms part of a multiple pregnancy which is endangering all the foetuses and the mother. Although the amendment expressly solves the problem that selective reduction does not end the pregnancy, there have been criticisms of the new Act's definitions.[44] For example, religious groups complained unsuccessfully that this would reduce the meaning of pregnancy to 'the gestation of a foetus which is discontinued by termination'.[45]

Ultimately, the Act would therefore appear to have come under the influence of arguments put forward by clinicians involved in fertility treatment rather than arguments proposing the enhancement of foetal and embryo rights along more religious lines.

Decriminalisation of abortion in France

In France, debate on abortion did not cease with the passing of the 1920 and 1923 laws. In the post-war period particularly, the laws were seen as being too restrictive by political parties on the left.[46] Between 1928 and 1933 in the Third Republic there were three backbench bills on abortion, one of which favoured liberalisation. Between 1948 and 1956 during the Fourth Republic there were four bills, one Communist-inspired in 1956, which aimed to extend the grounds for therapeutic abortion. Between 1961 and 1974 during the Fifth Republic there were seventeen bills, which intended to make the abortion laws less strict or to abolish them altogether.[47]

Opponents of abortion in Parliament, pronatalist organisations and religious groups saw contraception as a 'lesser evil', and they thus promoted it as a solution to the social problem of backstreet abortions. Contraceptive liberalisation was thus made available by statute in 1967, 1973 and 1974 to stave off liberalisation of the 1920 and 1923 abortion laws.

However, the French government could not prevent the abortion issue from looming on the political horizon of the late 1960s. Calls for abortion to be the responsibility of the woman herself; 'on demand' up to a certain time; and free came from a significant gathering of interest groups made up, in the main, of the growing French feminist movement, the MLF, from 1969, and the left-wing medical movement, Groupe Information Santé (GIS), from 1973. These groups demonstrated on the streets of Paris, and openly carried out illegal abortions with impunity. In an unreported case at Bobigny a minor who had had an abortion was acquitted and the two abortionists, the defendant's mother and her accomplice, fined and given a suspended sentence respectively. The tribunal believed there were extenuating circumstances, namely that the defendants had been unduly influenced by the open flouting of the law by feminists reported in the press. However, the illegality of abortion was still upheld. An abortion campaigner who had been carrying out illegal abortions was convicted on 8 May 1973, and in the same year a 16-year-old minor was sentenced to fifteen days' imprisonment for attempting to abort herself without success.[48]

The parliamentary bills on abortion published at the time evolved from those that were ostensibly an extension of therapeutic abortion by designating specific grounds, as in the UK, to those stipulating that abortion should be on demand. The former were the most numerous and initially determined the idea for law taken up by the government.

The government-sponsored bill of 7 June 1973, presented by the Justice and Health Ministers, MM. Taittinger and Poniatowski, also known as the Messmer Poniatowski Bill, was therefore similar to the Act of 1967 in the UK in that abortion was to be allowed on certain grounds. This could apply when the pregnancy threatened the physical or mental health of the mother immediately or in the future; where there was a serious threat of foetal abnormality; in cases of rape or incest. However, the bill was already more liberal than its counterpart in the UK, as the woman concerned could assess whether these grounds applied and give written confirmation of this to her general practitioner and choose the hospital doctor who was to perform the termination. However, both doctors still had to agree that the woman was legally entitled to an abortion. It was asserted that this would be a medical act and therefore reimbursed, something not in the final Act. Unfortunately, the majority (made up of many pronatalists and Roman Catholics) voted to send the bill back to a commission to try to stall the law or have it amended out of recognition.[49]

After the presidential election of 1974, the new President Valéry Giscard d'Estaing promised the liberalisation of abortion, but only as part of a whole package of policies designed to capture the female liberal electorate and it was at this juncture than the government further conceded and published a bill allowing abortion on demand. Members of the Socialist Party in the National Assembly had been the first parliamentarians to put forward the idea of abortion on demand when on 1 June 1973 they published a backbench bill based on the text of the feminist group Choisir (who had pleaded for the defendants at Bobigny), namely the annulment of all restrictive laws on abortion and contraception and abortion on demand up to the twelfth week of amenorrhoea, but between the twelfth and twenty-fourth week with the advice of one medical and one social professional provided by the state.[50]

The law 'relative à l'interrruption volontaire de la grossesse' was finally promulgated on 17th January 1975 ('loi Veil'). Article 317 of the Penal Code was suspended under the specific circumstances permitted by the statute.[51] It was more liberal than the previous bill as it provided for abortion on demand before a certain time. In Section II any woman whose pregnancy places her in a situation of distress ('détresse') was entitled to ask a doctor for an abortion before the tenth week of pregnancy (twelve weeks of amenorrhoea) (art. 1). The operation must be performed by a doctor in a public or approved private hospital (art. 2).[52] The doctor must inform the woman of the risks associated with abortion and the possibilities of adoption and state benefits for mother and child (art. 3). The woman or couple must then consult a social worker (art. 4). The woman must wait a week after her original meeting with the doctor to reconsider her request and then give him written confirmation of it (art. 5). The doctor must then perform the operation or find another doctor who will (art. 6). Minors must have the consent of one of their parents or guardians (art. 7). A doctor refusing to carry out an abortion must inform the woman at their first meeting; other paramedical staff such as midwives, nurses or auxiliaries need not assist with abortions; a private hospital may refuse to perform abortions, but a public one may only do so if another provides the service locally (art. 8). A woman must be informed postoperatively about contraception (art. 9). Figures on abortion must be sent to the regional medical inspector (art. 10). A foreigner must be resident for three months before being allowed an abortion (art. 11).

Dhavernas argues that the government was not bringing in abortion to increase women's reproductive rights but rather to create a law that would be respected and to ensure respect for the state. The Minister of Health, Simone Veil, emphasised that what was at stake was that people should respect the law and by association the authority of the state.[53]

Therapeutic abortion in France, abortion after the time limit of twelve weeks' amenorrhoea, is also provided for by the law of 1975 and is similar to the emergency procedures set out in the 1967 Act in the UK. It can be carried out after the agreement of two doctors, one of whom must be a hospital doctor, that there is serious danger to the health of the woman. However, it differs from English law in three respects. In France it may be carried out where there is a risk of incurable foetal abnormality; as long as written evidence of the consultation is kept by the woman and each of the two doctors after the operation. No upper time limit was ever set for therapeutic abortion, despite questions being raised at the time, especially in the Senate. Thus, on this ground, abortion law was more liberal in France until 1990. However, just as there was medical debate on the issue in the UK culminating in the 1990 amendments, French doctors are currently questioning the ethics of performing an abortion on a viable foetus and therefore advise the upper limit to be either twenty-two or twenty-four weeks' gestation, though this is left to medical discretion.[54]

In theory, therapeutic abortion can only be performed if there is 'un état de péril' (state of danger). Abortion before twelve weeks can be carried out where a woman finds herself in 'un état de détresse' (a state of distress). The difference between the two was decided at the Tribunal Correctionnel at Rouen on 9 July 1975. 'Danger' was taken to mean a threat to life, or having serious physical consequences, 'distress' as the result of social, family, financial and moral elements ('la conjonction d'éléments sociaux, familiaux, financiers ou moraux').[55]

As in the UK, the law medicalised abortion in France in that the operation had to be performed in a public or private hospital by a doctor. The French law differs from the 1967 Act in several respects, however. The French law paid lip service to pronatalism as well as medical viewpoints in that abortion information could only be obtained from doctors; all abortion numbers had to be collected and made part of an annual report on demography; consultation with a social worker and a week to reconsider the operation were made compulsory; and annually, abortions could not exceed one quarter of all obstetric or surgical operations. Finally, a clearly religious slant on respect for life is apparent in the very first article of Section I where it stated that the law guarantees respect for all human beings from the beginning of life, 'La loi garantit le respect de tout être humain dès le commencement de la vie'.

The 1975 law in France was only passed initially for an experimental period of five years. In 1979 the law was passed once more, with some amendments to the 1975 law: education of the population and families was to be provided for everybody by the state (art. 1); doctors, midwives and nurses were to be trained in contraceptive methods (art. 2); sentences and fines for criminal abortion were increased and Article 317 of the Penal Code was reinstated subject to the law on abortion (art. 3); if the week between meetings would jeopardise the ten-week limit, a doctor could perform the operation instead two days after their meeting with the patient ('entretien') (art. 6). A minor had to give her independent consent to an abortion, in addition to that given by one of her parents, and where no parental consent was available, a judge would apply an 'ordonnance de 1958 prévoyant "'l'assistance éducative"' (art. 8), whereby the court would decide what was in the child's best interests; if the 'chef de service' refused to set up an abortion centre in his hospital it was taken out of his hands and those chosen by decree, the administrative body in charge, 'conseil d'administration', would do so (art. 9). A parliamentary delegation to study demography was also set up (art. 13) to appease pronatalists.

The reimbursement of contraception and abortion were important to campaigners in both countries. In the UK abortion was available in theory from 1974 on the NHS, but in reality NHS provision has been limited. Things did improve during the 1990s. In 1997 approximately half of all abortions were performed in the NHS sector, one-quarter in centres contracted to the NHS such as the BPAS or Marie Stopes clinics, and one-quarter privately.[56] It was not until 1982 that free abortion became available in France. However, abortion was still not reimbursed as per other medical acts. Therefore, by Article 5 of the 'loi Roudy', state funds were allocated annually within the provisions of the Finance Bill. However now 80 per cent of costs could be reclaimed.

The most recent ammendments to French abortion came in the law of 4 July 2001, when, inter alia, the time limit was lengthened from 10 to 12 weeks of pregnancy.

The law on RU 486

In the UK a second late amendment to the 1967 Act in 1990 (ss. 1(3) and (3A)) was made to anticipate the introduction of the abortion pill, RU 486. It introduced a new ministerial power over approved places and medicines whereby RU 486 and possibly other 'medical terminations' would not have to be administered in a hospital or approved clinic. It did not deal with the problems of medico-legal arguments surrounding RU 486 and the IUD in relation to the implantation of the fertilised egg. Such arguments illustrate neatly the overlap between the contraception and abortion issues whereby questions have been raised about whether the IUD and emergency contraception act to prevent implantation or act on the implanted egg thus becoming liable under the Abortion Act.[57] Medically, emergency contraception is unlikely to constitute abortion.[58]

RU 486 provides abortion that is simpler, less risky, and less traumatic for women. Although without the need for surgery and a stay in hospital it would appear cheaper, the drugs have been expensive, and this has meant that access is more difficult for British women than their French counterparts.

In trials where RU 486 was used on its own (as mifepristone) it had a success rate of 80 per cent as long as it was used before five weeks of amenorrhoea. When combined with a prostoglandin (mifegyne plus gemeprost) it was found that abortions after six weeks of amenorrhoea were possible.[59] In April 1982, Beaulieu announced his synthesis of RU 486.

In September 1988 in France the abortion pill was introduced. It took six years for the drug to be commercially available in France as clinical development had begun in 1982 – as early as December 1982 the MFPF had invited Professor Beaulieu to a meeting on the subject. The health minister Mme Barzach was in favour of the drug as were the French National Ethics Committee ('Comité Consultatif National d'Ethique pour les sciences de la vie et de la santé', CCNE), who on 16 December 1987 pronounced in favour of its use within the law on abortion and under medical supervision in specialist centres. The CCNE also underlined the government's lack of support for any questioning of the 1975 abortion law or of 'pro-life' interest groups, in contrast to the British government in 1990.[60]

In France there was immediate controversy about the drug, which could have affected women's rights to the drug worldwide. On 26 October 1988 Roussel-Uclaf suspended production of RU 486 in the face of a threat to profits from American 'pro-lifers' boycotting their products. Fortunately, the drug was forced to be immediately reinstated by the Health Minister M. Evin after pressure from pro-Choice groups, or perhaps because the government had a 36 per cent stake in Roussel. The government again pledged its support of women's rights as Evin stated that a resumption of production was in the interests of public health, because abortion was a woman's right by law, and the drug was the moral property of women.[61] However, the Senate was less happy about the implications of making abortion easier for women and this led to such precautions as leaving the drug in a locked cupboard in a doctor's surgery from 1989.

In France, prostaglandins (which stimulate contractions), are already used for therapeutic abortions, and have advantages over solutions of saline, glucose or urea which can be dangerous to the woman.[62] However, the initial furore has led to certain other precautions limiting its provision in France. The strict method applying to the abortion pill in particular in France is that RU 486 has to be swallowed in front of the prescribing doctor, the woman has to give written informed consent, and two to three days later prostaglandin is given with instructions and further appointment.[63] Before they are given the drug, women also have to give written consent to surgical abortion in case the drug fails.[64] RU 486 is also only allowed to be used in abortion centres, is not on sale in pharmacies, and is only prescribed for five weeks' amenorrhoea, no later.[65] Interestingly, the medical professions have wanted to see more women taking it before the seventh week and at home, as this would reduce medicalisation and costs.[66] France has also banned women who smoke heavily or aged over 35 from taking RU 486, after a woman aged 31 who smoked heavily died of a heart attack following treatment with the drug.[67]

The French government was influenced in its endorsement of the drug by a survey in the *Nouvel Observateur*, which showed that most French women were favourable to the drug.[68] In its first year, 20,000 French women used the drug, it was prescribed in more than 793 licensed centres, and accounts for over 20 per cent of terminations.[69] Abortion rates are decreasing in France annually: there were over 130,000 in 1976 increasing to 180,000 annually between 1981 and 1983; this dropped to 160,000 in 1987.[70] Furthermore, the drug fits neatly with French legislation encouraging women to have early abortions. Unfortunately for British women, in contrast to France, access to medical abortion has been very limited. Of 220 clinics providing an early abortion service in 1991, fewer than seventy were found to have supplies of the drug. Three-quarters of abortions before the ninth week were carried out in private clinics, and it was estimated that very few used the drug. In non-NHS clinics, DOH restrictions deter women from medical abortions.[71] Although in the UK RU 486, introduced in July 1991, has been licensed for use much later than in France within the first nine weeks of gestation, and since 1995 to be used between 13 and 20 weeks (though not between 10 and 12 weeks), the estimated risk of haemorrhage has ensured that it must be administered in hospital, thus limiting women's freedom.[72] Use of the drug has been increasing but remains relatively small at 6.6 per cent of terminations.[73]

The Family Planning Association criticised the lack of availability of RU 486 in 1999.[74] This criticism was followed by guidelines issued by the RCOG who reported wide discrepancies in the range of abortion services in England and Wales and recommended that women should not have to wait longer than three weeks for an abortion.[75]

Competing rights and interests

In France statutory amendments to the original 1975 law were passed by Parliament in 1979 and 1982, but cases have only interpreted the law. By contrast the Abortion Act in the UK did not mean that attempts to adapt abortion legislation came to an end, whether through Statute or case law. The French Statute therefore dealt with a number of the details that in the UK were left to the vagaries of case law. Such rights concerned parental rights over minors; the rights of putative fathers; and the rights of doctors performing abortions.

Abortion provision for minors

What of parents' rights over their children? As regard minors in France, they need the consent of one parent in order to avail themselves of an abortion (art. 7). However, in the UK's Abortion Act 1967 mention was not made of minors. Since the *Gillick* ruling (*see* Chapter 2 for discussion of this case) English law may have become more favourable to a 'mature' girl under the age of 16 wanting an abortion against the wishes of her parents. As long as she is able to understand the physical and emotional consequences of abortion, she alone will be able to consent to the operation. If not, then a Local Authority could seek to use its inherent jurisdiction, as set out in the Children Act 1989 (Section 100(3)-(5)), taking into account the significant harm the girl might suffer if medical treatment, such as abortion, were or were not carried out.[76]

In an extreme case a doctor who carried out an abortion could be prosecuted for assault, but would not be guilty of criminal abortion. In *Re B (a minor)* (1991),[77] Hollis, J. held that an abortion could be carried out on a 12-year-old girl who, along with the grandparents with whom she lived, wanted the abortion, against the wishes of her mother, 'an abortion was in the best interests of a child aged twelve years ... in view of the risk of physical and mental injury to her health'.

The child was made a ward of court and Hollis, J. instructed that the child's views be independently obtained. Here it was not held that the child was mature enough to consent, but that the court should decide what the best interests of its ward were, taking into account her own wishes. He decided that what had to be taken into account were that physically abortion would be safer than pregnancy, and that, socially, teenage mothers had a high suicide rate. In comparison the trauma of abortion would be short-lived. Her age was also of importance as were the wishes of those around her. Arguably, the English law relating to minors is really just a further example of medicalisation, as the doctor – not the girl or her parents – makes the decision of whether a girl is mature as well as whether or not to perform the abortion.

Putative fathers and their rights

In the UK the rights of husbands were assessed in *Paton* v. *British Pregnancy Advisory Service* (1978).[78] Mr Paton tried to get an injunction in the High Court preventing his wife having what would otherwise have been a lawful termination. This was refused as the husband had no legal right to be consulted by his wife under the 1967 Act. The husband in this case then took the matter to the European Commission on Human Rights alleging a violation of his rights, under Articles 2 and 8 of the European Convention on Human Rights, to a family life and the child's right to be born. The court found against him on the grounds that following the 1967 Act abortion was allowed in the early stages of pregnancy and therefore the life and health of the woman superseded both of the rights claimed by the husband. One question that Sir George Baker P. at the High Court did not decide was whether, had the doctors approved the abortion in bad faith, a husband would be allowed an injunction to prevent an unlawful abortion. However, such a judgment would be unlikely to be given in time to prevent a woman from going ahead with an abortion before she could be stopped.[79]

Similarly, in C v. S (1987)[80] a woman's boyfriend initially had his application for an injunction refused by the High Court following *Paton*, on the grounds that he had no standing, then at the CA was refused the right as the father of the unborn child to contest the abortion. In this case, the rights of the putative father seem to have taken a backseat to questions of viability and lawfulness. A foetus of eighteen to twenty-one weeks was deemed not to be viable by Heilbron, J. Therefore, an abortion carried out on such a foetus would not be unlawful. The boyfriend in question had no grounds for an injunction on this basis. This was confirmed by the Attorney General's Reference (No. 3 of 1994).[81] This considered the case of a man who had stabbed his pregnant girlfriend causing the subsequent death of her child after it was born, due to its prenatal injuries. In this case Lord Taylor, CJ held that the foetus was not a person in being but was part of its mother until it had a separate existence of its own. The foetus could not be deemed to have been murdered – only the woman assaulted and damaged. Thus a foetus did not enjoy the rights of a person that is separate from its mother.

Men claiming rights as the fathers or guardians of their unborn children gain no more recognition under French law. The legal notion of 'détresse' as a ground for demanding an abortion is something entirely at the discretion of the woman concerned. Nobody can prevent her from aborting including her employer[82] and her husband.[83] The latter decision was disputed as being contrary to Article 4 of the 1975 law, which advised that a couple should participate at the meeting with the doctor to discuss abortion ('entretien'), but this decision supersedes any implications of father rights in that Article.[84] The most the husband can do is use as a ground for divorce the injury of having hidden the operation from him or having gone against his wishes. A husband who forced his wife to abort would have committed a serious injury against her.[85]

Medical professionals and abortion rights

What of the rights of doctors under the law on abortion? In R v. *Smith (John)* (1974)[86] a doctor in the UK was convicted of bad faith after performing an abortion. The doctor in question claimed to have used the statistical argument that continuing the pregnancy would be of greater risk to the woman than an abortion. This was a peculiar case of straightforward bad faith, but despite its rarity it has been claimed that this argument is used by unscrupulous doctors to provide abortion on demand. However, the decision as to whether to provide abortion actually lies very much in the hands of doctors. Not only is abortion largely only available privately in the UK, legislation in both countries also provided that medical professionals do not have to carry out abortion as they may conscientiously object to carrying out the procedure.

Moreover, to the detriment of women's reproductive rights, medical professionals can and do forego even this option in the UK, by lawfully refusing to carry out abortions by interpreting the grounds strictly and refusing to perform any abortions other than to save the mother's life or for foetal abnormality, thus depriving the legal right of women to abortion. Some consultants have even been known not to offer amniocentesis to their patients to prevent them being able to proceed to therapeutic abortion. However, there are legal rules in the UK which can tip the balance in women's favour. As far as a doctor who objects to abortion is concerned, it could also be argued that he must fulfil a basic duty of care to a pregnant woman over the age of 35 and offer amniocentesis, knowing that this may lead to an abortion in the case of foetal handicap. Other medical and administrative staff have less rights to refuse to participate in abortion provision.[87]

In France, as there are no grounds for doctors to interpret, those who 'object' to abortion can only resort to using the conscientious objection clause in the 1975 law. There have still been problems for women, however, in regard to the initial lack of government resources for the setting-up of centres, which was compounded by a reticence on the part of doctors, especially gynaecologists and those in charge of hospitals (unlawfully in many cases) to carry out operations *they* found medically unethical, therefore invoking the conscience clause (especially for married primipares and previous aborters). This was highlighted by the Nisand report of 1998 (*see* Chapter 5). However, the French model of conscientious objection is to be preferred to the British model as French women must be told in the first interview if the doctor will not carry out the termination.

Conclusions

In 1967 the UK was, to a large degree, revolutionary in its statutory liberalisation of abortion law. French women would have to wait another eight years for the *decriminalisation* of their abortion laws: from 1975 abortion became available at the request of the woman concerned. Despite abortion being available 'on demand' in France, is it actually more liberal than its English equivalent?

In both countries laws on criminal abortion are still in force: in France, Article 223–10 to 223–12 (old Article 317) of the Penal Code, in the UK, the Offences Against the Person Act 1861. The important phrase 'greater than if the pregnancy were terminated' does add a liberalising aspect to the English law after the twelfth week of pregnancy. Whilst in France, after twelve weeks amenorrhea, only therapeutic abortion may be carried out on quite limited grounds, though this has no time limit. In the UK a time limit of twenty-four weeks was introduced by Parliament through amendments in 1990, a reduction from the previous twenty-eight weeks limit. Abortion is also difficult to obtain in some areas of the UK. In France, however, abortion has only been reimbursed by the health service since 1982. The law on minors is more straightforward in France as they were mentioned in statute law thus, particularly since the *Gillick* case, provision is more likely to minors there. The abortion pill, RU 486, makes abortion simpler and involves less invasive surgery. Much better provision has been provided to women in France than in the UK, however. In both countries women's freedom to abort away from the machinations of fathers has thus far been ensured as fathers do not have rights to contest abortion in either country.

Damages can be claimed by the woman patient as with any other medical treatment, but claims have also been filed by the children born or damaged as a result of failed abortion (similarly there have been cases where damages have been claimed after failed contraception or sterilisation). This has led to debate about foetal rights conflicting with women's rights. Indeed in the later stages of pregnancy the United States has seen fit to interfere with women's rights by making foetuses wards of court,[88] and by limiting the actions of mothers through surrogacy contracts. In the UK there have also been cases where judges acting *in camera* have ordered women to undergo Caesarean sections against their will, though this has now been superseded by a (qualified) recognition of women's autonomy in childbirth as outlined in *Re MB* in 1997.[89] However, the rights of the foetus have been pitted against doctors' rights in terms of damages and the right to health once born, as opposed to women's rights and the right to be born. A woman herself has the right to sue the doctor concerned, to choose not to have children, and to have healthy children. In the UK the 1990 amendments did reduce the time limit for abortion thereby reducing women's rights as long as there was no foetal abnormality.[90] Nevertheless, abortion remains, for the time being at least, in the hands of the mother and her own environment rather than those of her 'unborn child'.

But there are features of the French law which might not easily come under the heading of 'liberal'. There is a statutory obligation on women in France to reconsider termination for a week (though this could be shortened to two days after 1979), alongside doctors having to detail to their patients the risks of abortion and the availability of state benefits for childrearing and adoption. This underlines, as with contraception, the emphasis in the French law on pronatalism rather than on the autonomy of French women, and contrasts with the English law.

Perhaps, then, neither country's abortion provision is more 'liberal' than the other. One overriding factor remains, however: abortion is available on demand in France. This constitutes a tangible recognition of women's reproductive rights.

This Chapter has given some indication of the relative influence of the interest groups concerned. Pronatalists and Roman Catholics were responsible for the restrictive French statutes of 1920 and 1923 and certain limitations present in the 1975 law. Despite this, French abortion campaigners and their left-wing allies did attain abortion on demand. In both countries, although statutory rights were enacted in 1967 and 1975, medical professionals have still restricted women's access to abortion, particularly through their use of the conscientious objection clause, in both countries. The policy process behind the abortion provision in the UK and France, and the interest group involvement in this, will be more closely examined in Chapter 5.

5

Abortion politics in development

Campaigns for the liberalisation of the abortion laws took place at different times in the two countries. In the UK[1] abortion and contraception campaigns were separate though concurrent. The UK abortion campaign began in the 1930s, with legislation being passed in 1967, and amended in 1990. In France, by contrast, campaigns on abortion did not begin until after the passing of the contraception law of 1967, resulting in legislation on abortion in 1975. In both countries, however, the interest group actors were similar. The abortion campaigns were led by women's rights campaigners, whose allies were primarily left wing. In France, these allies were joined by individual radical members of the medical professions. Their opposition remained the Roman Catholic Church, religious fundamentalists and the medical professions. In the UK, the medical professions spoke out against the idea of an abortion statute, and women's control of abortion as opposed to medical discretion, rather than against abortion *per se*.

When comparing campaigns around abortion in the two countries, it would appear that the timing of the law on abortion in each country, whether coming before or after 1968 when second-wave feminism had begun, had an effect on the lobbying methods, the resources and alliance-building capacity of pro-abortion campaigners. Hence, as the legislation that British feminists were trying to influence was passed in 1967 as opposed to 1975, those feminists who lobbied for women's rights in relation to abortion were first-wave liberal feminists. However, due to the input of radical feminism into the abortion campaigns in France, the unity and alliances of French feminists were weaker as compared to the UK. Radical feminism was only a feature of those abortion campaigns that took place in the UK after 1968 to prevent amendments to the Abortion Act 1967. However, the radical nature of the French abortion campaign served to ensure that abortion law after 1975 was more favourable towards women and feminist demands because abortion was provided 'on demand'.

This Chapter examines the structure, aims, methods and resources of abortion campaigners, their allies and opposition. The impact that campaigners were able to have on legislators, as evidenced by the parliamentary debates leading up to legislation is then assessed. In turn, the relevant abortion laws passed and their implementation is considered, with particular reference to the political and legal environments in which campaigners were operating. As in Chapter 3, which looked at the policy process around contraception and the relative influence of the different groups involved in campaigns on legislation, the aim here is to examine the most important campaigns around abortion, namely those that led to statutory amendment. Nevertheless, some brief comment is made on events which have taken place after that time.

Liberalism and reform in Britain

The first campaigners in Britain on abortion liberalisation were individual Malthusians who decided to turn their attention from birth control to abortion once other groups became involved in the former issue.[2] The more widespread action in support of birth control in the 1920s, with the setting up of clinics by the NBCC, also provided an impetus for debate on the abortion issue.[3] These campaigners therefore proceeded to set up the Abortion Law Reform Association (ALRA) in February 1936.

ALRA never enjoyed mass membership; indeed, it preferred to remain a small, knowledgeable and well-organised group – even by 1964 it had only 200 members.[4] However, its membership was politically radical relative to the general population.[5] In the 1930s, ALRA had been funded mainly by Janet Chance. When a new generation of members took over in the early 1960s their income increased dramatically as a result of an increase in subscriptions and donations from new members and wealthy sympathisers.[6]

As early as 1938, ALRA performed the task of trying to extend and affirm the law on abortion by using case law, in R v. Bourne, in a way that would have been much more difficult in the French codified system. Joan Malleson and Dr Aleck Bourne, a senior obstetrician, were both members of ALRA's Medico-Legal Council, which was hoping to extend the law by using a test case. Malleson was told by the Schools Care Committee of a 14-year-old girl who had been raped and was pregnant. She wrote to Dr Bourne telling him that 'Many people hold the view that the best way of correcting the present abortion laws is to let the medical profession gradually extend the grounds for therapeutic abortion in suitable cases, until the laws become obsolete, so far as practice goes'. She added that public opinion was bound to be on his side if he performed an abortion on the girl.[7] As detailed in the preceding Chapter, this resulted in an extension of the law, or, at the very least, a clear statement that abortion was available to protect the life as well as health of the woman concerned.

Immediately following the Second World War, ALRA was undecided

tactically as to whether they should rely on the development of legal precedents
or the drafting of a model parliamentary bill combined with political lobbying.
During the 1950s, many ALRA-backed bills were put forward, but more
importantly in 1948 and 1958 liberalising legal precedents were set. This meant
that in the 1960s ALRA could concentrate on parliamentary lobbying. The
coincidence of militant action, rather than reaction, in the 1930s and 1960s
was concurrent with the young age of the group's leadership. Those in society
who were helping to orchestrate social change in the 1960s were reflected in
the new leaders of ALRA – young, energetic, left-wing men and women –
who took over in the early months of 1964, spurred on by the public reaction
to the Thalidomide disaster of 1962, when abortion on health and eugenic
grounds became more acceptable. They also acquired a new, experienced
chairwoman, Vera Houghton, who had previously set up the International
Planned Parenthood Federation (IPPF).

To keep abortion in the news, ALRA emphasised current public fears, such
as those in 1961 to 1962 surrounding the Thalidomide drug. At this time,
abortion was not available for a deformed foetus and this raised questions in
the House of Commons following Kenneth Robinson's 1961 Bill.[8] They also
created news, such as on the widespread use and availability of noxious
abortifacient drugs. One important resource that ALRA often drew upon was
experience of lobbying Parliament. Their chairman, Vera Houghton, had
worked for the IPPF and their President was a distinguished lawyer, who
helped to draft numerous bills. Introducing bills was used from the 1950s as
a publicity exercise. Also, early failures taught the organisation who its allies
were in Parliament, how to use parliamentary procedure to advantage and
what sort of bills were capable of arousing support.

In several respects, ALRA found it necessary to pretend to be less 'radical
and fiercely feminist' than they in fact were.[9] The ALRA executive attempted
to play on the disregard by the establishment of radical groups by emphasising
their more conservative supporters and by dressing conventionally.[10] They also
spoke soberly on the need for abortion in serious cases of rape and incest,
and incessant childbirth in poor social conditions; the high figures and dangers
of illegal abortions; the fact that over half of the doctors that they surveyed
could not understand the present law; and the imposition that Roman Catholics
were attempting to make on others when liberalisation would not have to
affect them personally. They tried to present facts on which a majority of the
public could reach a consensus.[11] They also kept their legal aims discreet 'to
retain public support'.[12]

In relation to medical control of abortion, officially ALRA sought 'legalised
abortion when performed by a medical practitioner, subject only to restrictions
imposed by medical and humanitarian considerations'.[13]

Privately, ALRA had more radical ideas and were critical of the medical professions. They believed, however, that including the medical profession in its proposals was tactically necessary as their support would be needed in order to get the government to put abortion liberalisation on the political agenda. Some members held feminist beliefs that abortion should be on demand, as women should decide what happens to their bodies and cease to be subordinated to reproduction. Stella Browne, its most militant leader, believed in abortion rights up to full-term gestation. However, these demands were not spoken about in public campaigns so that respectability could be retained.[14]

Indeed, one of the most important disagreements between members of ALRA was on the question of the form that legislative change on abortion should take. This could be either repeal of the law up to a specified time in pregnancy, or reform to widen the permitted conditions for abortion. Their President, Professor Glanville Williams, proposed in 1963 repeal to allow abortion on request up to the thirteenth week and thereafter only to save the mother's life, as most illegal abortions, which were, after all, what the organisation was aiming to prevent, would not be reduced if only the more serious cases were allowed by reform. He was supported by some local groups and medical members. However, ALRA's executive were advised by members of the House of Lords in 1964 that the only type of bill that had any chance of success would be a reform bill that left the decision in the hands of the doctor, rather than the patient. This, therefore, became their main aim. 'With this decision ALRA therefore turned its back on a woman's right to choose.'[15] Thus the types of abortion cases they envisaged were: preservation of the woman's physical or mental health; in cases where there was serious risk of a defective child being born; in cases where pregnancy resulted from a sexual offence, such as rape.[16] Effectively, they wanted to extend the law of the time to include the ground of foetal abnormality and to have this enshrined in statute.

Radicalism and revolution in France

In contrast to the UK, campaigns on abortion in France did not really begin until after 1968 (the Thalidomide scandal appearing not to affect abortion debate there), though campaigners during debates on the liberalisation of contraception had criticised the laws of 1920 and 1923 for their social out-datedness, impracticality and austerity.[17] Indeed the campaign was provoked by second-wave feminists and the shortcomings of the contraception law of 1967. The inadequacy of the 'loi Neuwirth' provided a ground for those influenced by the new radical post-1968 politics to campaign on its behalf and to produce more radical positions on abortion than in the UK. It changed the remit of women's organisations campaigning on reproductive rights such as the MFPF, who spoke out more radically in favour of women's right to choose. They hoped that the implementation of the Neuwirth law within their clinics would eradicate abortion. They advised pregnant women to take the pregnancy to term and then come for contraceptives. It also led to the creation of the separate organisation, the ANEA. This was created by medical and legal leaders of the MFPF to research abortion. It believed that abortion could only be provided on certain grounds (therapeutic) and was a matter for clinical judgement.[18]

But in their first major campaign, the one from which the MLF was essentially born, feminists rejected old ideas such as those of the MFPF, and as a reaction to the inadequate 1967 Neuwirth law they placed the right of women to control their own fertility as the central tenet of the campaign against abortion. 'The question thus posed was less *when* (as it had been for the MFPF) and more *whether* to bear children; within this revision the rights of fathers and needs of the nation were clearly subordinated to the rights of women.'[19] Reproductive freedom was seen to lie at the heart of women's freedom: from the obligation of motherhood; from dependence on men; or from a feeling of isolation and guilt.[20]

Outside the MLF were mixed-sex pro-abortion organisations led by radical feminists, such as the 'Mouvement pour la Libéralisation de l'Avortement' (MLAC) from 1971; and liberal feminists, such as 'Choisir' from 1973; as well as sympathetic non-feminist organisations, such as the relatively radical medical group GIS from 1973. Some of these, such as 'Choisir', attempted to become members of the policy community and use conventional channels, methods and resources. Non-feminist organisations outside the MLF, as well as socialist feminists within it, saw abortion and contraception as class issues rather than women's rights issues. This led to differences among pro-abortionists about beliefs and strategies. There were also differences among feminists between socialists and radicals who believed that motherhood should be rejected in a capitalist society, and liberals who argued that the law needed only to be reformed to allow women to have reproductive choice. In the short term, however, and during campaigns, most feminists agreed on the need for reform of the law and what shape it should take.

The liberal feminist pro-abortion group, 'Choisir', was created in autumn 1973 by MLF members, MLAC and the Manifeste signatories.[21] It contained different strands of feminism and differences soon appeared within it.[22] 'Choisir' saw contraception as an important way to avoid recourse to abortion, but argued that women also needed clinically safe conditions in which to have abortions, even if contraception were widespread, because there would always be cases of rape, incest, failure of contraceptives, and misuse (particularly in the case of the Pill). It saw itself as a reformist organisation that was trying to help women.[23] It wanted the 1920 and 1923 laws on abortion replaced with a bill that it had formulated, which included social cases for the first time. This was important to it as it argued that most illegal abortions were for social reasons. Its members pointed out that women were having to pretend to their doctors that their life was in danger in order to get a therapeutic abortion.

Despite the fact that 'Choisir' was reformist and liberal, its actions leading up to the liberalising of the abortion laws were radical when compared to British anti-abortion tactics. For example, Choisir and MLAC decided to utilise an abortion case at *Bobigny* in November 1972 as a trial of the 1920 law. The way this trial was used contrasts with that of *R* v. *Bourne*, although the thirty-four years separating the two cases may have contributed to these differences. In the *Bobigny* case a woman and her friend were accused of performing an abortion on the woman's daughter. The aborted minor was acquitted, the two aborters only fined and given suspended sentences as they were presumed to have been adversely influenced by the campaigns surrounding abortion by radical feminists. The case provoked much public debate – the Conseil de l'Ordre spoke out against abortion and the MLF responded by occupying its Paris headquarters and organising a meeting of 2,000 people. The sentences passed were viewed by the public as extremely mild and were thus hailed as a victory for the pro-abortion campaigners. Campaigners themselves saw the *Bobigny* case as a turning point after which the 1920 and 1923 laws had been shattered and could no longer be applied in practice '(l)e jugement de *Bobigny* a fait éclater la loi, qu'on le veuille ou non. A partir de Bobigny, on peut le dire, il n'y a plus de loi de 1920. Elle a volé en morceaux'.[24]

Most of the campaigners in France were politically radical. MLAC published in *Le Nouvel Observateur* and *Le Monde* on 5 April 1971 'Le Manifeste des 343' in which women, including many celebrities, declared that they had had illegal abortions.[25] Again, this brought abortion, formerly a most private, taboo subject to public attention and was the catalyst for the abortion campaign to become a mass movement '(l)e choc provoqué par cette publication a cristallisé très rapidement un véritable mouvement de masse en faveur de la libération complète de l'avortement et de la contraception'.[26]

MLAC also set up the Centre for Sexual Information in Paris – a network of GPs, medical students and nurses providing abortions illegally by the modern Karman method of aspiration. These were performed for free or a small fee and were disguised as miscarriages in hospitals. This was to show that abortion could be simple and safe and did not necessarily have to be a medical issue – it could be performed for women by laypersons (though most of those carrying out the operation were medically qualified).[27]

Many of the actions of radicals were organised to cause press debate, for example during elections by forcing candidates to take positions and to put forward their own propositions on abortion. The MLF and other radical groups, it has been noted, rejected the idea of direct communication with the government, but liberal feminist groups like Choisir, did not, and indeed, as will be seen, were consulted by the government on the content of the law, as well as making use of policy community allies, such as the Socialists, who were more likely to have an influence on Parliament or become a member of the network, as the main opposition party, or after elections, in government.

That the aims of the campaigners in the UK and France were different was in part due to the influence of second-wave feminism in France. In the UK, though secretly, from the 1930s ALRA wanted extremely liberal abortion laws, and in the 1960s even their President, an eminent lawyer, preferred abortion on demand up to the thirteenth week (with therapeutic abortion after that time). Nevertheless, the British organisation deemed it necessary to tone down these aims to therapeutic abortion on certain grounds with medical involvement, in order to achieve legislation. In France, however, their aims were more radical and blatant, notwithstanding that the emphasis on feminism was similarly toned down in order to achieve legislation by the liberal reformist 'Choisir' and the socialist MLAC.

Correspondingly, the structure and methods of the French groups benefited from their context and acted more like a new social movement (NSM) (*see* Chapter 1) than in the UK. In the UK, ALRA began as a small, voluntary, privately funded organisation. The French groups, by contrast, were unstructured, non-hierarchical and personalised, 'movements', with self-help a priority. Nevertheless, both countries' groups, apart from the MLF itself, were mixed, middle class and made use of their 'professional' members. Both (apart from the MLF which was even more like a NSM and was aimed at women) also successfully employed such methods as using legal cases, parliamentary lobbying, utilising the media and public opinion polls (actually commissioned by ALRA) and attempting to sway the opinion of the general public and respected organisations. The public face of ALRA was much more conservative than that of French organisations, however, with the latter performing illegal abortions and campaigning publicly nationwide.

Neither in France nor in the UK were these groups 'insiders'. This was due in no small part to the radical nature of their aims and methods and their lack of resources. This was particularly the case in France. The 'outsider' status of campaigners was also a result of their being women's organisations, campaigning for women's rights, at a time when women were considered a minority interest and outside the parliamentary arena, even among the small number of MPs who were women. Moreover, in both countries the aims of the campaigners crossed sectoral boundaries of religious, social, economic and health policy sectors which made government response difficult and tardy (though once accepted by the government these were subsumed into the health policy sector). This does not mean to say that ALRA was conservative; for their time they were perhaps as radical as the feminists were to become in France at a later stage.

Campaigners and their allies

The alliances that campaigners are able to build around an issue are an important component of their political environment as they will tend to increase resources and the show of strength campaigners can display to any government. The interest groups with which abortion campaigners had the capacity to build alliances on the abortion issue were similar to those who allied with campaigners fighting for contraceptive liberalisation, and consisted of mainly left-wing groups. However, in the UK, the Anglican Church found it more difficult to support the issue of abortion. In France, by contrast, even some medical professionals were driven to speak in favour of abortion due to the rigidity of the French law, and due to the fact that the French debate took place several years later at a time when abortion had become more acceptable and safe due to the introduction of the Karman aspiration method, which could be carried out before twelve weeks of pregnancy.

In the UK throughout the campaign, ALRA's attempts to gain support and funding were fruitful, especially among women and the political left. In the early 1930s, it was individual women members of the Labour party who were also members of the Malthusian movement and in favour of abortion liberalisation who tried to gather support among sympathetic groups. These included Dora Russell, Frida Laski and Stella Browne. One important success was the support of the Cooperative Women delegates in 1934 of which there were 1,360. This group advocated the revision of the 1861 Act; abortion being treated as a normal surgical operation; amnesty for women imprisoned for abortion; the right of women to control their own bodies; the right of children to be wanted; and the need for a back-up when contraceptives failed.[28] ALRA's main aim was to harvest as much outside support as possible in order to show that more traditional groups in society, especially women's voluntary groups, were also in favour of abortion reform.[29] Whilst soliciting support, they also used the opportunity to raise funds.

In addition some of ALRA's more eminent members were individually in a position to meet with senior MPs, though as a group ALRA itself was outside the health policy community.

Many of the groups who lent support to campaigns in France generally supported the regulatory role of the legislator and of public institutions. One of the most important results of left-wing support in France, which far outweighed political support in the UK, was the support of François Mitterrand. In the presidential election campaign of 1965, as leader of the left coalition, he posed the social problem of 'backstreet' abortions and the need to change the laws of 1920 and 1923. On 1 June 1973, the Parti Socialiste (PS) put forward a backbench bill based on that of the campaign group, Choisir, demanding the annulment of all restrictive laws on abortion and contraception and abortion on demand up to the twelfth week. Between the twelfth and twenty-fourth weeks one doctor and one social worker would give their advice, though the final decision would be that of the woman. This would be reimbursed by the patient's medical insurance.[30] Choisir's draft law, however, was amended by the PS to include the notification of one parent in the case of a minor seeking an abortion.

But by far the most important members of the health policy community and the abortion policy community were the medical professions. A small number of these did in fact support ALRA in the UK, but not in sufficient numbers to be useful. This contrasts with the more confrontational tactics of some clinicians in France. As early as 1969, ANEA, composed mainly of GPs, presented a series of legislative proposals on abortion. They proposed abortion on specific grounds. The MLF rejected this text, arguing that therapeutic abortion would force women to give birth against their will '(e)nfanter reste donc un devoir, et forcer les femmes à enfanter contre leur gré reste la règle de l'avortement thérapeutique'.[31] In 1973, ANEA imitated the actions of the MLAC and MFPF and carried out abortions publicly, demanding that abortion be provided on more liberal grounds.

Another medical ally was GIS, essentially a reformist medical group with mainly male members 'who wanted to change the nature of medical practice (and) saw the issue of abortion in terms of what was wrong with medicine rather than in terms of women'.[32] In February 1973 (following the publication of the 'Manifeste des 343') GIS, consisting of 331 GPs (730 by April) admitted to having practised free abortions (for which they too were not prosecuted) and signed a manifesto asking for the legalisation of abortion up to the eighth week of pregnancy and stating that women alone had the right to control their own body and life. They accused some doctors, who refused to help, of medical negligence 'non-assistance à personne en danger', and others of profiting from secret criminal abortion.

In both the UK and France, then, abortionists gained support from many groups, usually from the left wing, including from lawyers, physicians, religious and political groups. Some of these were useful policy community members with concomitant resources. They were not necessarily 'feminist', agreeing mainly with the social aims of liberal feminist campaigners for abortion to be safer and more accessible, rather than including more radical claims for women to be able to control their own bodies away from any medical interference. In the UK more women's groups came out in support, though again for social, not feminist reasons as they were not feminist organisations. In France, political parties showed more solidarity with the abortionists perhaps due to their position in opposition and the more desperate need for a law at that late stage.

Opposition to abortion campaigns

Opposition strength is an important aspect of interest group debate, determining the strength of campaigners. In both countries, the main opposition to abortion reform came from within the medical professions and the Roman Catholic Church. By the 1960s in the UK, only the Roman Catholics could really have been said to have been a group which lobbied to prevent liberalisation in any shape or form in opposition to ALRA, and their opposition was weak and only mobilised after the 1967 Act to any large extent. In France those groups who were against abortion liberalisation reacted late in the day to the campaign that had built up around the MLF. It was not really until mid-1973 that they did and some might say this was too late to stop the momentum in favour of liberalisation. During the 1970s, right-wing Catholics in the French Parliament lost much of their stranglehold on policy networks, to be replaced by the centre; and from 1981 by the left when the Socialist and Communist coalition government came to power. However, pronatalists, Roman Catholics, conservative lawyers and clinicians were very much heeded by the drafters of the eventual law and played a central role as members of the policy network – their influence is apparent in the final legislation.

In France there was also an important pronatalist element within the opposition, in contrast to the UK, for whom abortion was even more important than contraception. This pronatalist argument was shared by the right wing, a group called 'Laissez-les-vivre' and the Communist Party (PCF). Following the pro-abortion Peyret Bill of June 1970, 'Laissez-les-vivre', was set up by Foyer, the Minister of Health belonging to the traditional wing of the centre-right party, the Union des Démocrates pour la République (UDR), which battled against the liberalisation of abortion.[33] The PCF equated contraception with sexual liberation, which it saw as 'bourgeois' and a ruse to weaken the numbers of the working class. It therefore opposed the legislative proposals for contraception of 1966 to 1967. It used its local 'policy community' power to prevent clinics being set up in the red belt Communist-run sectors of Paris. The PCF did not yield its firm stance against abortion liberalisation until 1973 when it accepted abortion only on serious socio-medical grounds, in the wake of the growth of socialist feminism within its ranks.

The Roman Catholic Church

In the UK the Roman Catholic Church in the post-war period was mostly concerned with the growing use of birth control and the increasing support this practice gained from established groups. Commentators such as Francome and Lovenduski have argued that the Church had a negligible influence on abortion in the UK until after 1967, but it did make its presence felt before this time, especially in the Labour party. 'The Roman Catholic Church watched birth control become publicly acceptable with growing alarm, and in conse-quence, hardly had time to notice the growth of the abortion law reform movement, which seemed as yet too insignificant to merit more than routine denunciation.'[34] However, despite being small in numbers, the Roman Catholic Church still 'constituted the major opposition and provided a basis from which opponents of change could work': mainly Roman Catholic organisations campaigned against birth control, such as Dr Halliday Sutherland's League of National Life 'the forerunner of modern anti-abortion movements'.[35]

Before 1967, the Roman Catholic lobby was badly organised while ALRA was strengthening its campaign with the public and with MPs. The former had the problem that their support of the law as it stood diminished any fervour they may have had in campaigns. Moreover, the Roman Catholic clergy, already discredited, made badly received, clumsy efforts to put their case.

When the Society for the Protection of Unborn Children (SPUC) was set up in January 1967 in response to the Second Reading of Steel's Bill of July 1966, Roman Catholics were therefore excluded from its Council. However, SPUC was accompanied by a new grass-roots Roman Catholic anti-abortion movement in 1967 that was always mentioned in the same breath which, despite SPUC's efforts 'made it much more easy to discount them'.[36] This was particularly easy in Britain where public criticism of Catholicism and the 'Irish problem' has been widespread.[37] Nevertheless, the organisation contained important and prestigious figures such as Anglican clergy and gynaecologists, including Aleck Bourne, who supported keeping the legal status quo. SPUC aimed to prevent abortion being given on social grounds and for foetal abnormality, but many of their tactics were incoherent, if dramatic. More conservative tactics included organised petitions, letter-writing and a Gallup Poll, which showed public support for a Royal Commission (which, if used, could have delayed the reform indefinitely).

In France, the moral discourse of the right and the Roman Catholic Church also played an important part in debates. As in other Roman Catholic countries, opposition to abortion and contraception in France was very much the domain of the Church in conjunction with the political right. The Roman Catholic Church remained very important in national life and national politics. General de Gaulle, his wife, and many of his ministers were devout Roman Catholics. In fact, traditional Roman Catholics, active on the political right, wanted existing laws to be more strictly enforced rather than reformed. 'This religious ethical discourse held morality as universal and as being religious, a morality that respects the right to life and considers the embryo to be a living being.'[38]

The 1967 Neuwirth law, along with increasing sexual liberation worldwide, had led to the *Encyclique Humanae Vitae* being published by the Church in 1968 denouncing contraception. This caused a massive reduction in the numbers of practising Roman Catholic women using contraceptives.[39] Similarly on abortion the Church felt that life was so precious that no parent had the right to decide on the life or death of a 'child' even where having another child might lead to severe social constraints on the rest of the family. The most serious inconveniences did not justify endangering life '(l)a vie est un bien trop fondamental pour qu'on le mette ainsi en balance avec des inconvénients même très graves'.[40] The widening of the debate by abortion rights campaigners contributed to the Roman Catholic hierarchy changing their objections to birth control from those based on the inadmissibility of separating sex from procreation through contraception, to those based on the question of when life began and the value of the embryo. Contraception became a much less potent issue to the Church when all its strength was needed to combat abortion.[41]

Medical opinion

Medicalisation, in theory and in practice, took a hold in the UK during the nineteenth century and the medical organisations were presumed to have a vested interest in all policies related to health. Eckstein has demonstrated how, with the institutionalisation of the British NHS in 1946, the role of the medical profession in the health policy network was permanently enshrined.[42] From the nineteenth century, the medical profession controlled the development of lawful therapeutic abortion and were left to do so by the State in accordance with medical self-regulation and management of the relationship the profession enjoyed with the government.[43] Medicalisation was more likely of abortion than contraception as abortion entailed a surgical operation. It was for this reason that doctors were even more important to feminists as allies on this issue.

In response to favourable judicial statements on abortion and state concern with maternal mortality, in 1932 the BMA set up a special committee to look at the law especially where it adversely affected poor mothers of ill health and who already had several children. In 1936 the Committee reported that they had estimated that between 16 and 20 per cent of pregnancies ended in abortion, either spontaneous or induced, and that most of these were induced.[44] In addition, they believed that the law was in need of clarification. They concluded that therapeutic abortion would be available in cases of rape under the age of consent; foetal abnormality; and perhaps, subject to public opinion, social and economic necessity.[45] Aleck Bourne was a member of the Committee. These views were somewhat radical for doctors at the time, as even by the 1960s they were still clinging to the legal status quo of case law – despite complaining about its lack of clarity – in preference to liberalisation and statute, as doctors preferred decisions on abortion to be left to clinical discretion.

The importance of medical expertise was becoming increasingly important to the public, and, in turn, the State, by the 1960s. Religion was on the decline and technology was gaining in favour.[46] Despite having a two-way relationship with the State, the health professionals in the UK enjoyed autonomy and self-regulation to a greater degree than in France. Within the policy community, then, different organisations such as the BMA and the Royal College of Obstetricians and Gynaecologists (RCOG) fought to ensure their own status against their rivals in order to be the most important member of the network on any given issue.

Though their membership ensured their consultation, their internal divisions weakened their influence in the face of the reforming zeal of the left and ALRA.[47] In April 1966, for example, the RCOG opted unanimously to retain the legal status quo as it felt such a dangerous operation should be left in the hands of a doctor, namely a consultant gynaecologist. If it became lawful, then it should only be available where there was 'substantial risk that the child if born would suffer from such physical or mental abnormalities as to deprive it of any prospect of reasonable enjoyment of life'.[48] They disagreed with ALRA's proposal of abortion being available for minors under 16 as this might lead, they argued, to demands being made on doctors, and promiscuity. They were more in favour of sterilisation as a form of preventive medicine being urgently legislated on than a new abortion law.[49] The BMA issued a similar report in July 1966 though without the demand that abortions should be carried out only by a gynaecologist, thus acting in their own interests in a similar fashion to the RCOG.[50]

French medical journals in the 1930s contained accounts of abortions carried out for serious medical reasons. In 1947 the Conseil de l'Ordre opposed expanding an amnesty for criminals to those who had been convicted for abortion.[51] In the face of the criminality of abortion and the strong opposition of the Roman Catholic Church, government and religious groups, in the early and mid-1960s, it ruled that contraceptive advice, the carrying out of abortions and changes in the 1920 and 1923 laws were not a doctor's province. Eventually, the right wing of the Conseil de l'Ordre obtained that sexual matters be dealt exclusively within the terms of their (medical) competence. In a communiqué on 23 October 1970, the Conseil stated in response to the first backbencher-sponsored bill on therapeutic abortion that respect for human life was a fundamental tenet of medicine, which included embryonic and foetal life.[52]

Despite the apparent increase in medicalisation in France at this time, the categorisation by senior members of the medical profession of abortion as a moral, not a medical act, prevented its absorption into the health service and delayed progress on liberalisation. It also forced radical doctors into needing to organise themselves separately from other camps, in contrast to the UK.[53] Opinion within the medical profession was, moreover, shaped by the fact that the French state did not provide any training for the medical profession in methods of birth control or sexual education, as they were not considered to be proper medical subjects. Thus doctors held opinions that were based on medical or social concerns, rather than religious or moral ones. This ignorance led them to see birth control as the work of 'quacks'. As we have already seen, they let their religious beliefs determine their attitude to the issue and to women coming to them for advice, whom they saw as degrading themselves.[54] In 1973, 10,000 GPs signed a manifesto asserting that abortion could not be morally considered a medical act.

When comparing the UK and France, it is clear that, in both countries, the opposition of the medical profession and the Roman Catholic Church was important. Both were in disagreement with the aims of the campaigners.

The Roman Catholic Churches in both countries were against abortion and promoted the idea of the right to life of the embryo. They did not want to see liberalisation, but more strict enforcement. In the UK, however, Roman Catholics had less influence on the central policy network: their influence was mainly in the local policy community in the Labour party, and they were preoccupied with birth control until the founding of an established opposition SPUC in 1967. In turn, the leadership of SPUC was concentrated in the hands of Anglicans and gynaecologists rather than Roman Catholics, but depended on the help of the Roman Catholic Church and agreed with many of their aims such as objections to abortion on social or eugenic grounds. The League of National Life was rather ineffectual and concentrated on gathering support through petitions and polls. Francome concludes that it was 'overall social conditions', such as the widespread resort to backstreet abortions among the lower classes, that acted against SPUC and in favour of ALRA.[55] By contrast, Roman Catholics in France were influential members of the policy community.

The medical professions in France appear to have been influenced by Roman Catholic moral doctrine on the life of the embryo, whereas their counterparts in the UK were more inclined to see abortion as 'immoral'. Both also saw abortion as non-medical and defended the legal status quo. The legal 'status quo' was, however, somewhat more liberal in the UK, where lawful therapeutic abortion was accepted as part of medical practice and included grounds of mental and physical health. Thus the British medical view was more liberal than that held in France. The conservatism of the law and its defenders in France created different incentives and structures for opposers and led to more radical groups being set up to challenge the authority of the Conseil de l'Ordre. The fact that the law ultimately was more radical in France, despite such strong opposition, is testament to the effectiveness of the illustration by radical feminists of the relative safety of the Karman method. The British campaigners could not benefit from this resource in the mid-1960s. This contributed in part to the more conservative law that was passed in the UK.

The medical professions had representation in the policy networks in both countries. Fellow members in France were the Roman Catholic Church and pronatalists. Though the government sanctioned the liberalisation of the French abortion laws against the wishes of the pronatalists and religious groups, the views of these groups were still largely heeded. Indeed, the lack of dispute following the law is evidence of their appeasement. They all benefited from the attributes necessary for such membership in terms of beliefs, structure, size, membership, expertise, and so on.

In France, the needs of the members of the policy network and thus the management of the relationship they enjoyed with the government ensured their influence on the law, even after the coming to power of the Socialists in 1981. Even then, though, as abortion was a conscience issue, much debate took place in Parliament, network members still managed to exert more influence than other groups represented there. This could well be due to the strength of the civil service in France, which drafted the legislation and advised ministers.

Parliamentary debate and the response of the government

Much of the parliamentary activity seen on both sides of the Channel on the abortion issue has been as a result of the initiative of individuals rather than of political parties. This is particularly true of the UK. This is partly due to the fact that abortion is a 'conscience issue', which crosses party boundaries and is difficult for governments to allot to a particular policy sector.

In 1937, the British government responded to pressure from women's organisations, maternal mortality campaigners and some physicians with the setting up of the Birkett Committee. The Committee reported in 1939. Its task had been 'to enquire into the prevalence of abortion, and the law thereto, and to consider what steps can be taken to secure the reduction of maternal mortality.'[56] It interviewed several women's organisations both for and against liberalisation. The Mothers' Union and the Union of Catholic Mothers wanted a more effective enforcement of existing laws as abortion constituted 'the wilful destruction of human life'. The National Council of Women, the Women's Cooperative Guild and the East Midlands Working Women's Association, among others wanted the legal grounds for therapeutic abortion to be extended to include socio-medical considerations.[57] The Committee accepted the views of the *Bourne* judgment and recommended that these should be written into statute, as it estimated that 40 per cent of abortions were illegal, more than the figure of 20 per cent estimated by the BMA. The Committee did not go as far as ALRA's suggestions, and rejected any idea of general legalisation as it believed this would encourage promiscuity.[58] The media in the 1930s very rarely mentioned abortion, as it was not a subject considered suitable for public debate. The government had no real desire to legislate, as is often the case when setting up a commission to investigate an issue. Fortunately for them, the Second World War intervened and no debate in the Houses of Parliament ensued.

From the 1950s in the UK, Private Members' Bills were presented in order to bring uniformity to the law, clarify it for doctors and reduce backstreet abortions. After the Thalidomide disaster in 1961 foetal abnormality came to the fore as an issue.[59]

In May 1966, David Steel, a Liberal MP, agreed to sponsor an ALRA bill, the Medical Termination of Pregnancy Bill having drawn third place in the Private Member's ballot, which proposed abortion for rape and on social grounds.

ALRA had been campaigning up until now, but their initial success ensured that other groups began their own manoeuvres. In November 1966, the RCOG and BMA issued a joint statement for the first time, which focused on Steel's Bill. Here, they argued that there should be at least two doctors involved in the decision-making around abortion, and that one of these should be a consultant or MOH-approved doctor. The RCOG argued that this consultant be a gynaecologist. (This was also advocated by the Church of England.) But, most importantly, as far as ALRA were concerned, the statement rejected the social ground of the mother's environment, as they felt these would lead to an unacceptably high demand, although it did recommend that a subclause should be added to allow a doctor to take into account a patient's 'total environment'.[60]

Throughout 1967, both sides campaigned and lobbied ferociously. ALRA concentrated on publicity by directing their efforts at doctors, MPs and the public. The medical bodies pressurised Steel personally to amend the social and consultant clauses. Steel responded by accepting their new sub-clause on 'total environment' and amended his bill accordingly.[61] But against the wishes of the BMA and RCOG, the idea of the 'future well-being' of the patient, her child and existing children was added to physical and mental health, as factors to be taken into account and a clause 1(1) (a) (ii) was added which stated that the doctor should take into account the patient's 'total environment actual or reasonably foreseeable'. In an accompanying statement, Steel referred to the influence of the BMA, RCOG and Church of England. He also appears to have been influenced by the Church of Scotland. He felt that the new extended clauses would allow for clinical judgement and could be interpreted widely or narrowly.[62]

Reformers were expected to compromise for the sake of reform. ALRA's position as a pressure group sponsoring the Bill had always been difficult. It was their task to brief him and to whip up support from parliamentarians to ensure safe passage of the Bill. But Steel saw the issue from an MP's point of view and wanted to gain support from the centre and not be seen as the mouthpiece of the group. Members of ALRA felt betrayed at the time, but later argued that this was a most astute decision 'In view of the tremendous effort which was later needed to get even the amended and watered-down version through Parliament'.[63] Both actions were in order to please the medical professions. It was individual doctors, including Dugald Baird rather than the BMA or RCOG, who directly influenced Steel. Baird, like the BMA, suggested combining medical and social grounds.[64] Between the RCOG and BMA the latter had most influence as Steel was persuaded that GPs would be more responsible for implementing the legislation than consultants.

In January it went to Select Committee. Here, to slow progress, the opposition tabled numerous amendments, made lengthy speeches and introduced many points of order. But only one amendment was finally introduced, that is, that nurses and doctors could refuse to operate on grounds of conscience.[65] The Bill was passed, supported by Labour members, by 163 votes to 83. As the Bill then proceeded back through Parliament, the votes against it increased.[66] Thus the opposition (SPUC and the medical professions) did have some success in creating fears that the Bill was too liberal.[67]

Despite opposition from Roman Catholics the Bill passed through the HL by 127 votes to 21 and an important amendment was introduced. Lord Chief Justice Parker pointed out that all the suggestions such as 'grave risk' or 'serious risk' would cause problems of definition in the courts. He proposed instead that the criterion should be where risk to life or injury to health was greater by continuing the pregnancy than by terminating it, often referred to later as the 'statistical argument'. In practice this would permit a quite liberal interpretation as pregnancy was always more dangerous than abortion. Opponents were caught out by this amendment, as part of their discourse had been that abortion was more dangerous than childbirth so they could not now argue that this was a 'liberal' amendment.[68] The liberalisation of this amendment was not intentional. It only became apparent with hindsight. The Bill received the Royal Assent on 27 October 1967 (though did not come into operation until 27 April 1968).

In France, the influence of the contraception debate and new radical political groups, such as feminists, began to effect even the right wing and override the wishes of the policy network from 1970. In July 1970, the Gaullist backbencher, Claude Peyret (who was instrumental in drafting the eventual abortion law) proposed a similar bill to that of the medical group ANEA, which became known as the 'Peyret text'. This text, however, omitted the social grounds found in the ANEA proposition. In December 1972, Peyret also presented a report to the Commission of Cultural Affairs, which they adopted. After the first actions of the abortion campaigners, the government itself was forced to take a stance on the issue and in 1972 the Health Minister, Boulin, prepared a draft bill modifying the abortion legislation, but ultimately decided against putting it before Parliament.

The 1973 legislative elections saw the parties forced into taking positions. In January 1973 President Pompidou agreed at a press conference that the law was out of date and would be revised after the legislative elections. Following the elections, on 16 May 1973 the Socialist party put forward an opposition bill. On 6 June, the Justice Minister, Jean Taittinger and the Health and Social Security Minister, Michel Poniatowski presented the government's own bill ('projet de loi no. 455 relatif à l'IVG'), which took up much of the Peyret text. It was the product of months of debate, consultation and commissions. It was essentially an extension of therapeutic abortion to include medical grounds.

Taittinger even went so far as to criticise the old legislation for being out of date and anti-women. He called it 'archaïque, inadaptée, inefficace, inhumaine, injuste enfin ... Qui fait la loi? Des hommes essentiellement. Qui la subit? Des femmes essentiellement'.[69] He believed abortion was a matter of individual conscience. He also pointed out at one point that if half of the Deputies had been women he would have been paid more attention. Poniatowski argued that the old laws were being openly flouted and were now untenable. These strong statements show the enormous swing in opinion in favour of liberalisation of a government minister – someone at the pinnacle of the policy community – that had taken place following the actions of interest groups in favour of liberalisation. The Bill was rejected by the National Assembly, however, some thinking it went too far, some not far enough.

The notice of the Assembly was drawn to a declaration on 4 June by 10,031 'pro-life' doctors in the Association des Médecins pour le respect de la vie in the press opposing abortion. This maintained that the life of the child was separate from the mother, to be protected by the doctor throughout its existence. The Deputies felt that the support of the medical profession was an absolute necessity.[70] Thus, as with many laws that pose problems for the authorities, the law was moved sidewards to be debated by the Commission des Affaires Sociales. Under its president, Dr Henry Berger, it was entrusted with the task of taking into account all the main social, moral, medical and legal arguments through consultation. From July to November 1973, it interviewed 148 people, most of them doctors, pronatalists and religious groups, though feminist organisations such as Choisir were also consulted.

'Pro-life' groups reiterated arguments in favour of not liberalising the law and for having a conscience clause or special 'abortion doctors' if it were liberalised.[71] The arguments of abortion campaigners were social and feminist (MFPF, MLAC, Choisir). They advocated abortion before twelve weeks on demand and after that in cases of foetal abnormality or mother's health; with a social adviser (ANEA); and for minors too (MFPF). They also pressed for more sex education and contraceptive provision.[72] Within the medical profession, differences emerged between the statutory professional body, the Conseil de l'Ordre, which oversees the application of the medical ethics in the Code de Déontologie, and the union representatives of French doctors. The Conseil referred to the basic medical ethic of preserving life, though this principle might be challenged if the foetus threatened the long-term health of the mother or was malformed. Doctors could only advise, while special abortion doctors should perform the terminations and other doctors should be allowed to refuse to perform the operation, if it were not an emergency. The medical unions condemned the Conseil as being unrepresentative and unrealistic. To them a new law should be for five years provisionally; a matter for the doctor's individual conscience but only performed by a doctor; was safe and simple before between ten and twelve weeks; should be on specific social and eugenic grounds; anonymous; and reimbursed.[73]

The Commission's report was published as the Berger Report ('Rapport no. 930') in January 1974. Debate was scheduled for spring 1974, but had to be postponed following the death of President Pompidou, which necessitated an election. Meanwhile in spring 1974 other bills put forward the idea of abortion on demand up to the tenth week.[74] During the campaign of May 1974, the candidates took positions on the issue. The difference between the left and right was the feminist issue of abortion being a woman's choice. The ultra-left fully supported all aspects of reproductive choice with abortion on demand at any time. Mitterrand (United Left), proposed the PS–Choisir bill with abortion on demand up to the tenth week. The extreme-right candidates opposed abortion.

During the presidential elections, the eventual winner, the right-wing Giscard d'Estaing of the Union pour la Démocratie Française (UDF), proposed four main principles on abortion as part of a whole package of policies designed to capture the female Liberal electorate. These were reformist rather than radical, but spoke of: respect for life; safe abortion; facilitation of motherhood; and a conscience clause for medical practitioners.[75] Electoral support increased for the Socialist candidate, Mitterrand, however. The resulting pressure forced Giscard d'Estaing to radicalise his campaign in women's favour. Subsequently, a female magistrate, Simone Veil, was appointed Health Minister by the victorious Giscard d'Estaing and assigned the task of writing a completely new government bill, which would allow the decision be that of the woman's alone, but which would rule out reimbursement. By choosing Veil, an outsider, Giscard d'Estaing weakened policy network members, such as the medical professions, but simplified the politically difficult task before him. At a press conference, Giscard d'Estaing also pressed the Assembly to vote for a liberal, not a repressive law, promising a moratorium on abortion prosecution until the new law was passed. What Giscard d'Estaing had also created was the world's first Minister for Women, Françoise Giroud, at the Secrétaire aux droits des femmes. Women's laws now constituted a new policy sector and women's rights groups now had somewhere to direct their lobbying. This was in addition to having a woman at the head of the policy sector on health, Simone Veil.

The law was only passed for a 'trial' period of five years, and only thanks to the Socialists and Communist Deputies by 284 votes to 189.[76] Four basic principles formed the foundations of the eventual law: abortion was to be a medical act to be practised in hospitals only; it was the responsibility only of the woman concerned (thus allowing women control only under medical supervision); it was a problem of conscience for the GP; and was an extreme solution that was no substitute for birth control.

The law 'relative à l'interruption volontaire de la grossesse', 'loi Veil', was promulgated on 17 January 1975. What appears to have been uppermost in the mind of Simone Veil was to learn from the mistakes of the last government bill, thus taking a liberal line between the two opposing camps and making use of the reported consultations in the Commission des Affaires Sociales during the reassessment of the Messmer–Poniatowski Bill. She proposed to allow abortion on social grounds in an attempt to control a social prob-lem[77] and to medicalise abortion by forcing the operation to be performed in a public or private hospital by a doctor, to prevent the damage to health of backstreet abortions, which put a financial strain on state resources. However, a conscience clause was inserted to allay the fears of the medical professions that they would become technicians, and abortion was initially without reimbursement so as to differentiate abortion from other medical acts. The fact that a woman could decide whether she was in a situation of distress avoided having to find specific grounds that the different factions heard by the Berger Commission could agree on and allowed a political consensus to be reached '(s)'appuyant sur les résultats des auditions (le gouvernement) recherche avant tout le consensus social qui devrait permettre son adoption'.[78]

Campaigns around implementation and post-statutory amendment

Since the passing of the statutes of 1967 and 1975, campaigns around abortion have continued, ostensibly around ensuring its implementation, and in relation to amendment campaigns. Analysis of these reveals the continuing influence of religious groups as well as clinicians.

In response to some expressed dissatisfaction over implementation,[79] and at the instigation particularly of 250 MPs concerned at abuse of the Act, the British government set up an investigative committee under Mrs Justice Lane in 1971 to inquire into its working. In April 1974, the Lane Committee unanimously approved of the Act and its provisions. They concluded that abortion should remain a normal medical act, but that NHS provision should be expanded. However, as a medical act, abortion provision should remain at clinical discretion.

With the passing of the 1967 Act in the UK, ALRA felt it had achieved its declared aim, and with the law on their side became complacent. Many members and donators thus abandoned the organisation between 1967 and 1972. The Lane Report met with the approval of ALRA.[80] The anti-abortion lobby benefited from this complacency, and between 1970 and 1980 there were no less than nine attempts at pro-life amendment in Parliament.[81]

In contrast to ALRA, the National Abortion Campaign (NAC) was the embodiment of feminist ideals of non-hierarchical, democratic organisation. Its members were radical and socialist and this often led to disagreement about alliances. As with the French campaigns in the early 1970s, this disunity weakened them to an extent in terms of their influence on legislation and their alliance-building capacity.

NAC adopted the policy and slogan 'Free abortion on demand – a woman's right to choose', translating feminist thinking on women's rights to control their own bodies and health without medical interference. Their long-term aims (as feminists) were to liberalise the Abortion Act to allow abortion up to term, and on demand to prevent it being used as a form of sexual control over women. With the existing law under attack, they had to contend in the short-term with defending the Act.[82] Alongside ALRA, the NAC (particularly its socialist rather than radical members) became an accepted part of the health policy community, even attending meetings at the Labour government's DHSS.[83] In 1977 the TUC and Labour party adopted defence of the 1967 Act as official policy and the parliamentary Labour party reminded MPs of this fact as amendments went through the House. On 28 October 1979, the TUC also organised the massive national demonstration against the Corrie Bill. During the 1970s, the lobbyists, for example from 1976 the Coordinating Committee in Defence of the 1967 Abortion Act (Co-ord), gained in experience and learned to use parliamentary procedure to their advantage with the help of Labour MPs as allies who 'whipped' their colleagues, by for example tabling numerous amendments at the Report Stage of the Corrie Bill to take up debating time.[84] The lobbyists also reported back all developments to NAC and other groups so that everyone was consulted. This ensured their success at defeating anti-abortion bills.

In addition, the main medical bodies now came out in support of the 1967 Act and against amendment. This support from members of the policy network was instrumental to NAC's success in resisting amendment at this time. The BMA openly criticised all clauses of the anti-abortion Corrie Bill in 1979. The RCOG defended the 1967 Act from 1974 on and opposed Corrie's major clauses except the reduction of the upper time limit from twenty-eight to twenty-four weeks. Marsh and Chambers related this change of opinion after the passing of the Act to the fact that clinicians were relieved at the disappearance of distressing backstreet and self-induced abortion with which they had had to be involved. Their initial fears that the Act might be abused had also been dispelled.[85] The Royal College of Nursing (RCN), initially in favour of amendment, changed its mind after 1977 and came out against restriction of the grounds for abortion proposed in the Corrie Bill. The Royal College of Midwives came out against amendment in 1977.

The more radical members of SPUC broke away in 1970 to form LIFE. This group campaigned against abortion in any circumstance, even to save the mother's life.[86] Independent from, but associated with LIFE and SPUC, 'The Association of Lawyers for the Defence of the Unborn' was formed in 1978. It aimed to inform and influence the legal profession and to provide legal advice for reformers. All these opposition groups were well organised to the extent that the National Pro-Life Committee was formed in 1974 to coordinate them. As will be seen, this degree of organisation contrasts with pro-life groups in France.

Despite the existence of these groups, and the extent of their organisation, Marsh and Chambers do not ascribe much influence to the Roman Catholic Church on MPs voting as references to their views were rarely made during amendment debates – the views of the BMA and RCOG counted for much more.[87] The pro-life lobby did not enjoy support for their radical aims from the medical professions either, thus MPs were reluctant to support them.[88] However, after initial failure the pro-life lobby learned from its mistakes and increased MP opposition to abortion during the 1980s by continuing to lobby on the issue in a more coordinated national fashion and on a step-by-step basis while their adversaries became complacent. There were also backbench attempts at amendment, for example the Alton Bill of 1986. They were eventually successful in 1990.

It was lobbying by pro-life MPs where they criticised parliamentary procedure for being unjust that persuaded Prime Minister Margaret Thatcher to allow for time to be set aside by the government for abortion amendment. This led to the Human Fertilisation and Embryology Bill having a title that appeared to envisage this: 'and the subsequent development of the embryo'. Roy Cunningham, a civil servant involved in the development of the debates on the Embryology Bill and abortion amendments, argued that the government in the late 1980s was not expecting to include abortion in the remit of the bill as they regarded it as a backbench issue and it had also been excluded by Warnock. In the HL a pro-Choice Labour peer, Lord Houghton, introduced a pre-emptive Private Member's bill (that gave effect to the suggestions of a Lords Select Committee Report of 1987). It attempted to detach the Abortion Act from the Infant Life (Preservation) 1929 for clarification and to introduce a time limit of twenty-four weeks after lobbying from the medical professions. This would also keep abortion separate from the embryo research issue. It passed all its stages in the HL.

The British government itself hoped to curb the pro-life lobby's attempts at amendment, but feared that abortion debate might swamp the Embryology Bill and thus set aside separate time for abortion to be debated by a system of pendulum voting on time limits between the extremes of eighteen and twenty-eight weeks. Indeed, the Leader of the House of Commons, Sir Geoffrey Howe, introduced a core clause in the Embryology Bill which closely resembled the Houghton Bill. Thus, the government was not necessarily in support of pro-life aims.[89] Morgan and Lee have argued that MPs' support for abortion was heavily influenced by their voting on research the day before, and that a time limit of twenty-four weeks was supported by the main medical bodies. They were swayed by arguments for genetic handicap, rather than women's right to choose, heard in the research debate.[90] Most of the MPs who did vote for abortion (and research) were from the Labour party. Fortunately this debate led ostensibly to a liberalisation of the law with the removal of the time limit for abortion in three cases. Pro-life resources were stretched between embryo research and abortion, which weakened their lobbying campaigns.[91] Since 1990 in the UK, attempts at amendment have not met with success. The threat to abortion rights is, however, ongoing. Moreover, lobbying at a local level has taken place by pro-life groups such as the group Precious Life picketing abortion clinics.[92]

On 13 March 2000, the RCOG also published national evidence-based guidelines on the care of women requesting induced abortion. Yvette Cooper MP, the Secretary of State for Health, told the House of Commons that these were to be used to 'promote the development of high quality services and take account of local needs and service provision'.[93] This would point to support being given to pro-choice campaign in the near future, at least while the Labour party still hold power in the UK.

In France the campaign for abortion liberalisation continued even after the 1975 law due to problems of implementation and because the 1975 law contained a clause that the law must be reconsidered after an interval of five years.

Feminist and allied groups campaigned after 1975 on two particular issues. The MLAC and MFPF tried to get the ten-week limit on abortion (twelve weeks after conception) extended as they argued it was too short considering the fact a woman could receive numerous refusals before finding a doctor to perform the operation. But their main fight was now the reimbursement of the fee (set at 400 to 700 francs), because abortion would not be considered a normal medical operation until this was achieved. They also contested the fact that abortions carried out on minors should have parental consent; and that information or publicity on abortion could only come from medical personnel or in designated centres

By this time, all the organisations had accepted the need for reform, although the Roman Catholic Church remained critical of the nation's political leaders for having introduced the legislation. Even the Conseil de l'Ordre approved of the law as it had reduced the medical injury associated with clandestine abortion. It was renewed on 30 November 1979, initiated this time by the Minister for Women and passed, once again, with opposition support. Unfortunately, the demands of the MLF and pro-abortion groups were ignored, despite being put forward by the left wing during the debate. No therapeutic abortion grounds were increased; the rules on foreign women were not relaxed. This may have been due to the concurrent widespread press reports on the *Pergola* case in which doctors were accused of illegal abortions, but for which there proved to be insufficient evidence.

Subsequently, in 1981, the Socialist government increased the budget of the Women's Ministry (created by Giscard in 1974), giving it cabinet status with socialist–feminist Yvette Roudy, at its head. This improved the standing of women's issues *vis-à-vis* other ministers in the government when demanding finance, and also created a wider policy community for women's groups. In

1982, Roudy attempted to put into effect one of the final demands of campaigners on abortion and pass a decree granting a lump-sum reimbursement
by the Social Security of fees paid for an abortion. The fact that she was using
delegated legislation to put into effect a demand put forward by women's
rights groups shows the increasing importance of such groups in the policy
community. This resulted in uproar from the medical profession and religious
groups that such an action was a 'banalisation' of abortion, and the government responded by publishing a bill to be debated in Parliament, but only
after the approval of a national opinion poll. Roman Catholics also marched
in Paris in April 1982 and bishops lobbied the government. The Health Minister
then announced in August the delay of reimbursement. In response, feminists
lobbied the left wing and marched in Paris themselves. This arguably helped
to sway the minds of the French government and reimbursement became
official policy after 1982.

In July 1999, professor Israel Nisand produced a report on abortion in
France for the Ministries of Employment and Health.[94] This report was liberal
in remit: it set out to identify and diminish any difficulties faced by women
in relation to the provision of abortion services in France. The main problems
Nisand identified in the report were several: many health clinic directors were
using what should have been only their own personal conscientious objections
to prevent any of their staff performing abortions. This was in addition to
the lack of doctors willing to perform terminations (due to a lack of militancy
and a lack of status now attached to administering them). This was driving
women to use the private sector. In turn, the private sector was accused of
not respecting the law or women's rights through a lack of information and
a lack in choice of method.

Nisand thus recommended that quotas of abortions carried out in public
centres should be stopped; that women's choices on methods needed to be
respected, including on RU486; that abortion law should be moved from the
Criminal Code to the Public Health Code; and that more information should
be made available to women about abortion and emergency contraception.
These recommendations were similar to those made by the pro-Choice group
Association Nationale des Centres d'IVG (ANCIC) in 1992, which had been
commissioned by the Secretary of State for Women. The Nisand Report,
however, was commissioned by two large Ministries who are extremely
powerful in the health policy community. It is thus very much to pro-choice
campaigners' credit that the Report speaks of increasing women's access to
abortion services and enhancing their rights. The Nisand Report was also,
however, hostile to the lengthening of time for abortion on demand from ten
to twelve weeks of pregnancy.[95]

Amongst pro-choice campaigners, expectations that the Nisand Report would amend the law of 1975 were high. When parliamentary debate was not forthcoming, the Socialist government were accused of ignoring the needs of the 5,000 French women who were currently having to seek abortions abroad as they were more than ten weeks' pregnant. The accusations came from women's magazines, family planners, pro-choice groups, abortion and contra-ception clinic directors, Socialist MPs, and in particular, Socialist women MPs who were members of the government's Delegation on the Rights of Women. Their criticisms of the government increased when the Conseil d'Etat ruled that secondary legislation authorising the supply of emergency contraception to minors by school nurses was *ultra vires* and could not be authorised by the government. As part of the criticism, Socialist MPs published their own parliamentary bill on abortion and emergency contraception.

This forced the hand of the government to publish a bill on abortion and emergency contraception. This became the law of 4 July 2001 on abortion and contraception. The Act would extend abortion on demand from ten to twelve weeks of pregnancy; extend provision to minors by ending the need for parental authorisation; end the criminilisation of publicity on abortion; make emergency contraception available to minors in pharmacists; and make emergency contraception available on prescription and without parental auth-orisation from school nurses.

Opposition to abortion is still very much in evidence in France. In January 1995, 15,000 anti-abortionists marched in Paris and staged sit-ins at clinics.[96]

The 2001 Act may therefore be a very important factor in protecting women's rights to abortion during any future debates on the re-examination of the bioethics laws in France. With similar aims to the RCOG Report of 2000 of improving abortion services, it illustrates that both British and French governments are currently in favour of abortion rights.

Conclusions

To conclude, when attempting to gauge the influence of campaigners on abortion law several points emerge.[97]

The extent to which abortion was prohibited in each country had an effect on those groups who campaigned around the issue. This meant that, in contrast to the UK, in France before the early 1970s, there was no campaigning group on this issue. As abortion was illegal in France, it was difficult for groups to speak out, let alone to be a member of a policy community on the issue. French feminists had to be much more radical to get abortion onto the political agenda, and had to wait until the political climate was more responsive. Ultimately, the members of other health communities extended their own influence over abortion at the invitation of the French government, though campaigners still had an influence on their remit. The inadequate legislative response of the French government to the contraception campaign actually had a radicalising effect on the campaign on abortion as the government could be seen to be being unreasonable. For example, as late as 1973 only 7 per cent of French women used a modern contraceptive method, and those who did not were usually working-class women (who therefore had to resort to illegal abortions due to their hardship). This predisposed non-feminist groups to support feminists in their campaign.

It is clear that both countries gave much weight to the opinions of the medical professions and religious groups. In France, in addition, pronatalists and Roman Catholics had a strong influence. However, campaigners in both countries initiated debate by getting it onto the political agenda, which ultimately determined the final structure of the statutes passed.

The contemporaneous political and legal environments appear to have been more important in relation to the passing of abortion law than of contraception law, perhaps as abortion was seen to be a more serious issue politically.

In relation to the political environment in the UK, at the time of Steel's Bill a number of elements combined to ensure its success: the HL had already reformed such controversial issues as homosexuality and capital punishment and had accepted abortion reform; the composition of Parliament was younger and more radical than before; Kenneth Robinson was now Minister of Health; Roy Jenkins, a supporter, was Home Secretary; the government's position was one of 'benevolent neutrality';[98] public opinion showed support for reform; after the First Reading in July 1966 most non-Catholic churches came out in favour;[99] ALRA's chairman's husband was in the cabinet; due to the timing of the election, the bill coincided with a long parliamentary session;[100] and John Silkin, whose father had introduced abortion reform bills, was government chief whip.[101] Another important factor that led to this bill's success was that the Roman Catholic opposition was badly organised.

In France, elections in 1973 and 1974 played a particularly important part, politically, in the events leading up to the passing of the liberalising statute of 1975. Giscard d'Estaing had to legislate on abortion following the presidential elections as a fulfilment of his promises to women and voters. He also used abortion as a flagship for his general reformist 'décrispation' policies at the beginning of his term in office. This was also done at the beginning to make use of the parliamentary majority as is often the case in majoritarian systems, though he needed left-wing support to have the law passed eventually. Only during cohabitation in 1986, did the right-wing Prime Minister moot a challenge to reimbursement but backed down in the face of public and parliamentary opposition. This provides evidence of the support for abortion, which remains at a national level and the dwindling strength of the Roman

Catholic Church in the policy community. The political environment in France also enabled 81 Deputies to challenge government law leading to a conclusive ruling by the Constitutional Court that there were no constitutional rights to life for the unborn child. The French process was on the whole much more open to negotiation, with the process of debate in the form of a five year re-examination written into the law. Debate also took place in 1982, though this was on reimbursement, rather than the law itself.

Despite the fact that the UK is not a Roman Catholic country, Roman Catholics did play an important part in the abortion debate there. Their initial failure was arguably due to the fact that they did not begin lobbying in earnest until after the law had been passed. It was the conflict between women's reproductive rights and embryo rights that led to abortion amendment in 1990 with the passing of legislation on new reproductive technologies. However, the strength of Roman Catholic and other religious groups was highlighted when they successfully lobbied the government to allow debate on the 1967 Act in 1975 and 1990, making use of British parliamentary procedure to threaten abortion rights. Fortunately, in 1990 this backfired somewhat as it led inadvertently to liberalisation, due to the lobbying of women's rights campaigners and their medical and left-wing allies.

During debates on abortion the medical professions of both countries can be seen to have exerted pressure successfully. Such influence was also evident during the lobbying process on the liberalisation of contraception. During the passage of the Abortion Bill in the UK, Steel altered the social clauses of the bill in order to win the approval of the medical professions and garner the further support of those who would vote for a bill that had met with medical approval,[102] thus condoning the medicalisation of the abortion issue.

In France, too, the medical professions were influential, though it is more difficult to separate their aims from those of pronatalists or religious groups. Arguments advanced by the Conseil de l'Ordre and religious groups in the Berger Report re-emerged in the 1975 law. Such points included the idea that the fundamental respect owed to life should form the backbone of the law; that a woman seeking an abortion must take a week to think over the operation; and that doctors should be able to refuse to perform the operation. The arguments of pronatalists that were accepted by legislators were numerous. These included: that possibilities for adoption must be offered to women; risks of abortion must be 'explained'; figures on abortion should be monitored by central government; and that abortion must only constitute a quarter of all obstetric operations. Finally, it was doctors' unions who spoke to the Berger Commission of wanting to see a five-year trial period and abortion before ten to twelve weeks, and these points also re-emerged as part of the 1975 law on abortion.

Nevertheless, in both countries, the legislation on abortion has been an undeniable gain for women. Abortion is now legal, available to all women of whatever social class and completely free of charge.

Unfortunately for women and pro-choice campaigners, women in the UK do not have the right to choose an abortion, it is only *available* to them in theory, and they must rely on the opinions of the two doctors concerned. In addition, the NHS is not obliged to provide free abortions, which has led to an average of 50 per cent and in some areas 90 per cent of women having to pay for theirs. Lovenduski concluded that, as in France, the Abortion Act was merely 'posturing' on the part of the government,[103] and another example of the government rhetoric referred to in policy community theory.

Those groups who campaigned for the liberalisation of abortion included first-wave liberal feminists in the UK before 1968, and second-wave liberal, as well as radical, feminists in France where campaigns took place after 1968. In the UK, the campaign lasted ostensibly from the 1930s up to the Abortion Act of 1967 and after that time in relation to implementation and amendments, most notably in 1975 and in 1990. In France, the abortion campaign had a different timescale, lasting from the 1950s to 1975, then to 1979 when the original 1975 law came up for renewal and then in 2000.

The influence of radical feminism on the abortion debate is therefore only apparent during the amendment campaigns in the UK. This had an effect on the methods and resources used by pro-Choice group before 1967, their alliance-building capacity and their effectiveness. ALRA, for example, were hopeful that sympathetic doctors would take advantage of the vague wording of the Act and sanction abortion requests and to some extent these hopes were realised.[104] Nevertheless, those groups which were available to ALRA as allies were only slightly useful.

In France, by contrast, radical feminists played an agenda-setting role in that they radicalised the aims and methods of liberal feminist campaigners and their allies. Not only did the government therefore invite liberal feminists such as Choisir, and their allies, for consultation by the Commission of 1973, but their arguments also contributed to the text of the 1975 law more than other extreme viewpoints for or against. Thus the health of the woman seeking an abortion was safeguarded by the law; abortion was available *on demand* before twelve weeks' amenorrhoea, a social worker had to offer advice; and contraception was also offered (though minors needed parental consent and doctors supervised and limited the remit of the woman's demand for termination).[105]

The French government was forced into such legislation by the political uproar created by the MLF, the MLAC, GIS, Choisir and MFPF and ultra-left after 1970.[106] Abortion was on the agenda and public opinion was shifted from the right to the centre. On this, there is a consensus among commentators.[107] This underlines the importance of radical feminism, as predicted by the feminist literature, despite problems of disunity, and was especially remarkable given the legal advances that had to be brought about by abortion campaigners in France.

As with contraception, radical campaigns initiated a wider public debate on sexuality and motherhood. In France this was a particularly successful and important achievement for women as it forced these issues into the political arena, leading ultimately to such achievements as the Ministry for Women's Rights in 1981, whose descendants initiated liberalising amendments to the 1975 law in 2000. The abortion campaign can also be seen as an attempt to bring life to the radical ethos of the personal being political.[108] However, it was not the only important factor behind change. Commentators from the MFPF have themselves pointed out that '(g)iven the plurality of motivations ... the contemporary women's movement cannot be said to have dominated the universe of political discourse'.[109] Economic, political and ideological necessities also carried much weight: '(i)l répondait aussi à des nécessités économiques, politiques et idéologiques, qu'il faudrait analyser de près.'[110] Moreover, such changes in discourse are precarious: the State can revoke what is given; allies can move on, leaving a weakened interest group in their wake; and the old enemies remain ready to reassert themselves with their familiar homilies on women, patriotism and the family.[111] Political debate and conflict on abortion law continues in both countries to this day. They have not been abated by developments in embryology and infertility treatment. Such developments, with their consequences for reproductive rights and medicalisation, come under closer scrutiny in the following two Chapters.

6

Assisted conception and the law:[1] medical gatekeepers and embryo status

As we have seen throughout this book, governments have overseen the enactment of various statutes and the development of case law, both of which have attempted to deal with the various problematic social issues raised by reproduction. I have argued that this has invariably been at the behest of interest groups who have been involved in political campaigns around these issues. As a result of reproductive campaigns, contraception law offered to women an important measure of control over their reproduction that they had not previously had. With abortion law, rights pertaining to reproduction offered to the unborn child some protection and status, but it also established women's rights which could not be superseded by the child.

Assisted conception has offered new medical and technological possibilities. It has made it possible for a woman without ovaries to carry a child; for a woman without a womb to bear a genetically related child; for couples who suffer from a genetic disability to bear children that will not similarly suffer. Such possibilities, however, have thrown up social, ethical and legal problems surrounding the donation of human gametes and embryos, the resultant family relationships, patient treatment and embryo research. The law has attempted to offer some answers to these problems in the way of guidelines to medical practitioners, the protection of women patients and the enshrinement of embryo rights, yet problems and questions continue to surface.

In both countries, there were debates from the early 1980s about the requirement for the regulation of assisted conception by legislation. Doctors working in the field were themselves largely in favour of self-regulation. Conversely, others believed that legislation was necessary as they saw the technologies as, alternately, unnatural and immoral, dangerous and costly. Moreover, it was argued that the individual should have the right to decide, and that doctors should not be able to conceal from public view a wide range of matters which should be more democratically decided. Finding a legal solution that would satisfy all parties was not an easy task and approaches to legislation have differed in the two countries. In France, only piecemeal regulation existed before 1994, in contrast to the UK's Human Fertilisation and Embryology Act 1990. The original French approach was much more ambitious and all-encompassing, which may have been a factor in the relatively long delay before the passing of the 1994 bioethics laws. Particularly before the passing of statute there were several court cases on artificial insemination by husband or donor (AIH and DI, respectively) and on surrogacy. There has also been considerable legal debate in academic and parliamentary circles, much of it at the instigation of successive governments. Such debate continues apace.

In this Chapter it is my intention to outline briefly the regulatory framework of assisted-conception law in Britain and France. I then go on to examine in more detail each specific variation of law on assisted conception in the two countries, namely gamete donation, *in vitro* fertilisation (IVF), surrogacy and embryo research, with particular emphasis on differences between the legislation of the two jurisdictions, and the consequences that these particular issues have for women's reproductive rights.

Regulating assisted conception

The Human Fertilisation and Embryology Act 1990 provided statutory regulations governing donor insemination, embryo research, and IVF in the UK. It not only covered IVF, which, it could be argued, was an invasive and experimental treatment and thus in need of regulation, but also embraced all other gamete donation under one assisted-conception heading. This therefore brought donor insemination under tighter controls but also limited women's freedom of access.

The Act brought into being a new independent licensing authority, the Human Fertilisation and Embryology Authority (HFEA), whose structure was closely based on that of the Voluntary Licensing Authority (VLA). Its membership is chosen by the Secretary of State and is renewable every three years. It must be made up of men and women at least half of whom have not been registered medical practitioners, kept or used gametes outside the body, or funded such research. But there must be at least one person from each of these categories who altogether form at least one-third and not more than half the membership, but they cannot be appointed chair or deputy chair. MPs are not eligible for membership.

Under the Act, assisted conception is regulated much more thoroughly than previously. The HFEA can issue three types of licence, one of which covers IVF treatment (renewable after five years). The treatment licence will be

necessary for DI, donor gamete intra-fallopian transfer (GIFT) and egg donation, as well as IVF. Unfortunately, however, the Authority is itself funded by
the collection of licence money, thus, some have argued, encouraging it to
grant such licences. The HFEA controls treatment and research through powers
provided by the Act directly, by regulations given by the Secretary of State
and through its own directions and Code of Practice. Infringement of this
Code does not constitute an offence but may impinge on the granting or
renewal of the required licence. The Act provides powers in addition to that
of licensing whereby HFEA members may at any time visit and inspect premises
and may confiscate and take away anything they think relevant to their task
(s. 39). Centres are inspected before licences are granted.[2] Licensed activities
must take place in authorised premises with a named person responsible and
trained staff. There is a complaints procedure, with a senior member of staff
acting as complaints officer in each centre, whereby complaints must be
processed swiftly with written reasons for their action. Complaints can be taken
further than this, if necessary to judicial review. Doctors have a conscience
clause available to them (s. 38), as with abortion.

In the UK the 1990 Act now ensures that written and informed consent
from women patients is obtained before treatment, which is to their benefit.
It is mandatory (Code of Practice, Part 4) to give clear, relevant information
by a trained person before consent is given. This information should include:
the limitations, possible outcomes, and 'variations of effectiveness over time';
the possible side effects and risks to child or woman including those of multiple
pregnancy; the length of time and disruption to domestic life; the techniques
and pain and discomfort; the possible deleterious effect of storage on gametes
and embryos; the alternatives including non-licensed infertility treatments;
counselling; cost; the legal situation of parents; the ensuing child's right to
seek information; the extent to which information can be stored and used;
the liability of the centre to the child; the number of attempts that should be
made. Unfortunately for women, counselling (Code of Practice, part 6) is not
mandatory for patients, only available.

In France, two government decrees were issued in April 1988 (88–327 and
88–328). They established the Commission Nationale de Médecine et de
Biologie de la Reproduction (CNMBR), with power to license a limited number
of public and private clinics to undertake specific methods of assisted conception (subject to certain conditions concerning qualifications of personnel and
standards of equipment) and to check success rates and produce an annual
report on clinics. It thus equated roughly to the HFEA in the UK. This
institution became the Commission Nationale de Médecine et de Biologie de
la Reproduction et du Diagnostic Prénatal (CNMBRDP) from the time of the
Bianco Bill of 1992, from which time the issue of prenatal diagnosis was added

to its remit. The decrees were not implemented before a further much-contested decree of September 1990.[3] Their declared aim was to institute quantitative and qualitative controls. These were followed by a clause regulating sperm donation in a general social services law in 1991.Though this legislation may look extensive, in fact it only instigated licensing and did not put legal regulation or patient rights onto a statutory footing.

The methods of debate on assisted conception in France contrast with those in the UK, where debate and the formulation of legislation concentrated almost wholly on the Warnock Commission and were resolved by the 1990 Act. The French government instead dealt with assisted conception throughout the late 1980s in an ambitious and far-reaching way which involved lengthy and in-depth interest group consultation throughout the policy community and various committee reports (*see* Chapter 7).

The French finally passed three separate statutory laws on bioethics in July 1994.[4] The first to be passed related to the use of information held on computer about patients involved in assisted conception and research.[5] This was passed with little resistance and will not be looked at in detail here, besides my acknowledgement that medical and ethical issues involving confidentiality and computer data have played a part in debates on assisted conception. The second statute related to the respect to be accorded to the human body as regards donation, surrogacy, and genetic research and thus made additions to the Civil Code.[6] The third statute related to donation and use of the human body and its parts, regulated assisted conception and prenatal diagnosis, embryo research and gene therapy, and made additions to the Public Health Code.[7] Here, I refer to the 'Statute on respect of the human body' (94–653) and the 'Statute on donation and assisted conception' (94–654), respectively.

Gamete donation: parenthood, anonymity and consent

Legislators faced with the growing demand for medically assisted conception have attempted to formulate regulations for what is in essence a growing medical industry. But this particular industry has given rise to a series of thorny ethical issues. In the area of donation, the gamete used to create an embryo is invariably, by necessity, donated. The genetic parent of the resulting child will therefore be different to the eventual social parent who takes the child home. The practice of gamete donation thus raises many questions. If somebody's sperm or ovum can be given to another person in this way, what is the nature of humanity or humanness? What is a family? Who is the true parent of the child? Should children be told that their genetic parent is not their social parent? Do donors need to remain anonymous?

Gametes may well have a special status because they are of human origin.

They also contain genetic material. For some, they also hold special meaning because they are part of the procreation of a new life, and are helping another person to create this new life. For most of us, then, human gametes are distinct from other human body parts and from non-human gametes and merit the particularly restrictive provisions governing their use, the resulting offspring, and their 'parents'. It could be argued that the donation of gametes objectifies them and assimilates them to property. However, the stipulation in both countries for informed consent before donation, underlines that the law holds donors to be social persons and gametes to be more than a mere clump of cells. Legislators have to some extent assured their humanity in this way.

In the UK, debate centred on the formal regulation of DI. There were fewer legal cases on DI in the UK, in contrast to France. The earliest relevant case was *Maclennan* v. *Maclennan* (1958) from Scotland, which ruled that DI without a husband's consent did not constitute adultery as a ground for divorce. Indeed, before the 1990 Act there was a lack of specific management in the UK of DI in contrast to France.[8] The Warnock Committee was in favour of the use of donation to combat genetic disease, with sex selection to be kept under review by the licensing body. Frozen eggs were not to be used for therapeutic purposes due to the medical risks involved with this, which was also to be kept under review.

Section 13(6) of the 1990 Act in England therefore requires consent, after the opportunity for counselling has been given, from donors of sperm, eggs and embryos, before the latter can be used for treatment, donation, storage or research. To ensure their informed consent, donors of gametes (or embryos) must be told, *inter alia*, about the possible uses their gametes may be put to and their legal status as parents.[9] Under Section 12(e) donors are not to be paid and may only have their expenses reimbursed up to £15 or treatment in kind, though the HFEA is currently considering whether payment should be prohibited.

One of the major concerns of the HFEA has been to ensure the quality of gametes. Therefore donors are screened under the 1990 Act: they must undergo medical tests for heritable disorders, transmissible infection and fertility; be over 18 and under 35 for women, or under 55 for men (unless there are exceptional circumstances); be capable of giving a valid consent; provide a medical and family history; their GP must express his or her opinion; their family status and personal attitude toward donation must be taken into account. Much discretion on donation has been left up to the HFEA in the writing of the Code of Practice and beyond. The Authority has therefore a very powerful role in the regulation of donation.

The issue of whether a human could donate his or her own body part and could consent to that, has been much more of a philosophically problematical issue for French lawyers and ethicists. Important principles have existed in the Civil Code since the 1789 Revolution which impinge on donation: the freedom and privacy to do what one likes with one's own body ('liberté de disposer de soi'); the unavailability of the body ('indisponibilité du corps'), which replaced the superior status of the Church and the soul with that of man and his body. Having gained in importance and status, the body could not be commercialised, contracted, enslaved, separated or tampered with in classical civil law and private law – it was not a thing ('une chose') under Article 1128. Following codified law, therefore, any products of human origin could not be bought or sold, nor could the human donors or their inheritors profit from their production, although the donors could be informed of the intended use. The only exceptions to commercialisation of human products were if they were for therapeutic or diagnostic purposes (not cosmetic), or very small in size, such as genes produced by naturally sourced micro-organisms (which have been patentable in Europe since the 1960s).

In terms of the law on consent, a patient in France, or his or her guardian, must authorise treatment through the giving of their consent, written or otherwise, under the 'loi du 29 mai 1951'. Risks must also be explained to a patient.[10] The 'loi du 20 décembre 1988', 'loi relative à la protection des personnes qui se soumettent à un essai biomédical' ('loi Huriet'), specifically provided for free and informed consent before medical treatment. The 1994 laws themselves treat the issue of consent seriously, counselling less so, relative to the 1990 Act.

French law on donation has existed since the Barzach decrees of 8 April 1988.[11] These then became Article 13 of the law of 31 December 1991 (No. 91–1406), which dealt with the issue of donation as part of a law dealing generally with health matters. The law provided for the licensing of the recovery, treatment and storage of donated sperm by the Minister of Health, with detailed arrangements to be fixed by decree by the Conseil d'Etat. Licences were to be renewed every five years. Donation must be free and fresh sperm not used. Sanctions were imprisonment and hefty fines.[12]

The bulk of gamete donation law in France is now dealt with by the 1994 statute on donation and assisted conception.[13] Article 10 reaffirms the regulations pertaining to donor insemination which have operated under self-regulation by the largest and government-approved donation body CECOS, in relation to consent before donation, anonymity and a ban on payment. Most importantly, and on this the regulations in France on donation contrast with the UK, gametes may only be donated from one set couple to another: a donor must now be a father or mother in a couple and have the written consent of their partner to donation. The partner of a gamete donor has as much right to revoke his or her consent as the actual donor, at any time before fertilisation. Once an embryo is created, the embryo 'belongs' to a particular couple having treatment.[14] In Britain, by contrast, centres are only advised to encourage donors to obtain partners' consent.[15] Prior to the passing of the 1994 statutes, a handful of French clinics carried out insemination and did not follow these CECOS-inspired rules.[16]

Before 1994 only the informed consent of the woman who had the donated gametes, or embryos created from them, transferred to her body was lawfully necessary, rather than the consent of the actual donor and the donor's partner.

Previously accepted certainties about parenthood have been overshadowed by assisted-conception treatments. The use of donor gametes has thrown up difficult philosophical questions about the constitution of the family and parental status. Various new regulations have been introduced which attempt to clarify parenthood. In both countries, legislators have instigated the rule that a donor can never be the parent where the donation and treatment are carried out in a licensed clinic and the donor appropriately consents and remains anonymous. The legal parents of the assisted-conception child are set out as soon as treatment begins: a 'child' belongs to one set of parents rather than any other from before its conception at the time of gamete selection, the exception to this rule being in the use of surrogacy. The use of donor 'parents' has turned long-established and accepted rules on filiation or parenthood in France upside down as biological 'facts' are no longer as tenable.

On the question of motherhood, rules have been identical on either side of the Channel since 1990. Under Section 27 of the 1990 Act and Article 374 of the French Civil Code, the woman who gives birth to the child is considered to be its mother. This applies whatever the genetic make-up of the child, in other words, whether or not the original ovum was genetically the product of the birth mother except that in certain surrogacy arrangements (using ova or womb donation) the commissioning parents can apply for a 'parental order' (s. 30) (*see* p. 154). This rule has had to be instigated in regulations governing assisted conception because the use of donation has resulted in an anomaly, which could not have existed previously, whereby a woman who gave birth was not necessarily the genetic mother of that child. The child could be the product of a donated ovum or a donated embryo. The birth mother in France, however, has had the ability to remain anonymous for the past 200 years ('accoucher sous X'). This has been an accepted practice as it was thought that a woman who did not want a child, or to be seen to have given birth to an illegitimate child, might seek to destroy it either at birth or before. Such a child in France would then be legally motherless in the sense that its birth certificate would not acknowledge any woman by name as its mother.

Until 1987 in the UK, the donor of sperm remained in law any ensuing child's father – no father was registered on the birth certificate therefore because sperm donors remain anonymous. Any husband registering himself as the father would be committing perjury by so doing. Section 27 of the Family Law Reform Act 1987 clarified the matter somewhat and provided that, where the woman's husband had consented to DI, the child should be treated as his natural child.[17]

Section 28 of the 1990 Act applies to assisted conception fatherhood in Britain. Section 28(2) re-enacts the provision of Section 27 of the Family Law Reform Act 1987 whereby the husband is presumed to be the father of any child his wife gives birth to, unless he can prove that he did not consent at the time of treatment. Section 28(3) extends this to partners within unmarried couples, where they are seeking treatment together and the male partner is infertile. There is no requirement to seek consent but it is normal practice. Under Section 28(4), if the husband or partner does consent only he is the father. If he does not, he may accept later that the child is his. Under Schedule 3 of the Act, the donor is never the father if the donation and treatment are carried out in licensed clinics and if the donor appropriately consents. This can therefore in theory lead to legally fatherless children where the husband or partner proves he has not consented.

In France the issue of fatherhood or filiation has been more problematic for legislators due to pre-existing legal principles. From the 1800s, the law on filiation established the presumption of paternity to eliminate disputes within families and to favour patrimony. The child conceived during the marriage had as its father the husband of its birth mother. The child born 300 days after the dissolution of the marriage was legitimate. The child born before 180 days of marriage was legitimate unless contested by the husband. The use of the assisted-conception procedure whereby donated gametes, which could be stored for several years before being used to create a pregnancy, thus presented problems.[18]

Article 10 of the 1994 statute on respect of the human body refers specifically to filiation in the case of donation. None is established between a donor and offspring. Laws on filiation in France previously applied only to men, as the law on birth mothers has existed for almost two centuries. Although ova donation is less important numerically than sperm donation, perhaps due to the much more invasive procedure it necessitates, its introduction has meant that both fatherhood and motherhood are now contestable where assisted conception has been used.[19]

In both countries, then, legally fatherless children can be created where the husband or partner proves he has not consented. In France, a legally parentless child can also be created if its mother gives birth anonymously.[20]

So, it would appear that informed consent has been introduced in both countries as a precaution against conflict around the question of fatherhood and to ensure agreement about treatment between a couple using a donor. This is further reinforced by the legal stipulation that donors must remain anonymous. In this way, there is no question of them being held to be the parents of the assisted-conception child produced. Psychological studies on adopted children have shown the value of telling children the truth about their origins and adopted children have been given the right to such information.[21]   In practice, however, it would appear that parents of assisted-conception children do not intend telling those children the truth. Should children be told that their genetic parent is not their social parent? Do donors need to remain anonymous? Many donors themselves would wish to remain anonymous and not have any relationship or give inheritance rights to children resulting from their donation.

Under the 1990 Act (s. 13(2)), licensed centres must keep records of the users of their services, the donors' names, the child's name and which services were used and the names of those whose consent was required (for 50 years). Under Section 31(4)(b), information will be available to the 18-year-old assisted-conception child, or younger, planning to marry, after counselling. This does not force parents to inform their children but will avoid consanguineous marriage, as the two people are entitled to information on whether or not they are related. Section 31(4)(a) provides that any information the Authority decides to give may include identifying information (though not retrospectively). No regulations have yet been issued by the HFEA under Section 31.

The idea of there being a right to know genetic and personal information in parliamentary debates in Britain was based on a European Court of Human Rights case, *Gaskin* v. *UK*.[22] This held that Article 8 of the ECHR, demanding respect for the private life of an individual, required that all people should be able to establish details of their identity as individual human beings.

Legal debate in France on the issue of the right to know has followed similar lines to the British debate.[23] Braibant's was the only Report to disagree with medical opinion on the need for donors, and argued that donation of ovaries and sperm should not be anonymous so that children could know their biological origins. Article 2 of the 1994 statute on donation and assisted conception goes further than the English law and ensures complete anonymity to donors. This means that children born as a result of donated gametes would never be able to know their genetic identity or their natural parents. Under Article 10 of this statute, the only time non-identifying information may be given to children resulting from donation is on the grounds of therapeutic necessity and subject to clinical discretion. Indeed, the application by French Deputies to the Constitutional Court of July 1994 was devoted partly to the issue of anonymity. The lack of information for assisted-conception children provided by Article 10 was seen as an attack on the right to health of the child and the exercise of its free will. This was against the 'principe de responsabilité personnelle' (principal of personal responsibility) in the Civil Code and the 'loi du 16 novembre 1912', which allows for the search for paternity.[24]

In order to cement the relationship of the social father, it has been decided in England that the child will have no claims on the biological father and will only have access to the most meagre information on him, and in France that there will be complete anonymity. This contrasts with laws on adoption, whereby adoptees have access to information on their mothers, something that has been accepted as necessary to the children concerned.[25] Despite the conclusions of psychologists, legislators have seen fit to prevent the assisted conception child from knowing its genetic parents, or even, in France, its genetic identity. It would appear then that parents and legislators alike would rather not respect their child's 'right to know' and are instead respecting the rights of parents. This appears to be anomalous with other attitudes in the French Statutes in relation to the respect of the child, for example in the 'projet parental', but may well sit nicely with their historically pronatalist family policies.

The ethical and legal issues of humanness and parenthood have played a large part in debates on both sides of the Channel in relation to the use of gametes after the death of the biological parent of those gametes, donated or not. These have been further complicated in France by the issue of filiation. In both countries the legal regulations surrounding postmortem insemination have been hotly disputed, as semen has been donated in larger quantities than ova, and ova cannot generally be frozen. Post mortem insemination raises questions of the wishes on the part of the genetic father whose sperm might be used, and indeed of the mother of any resulting child. Would he still want his child to be born when he was dead? Why would a woman insist on having children by an ex-partner after his death? Why does she not move on to a further relationship that can provide a more stable family environment? Would this not be of more benefit to a child's psychology? Legislators on both sides of the Channel have seen fit to make use once more of the law on consent in an attempt to solve some of these issues.

As far as English law is concerned the posthumous use of sperm or embryos creates fatherless children as death legally ends the marriage;[26] the child will be a non-marital child with no rights to claim against his genetic father's estate under the 1990 Act. Schedule 3[27] of the Act further provides that any 'donor' of gametes or embryo must provide informed consent for the use of these after their death or incapacitation, as they are then no longer in a position to use their right to vary the terms of their consent or to revoke it.[28] This use also depends on clinical judgement, with the power to decide on treatment lying ultimately with the doctor, not the woman patient. The clinician would then have to take into account the welfare of the prospective child and the need of that child for a father under Section 13(5). This also applies to ova or embryo donation. Ultimately, English law does allow postmortem insemination and embryo transfer.

During 1996 these regulations on the postmortem use of sperm resulted in a very public legal wrangle whereby Diane Blood applied for permission to use her husband's sperm after his death. At Mrs Blood's request, sperm was removed from her husband while he was in a coma two days before his death. Although in this particular case there was no infertility and the sperm was not from a donated source outside the couple, the regulations of the 1990 Act and the HFEA still applied as soon as the sperm was stored. The HFEA initially ruled that treatment could not be carried out as there was no firm evidence that informed consent by Mrs Blood's husband to postmortem insemination had been obtained under Section 4(1) of the Act. The Authority also refused to allow release of the sperm for treatment to take place elsewhere in Europe. Mrs Blood sought judicial review of this decision arguing that Mr Blood had intimated his consent. In October 1996 the High Court agreed with the HFEA.[29] At the Court of Appeal in February 1997, however, Mrs Blood was accorded the right to take the sperm abroad under European Community law [30] and receive medical treatment in another Member State.[31]

In France too there have been cases of women who, like Diane Blood, have wanted to use sperm after the death of their partners and several couples have wished to be able to keep sperm in storage for use in case of the premature death of the husband. In the *Parpalaix* case [32] the refusal of the donor insemination centre CECOS to hand over the sperm of a dead husband to his widow was deemed unlawful by the court. Under contract law, [33] the contract between CECOS and the Parpalaix couple obliged CECOS to hand back the sperm as the couple had not been made aware of CECOS objections to posthumous insemination. The court was influenced by the fact that the couple were married and that procreation was an object of marriage. This resembles the possible thinking behind the Court of Appeal judgment in the *Blood* case. Here, a very interesting construction was put on Mrs Blood as the 'ideal' mother who had undergone a very traditional marriage service. In addition, it was held in *Parpalaix* that the wishes of the dead man could be inferred via the testimony of others, and similarly in *Blood* that the unlawful taking of sperm would not recur, that the approval of the use of Mr Blood's sperm would not set a precedent, and that therefore the HFEA should have been prepared to take Mrs Blood's evidence of her husband's wishes into account.

However, the *Parpalaix* ruling has now been replaced by Article 10 of the

French statute on respect of the human body. The consent necessary for each insemination and for each embryo transfer is now revoked after the end of a marriage or stable relationship, including after the death of one of the partners of the couple undergoing assisted-conception treatments using a donor. (Unless of course treatment has already begun with that donated gamete.) This is because treatment can only be given to a couple initiating a 'projet parental' or parental undertaking together, in other words both setting out to be a parent-couple of any resulting child. Accordingly, it would appear that a French Diane Blood would not be able to gain access to the stored semen of her dead husband or partner, whether or not it could be proved that he had given his consent to postmortem insemination, because he could not be there in person to consent to the insemination or embryo transfer taking place. Nor could a French Mr Blood use a surrogate to gestate an embryo that had been created from his dead wife's ova, or had been donated to the couple.

One legal commentator in France has expressed the view that the 1994 statutes do not solve the problems of postmortem insemination or postmortem embryo transfer within marriages, and that these are still subject to the Civil Code.[34] Even if this were the case, and although the Civil Code has been interpreted by judges in various ways, the vast majority of judges have followed the same line as the 1994 statute, namely that both partners in a couple need to be present and consenting at the time of embryo transfer or implantation into the mother of the future child. For example, in the *Pires* case,[35] the judge held that: under Article 315 of the Civil Code the delay between fertilisation and pregnancy negated the legality of the fatherhood of the dead husband; that two people were necessary to agree and consent to create a child and claim a right to parenthood; and that the presence of both partners was necessary at embryo transfer to ensure the filiation or parenthood of the ensuing child.[36]

On the issues surrounding donor insemination, then, largely similar results have come from quite different approaches. Legislators on both sides of the Channel have attempted to deal with the difficult questions of humanness and parenthood through strict regulations governing informed consent. This attitude would also appear to have coloured attitudes towards requests by widows for postmortem insemination where stress has been laid in both countries on informed consent. The stress is slightly different between the two countries. In Britain that consent is to the use of the gametes after the death of the donor, whereas in France the consent must be given at the time of their use, namely at the time of embryo transfer to the uterus. If a British man consents to the postmortem use of his sperm by his wife, she may go on to use them, though this use ultimately lies at the discretion of the medical personnel. Her French counterpart is not in a position to do this, despite the vagaries of

French jurisprudence. It has also been felt in both countries that clarity about parenthood was so important to society and to the child's status that donor anonymity had to be ensured at the expense of the claims of the child to have a psychological need to know about his or her true biological origins, about his or her assisted conception and his or her difference from his or her parents and from 'normally' conceived children.

Access

Several different kinds of people are now turning to artificial techniques to assist them in their quest for a child. Some of these people may be infertile, others may be seeking to avoid passing on a genetic disorder to their offspring, and yet others may not want to engage in heterosexual sex. An important issue for these people has been access to the new technologies. Those who do not fit with accepted ideas of parenthood have found themselves refused treatment according to strict and often questionable criteria which could dash any hopes they had for a family and nullify their past efforts. These criteria have led critics, such as feminists, to pose questions such as who controls access to assisted conception? Who has the right to set criteria whereby single and lesbian women are excluded from assisted-conception treatment? [37] Such regulation is especially questionable when nature does not prevent single or lesbian women from becoming mothers.

Neither British nor French patients who go to clinics in search of medical help to conceive are completely free to pick and choose the services on offer. The British and French Establishments have seen fit to limit and regulate such access. Moreover, the methods of limitation chosen differ markedly in the two countries: the same person would not necessarily enjoy the same right to treatment in both countries.

In the UK, Warnock recommended that DI should only be administered by a registered medical practitioner, with legislative control over 'do-it-yourself' kits under the Medicines Act 1968 (such kits had been advocated to single women by feminists). The issue never received as much attention from Parliament, interest groups and the government as did embryo research and surrogacy. However, the White Paper introduced the idea of the Statutory Licensing Authority (SLA) drawing up a Code of Practice to be laid before Parliament and to cover, *inter alia*, the screening of donors. The issue of offering DI to single women was not as important at this juncture however, and several clinics were happy to do this.

It was therefore no small step when such restrictions on women's rights were actually included in the 1990 Act in the UK.

Section 13(5) of the Human Fertilisation and Embryology Act 1990 requires that the welfare of the child be taken into account when assessing suitability for all licensed treatment 'including the need of that child for a father'.[38] In debates in Parliament the original intention by interest groups to outlaw all single and lesbian mothers from DI failed and Section 13(5) is a compromise. This has, however, been charitably interpreted by the HFEA. In its Code of Practice it has therefore alleviated any threat to single mothers-to-be to some extent by accepting that there might not be a husband or partner, and allowing centres to consider, in such a case, 'whether there is anyone else within the prospective mother's family and social circle who is willing and able to share the responsibility for meeting those needs and for bringing up, and maintaining and caring for the child'.[39] However, the relevance of the need for a father at all is questionable.

Part 3 of the Code of Practice lists long and detailed guidance for centres to follow when taking account of the welfare of the child. Some of these are perhaps unnecessary considering the efforts that potential parents put into infertility treatment, for example, commitment to bringing up a child or the ability to meet the needs of the child. Others are certainly of a social nature, such as patients having had children removed from their care or evidence of a previous or relevant conviction.[40] Who should make the final decision based on such criteria? Can such decisions be left to the medical personnel involved, even assisted by an ethics committee? Even GPs and 'any individual, authority or agency' are to be asked their opinion as to the suitability of parents, and account taken of the fact that a patient has not consented to this.[41] Even those services not requiring a licence need to use criteria for their donors, for example, if the insemination following sperm donation is to take place in a licensed clinic. Donors of embryos must be having treatment themselves. Moreover, though the prospective parents under review have the opportunity to give their views and to meet objections, their 'assessors' include any person at the clinic who has come into contact with them and confidential information from an outside source can also be discussed with the medical team involved.[42]

Access to IVF has been limited further by the attitude of the British government to health service provision. Local health authorities have limited resources. A low priority has thus been given to an illness that is not life-threatening and the treatment of which can be extremely costly.

In NHS clinics, therefore, criteria which restrict access have been even more stringent in order to limit spending. By way of example, the criteria at the NHS-funded IVF Unit at St Mary's Hospital in Manchester in 1984 and 1985 included that the couple be in a stable relationship, childless and resident within the area covered by the Regional Health Authority, with a limit set on treatment cycles to three per couple.[43] The 1990 Act does not indicate how a review of a decision to refuse licensed treatment services to a woman or couple might be brought. It is obligatory, however, to establish and use an ethics committee to oversee the management of individual cases.[44]

One obvious avenue of redress for women or couples refused treatment is to seek judicial review of a clinic's decision to refuse treatment. Given the relative liberality within the private sector in relation to access to treatment, disaffected patients are much more likely to have been refused treatment by the NHS. Their prospects of success in the courts are slim. First, the courts have consistently declined to force health providers to reorder their general priorities for treatment.[45] Second, so far, attempts by individuals to upset clinics' judgments as to their suitability for treatment have been unsuccessful. In R. v. St Mary's Ethical Committee, ex parte Harriott[46] Schiemann, J. explicitly endorsed an NHS clinic's freedom to take into account the potential parenting skills of the couple and to rely on evidence of past conduct to judge those skills as wanting. A significant amendment to the HFEA Code of Practice in December 1995 was the emphasis on the age of the patient and their 'likely future ability to look after or provide for a child's needs'.[47] In R. v. Sheffield Health Authority, ex parte Seale,[48] Auld, J. upheld an age bar of 37 preventing older women from being afforded IVF. Only a judgment no reasonable clinic could possibly arrive at in rationing its resources would be struck down, he said. The woman reported in 1994[49] as complaining of a treatment refusal based on her husband already having a child by a previous marriage would have been unlikely to find comfort in the courts. The British patient is required by law to submit to an assessment of suitability for parenthood. In the private sector that assessment may well be minimal. Within the NHS, rationing of resources has meant that poorer patients may be ruled out of contention for treatment unless they are part of a conventional heterosexual couple, young and have no other children by their current or prior relationship.

The French position on access is very different.

The law imposes stringent rules excluding from access to treatment any patients who do not seek treatment as a heterosexual couple seeking to replicate a conventional nuclear-family structure. But, if patients meet that standard, the methods of funding treatment ensure that poverty is no bar to access. French patients may only be treated within a 'projet parental' (parental undertaking). All treatment must be given in the spirit of a particular couple's undertaking to be a parent. Under Article 8 of the statute on donation and assisted conception, assisted reproductive techniques (ARTs) or a created embryo can only be used to help a couple have a child or to prevent the transmission to that child of a particularly serious illness. This man and woman must not only be alive at the time of any treatment cycle, but also of procreating age (pre-menopausal), married or cohabiting for more than two years, and giving their annual written, informed consent beforehand to embryo transfer or AI.

Also under Article 8, an embryo can only be created to satisfy that particular couple's use of a treatment cycle to achieve a conception, gestation and then a child. Each couple is entitled to four treatment cycles or five years of treatment. As a general rule, couples undergoing treatment may only use one donated gamete, rather than both. In exceptional circumstances, an embryo can be donated to a couple undergoing treatment by another such couple who have tried assisted conception without success. Both members of the donating couple must give written consent to donation of what is in effect 'their' embryo, whether the original gametes were donated or not.

In addition to the 'projet parental' being introduced by the 1994 statutes, the final part of Article 8, which deals with counselling, also serves to make life more difficult for French patients trying to gain access to treatment. Under the 1990 Act in the UK, counselling has to be provided to all patients receiving treatment in a licensed clinic. Patients themselves, particularly in the UK, have campaigned for this to be introduced in clinics in order for the more difficult aspects of treatment to be discussed, such as the low success rates, the invasive surgery and the psychological problems associated with 'failure'. In France, counselling was not taken up until parliamentary debate took place in the run-up to the passing of the 1994 statutes themselves.[50] Unfortunately for patients, the French form of 'counselling' is a double-edged sword. The purpose of these sessions is to inform the couple of the low success rates, the difficulties of treatment, the law and what treatments involve. Their other purpose, however, is to verify the motivation of the couple and to inform them of the possibilities of adoption.[51] A month waiting period must then follow, which can be lengthened by a doctor, before written confirmation that treatment is to be allowed is given. This form of 'counselling' in France may only serve to deter couples, rather than help them in their decision-making or even contribute to an informed consent, especially those who do not fit the ideal model of parents-to-be.[52]

Surrogacy

In surrogate motherhood, a woman gestates a child with the intention of relinquishing it at its birth to a specific parent or parents. This enables couples who are biologically unable to reproduce by themselves to have access to parenthood. It also provides the means whereby single men, homosexual or heterosexual, can have a child that may be genetically related to them when they are not in a relationship with the birth mother of the resulting child.

Fears have been expressed in relation to surrogacy. Opponents have called it immoral and unnatural. Utilitarian ethicists have argued that it is better for a child to be born by artificial means than not born at all.[53] Feminists have pointed out that it is the women who carry the child to term who suffer most at the hands of surrogacy as their bodies are being treated like mere vessels; contracts are used to force surrogate mothers to hand over babies they themselves have given birth to; and commercial surrogacy can exploit under-privileged women as they are the most likely to be attracted to the idea of payment for pregnancy. For genuinely infertile women, however, surrogacy can offer hope and even radical feminists have recognised that women can be willing to perform this service for compassionate reasons.[54]

Generally, there has been a similar approach to surrogacy from governments in the UK and France. It has not been banned outright, but has been strictly regulated in both countries with commercialisation outlawed and contracts unenforceable, in the UK through express legislation. This is therefore a bonus for women and a reduction in medical power through the outlawing of agencies.

The majority in Warnock wanted to ban all third-party intervention in surrogacy arrangements, while the minority sought formal regulation. This would have gone further than the eventual Surrogacy Arrangements Act 1985 which outlawed commercial surrogacy. It was still seen as extreme and premature by some medical and legal commentators.[55] Section 36(2) of the 1990 Act now also extends the meaning of the 1985 Act to include treatments not included in 1985, therefore not only embryo transfer but also the placing in the surrogate mother of a fertilising egg or gametes.

In France, the Braibant Report recommended that existing civil law dictated that surrogacy was condemned, but not banned. This means that commer-cialisation is outlawed and that the birth mother is considered the mother of the child.

However, rather than statute it has been case law in both countries that has been of most importance as far as the development of law is concerned. Ultimately, the legal status of surrogacy has been dealt with in a much less thorough way than other aspects of assisted conception in both countries.

Commercialisation

Warnock accepted that surrogates could act out of generosity, as feminists have pointed out, and that commercialisation did not necessarily spell exploi-tation of the surrogate.

The Surrogacy Arrangements Act 1985 makes it a criminal offence for any third party to advertise or receive money for setting up a surrogacy arrange-ment. No offence is committed by the couple or the surrogate. Adoption laws make it a criminal offence to give or receive any unauthorised payment in relation to the adoption of a child or transfers of parental responsibility.

The Act leaves open to question the legal position of professionals, such as doctors or lawyers and their fees therefore. Theoretically, doctors could give general advice and support but not paid 'intervention on behalf of any of the principals'. This could exclude counselling and supervision.[56] However, as long as doctors do not actively procure the surrogate, counselling of both the surrogate and the couple may be legal and is carried out in practice in the UK, for example at the fertility clinic Bourne Hall. In the UK, the Brazier report, *Surrogacy: Review for Health Ministers of Current Arrangements for Payments and Regulation* (Cm 4068), of October 1998 recommended that the law should ensure that surrogates were only being paid genuine expenses incurred by pregnancy. This would avoid turning children into commodities. It was also critical of the lack of registration of the non profit-making agencies such as Childlessness Overcome Through Surrogacy (COTS) and argued for a Code of Practice to be drawn up overseeing surrogacy arrangements in the UK and for a new Surrogacy Act incorporating these recommendations.

In France, the CCNE expressed disapproval of surrogacy in an Avis of 23 October 1984, where it wished the law to remain as it was and to discourage surrogacy because of the legal, social and ethical problems it created. These were seen to relate to commercialisation, the exploitation of surrogates, the possible abandonment of the child, disputes over adoption and parenthood and the inability of the child to trace its origins if it is abandoned by the birth mother. The Braibant Report proposed to create a specific crime of surrogacy to facilitate the repression of those encouraging such a practice. Like the 1985 Act, this was aimed at suppressing surrogacy agencies and third-party commercial involvement and making contracts unenforceable. This was, apparently, in order to protect women from exploitation.[57]

The crime of being a surrogacy agency was found in two important cases in 1988 and 1989 which then appear to have set the tone for a general legal condemnation of surrogacy.[58] These two cases concerned a group of agencies finding and remunerating surrogate mothers on behalf of commissioning couples – Alma Mater, les Cigognes, l'association Sainte-Sarah and the sperm bank CEFER. The associations were refused a licence to operate by each successive court for several reasons: the human body could not be a product to be bought or sold (art. 322–9 c. civ); a mother could not be paid to give away her child or forced to procreate through insemination (art. 353–1, 2, c. pén); she could not decide to give her child and parental responsibility for it to someone else (art. 376 c. civ); the arrangement for abandonment constituted a contract rather than an act of free will, despite the claims of the defence, because it necessitated the handing over of the child; the donation of human parts such as blood did not come into the same category as surrogacy as they are therapeutic treatments whereas surrogacy is not a treatment for sterility (art. 209–15 c. santé publique). The Cour de Cassation also pointed out that a surrogacy arrangement constituted abandonment despite the fact that the child was claimed by its father because the agencies existed for the sole purpose of causing children to be abandoned by their mother – they were creating abandonment. The association Alma Mater had even been accused of claiming that the surrogate had been inseminated by the male partner of the commissioning couple when this was not the case, thus breaking the laws on adoption. It was also pointed out that the right to found a family under Article 24 of the international agreement of the UN of 1966 and the ECHR did not give any couple the right to have a child through someone else.

Finally in 1994 the statute on respect of the human body, Article 4, outlawed commercial surrogacy agents.

Contracts and their enforceability

Warnock came out against commercial surrogacy and considered that such contracts were unenforceable, void and illegal as contrary to common law and the Children Act 1975, whereby agreement to transfer parental rights is an offence. Indeed the outlawing of surrogacy can be seen as a means of protection for the embryo as it cannot be commercialised. Neither the surrogate nor the commissioning couple can sue one another or attempt to enforce a contract through a court for payments or for the child itself. This was further underlined in specific relation to surrogacy by the Surrogacy Arrangements Act 1985, and reinforced by Section 36(a) of the 1990 Act which added a new Section 1(A) to the 1985 Act. This applies to all forms of surrogacy regardless of whether the surrogate is the genetic mother or not.

Any contract in France between the commissioning couple and the surrogate is null and void because a person cannot be given away or sold for reasons of public order (art. 1128 c. civ). The surrogate has automatic parental rights over the child, as its birth mother (art. 374 c. civ). Any person or agency attempting to arrange the abandonment or adoption of a child is liable to a fine or imprisonment (as in this country) under the Penal Code Article 353–1 and Civil Code Article 1128. This was reiterated by the Sapin Bill of 1992 and Article 4 of the statute on respect of the human body 1994.

Who keeps the baby if disputes arise?

This issue is of crucial concern to women. The 1985 Act in the UK and codified law in France has ensured that any contract or agreement is unenforceable should a surrogate change her mind and refuse to hand over the child. This was reinforced in English law in 1990, as Section 36(a) of the Human Fertilisation and Embryology Act now amends Section 1A of the Surrogacy Arrangements Act 1985. In both countries the mother is considered as she who gave birth to the child, and no other woman: in the UK, in Section 27 of the 1990 Act; in France, Article 374 of the Civil Code. However, there remains the potential for disputes in the UK over custody and access, which the 1985 Act did not clear up. Even after the 1990 Act, disputes such as these remain very much a matter for the judiciary.

Cases in the UK have indicated that to judges the rights of the *child* are considered as superior to that of the commissioning parents and the surrogate when it comes to deciding who should keep the baby after birth. Such rights appear to be considered to be that the child should be kept by the surrogate mother should a dispute arise, as evidenced by the 1990 Act as well as case law, unless she would be considered to be an unfit mother, surrogate or otherwise. In *A* v. *C* (1978) a surrogate bore a child whom she had conceived through DI, using the commissioning father's sperm. The father attempted to force her to hand the baby over through the courts. The Court of Appeal refused to do this and further removed access granted by the High Court. Again in *Re P. (Minors) (Wardship: Surrogacy)* (1987) Sir John Arnold P. refused to force the handover of twins born from DI using the commissioning father's sperm.[59]

In France the claims of the birth mother override all others whether or not her ovum was used. Indeed if the surrogate refuses to hand over the child and is married, she and her husband can legally override the claims of the commissioning parents as the child is considered in law to be the illegitimate adulterous child of the commissioning father (if his sperm was used) under Article 334–9 of the Civil Code.[60] However, there do not appear to have been any surrogacy cases where the birth mother has refused to hand over the surrogate child.

In both the UK and France, then, it is the woman who carries the child who is considered in law to be the mother of the child and indeed the law appears to have favoured surrogates. However, it is not certain that in a dispute of this sort in France custody would be awarded to a single surrogate mother. Though the 'birth mother' rule prevents a child becoming a pawn between disputing adults it is unfortunate for the commissioning parents who are perhaps desperate to use a method that will provide them with genetic children and who have found a willing participant. For the surrogate, coun-selling has been advocated, perhaps along the lines of adoption. The law itself however does not guarantee a successful outcome to a surrogacy arrangement.

Handing over the baby

Where there is no dispute in surrogacy arrangements, the surrogate is happy for the commissioning couple to apply for adoption and make the child legally their own.

In the UK, under the Adoption Act 1976 only a court may authorise a payment in relation to the child being adopted or handed over. Thus any payment made to the surrogate must not be found to include an illegal payment, subject to a criminal prosecution. In two English cases, the same judge, Latey, J., has made important judgments that have been considered to be tolerant. *In re a Baby* (1985),[61] before the Surrogacy Arrangements Act, the local authority concerned made the baby (the result of DI using the commissioning father's sperm) a ward of court. The judge argued that the ethics of the methods and commerciality of the surrogacy arrangement were not for him to decide. He therefore agreed to the handover and granted custody to the commissioning parents, as this was in the best interests of the child. In the case of *Re an Adoption Application (surrogacy)* (1987)[62] the parents had tried to adopt their surrogate baby and acquire parental rights. They had been formerly turned down for adoption due to their age and the fact that they had been divorced. But Latey, J. argued that surrogacy itself was not outlawed, only commercial surrogacy. He found they were not in breach of adoption rules, allowed them to adopt as the child was settled with the parents, and held that the payments to the surrogate were for expenses and could be approved by the court.

As noted under gamete donation, according to Section 30 of the 1990 Act a court may now make a parental order for a child whose creation is the result of some form of assisted conception to be treated in law as the child of a commissioning couple involved in surrogacy. This now offers a limited alternative to adoption. This was an amendment serving to sit alongside Section 27, which asserted that the birth mother alone was the mother of the child. It is a substitute to having to adopt what many couples saw as already their child. This is provided that an application is made within six months of the birth; the couple are married and resident in the UK, over 18 and have the child with them. The parties involved must show they agree and the surrogate cannot consent until six weeks after the birth. It should be noted that the Section 30 parental order would not have been available to the couples in the above cases as the surrogacy must involve some variant of assisted conception. It is perhaps a pragmatic compromise that attempts to balance the rights and interests of the birth mother and commissioning mother in line with case

In France, case law, rather than statute, has set out the law on the question of adoption by commissioning parents. Since before surrogacy a birth mother has been allowed to refuse to declare herself as the mother of the child on the birth register and the child is then registered as being of a 'mère inconnue' in order that the child may be adopted by parents in more fortunate circumstances and perhaps to prevent infanticide and even abortion. False declaration is a crime ('supposition de part'), punishable by between five and ten years' imprisonment.[63] It is possible for parties to a surrogate agreement to arrange for the birth to be anonymous, where the father then claims the child as his own (art. 374 c. civ), if he has not already done so before the birth, and organises for his wife to adopt the child. This would create difficulties for any woman who wished to change her mind after the birth, and strips her of her right to retract her consent up to three months after the birth.

Courts in the mid-1980s looked favourably on adoption where the commissioning couple applied to adopt as long as the couple conformed to accepted adoption requirements: where the commissioning father was genetically related, the mother was not registered at birth and the couple had possession of the child ('possession d'état') for a length of time, or with the consent of the biological father and the surrogate mother, although the latter has three months after the birth in which to change her mind as with usual adoption arrangements (art. 348–3, c. civ). However, such an adoption approval is dependent on the whim of the civil tribunal and is judged according to the best interests of the child. Nor is it open to unmarried couples, as adoption by the birth mother would take away rights from the genetic father, and they cannot both adopt the child, thus they must be married to both adopt.[64]

However, case law judgments imply that surrogate arrangements followed by adoption are unlikely. In 'Cour d'Appel de Pau, 19 février 1991' the rejection of an application to adopt by a lower court ('9 octobre 1990') was reversed and 'adoption plénière' by the commissioning mother was allowed to go ahead.[65] The Appeal Court reasoned that courts could not make law, only interpret it and the existing law was only on adoption, though contracts were certainly null and void. Referring to United Nations Conventions[66] on the interest of the child being paramount when deciding on its fate, they decided that the commissioning couple conformed to adoption requirements and so allowed 'adoption plénière'.[67] However in a later judgment on 31 May 1991, in a similar surrogacy case in terms of birth registration and care provided since the birth, adoption was rejected by a superior court, the Cour de Cassation.[68] The Cour de Cassation here aimed to give a definitive legal judgment as it found that the reasons given by the Cour d'Appel were contrary to those given when the Alma Mater agency was dissolved – the only purpose of this birth had been to contract to abandon a child. This was contrary to the principles of public order ('ordre public'), non-transferability of the human body ('indisponibilité du corps humain et de l'état de personnes') and adoption.[69]

The law on surrogacy and adoption now appears to be similar in both countries. In the UK Section 30 of the 1990 Act as regards a parental rights order is similar in substance to adoption, though different in form, while in France the commissioning father is often registered on the birth certificate (though the more usual 'adoption plénière' has not been permitted). However, in the UK both of the commissioning couple are acknowledged as parents whereas in France the commissioning mother has no legal relationship to the child unless a sympathetic court rules in her favour.

Embryos and personhood

The use of medically assisted conception from the 1980s has meant that gametes can live outside the human body for the first time. As we have seen, the storage and donation of these human genetic products have raised questions regarding humanness and parenthood in relation to their insemination. Assisted conception has also provided methods whereby these gametes can go on to be fertilised outside the body. An individual human thus begins its life in a Petri dish. But is this oocyte or 'pre-embryo' the same as the person born some nine months later? Or does it have a status separate from other people? Should such status mean the law should guarantee preservation of the embryo in all circumstances? Is the embryo equivalent to a 'thing'? Does the embryo belong to people as property does?

In debates on the embryo and its use in assisted conception, adversaries have argued with each other about the status of the embryo, its humanness or otherwise, and the extent to which assisted conception should be allowed to utilise embryology techniques. This is an important issue in relation to women's rights as women's bodies have historically been pitted against those of the unborn child and now embryo. Thus it is important to assess what legal status the embryo has acquired through law on assisted conception.

In the legal debate on the embryo, certain issues have come to the fore: embryo donation, embryo storage, and embryo research (including treatment). French statute is much stricter than English law in setting firm rules as to treatment regulation and increased codified protection of the embryo. The 1990 Act in the UK is more of a framework within which self-regulation is the rule. Women's rights have been threatened by the repercussions for abortion of debate on embryo status. Women patients have been affected in so far as their choice of treatment has been limited.

Legislators in each country have dealt with the issue of the classification of the embryo as a person or thing in crucially different ways. The pragmatism of the common law has enabled the English to avoid having to classify the nature of the embryo. For example, the 1990 Act[70] affords civil liability to the child damaged as a result of treatment. This is an extension of the Congenital Disabilities (Civil Liability) Act 1976. It provides for damages if a child is born disabled as a result of an act or omission following the selection, keeping or use of gametes or embryos or if there has been negligence or a breach of statutory duty to one or both parents, and/or which if injury had occurred would have given rise to liability. The defendant must be liable in tort to one or both parents. The Act does not discuss the issue of product liability in relation to embryos within the meaning of the Consumer Protection Act 1987, however, where for example an embryo implanted into a woman damages her health. Following R v. *Tait*,[71] where a five-month-old foetus was not a person for the purposes of the Offences Against the Person Act 1861, an embryo cannot be a person. Moreover, the Court of Appeal in 1994 reaffirmed that under English law the foetus (or embryo) was not a separate person from its mother, but was rather one of two things: either an integral part of its mother, or in co-existence with its mother, in other words 'not-one-but-not-two'. Both approaches were compatible with the Abortion Act 1967, which permitted women, on public policy grounds, to allow clinicians to harm their foetuses.[72] Such questions were left unclear by the 1990 Act, however.[73]

French legislators have been hard pressed to formulate guidelines for assisted conception, not only with the difficulties of amending Codes and having to formulate law for new types of medical technologies, but also because French law is based on Christian tradition which makes it a sacrilege to own or sell or commercialise the body, even one's own body. Under French law, therefore, the embryo must be categorised as a person or as a thing. As in England, embryos in France have rights as people that are contingent on being born and being viable which means that women's rights outweigh them. They have a right to inherit, to not be murdered and to damages after birth. Pre-embryo rights are even less than those of the foetus or newborn.[74]

Under Section 14 of the 1990 Act in England a licence is required from the HFEA (renewable after ten years) for the storage of gametes or embryos or both. Under Section 14, gametes may be stored for ten years embryos for five years.[75] In 1991, regulations were published which allowed the statutory storage period for sperm to be extended beyond ten years for men under 45 whose fertility was likely to become impaired after medical treatment, to allow them subsequently to have children with their partner.[76]

In August 1996, those embryos which had been stored for five years, and had been put into storage before the implementation of the Act on 1 August 1991, were due to reach the end of their storage period and be 'allowed to perish'.[77] In May 1996, the government attempted to appease national and international objections to the destruction of such stored embryos and to take account of other circumstances besides those catered for in the 1991 Regulations.[78] They therefore introduced regulations to extend the storage period for embryos to 10 years provided that the donors of gametes consent in writing at the time of storage or before the end of the five-year period.[79] This only applies to the storage of an embryo that has been earmarked for the treatment of a particular woman until she reaches the age of 55,[80] although control over the storage or any use of the embryos remains dependent on the consent of the gamete providers.[81] The new circumstances in which storage may be extended are if a gamete provider or woman being treated might, now or in the future, suffer from impaired fertility, or transmit a genetically defective gene to a child, or become prematurely and completely infertile.[82]

Numerous texts have been published elaborating the French position on the issue of embryo storage. In the two Avis of 1984 and 1986 issued by the CCNE,[83] the freezing of spare embryos in licensed centres was endorsed due to the risks inherent in the IVF process for women. This procedure was to be carried out only if the centre could improve the woman's chance of success, for up to twelve months, with the consent of the couple and for their use only. It advocated that the first transplantation should take place within six months of freezing to prevent storage for convenience and damage to the embryo. The Braibant Report in 1989 thought that the period during which the parents could authorise the storage of their embryos should be five years rather than one or two to fully enable them to have their own children, but prevent 'stockage' of embryos. After five years they should be destroyed.[84] Under Article 9 of the 1994 statute on donation and assisted conception, embryos must now be destroyed if they have been stored for five years and have been 'abandoned' by the couple undergoing treatment as part of a 'projet parental' due to their lack of agreement or consent as to the fate of the embryos, or due to their disappearance, or to an end to their status as a couple, and a receiving couple to whom their embryos can be donated cannot be found. There is a difference in status, therefore, between those embryos which were put into storage after the implementation of the 1994 laws, and those already in storage at this time. The latter were due for destruction after the five-year limit. Their fate will not be decided, however, until the bioethics laws come up for their scheduled re-examination. This is not now due to take place until after the presidential and legislative elections of 2002. Some have spoken of the revision not being likely before 2003.[85] Debates at that time will almost certainly reflect those which took place in Britain during the summer of 1996.

On the issue of embryo donation, the 1990 Act in England authorises donation after appropriate counselling and consent, with the embryo being 'allowed to perish' when no consent can be procured.[86] The ensuing child is considered in law as that of the recipient couple subject to the requirements of Sections 27 and 28 regarding the birth mother, the consent of the father, whether married or not, and providing the child is not then adopted. As with gamete donation, the embryo donor remains anonymous and does not have any rights in the child. Succession rights begin at birth, not at fertilisation.

Since the early 1980s in France government bodies have been in favour of strict limits on embryo donation arguing that it should not be commercialised and should involve the consent of donor and recipient and be part of a 'projet parental'.[87] Under the 1994 statute on donation and assisted conception, embryo donation, as with storage, are only available as part of a 'projet parental'. The 1994 statute on donation and assisted conception, Article 8, stipulates guidelines to follow in situations when the couple do not use their own embryo. In exceptional circumstances, both partners may give written consent to donate their stored embryo, anonymously, to a particular couple for whom ART without a donor and as part of a 'projet parental' has already been unsuccessful. Once an embryo has been created, the control over its fate as regards storage or donation passes from the gamete provider to the couple having treatment as part of a parental undertaking, and passes from one such couple to another such couple, if donated. This contrasts with the power of gamete providers under the 1990 Act in England to vary their consent to embryo storage.[88] If a partner dies, the survivor is to be asked to donate by a judge, who will check the criteria of the receiving couple to see whether they can offer to any resulting child suitable familial, educational and psychological conditions. It should be borne in mind that these strict criteria on embryo donation have been put in place when only a handful of embryos are actually made available for donation each year.[89]

The 1990 Act does not prohibit embryo research in England and any research carried out under the Act may indeed be harmful to that particular embryo. The Act does give the *in vitro* embryo legal protection for the first time, however. Research licences (renewable after three years) are only allowed for each specific research project which must be directed towards one or more of a defined number of aims – advances in the treatment of infertility; congenital disease; miscarriage; conception; and gene chromosome abnormalities. However, the Authority is given the power under the Act to extend these aims under the regulations it sets. In theory, then, the scope of embryo research possible in Britain is wide.

A significant legal principle in French law which impinged on embryo research was the 'indisponibilité du corps': that the human body cannot be interfered with and is not a 'thing' under Article 1128 of the Civil Code. The human body can only be interfered with if this is medically therapeutic for that person. Accordingly, under the French statute on donation and assisted conception, Article 8 completely prohibits embryo research unless, in exceptional circumstances, the couple give written consent and the research is for medical ends and is not harmful to that embryo. This appears to create a situation where the creation of embryos for research is outlawed, in complete contrast to English law. If the French law is interpreted literally no basic research is allowed. This creates a situation where a clinician would have to argue that a particular form of research was not medically harmful to that embryo. An anomaly is also created whereby preimplantation diagnosis on cells removed from an embryo for eventual transferral to the uterus is lawful as it is therapeutic for that embryo, yet can only be done where there exists a risk of transmission of an incurable disease from parent to child.[90] This has led to a much more difficult situation for French researchers, in comparison to their English counterparts. Moreover, Article 2 of the French statute on respect of the human body states that 'the law ensures the primacy of the person, prohibits any violation of the dignity of the person and guarantees respect of the human being from the beginning of life'. The statute does not, however, specify when exactly that life begins.[91]

On 27 July 1994 the Constitutional Court responded to two 'Saisines' (or referrals to it that had been made by parliamentarians) at the end of the parliamentary debates on the assisted-conception bills, as to the constitutionality of assisted conception, particularly with respect to embryo research and the extent to which this impinged on the constitutional protection of a right to life. The decision handed down by the Constitutional Court was that it was satisfied that there were numerous safeguards in the laws in relation to assisted conception treatments, and accepted that Parliament had not decided to extend to embryos *in vitro* the principle of respect to all human life from inception (as stated in the Civil Code and the 1975 abortion law) and indeed that the bioethics laws were specifically in conformity with the principle of protecting human dignity.[92]

In consequence the *in vivo* embryo enjoys more rights than its *in vitro* counterpart. It would appear that the French have fudged the issue of whether the *in vitro* embryo is really a person or a thing, and have worked their way around the existing legal principles that have dogged attempts at assisted-conception laws. They have afforded protection to the embryo through penal sanctions and the necessity of consent, yet have allowed the embryo to be stored, donated and destroyed according to the desires of its parents. There is a lack of a limit in the French laws to the number of embryos which can be transferred to the uterus during a treatment cycle, thus necessitating selective reduction of a large number of embryos.[93] It is left to medical discretion as to whether research on an embryo is harmful to that embryo.

When the French bioethics laws were passed in July 1994, legislators were mindful of the need for further detail on the subject of embryo research. Article 8 of the French statute on donation and assisted conception thus stated that more specific guidelines were to be published in due course by the Council of State. These were eventually published in the form of decree in May 1997.[94] Now inserted into Article 8 of the statute on donation and assisted conception is the clarification that the medical study of human *in vitro* embryos can only be carried out for one of the following purposes:

> it has a direct advantage for the embryo concerned, *most notably in that it increases its chances for a successful implantation* (my italics);
>
> or it contributes to the improvement of medically assisted procreation techniques, notably the development of knowledge on the physiology and pathology of human reproduction;
>
> no study may be undertaken which attempts to or carries the risk of altering the genetic make-up of the embryo, or might alter the embryo's developmental capacity. Acts carried out as part of biological diagnosis on cells taken from the *in vitro* embryo do not constitute studies in the sense of the present Section.

This would appear to have clarified the position somewhat for those seeking the necessary approval for a research project from the CNMBRDP. Most notably, the stipulation that the research in question must be therapeutic for the embryo is more closely defined as having to improve its chances of implantation when it is transferred to the woman's uterus, or improve techniques of assisted conception.

The French law on embryo research has now begun to resemble its English counterpart much more closely. Under the Human Fertilisation and Embryology Act 1990 research licences are only allowed for each specific research project which must be directed towards one or more of a defined number of aims – advances in the treatment of infertility; congenital disease; miscarriage; conception; and gene chromosome abnormalities [95] and to increase knowledge about the creation and development of embryos.[96] These are similar to the French stipulations that embryo research should contribute to the improvement of assisted-conception techniques and the development of knowledge on the physiology and pathology of human reproduction. However, the French guidelines of 1997 are in fact less specific than the 1990 Act and remain unclear. Moreover, the stipulation in the French law that research should be therapeutic to that embryo still stands, and would seem to indicate that the scope of embryo research theoretically possible in Britain is still much wider than in France. The French law after 1997, therefore, prohibits destructive research for the purposes of improving medically assisted procreation, understanding genetic disease or enabling the improvement of contraception.

A further legal anomaly on the issue of embryo status is that pertaining to prenatal diagnosis. In May 1997 two decrees were also published on this particular issue.[97]

Under Article 12 of the statute of 1994 on donation and assisted conception, preimplantation or prenatal diagnosis refers to the detection of a particularly serious affliction in an embryo *in vitro* or a foetus *in utero*. Under Article 14, the couple whose embryo or foetus is being 'treated' must have a strong probability of giving birth to a child afflicted with a particularly serious genetic disability, recognised as incurable at the time of diagnosis. The aim of prenatal diagnosis must only be to diagnose, prevent and cure any disability.

The two decrees of May 1997 on prenatal diagnosis actually say little of substance on the issue of embryo research. They are mainly concerned with outlining the tasks, staffing and licensing of the multidisciplinary centres that carry out prenatal diagnosis. What is noteworthy, however, is the fact that they restate the anomalous position of prenatal diagnosis whereby the taking of cells from an embryo for such diagnosis is lawful as it is deemed to be therapeutic for that embryo. Preimplantation diagnosis can only be carried out where there exists a risk of transmission of a genetic disease from parent to child that is incurable. Such a necessarily incurable disease cannot be 'treated', and the embryo itself cannot benefit from preimplantation diagnosis. Only an embryo that is free from the genetic disease can benefit from such 'treatment' as the only 'therapy' available is termination or destruction. This may benefit the parents but how can it be said to be therapeutic for the embryo itself? The decrees merely reiterate this legal anomaly.[98]

On the whole, the 1994 laws in France appear to try to protect the embryo more forcefully than the 1990 Act in relation to donation whereby an embryo must be donated from one couple to another, and in relation to research whose regulation is considerably more strict to the extent that basic research would appear to have been completely outlawed. As with the other legal issues raised by the new techniques of assisted conception, in France constitutional principles have complicated the legislating process for parliamentarians. The idea of embryo storage has also created fierce legal debate in France due to the question of whether you can destroy or dispose of abandoned frozen embryos as if they were things rather than humans. Again the constitutional idea of a human being never legally being construed as a thing impinges on this law. Academic lawyers have concluded that the issue has not been solved by the 1994 laws. This question led to a referral to the Constitutional Court to decide on the constitutionality of embryo storage, disposal and research. Whenever the laws come up for debate again, the question will be central.

A comparison of the English and French responses to the question of embryo status, particularly in relation to research, leads to the conclusion that the embryo is a good deal more valued and protected under French law than English. This 'value' does not mean, however, that the value of the embryo is closer to that of the born child in France. Personhood is dependent on birth and viability in both countries.

Conclusions

The 1990 Act in England and the 1994 statutes in France have both been described as occupying the middle ground between prohibition and permissiveness. Legislation took some eight years to reach the statute book in the UK. In France the process took still longer, and amendments to the present statutory laws may yet take place. The delay in both countries meant that, almost by necessity, self-regulation by the medical professions has been condoned by governments. Legislators in both these countries have made use of rules on informed consent; have restricted access; and have left important questions to the vagaries of clinical discretion. Consent law in both Britain and France, particularly in relation to donation and embryo research, has provided a means of assuring personhood as well as parenthood. Yet there are important differences between the two debates. The French have been dogged by the difficulties of working around constitutional principles, though ultimately these have provided safeguards. The English, meanwhile, have adopted a more pragmatic line. Moreover, one important difference stands out: the uncompromising outlawing of embryo research in France, in contrast to Britain, alongside the restrictions on access provided by the 'projet parental', have determined that the French have emphasised the interests of the child much more than their English counterparts. The law as it now stands on assisted conception does have safeguards in relation to women patients in both countries, as clinics have to be licensed. There are limitations however as to how far licensing rules are reviewed and controlled, though the licensing bodies, especially in France, may have a medical bias. Neither is counselling in either country mandatory, with French consent law on treatment not being stringent enough. Consent in relation to donors has been improved in France, making fathers less able to disown their offspring, in women's and children's favour. To children's detriment however, for the present, donors remain anonymous in both countries.

Surrogacy has been objected to particularly by feminists. It has not been specifically prohibited in either country however, though commercialisation and contracts have. Surrogacy law in the UK may have unfortunately restricted a surrogate's access to counselling and supervision. Embryo rights could also be said to have increased through the interdiction of commercial surrogacy, though in reality both countries' laws on adoption have merely been extended to the practice of surrogacy and on this issue the interests of the child have become paramount when deciding questions such as custody. Indeed it is debatable whether such details as the Section 30 parental order in the UK are anti-women at all if those women are infertile.

Clinicians in both countries who spoke out in favour of self-regulation will have been left dissatisfied. Likewise patients who wanted unlimited access. The only group which might see one country's laws as being marginally preferable to the other's might be those in France who support the rights of the embryo and the welfare of the child. However, this group is expected to oppose the French statutes when they re-emerge for debate in 2002/3 as vehemently as they ever have. A more detailed examination of the arguments of such groups and their role in influencing the content of laws is the task of the following Chapter.

7

The delivery of assisted-conception regulation

As the twentieth century was entering its final two decades, a new reproductive issue entered the fray of reproductive policy-making: that of assisted conception. The many issues that this raised instigated a relatively swift statutory response from both the British and French governments. These were examined in the preceding Chapter. But what of the policy debates surrounding this new legislation? The positions assumed by those interest groups involved were often diametrically opposed one to the other. Indeed, their groupings and discourses echoed those previously seen in the conflicts surrounding the reproductive rights issues of abortion and contraception. Women's rights campaigners, medical professionals and religious groups all played important roles. Those campaigning on the issue of women's rights lobbied principally on the issues of medical and governmental attitudes toward assisted conception, embryo status and treatment services. Religious groups remained concerned particularly with the status of the unborn child. In relation to assisted conception this translated into support for the embryo. The medical professions, for their part, sought to improve services and to maximise self-regulation, often, interestingly, alongside more 'liberal' feminists (see below for definition of liberal in this context). This was the case for both of our countries.

In this Chapter an attempt is made to assess the influence of those interest groups campaigning for women's rights in this area, relative to that of other significant groups in the UK and France. This entails an examination of the opinions and methods of women's rights campaigners, those of their allies, the medical profession and religious groups (the latter two as members of the policy network created around this issue). This is followed by an appraisal of parliamentary opinion and debate at the drafting and consultation stages leading up to the debate on legislation on assisted conception in 1990 in the UK and in 1994 and 1999/2000 in France. The format of the Chapter is thus comparative at each stage of analysis in order to assess the reactions of the British and French governments to the different opinions raised in lobbying and campaigns. Whose opinions carried most weight? What effect did this have on legislation?

Feminists and assisted conception

It was not felt necessary to explain in detail the different feminist opinions on contraception and abortion. However, the opinions of different feminist strands on assisted conception have been more problematic for feminist campaigns and lobbying methods.

Feminists have produced strongly argued critiques on both sides of the Channel. They have injected an element of sociological and ethical criticism of assisted-conception practice into intellectual debates, though have had less impact on the political stage. That is not to say that others have not voiced similar concerns. Nonetheless, feminist critiques did translate into political action.

As in earlier chapters, the typology of 'liberal', 'socialist' and 'radical' helps to define an attitude to lobbying prevalent among different types of groups, as well as delineating boundaries between beliefs and ideologies (though there may well be less and less mileage in this terminology with the onset of postmodern feminism).

The majority of feminist commentators who have spoken out vehemently against assisted conception and who have rejected outright new reproductive techniques associated with assisted conception I have termed 'radical' feminist. In contrast to this view, there is also evidence of a more sympathetic and favourable view towards infertility and in lobbying, by feminists who are therefore referred to here as 'liberal'. Liberal and socialist groups have been much more willing to participate in the policy-making process as lobbyists, in contrast to radicals. In France, too, campaigners have spoken out against assisted conception: liberals or egalitarians criticising medicalisation particularly; radicals from a more essentialist stance, which emphasises womanhood and naturalness.[1]

Radicals in the UK and France have also expressed fears that medically assisted conception might cause women to become, once more preoccupied with motherhood.[2] They have reproached women for lacking a common reproductive consciousness and for concentrating on their own individual choice.[3] Surrogacy has been likened to prostitution with women selling their bodies, and the poorest women being exploited both by society and by other women.[4] For this reason, research should rather be into the reasons for infertility – social or iatrogenic – social change and the facilitation of adoption.

More liberal feminists have argued that in a future scenario radical feminists had nothing to fear from the technologies themselves but from their use. Thus women who claimed to possess embryos or that sex-selective abortion was wrong risked increasing rights for embryos and threatening abortion rights.[5] Science had assisted women to gain control of their reproduction through the medical development of contraceptives, analgesics, amniocentesis and abortion. The problem was not science itself but that men, particularly medical men, had too much power over it, and that women were socially conditioned into motherhood.[6]

Three particular threads emerge from an analysis of feminist debates on assisted conception: first, their critique of services for the infertile; second, their criticism of the attitudes of clinicians and governments to assisted conception; and third, their emphasis on the growing threat of embryo status. It is important to note that liberals and radicals were equally critical on the issues of medical and governmental treatment of assisted conception, and embryo status. It was on the issue of services for the infertile that liberals and radicals in both countries particularly disagreed.

This split between strands or factions mirrors earlier campaigns on abortion, when difference and, consequently, political disunity and weakness were also apparent. As discussed in Chapter 5, the French abortion campaign of the early 1970s, for example, saw liberal and socialist feminists prepared to form alliances with clinicians, politicians and parliamentarians, while radicals used political techniques of direct action outside the parliamentary arena. This political disunity has been particularly apparent since the emergence of radical feminism in the 1960s.

On services for the infertile

The prevailing attitude among feminists before the 1980s had meant that historically infertile feminist women had felt stigmatised for their desire for motherhood. Naomi Pfeffer, in particular, has pointed out how this prevented any examination of the causes and consequences of infertility by feminists.[7]

Some feminists therefore began to advocate a more sympathetic attitude towards the women who wanted to use new reproductive techniques, and argued for an improvement in such services rather than their eradication. This would take account of the pressures such women were under from husbands, society, profit-making clinics and status-seeking doctors to reproduce genetically rather than adopt. Feminists had to realise, it was argued, that only certain women were 'coerced' into motherhood: 'undesirables' were dissuaded from it. Nor were infertile women irrational to want children. Nor was adoption a simple alternative. All women underwent pronatalist pressure.[8] The desire for a child can be due to several reasons: lack of fulfilment, loneliness, social pressure, necessity or choice; or even a desire for immortality, a fulfilling human experience and adventure. Adoption did not fulfil all of these desires.[9]

In France the 1988 MFPF conference also concluded that the desire for a child was in itself legitimate, but was the product of multiple social pressures. Despite the presence of infertile women at the conference, this was not an attempt to bring feminists and the infertile closer together, a move which had never taken place in France, according to French feminist academic Françoise Laborie when interviewed in 1990. Thus, for the MFPF, individual women should have the right to choose (an echo of the abortion slogan). To help them choose though they needed to be well informed. The MFPF reiterated their support of the right to choose and the improvement of centres offering infertility treatment through the new government bills, when they were consulted by the French government's investigative committee, OPECST in April 1992.[10]

'Liberal' feminists in the UK considered that women needed a better range of services, with an improvement in research, the introduction of independent women counsellors and an emphasis on improvement to make assisted conception safe and successful with full access and consent.[11]

> There should be full discussion and planning of infertility services, at all levels, rather than their growth being the haphazard result of individual consultants' interests. The DHSS should issue clear guidelines on development and funding ... Districts should include a section on infertility services in their strategic plans. The implication for the NHS of any arrangements with the private sector should be closely examined and such arrangements should be the subject of policy decisions, not left to individual consultants.[12]

In France, although the infertile and their feminist allies were less well organised, they too campaigned for better treatment. Here again we find the argument that, as patients, women were losing out due to a lack of information on infertility and treatment and a lack of independent counselling being provided by clinics.[13] On prenatal screening for genetic abnormalities, for example, women patients lacked support and objective counselling when such screening could lead to ideas of perfection and eugenicism. Also more information could be given to potential patients on other options such as adopting Third World children and other life options.[14] Forcing anonymity on all donors was paternalistic and perverse.[15] More DI centres needed to be set up, at which counselling should play a much more important part.[16] At the MFPF conference on assisted conception in 1988, a psychoanalyst and psychiatrist argued against the anonymity rule as her experience with adoption had shown that it was necessary for men to recover from associating infertility with virility, and for the couple to come to terms with their childlessness.[17] Others too argued that the French government's Braibant Report of 1989 needed to be amended to include a clause taking account of the state of mind of women having to consent when they had just undergone serious experimentation.[18] The empowerment of the assisted-conception patient was thus important.

In the UK the fact that most treatment was only available privately also affected the stance of feminists. Liberal feminists argued that feminists should extend the debate to the need for a high standard of care, and access for all women and therefore for better management of NHS resources.[19] They questioned the amount of resources that were being put into researching such techniques as IVF, instead of researching the causes of infertility.[20] The issue of money being spent on the causes of infertility and sexually transmitted diseases (a suggested cause of infertility), rather than on assisted conception, was important in France, too, where the government was accused of pronatalism and of spending vast amounts merely to increase the birth rate.

On medical and governmental attitudes to assisted conception

Linked to this criticism of treatment availability has been an issue on which all feminists have agreed to a large extent: their objection to the increasing use historically of medical technology in reproduction of which assisted conception can be seen as the latest manifestation. It was argued that assisted-conception treatments were thus reducing women's control over their bodies and a woman's special function, by 'industrialising' reproduction. Women were again being excluded from medicine, except as recipients, by patriarchy. Chatel spoke of the medicalisation of procreation and the replacement of holistic, social or human symptoms of pregnancy and parenthood by totalitarian veterinary prescriptions.[21] Many questioned the ethics behind the absolute faith of society in clinical judgement[22] and the lack of government control over the false representation by doctors of costly, experimental, unsuccessful and dangerous techniques that raised false hopes among the infertile.[23] Assisted-conception techniques could cause side effects such as hyperstimulation, as well as multiple pregnancies, premature babies, malformation and death. The donation of sperm and eggs was also seen as increasing medical control, and as being eugenicist as doctors might be inclined to select donors from the white, middle-classes, and from married men and women.[24] Embryo transfer had at this time, moreover, led to a relatively high number of abnormal pregnancies and to miscarriages.[25]

Governments in turn were accused, just as were the other members of the policy network on assisted conception, of being biased and in league with the medical professions in both the UK and France.

The first governmental response to assisted conception in the UK was the Warnock Report in 1984. The Report was criticised by radical feminists for attempting to normalise through legislation attitudes that were not widely held: of not questioning the need for assisted conception, but merely the regulation of it; of ova donation ignoring the possible coercion and exploitation of women; of regulating DI unnecessarily out of hostility to single women; of concentrating on ethical rather than social issues of relevance to women; and of emphasising traditional family values. Such campaigners criticised parliamentary intervention as they saw Westminster as male dominated. They were advocates of what they saw as reproductive freedom, rather than regulation.[26]

In France feminists were suspicious of governmental and medical motives to fund and encourage assisted-conception clinics because of their pronatalist reputation, especially at a time of scarce health resources. At the forefront of feminists' minds were government attempts to reverse the fall in the birth rate.[27] Moreover the State did not collect reliable data and provided only discretionary guidelines for clinics on the provision of data.[28] This led to the conclusion that statistics were chosen to benefit groups such as the medical professions and pronatalists rather than the infertile, and that decisions were being made without their full social implications being thoroughly investigated '(q)uel groupe de pression opère, brusquant les décisions, refermant le dossier de nos interrogations avant que les enjeux sociaux et les implications de ces choix n'aient été clairement envisagés?'.[29] They also condemned the publication by the media of pictures of smiling babies and sympathetic doctors; and reports of research that doctors claimed would help infertile women and cure 'hereditary diseases'.[30]

Criteria being used in both countries were seen as social and eugenic, to the detriment of women and society.[31] The medical professions were controlling access, sanctioned, in France, by the pronatalist government.[32] Clinicians were criticised for seeing experimentation on women as 'natural' and on men 'artificial', regardless of the infertility in either gender.[33] Moreover, eugenicism was being legitimised by government legislation.[34]

On embryo status

In both Britain and France there was less disunity among radical feminists, liberal feminists and infertile women on the issue of embryo status. Very few wanted to see any increase in legal status for embryos donated, stored and most especially researched upon. Liberals and many infertile women who campaigned for women patients to receive the best treatment were in favour of research being carried out on embryos rather than on infertile women, and on embryos being donated and stored to improve the chances of a successful pregnancy. For liberal and radical feminists, especially in the UK, it was feared that increasing the rights of the embryo *in vitro* might in turn increase those of the embryo *in vivo* and jeopardise women's abortion rights.

Certain modern techniques designed to ensure viable pregnancy increasingly pitched the rights of embryos and of women against each other.

Embryo research necessarily makes use of women's bodies to create the embryos, as does foetal surgery and foetal monitoring, thus potentially reducing women's rights. With advances in intra-uterine therapy and surgery that can be beneficial to the embryo, the rights of the mother may in future be diminished, especially if separate doctors are treating mother and embryo and wanting to fulfil their moral and legal duties to each.[35] It was feared that gene therapy, using embryonic tissues, would lead religious groups to attempt to redefine the legal status of the embryo. This would create problems for women carrying an 'abnormal' foetus; women needing treatment that might threaten her foetus; and for pregnant women generally who might be forced to protect their foetus by law.[36]

A small number of feminists have argued that increasing embryo status did not necessarily threaten women's rights. Such feminists are harder to categorise, but were more likely to be radical and French. They did not involve themselves directly in parliamentary lobbying or take account of the threat to abortion rights. They therefore saw it as 'humanitarian' to prevent commercial and medical experimentation on embryos,[37] and to prevent any attempts at what they saw as 'eugenicism'.[38] Although embryos were not as much persons as their mothers, nor were they mere bunches of cells whose disposal required no respect for human dignity. This was not only because embryos might arguably be capable of suffering, but because the fate of other 'less than full persons' such as the comatose or the handicapped depended on how we decided to treat the embryo.[39] Some believed that defining legal status for frozen embryos would define general 'humanness' and prevent eugenicist research. Such arguments were seen less often in the UK, where there was a more tangible political threat to abortion rights due to the political expediency of the Thatcher government in 1990.

For the most part, however, feminists have viewed embryo rights as a threat to women's rights and have argued against any proposals for protection of the embryo. They have contended that women, rather than medical professionals, should retain rights over embryos for as long as these depended on women's bodies for their continued development,[40] and that, consequently, any law should only state who would make decisions on research rather than establishing status for the embryo. Thus the MFPF conference in 1988 concluded that the debate must be transferred away from protecting the rights of the embryo to those of women.

On the effect on abortion rights

In both countries many feminists would agree with the philosopher John Harris on 'personhood'[41] that legalised abortion gives women the choice of whether to bear children or abort them; they argue that a woman is definitely a person, whereas an embryo may not be. Therefore, they cannot see how the choice of the woman can *ever* be subordinate to the life of the embryo and believe it to be hypocritical to allow abortion in some cases and not in others. Thus feminists have made connections between their criticism of embryo status and the effect such increased status might have on abortion rights.

But this link was not made universally by feminists, particularly not French feminists, nor by infertile patients themselves. Though some made this connection, it was also of relatively less importance in debates on assisted conception than issues of access or embryo research. Earlier fervent and mass debate on abortion contrasts with the type of debate seen on assisted conception by campaigners. Why were these differences apparent? The abortion and contraception issues came to a head after 100 years of discussion. It was simpler to grasp abortion techniques and their use of technology, as well as their possible effects on women. Perhaps abortion and assisted conception also differ because of the generation gap between women who go through IVF failure and those much younger women who are more likely to be actively mobilised in demonstrations which have often been organised by networks of university students and graduates. Other potential campaigners – infertile women themselves – may have been too exhausted to get involved because treatment is so arduous or have been convinced of the positive media image given to contraception.[42] Nor would such patients have wanted to alienate their doctors by complaining mid-treatment. With time, the earlier generation of feminists from the 1960s and 1970s had also changed their views on motherhood – by the time they were in their thirties they were more in favour of having children, thus putting infertility and assisted conception onto the agenda. Thus abortion did not become a central issue in debates, despite the risks posed by increased embryo status.

Most importantly, the issues around assisted conception were so numerous and complex that it was easy for feminists to disagree on them. This was especially the case during the 1970s and 1980s after the second-wave feminist movement split into different strands, each with its own loyalties.

In France, abortion was not linked by feminists to assisted conception to as great an extent as in the UK. The possible reasons for this are unclear. At the MFPF conference in 1988, for example, Gavarini argued that abortion and assisted conception were fundamentally different: the foetus had material and ontological status, whereas the status of the embryo was merely theoretical and potential.[43] Dhavernas[44] was one of very few French feminists to recognise the inherent threat to abortion. She argued that this was coming from echography which allowed the foetus to be seen as if separate from the mother,[45] and medical exhortations to mothers to talk to their foetuses. There was no proof that this was a two-way exchange, in reality the foetus only existed if the mother allowed it by deciding to continue with her pregnancy. By separating the issues, French feminists who came out in support of the embryo do not appear to have taken into account the possible threats to women's autonomy of the linking of *in vitro* and *in vivo* rights.

The genesis of assisted-conception regulation: the battle for influence

As detailed in Chapter 1, the success of interest groups in the consultation period of the policy-making process depends to a large extent on the sort of group that they are. This is determined by their aims, membership, structure and methods. In addition, the resources they have access to will also determine how seriously they are taken by the government during campaigns. Analysis of this aspect of the policy-making arena is therefore important in order to assess influence on policy and legislation.

The same method of analysis is also a useful tool in examining groups that were in opposition to women's rights groups and their allies, namely religious groups particularly as well as some medical professionals. The structure of campaigning interest groups, and their allies, can then be analysed to ascertain how far women's rights campaigners had an alliance-building capacity or had an indirect influence on any legislation that resulted. Differences between the campaigns of both countries are striking, as the abortion issue became an important feature of debates in the UK and determined the tenor of campaigns, particularly as regards the input given by British feminist groups. In contrast to the issues of contraception and abortion, left-wing allies outside Parliament were less obviously an important part of the political environment within which campaigns around assisted conception took place. Arguably, this is because assisted conception came onto the political agenda and reached parliamentary debate in only a decade with the State appearing to feel an urgent need to respond and to formulate legislation. This also meant that there was no legal provision yet enacted against which feminists campaigned and which could form the legal backdrop to campaigns. Again, this contrasts with the contraception and abortion campaigns of both countries.

Feminists as interest groups

Groups active in this area were, broadly, either radical or liberal (this includes socialist) in nature. The majority of radical feminists in the UK and France believed that it was essential to persuade governments to outlaw assisted-conception practices altogether through radical pressure group action on the peripheries of any policy area, and to dissuade women from using assisted conception. The most active radical group internationally, with British and French members, was the Feminist International Network on Reproductive Rights and Genetic Engineering (FINRRAGE). The group published mainly in academic, feminist circles, including a journal, RAGE (Reproductive and Genetic Engineering), with international radical feminist contributors.[46]

Another radical group in the UK was the Women's Health and Reproductive Rights Information Centre (WHRRIC). This group came out of campaigns on abortion. In 1983 NAC split over the issue of widening campaigns from abortion to reproduction generally. From 1988 the new group was called WHRRIC.[47] It aimed to enable women to make informed choices in a woman-centred self-help framework.[48] Its particular concerns were the threat to abortion of embryo status and access to assisted conception for single and lesbian women, rather than the improvement of services for the infertile. It produced information, ran classes, conferences and provided counselling. Though it did provide some support for infertile women, probably because of the presence of at least one infertile woman on its staff,[49] because it was radical in nature it did not campaign. However, it did urge women to support campaigning organisations who were pro-choice (Co-ord, NAC), and who supported the rights of the infertile (the medical group PROGRESS, the National Association for the Childless), as well as the group FINRRAGE.

Both of these radical organisations criticised the Warnock Report for its tolerance of medical power and emphasis on embryo rights. Feminists of a more liberal persuasion were not averse to campaigning on assisted conception. Their lobbying in Parliament was centred on the issue of the access of single women to infertile services, particularly DI. They also campaigned in the UK on the issue of abortion in so far as it was affected by the issue of embryo status. Among those who campaigned, there was a consensus, especially among established pro-choice groups, that anti-abortionists not only objected to research on the embryo and wanted to establish legal status to protect the embryo, but that they were using this issue as a springboard to amend the Abortion Act. Initially, anti-abortionists continued their backbench attempts at this, but persuaded the government to enable parliamentary time to be set aside to ensure that MPs were able to vote on the issue. Liberal feminist campaigners on assisted conception, who were also pro-choice, thus allied themselves with those in favour of research from an early stage after the Warnock Report when they realised these dangers. In the process such groups allied with medical institutions, of which radical feminists were strongly critical. Thus the fertility specialists' group PROGRESS and abortion-choice groups campaigned together.

Women In Medicine (WIM) were committed from 1981 to improving the practice of medicine for women as doctors and patients; providing support and a political voice for their members; and countering discrimination against women in medicine. They were a national feminist network run by a collective for women doctors and medical students (but open to all sympathisers). They did not campaign nationally on the 1990 Act, but their London branch sent letters to MPs who had previously abstained from voting on the Alton Bill. They were helped with information from the Stop the Amendment Campaign (NAC) and the Campaign for Access to Donor Insemination (CADI). They corresponded with Lord Houghton, a Labour peer whose Bill aimed to divert attention from the proposed tabling of abortion amendment to the 1990 Act. Their campaigns essentially concerned the Early Day Motion 1324 on the denial of DI to lesbians and unmarried women.

Another liberal campaigning group was the Campaign for Ethics in Research (CERES), set up in 1989. It campaigned for medical research, including that associated with reproduction, to become safer and more efficient and to be more lay-centred. CERES was essentially women-led and funded by subscription. It was rather more liberal than radical feminist in its campaigning strategy, if not its aims. Its methods included lobbying government on Department of Health policy and responding to official reports, such as the Warnock Report. Despite its complaints about a lack of permanent representation, CERES became an accepted member of the wider policy community on research issues and was consulted on issues in the assisted conception arena of gene therapy, infertility treatment consent forms, Human Fertilisation and Embryology Authority (HUFEA) guidelines, and membership of local research committees.

Another set of groups to feature in the landscape of assisted-conception policy debate were those set up to offer support to the infertile. These were not feminist and their campaigns were low key. They had no real experience of campaigns involving Parliament and essentially lobbied at the local level.[50] Indeed, the small, mixed and non-feminist group, National Association for the Childless, only began to question medical power after the issue came to the fore.[51] Many of their aims coincided with those of medical professions. FACT (Fertility Action and Campaign for Treatment) argued that infertile women should be entitled to as many embryos as they could pay for as this constituted freedom of choice.

In France, by the 1980s, the feminist movement had very few interest group resources at all and there were many constraints on those they had. But, as in the UK, liberal feminists did have allies among the professions such as Marcus-Steiff, a sociologist who published attacks on the misleading nature of fertility clinics' success rates; Marie-Angèle Hermite, a pro-choice lawyer; and the IVF doctor Jacques Testart. A few feminists published in journals and books. They also held conferences, although this did not produce campaigns. Their active influence was therefore limited. Passively, their influence could only be indirect as they were neither formally consulted nor in the policy network.

From the early 1980s, individuals in France attempted to initiate a feminist debate on the issue. But debate only ever took place within academic circles, and mainly by radicals who were against government lobbying. For example, the influence of the (only indirectly feminist) Centre national de recherche scientifique (CNRS) academic research group on the government, which aimed to improve services, began to take effect only in 1990, and this after many years of using the media to criticise the misrepresentations of fertility treatment by the medical professions.[52]

A French feminist conference organised by the MFPF in June 1991 had little influence on the government. This international feminist conference was funded by the Women's Rights Ministry, among others, which showed interest in the issue of the improvement of services, but by this time unfortunately no longer enjoyed power or prestige within the government. However, along with the Ministry of Social Affairs which was involved in the authoring of government bills on assisted conception, it did fund a film at the conference depicting the plight of IVF patients. It is unlikely that their British counterparts would have done the same. The film presented a liberal point of view of improving services, as opposed to a radical one calling for the elimination of assisted conception.

The MFPF was invited by the media to publicise its position. It also lobbied the Comité Consultatif National d'Ethique (CCNE) annual public meeting, the Journées Nationales d'Ethique, and at meetings of the Parliamentary Higher Council of Sexual Information. However, in 1986 feminist writer, Decluze,[53] complained that the CCNE annual public meeting was not in reality a forum for public debate or consultation. The public were represented by only two parliamentary Deputies; the proportion of women was too small; and if anyone in the room posed an awkward question they were simply told that the CCNE disagreed or told the CCNE *might* consider that in the next session. Women members up to that time had also been criticised by feminists for representing professional interests only. Therefore those French feminists who aimed to improve infertility treatment rather than eradicate it hoped to persuade individuals chosen to sit on the CCNE or consulted by that body to campaign on their behalf. In this way a more satisfactory bill might be produced that took women's health into account.

For example, in 1989 the Women's Rights Ministry organised a consultation with those opposed to assisted conception (sociologists and doctors), IVF patients, IVF practitioners and lawyers. From this, they produced a document which took account of women's points of view as regards risks, dangers and the procedures involved. In charge of the 1989 document was a philosopher

Renée Dufourt who became a member of the CCNE in 1990 and it was then hoped by feminists that she might be the first member to represent women's interests.

Others responsible for the assisted-conception bills, notably the Communist member of the Conseil d'Etat Guy Braibant, were criticised for ignoring women. Only Franck Serusclat, Socialist Deputy, sent a representative to listen to critics of IVF, including feminists, whose opinions may well have influenced the content of his bill and later government committee reports to which he had contributed. Laborie spoke in July 1999 of women Deputies and ministers who were completely ignorant of feminist criticisms even by the late 1990s.

Infertile women also campaigned in France. The group Association Pauline et Adrienne was set up by an infertile woman, Chantal Ramogida, named after twins she gave birth to after treatment at a non-licensed clinic. When the government proposed to limit non-licensed centres, she campaigned on their behalf. She was supported by doctors and received 3,000 letters from infertile couples who criticised their treatment and the extra costs. The organisation received much media attention. It preferred infertile women to have as many IVF attempts as they wished without government regulation. The group, however, were also against abortion and were potential allies for the Roman Catholic lobby. This is despite the fact that they believed that they should control the amount of embryos implanted, thus discarding any 'spare' embryos. This group was consulted by the government as recently as 1999.[54]

Though there was, then, feminist interest group activity in France and Britain during legislative debates on assisted conception, these were restricted to the outer margins.

The medical professions and assisted conception

The activities of feminists' rivals, and sometime allies, were much more central. The majority of clinicians dealing with infertility were in favour of recent developments in reproductive technology. Such professionals argued in support of their own freedom to carry out such treatments in so far as these benefited medical progress and the psychosocial needs of infertile patients. These views were expressed both in writing and in parliamentary campaigning.

From the 1980s onwards, both the British and French governments largely sanctioned self-regulation and clinical discretion.[55] (Many clinicians continued to feel their discretion threatened, however.) This was further endorsed by the expressions of public confidence in the integrity of assisted conception practitioners, especially doctors treating the infertile. Much of the media coverage depicted pictures of contented parents and healthy babies. This was a useful resource.

The official medical position in the UK

An original aim of the important medical interest group PROGRESS (containing liberal feminists), was for one body to oversee IVF doctors.[56] The Medical Research Council (MRC), RCOG and PROGRESS took up the idea in response to the restrictive clauses of the Powell Bill of December 1984, which advocated that each IVF attempt should need the permission of the Secretary of State. To them a licensing body would instead give 'the greatest flexibility to allow new techniques, or advances in existing techniques, to be applied quickly and without constantly changing the law'.[57] It was also self-legitimising 'The setting up of such an Authority clearly demonstrates how committed the professions are to a critical assessment – from a clinical and medical research standpoint – of their work'.[58] They therefore drafted a new clause to the pro-life Powell Bill that would replace the authority of the Secretary of State with that of a statutory licensing authority that was independent and answerable to Parliament, to regulate and monitor practice in research and IVF services. The minister was not considered capable of this role as he would act alone, without medical qualification or advice and in a political manner. The SLA however would have 'a significant representation of scientific and medical interests among the membership',[59] and thus have access to such advice. To gain public confidence these medical interest groups suggested that lay interests should be substantially represented with a lay chairperson, who would be in a position to give ethical and moral guidance to practitioners and researchers. This was instituted in April 1985 as the VLA and the idea of Parliament recognising such a body and setting up a Statutory Licensing Authority became part of the pro-research medical campaign and was ultimately successful. Almost half of the original members of the VLA were women, however, including the chairperson, Dame Mary Donaldson GBE.[60]

The VLA, later the Interim Licensing Authority, therefore embodied the objectives proposed by the medical group PROGRESS: it had a Code of Practice on research related to human fertilisation and embryology; IVF researchers were approved and licensed; licensed centres were visited; reports were made for the MRC, RCOG and Parliament; each centre had a local ethical committee, which concomitantly reviewed research proposals; each separate research project was licensed; consent had to be given for treatment and disposal; no more than three embryos could be transferred into the uterus. It also distinguished in relation to research between embryos and conceptuses by referring to embryos before the age of 14 days as 'pre-embryos' in the ILA Guidelines of 1990. A proposal that was included in the Embryology Bill was the licensing of specific women to have IVF and embryo insertion. Challoner puts forward the case that the medical professions made much use of the media in the UK, including television chat shows and documentaries. Robert Winston, fertility specialist, became a household name, alongside those of Steptoe and Edwards. One pro-research BBC documentary was shown on a continuous loop at the House of Commons. The pro-research camp itself also profited from alliances with genetic researchers and the concurrent successes of two pregnancies which had used experimental preimplantation diagnosis. This gave an added boost to their arguments '(f)or here was the potential to ensure that no embryos with genetic diseases would ever get to the stage where abortion was an option'.[61]

Insemination and IVF in France: a difference in clinical opinion

IVF has largely been provided in France on a private basis (though reimbursed by the government). Its practitioners, including IVF pioneer René Frydman, have campaigned to retain the status quo and to avoid legislation.

DI has been provided, by contrast, in CECOS centres in a conservative and pronatalist fashion to childless couples where there was male 'medical' infertility. Differences are apparent between the arguments of doctors like Testart who criticised donation but advocated intra-cytoplasmic sperm injection (ICSI) within couples, and bodies such as CECOS whose members support gamete donation but who are critical of the use of ICSI without further research.[62]

These differences have weakened the position of DI doctors in debates.[63] However, the many organisations set up in France in the 1980s and 1990s to represent infertility specialists, both practitioners and researchers, have been able to settle such differences and consolidate in one organisation in the late 1990s, the French Federation for the Study of Reproduction (Fédération Française d'Etudes de la Reproduction).[64]

A moral minority

In both countries only a minority of doctors have spoken out against assisted conception. Their objections have been based largely on moral grounds in defence of the embryo. Such doctors have often had personal connections to the Roman Catholic Church or the pro-life movement. In moralising tones they have expressed misgivings about the ease with which couples could use assisted conception, and accused them of using it for convenience.[65] The pro-life medical group Association des médecins pour le respect de la vie sought judicial review of the government decrees of 8 April 1988 on gamete donation. The Conseil d'Etat, however, on 21 July 1989 ruled that the decrees were admissible. This is an example of pro-life doctors in France attempting to use the courts as one of their lobbying methods.[66] More importantly, however, their membership of government bodies such as the CCNE has ensured that their opinions have been officially sanctioned.

Medical and feminist lobbying

In the UK allegiances between doctors and feminists were forged on the related issues of embryo research and abortion, but those feminists who wanted to see an improvement in services found allies here too. An IVF doctor in the UK complained that due to the lack of resources allotted to the treatment, 'By a chapter of accidents rather than any sinister design of its own the medical profession does indeed find itself cornered into the position of selectively breeding from the childless of the UK on no other basis than their ability to pay'.[67] They also advocated independent and skilled counselling.[68] Most IVF doctors, however, preferred self-regulation to legislation. In lobbying, medical professionals naturally focused their activities on issues which directly concerned them and the joint lobbying of feminists and clinicians was essentially a partnership of convenience. This involved service provision, and especially government attempts at regulation of embryo research.

The British campaigning group PROGRESS dates from summer 1985 and its first propositions were echoes of liberal feminist demands in that they advocated research into causes of infertility; services to be free of charge and without restriction; with no time limit on embryo research; or any embryo status. PROGRESS also advocated that the fewer legal changes there were, the better. They also wondered who would control the controllers, which, as has been noted, led to the setting up of the VLA.

PROGRESS was an umbrella group concerned with infertility and with disability, genetic malformations and embryo research modelled on Co-ord in response to the Warnock Report and possible legislation, such as the Powell and Duke of Norfolk Private Member's Bills. Its founding members included WHRRIC, ALRA, the MRC, BPAS, gynaecologists (including the fertility specialists Peter Baude and Robert Winston), geneticists, embryologists, lawyers, the FPA, MPs from both sides, MENCAP, BCC and Labour Abortion Rights Campaign (LARC).[69] Later it was supported by Baroness Warnock and the BMA.[70]

Member organisations campaigned at the local level with MPs and the press to counter the LIFE and SPUC pro-life lobby. They attempted to arouse sympathy by detailing the need for embryo research to improve IVF and to prevent congenital handicap.[71]

In France, media attention was given to critics who were sociologists and feminists, when renowned IVF doctor Jacques Testart, who, with René Frydman, produced the first 'test-tube baby' in France in 1982, published a book in 1986 advocating a moratorium on research, and one in 1992 criticising the eugenicism of the new technologies.[72]

He denounced with them the low success rates, health risks and lack of regulation of IVF treatment, medical power and misrepresentations, potential effects on future children, and the issue of treatments being allegedly used by people for reasons of convenience rather than for medical treatment. This resulted in a public debate between objectioners and practitioners.[73] Testart attacked practitioners, who were members of the policy community and therefore could initiate change and allow opposition or open objective debate, but tolerated neither, even among the medical profession, and certainly not from outsiders such as sociologists, 'Ils feignent de répondre à nos arguments, mais ne font que défendre leur désir de continuer à fonctionner entre soi, dans l'autosatisfaction et le corporatisme'.[74] Testart pointed out that the development of assisted-conception technologies was forging ahead without their effects on society having been thoroughly researched. Such effects could be physical or mental for those IVF children, who had been sexually selected or narcissistically cloned, for example. Similar effects could be felt by traumatised unsuccessful infertile patients. Equally, assisted conception could have social and eugenic effects. The government in turn was criticised by Testart for allowing this to happen. Their guidelines were seen as being 'too little, too late': 'Faut-il préciser que ces règles minimums ne sont pas respectées partout, et que personne ne s'en inquiète?'.[75] He went as far as to say car mechanics would not treat cars the way IVF doctors treated women.

In 1999 Testart remained critical of the relentless pursuit of science. In this way he continued to share the criticisms of feminists. However, he was conservative and paternalist on certain issues. He advocated gamete research rather than embryo research.[76] He was critical of the French licensing authority set up by the 1994 bioethics laws and of the CNMBRDP for their lack of medically qualified and autonomous members as it made them less likely to refuse to award licences.[77] For him, embryo research and pre-implatation genetic diagnosis (PID) were eugenic, and fertility treatment should be given ideally to fulfil the desires of a particular couple to procreate. Testart was therefore a supporter of the experimental ICSI treatment (which fertilises an ovum using one motile sperm), because it promoted procreation within a couple and avoided donation.[78] A feminist alliance with such a clinician, even radical feminist, might well sit strangely.

Religious opinion on assisted conception

Religious and moral opposition to assisted conception has been very much in evidence during parliamentary debates in both the UK and France. Despite calls by feminists to place women at the centre of debate on assisted conception, in both countries much of the discussion held by religious groups has centred on the rights of the embryo. Women can defend themselves, embryos cannot, they argue. Fears of eugenicism and, especially on the Continent, memories of Nazi human experimentation, have led to a demand for caution. This has meant that religious groups, particularly the Roman Catholic Church in France and the Anglican Church in the UK, have been accorded a privileged position within the policy community, more so indeed than on the previous two conscience issues of contraception and abortion.

The Roman Catholic Church in France and in the UK has objected to the unnatural use of artificial insemination by the husband (AIH) or by a donor (DI), to ovum or embryo donation and to surrogacy (womb lending or leasing). It has objected to the masturbatory act involved in AIH, and does not believe in any third party being involved in the act of procreation by a married couple, especially when that third party's genes are brought into the family. This is seen as a potential source of dissension and disunity.

In relation to the question of embryo rights and protection, mainstream Roman Catholicism has emphasised that life is 'a gift from God' and is therefore sacred. Life is also seen to begin at conception when a unique individual with its own genetic patterns and soul is created. Thus any attempt to end life after conception is seen as sinful. The only exception permitted by the Church is that of an operation to remove a cancerous womb from a pregnant woman which inadvertently kills the foetus or embryo, because here the primary purpose of the operation is to remove the cancer. This is evidenced by publications from the French Roman Catholic Church such as a document in 1984 from the Commission épiscopale de la famille,[79] and a Papal Encyclical in March 1995, *Evangelum vitae*, which called the use of human embryos or foetuses as objects of experiments a crime against their human dignity.

The Protestant Church has been much less critical of assisted conception. It has merely stressed the need for donors and recipients to be aware of the responsibilities of their actions. In this vein, it has stressed the need for the ensuing child to trace its genetic parents. Non-Catholic Christian Churches, such as the Anglican Church, have accepted contraception and abortion to save the mother's life even though they believe that the embryo deserves respect as an ensouled individual, although not necessarily from conception. The French Protestant Church has appealed for the affective side of reproduction to be emphasised more often and for the possibility of adoption to be made easier. However, assisted conception has been approved of as a method of helping infertile couples as long as it is strictly regulated to allow for counselling, with strict criteria on infertility and status, and anonymous and non-commercial donations.[80]

Religious groups and lobbying

The pro-life lobby would appear to have had much less influence in the UK than in France. British Roman Catholics, who have played an important role in this lobbying group, have not enjoyed the status of being members of the policy community as their French counterparts have. Roman Catholicism is a minority religion in Britain. Additionally, throughout history, British Roman Catholics have had less status as the shadow of the religious 'Troubles' in Northern Ireland has hung over successive governments who have considered consultation with Roman Catholic groups, relationship management with Northern Irish Protestants has thus been safeguarded. The animosity of the British general public toward Roman Catholics led to the organisation SPUC feeling it expedient to have a separate identity from the Roman Catholic Church in order to attract more support for its pro-life arguments. Indeed, Pfeffer (interview, 1991) argued that the very reason Roman Catholics, particularly those within the organisation LIFE, have themselves campaigned so vigorously on abortion and the embryo issue was due to their feeling of exclusion from British politics generally.

Groups in the UK who campaigned against embryo research thus had to concentrate on public pressure and parliamentary lobbying in opposition to assisted conception. Within a year of the Warnock Report, Enoch Powell MP introduced a Private Member's Bill, the Infant Life (Protection) Bill (1985) attempting to ban all embryo research and severely restrict IVF provision. The Bill ran out of time at Second Reading. This inaugurated an anti-research campaign to ban embryo research and to reduce the time limit for abortion, which was supported by the Roman Catholic Church, SPUC and LIFE and was militant, tightly organised and well-funded. Sensational tactics included the posting of a full-size plastic model of a twenty-week old foetus to all MPs on the morning of the House of Commons debate on embryo research. Personal abuse of opponents was also common.[81] This was often counter-productive as it was considered unreasonable by the MPs voting on the issues.

Pro-life groups in France also argued that dangers are inherent for the human embryo in the provision of assisted conception and embryo research, as well as abortion. They have also therefore argued in favour of the restriction of assisted conception through legislation. By contrast, however, the French government insisted that the question of abortion would not be brought up in Parliament. Without this their lobbying scope was much more limited than that of their British counterparts.

Assisted-conception regulation: the government response

It took less than a decade for the issue of assisted conception to reach the parliamentary agenda, in contrast to the much longer time taken for the issues of contraception and abortion. Throughout this time, and in both countries, there has been continuous formal debate and report-writing involving interest groups, both insiders and lobbying outsiders. In addition there has been parliamentary debate in both countries which interest groups have attempted to lobby. Despite these forums the policy network members on this issue – composed largely of religious groups, pronatalists in France, and the medical professions – appear to have been recognised and consulted. Thus the pre-existing health policy network was in effect simply extended to take on board the assisted-conception issue. Pronatalism has been much less apparent within political parties at the end of the century. Assisted conception has been seen essentially as a moral or more particularly a medical issue rather than one of women's rights.[82]

Before the development of IVF from 1978, treatment available for infertility was rudimentary. Much of this was limited to basic investigations to discover whether the cause could be found. Any subsequent treatment was limited to such things as DI. In her very informative analysis of the political history of reproductive medicine, Naomi Pfeffer details how in the 1950s the Feversham Committee was appointed by the UK government to examine the law on donor insemination after the 1958 *Maclennan* divorce case in Scotland (*see* Chapter 6) found that DI without the husband's consent did not constitute adultery. The Feversham *Report of the Official Departmental Committee on Human Artificial Insemination* noted that 1,150 DI children were then living in the UK. However, infertility treatment was far from widely available. Only a handful of British doctors claimed to offer DI in 1948, and only twenty in 1958.[83]

Despite this lack of provision, Pfeffer details the widespread condemnation of such treatments by the British public particularly as fears about male virility were fuelled by the idea of male infertility and the need for donor insemination. Although contraceptive treatment was funded by the NHS after its reorganisation of 1974, infertility treatment was not included in this provision. What treatment there was, therefore, was largely available only from private consultants. This was the case until the early 1980s in the UK.

In France, in contrast to the UK, both DI and IVF were fully reimbursed by the French state from the late 1970s. Sterility was seen as an illness in France, with assisted conception as one form of 'cure'. Indeed, it was during debates on the 1975 abortion law that the policy of state funding for sterility was initiated in order to appease pronatalists in Parliament.

There has been much demand for treatment in both countries. In 1996, 5,397 children were born as a result of assisted conception in the UK with a live birth rate of 14.7 per cent per treatment cycle.[84] In France between 1973 and 1990, 20,000 DI babies were born through the CECOS, and between 1982 and 1999, 40,000 treatment cycles were carried out successfully. In 1988, as much assisted-conception treatment was carried out in France as was carried out in the USA, whose population is five times greater, and 80 per cent of this was IVF treatment.[85]

There have also been long waiting lists for treatment in both countries. This has been particularly evident in the UK at the few clinics that have offered infertility treatment on the NHS since the late 1980s. Medical professionals in clinics have therefore been able to impose their own strict criteria. These have been based on age, length of time infertile, weight and length of time in a stable heterosexual relationship. Such criteria arguably border on the social rather than the medical, and are often based on criteria for adoption. Indeed, clinical self-regulation has been the norm for assisted-conception provision. The rather moralistic French association, CECOS, has, for example, enjoyed a monopoly of frozen-sperm provision to IVF clinics and of donor insemination treatment, despite being self-regulated for many years.

The UK's Warnock Report of 1984 (*Report of the Committee of Inquiry into Human Fertilisation and Embryology*, Cmnd 9314) showed a clear bias towards the arguments proposed by the medical professions from the beginning. Warnock advocated that both private and public services should continue, though with more attention being given by health authorities to the setting-up of NHS infertility clinics with counselling and full, informed consent in writing. All clinics would be regulated by a statutory licensing authority with a lay chairman and significant lay representation.

The only issue the British government felt strongly enough about to legislate on immediately was commercial surrogacy, and this led to the Surrogacy Arrangements Act 1985, apparently in the face of media coverage of surrogacy procedures such as that involving the British surrogate Kim Cotton.[86] Other aspects were regulated by the medical professions themselves until the passing of the Human Fertilisation and Embryology Act 1990. The government did publish two further consultation documents in the interim – a Green Paper (Cm. 46) and a White Paper in 1987 (Cm. 259),[87] which closely followed Warnock in most details. There were two formal rounds of consultation on the Warnock Report initiated by the Department of Health. The first of these was immediately after the Report was published in July 1984. The second came with the publication of the Green Paper which asked for opinions on, *inter alia*, licensing systems and donor anonymity. Both these consultation exercises had a very large response from the medical and scientific bodies, pro-life groups, adoption and child care organisations, voluntary organisations, women's groups, churches and legal bodies. In addition, some informal consultations were held with the medical groups MRC or RCOG on particular detailed administrative points of policy. There were also a number of informal consultations with the interim licensing authority to tap into their experience of licensing embryo research and infertility treatments. The White Paper then came out in support of a statutory licensing authority. A clear medical influence can therefore be seen.

In debates in Parliament on the Warnock Report and White Paper, MPs concentrated on embryo research as well as surrogacy – the issue of infertility services was not seen as particularly important at this time. Both research and surrogacy were seen as objectionable practices – most of those who spoke out at this stage expressed fears of the consequences of research and commercial surrogacy for the embryo and child.

Embryo research and abortion apart, the rest of the bill was a straightforward government measure on which the government's proposals had been set out in the 1987 White Paper. Some comment on that was received but in fact public attention and the parliamentary debates focused predominantly on the two 'conscience' issues, to the extent that there was relatively little consideration of the other issues. The one exception to that is perhaps the issue of the availability of information about donors. Here the medical bodies who were involved in infertility treatment were firmly in favour of anonymity to ensure the supply of donated sperm necessary to retain the high number of treatments that were carried out. Bodies like the British Agencies for Adoption and Fostering and the British Association for Social Workers took the opposite position, feeling that it was not in the interests of the child. Here the British government came out in support of medical arguments by retaining donor anonymity and by preventing any retroactivity should Parliament eventually remove donor anonymity. Again medical influence can clearly be seen.[88]

The influence of religious groups during parliamentary debates is also in evidence. Such groups advocated limits to treatment in relation to embryo research and access. The government itself did not take a stance on research, but notice was taken of religious arguments about the importance of the research issue when the government decided to leave the issue to a free vote in Parliament, as a 'conscience issue' with the rare procedure of having a section on research with alternative clauses on which MPs were to vote. Additionally, the only real amendment to the original bill was that on the welfare of the child, with account having to be taken of that child's need for a father. Furthermore, in contrast to France, religious groups also persuaded the government to debate and amend the 1967 Abortion Act.

Major commissions that included members of both the National Assembly and the Senate were set up by French governments to examine assisted conception and to produce reports. On 25 February 1983 President Mitterrand had set up by decree the permanent national ethics committee, the CCNE.[89] The task of the CCNE was to give 'Avis' on any moral problems arising from research in biology, medicine and health.[90] These Avis were not meant to have the force of law (under Article 34 of the Constitution only Parliament could formulate law on fundamental civil liberties). They were attempts to form a moral basis for future legislation and practice as it developed[91] and many followed a pro-nuclear family line. Before each Avis, much private consultation took place with interest groups invited to contribute their opinions.[92] With the backing of the CCNE, and at the behest of the then Prime Minister, Jacques Chirac, the Conseil d'Etat produced a report along largely similar lines, on 25 March 1988, entitled *Sciences de la vie: de l'éthique au droit*.

Six months later, in September of 1988 the new Prime Minister, Michel Rocard, requested a member of the Conseil d'Etat, Guy Braibant, to head an interdisciplinary group and prepare a Green Paper ('avant projet de loi') on 'bioethics and the rights of man', to pre-empt the possibility of backbencher bills being tabled.[93] The Braibant Report was published in March 1989 and entitled *Sciences de la vie et droits de l'homme*. It was based primarily on the CCNE findings except that it was not deemed that the human person deserved respect from conception. It would have strictly regulated the practice of assisted-conception treatment within a wide framework of new rights relating to bioethics and the human body. The principles behind it were that assisted conception could only be a cure for infertility, not as a method of convenience; that a child needed a father and a mother; that individual desires could not be respected ad infinitum; and that the legal status of children born as a result of assisted conception should equal that of other children. The relationship between women's rights and assisted conception, and issues such as the adverse effects of reproductive technologies on women's health, were not directly addressed.

In 1989 and 1990 the Ministries affected by the Braibant Report disagreed over whether it should be put before Parliament as they wanted further debate. Their criticisms were endorsed by the Conseil d'Etat, the CCNE, the Prime Minister and, most notably, representatives of the medical profession. The legislation on assisted conception was further divided by government Ministries into three separate bills in 1992 (No. 2599, Sapin Bill, on donation; No. 2600, Bianco Bill, on use of the human body; and No. 2601, Curien Bill, on data use). Additional reports were then commissioned to allow parliamentary debate and consultation to take place. This resulted in the Lenoir Commission (1991), Bioulac Commission (1992), Serusclat/OPECST Commission (1992).[94] Though often of a different nature or political persuasion these bodies reached very similar conclusions based on pre-existing Code law and medical ethics and advocated that assisted-conception treatment be given only within a framework of consent, anonymity, non-commercialisation and the parental undertaking of a particular couple or 'projet parental'.

The three draft bills on bioethics themselves were debated and approved by the National Assembly in late November 1992, with the majority of the

RPR, UDC and UDF abstaining.[95] They were blocked by the Senate however. It was the Mattei Report in 1993, authored by the Roman-Catholic medical politician, and arguably his own personal pleadings in Parliament that the embryo would not be harmed by assisted conception which ensured the passing of the bioethics laws in 1994.[96]

These are due for full re-examination by both Houses in France in 2002/3. To this end OPECST was commissioned once again at the end of 1998 to carry out consultations in order to assess the working of the 1994 laws in relation to scientific progress and to inform Parliament. All those selected for consultation by OPECST were representative of their profession or from a group representing a particular medical complaint: a small number of groups representing transplant societies, the infertile, lawyers, ethicists and government quangos such as the CCNE. The vast majority of the interviewees were medically qualified or medical practitioners. The Conseil d'Etat also produced a Report in May 2000 entitled *Les lois bioéthiques: cinq ans apres*, which set out what the Council thought the most pressing issues to be debated during any re-examination of the 1994 bioethics laws.[97] It asked whether reproductive cloning ought to be prohibited. Should embryo research be authorised? On what therapeutic grounds? And how would this fit with the idea of protecting the *in vitro* embryo? How could genetic engineering avoid bringing about discrimination? How to square the European Directive of 6 July 1998 on patenting of biotechnological inventions with the idea, important with respect of French constitutional law, of the non-commercialisation of the human genome? Such questions may provide a framework for any parliamentary debate which takes place in the near future. It illustrates the wide-ranging perspective on bioethics taken by the French in debates, though shows an ignorance of any concerns that may have been being expressed by women patients.

Why did the French take so much longer than the British to legislate on assisted conception? The establishment of the many advisory bodies of the 1980s served to forestall legislation for numerous reasons. Though in the UK, Royal Commissions and their like have been used on occasions to study social issues, such institutions as the Braibant and Lenoir Commissions were unusual and unfamiliar in France. Indeed, the Braibant Commission was considered a type of institution worthy of the formulation of legislation on human rights to commemorate the 200th anniversary in 1989 of the Declaration of the Rights of Man of the French Revolution of 1789.

The Reports published by these various bodies were also legal firsts for France. They were ambitious and far-reaching, involving lengthy and in-depth interest group consultation. They contained ethical and medical principles which were not covered by their British counterparts, such as organ donation and computer databanks. The scope of the legislation increased the amount of possible objections to any parliamentary assisted conception based on it and further delayed their legal resolution.[98]

The French legal system is a finely balanced codified system which attempts to cater for all eventualities before they arise. In cases before the courts, the law is applied rather than interpreted and is meant to be read as a coherent whole. Any change to the law thus has the potential to upset that balance which has discouraged legal commentators from endorsing change. Law on assisted conception would have had repercussions for this balance especially as the medicine behind it appeared to be continually throwing up new legal quandaries that needed to be resolved. Moreover, codified law necessitated a parliamentary and public consensus that on assisted conception proved difficult to obtain. It was more difficult therefore for the French to legislate on assisted conception. The Conseil d'Etat itself pointed this out in its Report of March 1988.

Finally, fundamental to any legal solution sought by commissions in France was the need to take account of the numerous far-reaching legal principles upon which French law was based particularly in relation to human rights and therefore inherent in any legal framework set up to deal with assisted conception. The legal principles that formed the foundation of the Braibant Report in 1989, for example, and which have been enumerated by successive commissions were: the right to respect of one's body ('droit au respect de son corps'); consent before the use or handling of one's body ('nul ne peut porter atteinte à l'intégrité du corps humain sans le consentement de l'intéressé'); the special nature of human parts and organs such that they cannot be assimilated to other heritable goods ('les organes et les produits du corps humain ne peut faire l'objet d'un droit patrimonial); the dignity of a dead or living person; the respect of existing family structures; the right to treatment; the right to a private life; freedom of research; and the protection of the human race. Such issues may well have been more relevant during UK parliamentary debates had the Human Rights Act 1998 then been in force. It may well be deemed of importance in any future case involving assisted conception and rights.

Debate at the parliamentary stage highlights the opinions of interest groups and members of the policy community in relation to the specific aspects of assisted conception treatment. The extent to which these opinions were supported by Parliamentary and legislative bodies reveals their influence on the final content of the bioethics laws of both countries.

Donation

On the issue of donation in the UK, at the Report Stage a motion for more information to be made available to DI children was defeated – it had been supported by groups such as adoption and infertility organisations, with counselling for donors and recipient parents.[99] It was therefore the medical professions who were influential here.

With the French law on donation in December 1991, there was no parliamentary debate as it was inspired by the Health Ministry. There was however intense media debate at the time, which praised CECOS methods. CECOS influence is also evidenced by the content of the law in that fresh sperm was banned, AIDS and HIV were to be tested for, and donations limited in number. IVF doctors appear to have been less influential on this issue as patenting of human body tissues and organ traffic were banned as a result of the lobbying of religious groups. Similarly, the Sapin and Bianco Bills of 1992 followed a CECOS framework of non-commercialisation, anonymity and filiation. Boutin, Roman Catholic Centrist Deputy, tried to introduce an amendment to prevent donor anonymity and allow DI children to know their origins. This was rejected so as not to deter donors and to give the social father precedence over the biological father. However, sanctions were reinforced. This points to the influence of religious groups.

Much criticism of the French regulation of donation was evident in 1999. Lawyers and psychologists argued forcefully against anonymous donation and of the need for a child to know its origins. In their view, the bioethics laws favour the best interests of the adult patient rather than the ensuing child.[100] CECOS also pointed out to OPECST in 1999 that the law could be changed to reflect the practice in CECOS clinics of allowing donors to be single people as well as those in couples, reflecting the increase in numbers of single people in French society at the end of the 1990s.

Government organisations such as the CCNE and the CNMBRDP, alongside clinicians and infertile patients' groups, also pointed out the shortcomings of the regulation of egg donation after 1994 as the amount of potential donors was drastically reduced.[101] CECOS indicated to the OPECST Commission that they had evidence of the unlawful donation of ova as a result of ova donors' expenses not being met and advertising being banned. Ova donation from a stranger was very rare and IVF couples were reluctant to donate their own. Couples were therefore being encouraged by clinicians to find ova donors, which flouted the rules on anonymity. Couples were also paying ova donors' expenses.

OPECST in 1999 described in detail how the prevalence of ICSI treatment in France would soon surpass that of DI and might soon obviate the need for donors. In fact the law encouraged the use of ICSI to the detriment of patients as it only allowed recourse to a donor after treatments using the couple's gametes had been exhausted. Both the CCNE and Dr Jegou, a member of the medical group INSERM (Institut National de la Santé et de la Recherche Scientifique), pointed out how ICSI treatments were not being followed up and their use was being sanctioned. This, despite the necessary safeguards such as animal research not having been carried out. The risks of ICSI – male sterility and genetic abnormalities – were not being fully explained to couples that were offered the treatment.[102] This critique of the use of ICSI was a criticism of the medical professions and their practice. As indicated earlier, the medical professions themselves are split on this issue in France. Although a government body is critical of practitioners in this respect, their arguments indicate that they are seeking to protect the interests of the child rather then the women patients who are undergoing experimental treatment. As it is primarily religious bodies who have sought to 'protect the child', then their influence as opposed to that of feminists is evident here.

Access

In the UK an attempt was made during the final debate in the HL by Lady Saltoun to restrict access to DI to married couples, to prevent access to single women and lesbians. Generally, debate in the HL concentrated on the short-comings of single mothers, but prejudice against homosexual parenting was also apparent. This was defeated by only one vote and ensured government notice of the issue in the House of Commons. This led in turn to a requirement in the Code of Practice for account to be taken of the welfare of the resulting child and any existing children when considering the suitability of patients for such treatments. This was then strengthened at the Report Stage in the House of Commons by an amendment which defined that welfare as the need of the child for a father. This may rule out single or homosexual potential parents though other family members can be considered as a substitute. A pervasive conservative and religious influence is therefore apparent.

The French went even further than the British in restricting the access of single women and homosexuals not only to DI but also to all types of treatment by applying a new term to assisted-conception treatments, in that they had to be part of a 'projet parental'. This was all-encompassing and covered the donation as well as the use of gametes but especially restricted access. The Minister of Health, Bernard Kouchner, proposed in the Bioulac Report that Article L. 671–2 of the Public Health Code could be rewritten so that the term 'sterility' was replaced by 'infertility', in order to limit assisted conception to couples both of whom are of the right age to procreate, living and consenting.[103] He argued that allowing postmortem insemination would put into question the basic principles of the bioethics Bills, and stated his opinion that procreation involved two people but death was never part of the equation '(u)n enfant se fait à deux, mais pas avec le mort'.[104] Furthermore, OPECST suggested amend-ments to Article 1 of the Bianco Bill that assisted conception could only be for the specific 'projet parental' of a couple. In relation to donation, both couples must be living and 'consenting' at the time of treatment.[105] An even greater religious influence is therefore apparent in France on the issue of the welfare of the child and parenthood than in the UK.

OPECST in 1999 argued for a clearer definition of infertility among practitioners in France with criteria being established that would be followed across the country.[106] This criticism of clinical discretion might well be strongly objected to during any re-examination by Parliament, and indicates some influence of those more generally critical of clinical practice such as feminists, or as is perhaps more likely, religious groups. Arguments put forward by more liberal commentators on infertility practice in France, included that by Chantal Ramogida who advocated that the cohabitation period, necessary under the 1994 laws before couples were given access to treatment, be reduced from two years to one year for older couples.[107] Such arguments put forward by the infertile were ostensibly ignored, however, in the final Bioulac Report. One interesting contrast to treatment in the UK is that women up to the age of 42 have access to IVF and are reimbursed in France, and indeed OPECST noted that, according to medical opinion, this might still be too young.[108] A victory for liberal feminists and infertility patients, perhaps, then. Or perhaps for pronatalists.

In vitro fertilisation

It is on the issue of IVF services, which particularly affects women, on which liberal feminists have principally campaigned. Although at the time of writing, GIFT is now used less often as a treatment for infertility, the passage of this issue through the British Parliament is informative. At the Committee stages, members of both Houses put forward amendments for GIFT to be included in debates, with the Standing Committee dividing equally for and against. It was the Health Minister, Virginia Bottomley, who made it clear that the government would resist the inclusion of GIFT and Lord Mackay complained that including it was far beyond the original intention of regulation in the White Paper.[109] This is despite the fact that GIFT shares the same risks and ethical problems as other treatments and needs regulation. Some have argued that it was excluded solely at the behest of the medical professions

> In respect of GIFT alone the government developed an extraordinary auditory defect. The careful formulation of policy advice based on scientific or biological criteria from interested parties such as the ILA, MRC, embryologists, and those working in infertility, threatened to deafen those who came with an open mind and to drown out the issues of philosophy and ethics to which the legislators were more properly tuned. With GIFT that advice went unheeded.[110]

In relation to the improvement of services, the British Labour party were in favour of creating more infertility services on the NHS [111] and tabled an amendment during debate on the 1990 Act aimed at forcing regional health authorities to improve their record on provision.[112] Labour MP Frank Dobson sent out questionnaires to IVF clinics in the UK, and produced a report entitled *Infertility Services in the NHS: What's Going on?*. It concluded that under-funding was 'having serious consequences on staff morale and patient well-being throughout the UK'. [113] However, left-wing and feminist campaigns to improve access to services in this way failed.

In France, some notice was taken of criticisms from feminists and their allies about the dangers of the unproven treatments for women patients. The CCNE in May 1984 wanted to stop any more clinics being set up as they considered IVF to be a serious, costly, risky technique that laid too much emphasis on reproduction. In December 1986 the CCNE recommended that IVF centres should be licensed and approved of by the CCNE, with frequent inspections. Due to the experimental and onerous nature of IVF they advised that more emphasis be laid on other treatments and the causes of infertility. In addition, the government wanted to add to the membership of CNMBRDP so that besides practitioners, there would be representatives of affected administrations, and family associations, though here perhaps increasing the influence of religious groups as opposed to that of women's rights campaigners.[114]

Unfortunately, much criticism still appeared in the OPECST Report of 1999 of the licensing instigated under the 1994 bioethics laws: the CNMBRDP was targeted for lacking in numbers of qualified staff with which to administer licenses. This body itself complained in 1997 that practitioners were continuing to carry out unlicensed activities due to the ineffectiveness of the licensing system. CECOS director, Pierre Jouannet, suggested that the French adopt an autonomous body akin to the UK's HFEA with public consultation and the setting out of a national Code of Practice.

Another aspect of fertility treatment to come under fire from OPECST, the CCNE, the Conseil de l'Ordre, and the National Medical Association, the ANM, in 1999 was the lack of regulation of ovarian hormonal stimulation in the bioethics laws. Its dangers for women's health were pointed out and the fact that it was being prescribed for women by non-licensed clinicians in the doctor's surgery.[115] Arguably, this shows the influence of feminist criticisms of the dangers of hormonal stimulation. Unfortunately, it was not until medical groups made the same criticisms that the government took notice.

Surrogacy

The UK's Surrogacy Arrangements Act 1985 left much discretion to voluntary agencies to administer surrogacy in a non-professional, non-regulated and non-monitored way. The statute was passed in Parliament relatively hastily in the face of public and media exposure of commercial surrogacy arrangements being carried out in Britain at this time, particularly that involving Kim Cotton. Fears were expressed during the 1990s that, in spite of the 1985 Act, problems remained. Margaret Brazier, for example, pointed to the disparity of financial bargaining power between the surrogate and the commissioning couple, the dangers of self-insemination for women and the lack of time for reflection by the surrogate about the handing over of the baby.[116]

Brazier was part of a team commissioned in October 1998 to investigate the practice and regulation of surrogacy in the UK, particularly the question of payments to surrogates. As with previous government debate on surrogacy, this was essentially a knee-jerk reaction to media coverage in 1996 and 1997.[117] They reported that there was a paucity of information on surrogacy due to it only being available from non-professional surrogate agencies, such the largest surrogacy agency in the UK, COTS founded by Kim Cotton. After consultation with groups involved in the surrogacy process, and official medical groups, the Commission recommended that payments to surrogate mothers should cover only genuine expenses and additional payments should be prohibited by legislation. Practice should be governed by a new law and Code of Practice which would be binding on registered agencies.[118] In the light of this report, Kim Cotton resigned from COTS in May 1999 arguing forcibly that surrogacy would be driven underground through a restriction on payments. Despite Kim Cotton's misgivings, the Brazier Report did avoid falling into the trap of assisted-conception regulation generally, by advocating social regulation of surrogacy, as opposed to its control being governed by clinical discretion.

In France both the government and Parliament strongly criticised surrogacy, particularly commercial surrogacy. It was particularly criticised by individual women parliamentarians as being exploitative of surrogates themselves and that laws should be amended to make adoption and paternity more favourable to infertile women, with more research undertaken into the causes of infertility.[119] These echoed some of the criticisms of women's rights campaigners themselves. Official government bodies such as the CCNE in 1984 and the Conseil d'Etat in 1988, however, criticised surrogacy from the point of view of the interests of the child. Both the case law outlawing commercial surrogacy and the Sapin Bill of 1992 were borne more out of the idea that the law should prohibit the 'trafficking' of children rather than out of support for women's rights.

Embryo research

In the UK it has been argued that 'The passage of the HFE Bill ... showed both Parliament and government successfully responding to a new situation, forced on them by the imperatives of science and medicine, through a combination of the traditional instruments of policy-making and a careful adaptation of Parliamentary procedures'. [120] The clause of the Bill that detailed the permissibility of embryo research was prepared in two alternative forms, one permitting research, the other forbidding it. Any other changes required a cumbersome amendment process. Hence it is hardly surprising that attention should focus predominantly on the clause on embryo research.

Throughout this time the pro-life lobby was sponsoring Private Member's Bills. The first was Enoch Powell's Unborn Children (Protection) Bill (18 January 1985), which was defeated but gained a Second Reading. This was followed by others of the same name in the House of Commons on 21 October 1985, 4 December 1985, 10 December 1986, 28 October 1987, May 1988, and in the House of Lords in February 1989 (which also got a Second Reading). Their aim was to ensure approval from the Secretary of State for IVF, and possession of the resulting embryo. IVF would only be available to married women and the only use that could be made of the embryo would be implantation, defective or not. This is despite the fact that implanting a defective embryo would have had serious implications for the women concerned. Moreover, IVF would have been impractical considering the demand for IVF and the variety of physical complications and treatments necessary for its success. Despite this, the Powell Bill received a Second Reading with a majority of 172.

The Warnock Report and the White Paper proposed that the embryo should be able to be bought and sold by licensed centres, but only to cover 'reasonable costs'.[121] The idea of a fourteen-day time limit for embryo research was put forward by the medical groups the BMA, MRC and Royal College of Physicians in both 1982 and 1983.[122] This received a resounding endorsement from MPs on 23 April 1990 by 364 votes to 193 (the vote was 234:80 in favour in the HL). Those who spoke in favour of research during the debate included the Health Secretary, Kenneth Clarke; his deputy, Virginia Bottomley; and the Labour spokeswomen Jo Richardson and Harriet Harman (the latter having argued for women's rights throughout debates on the Bill). Clarke, in his speech, effectively repeated the arguments put forward by PROGRESS in favour of research.

The fate of the embryo, and its supporters, was sealed when the UK issued a two-line whip which expected government MPs to vote with their party. In other words, they should ideally vote in favour of providing treatments and allowing embryo research. Some pro-life MPs were therefore forced either to abstain or to vote against their beliefs. In the House of Commons 303 MPs voted in favour of the Bill and 65 against. Similarly in the House of Lords, treatment which included embryo research was given the final go-ahead.[123] The influence of medical groups was clearly in evidence.

The initial period of public debate in France, from 1982 to 1992, consisted of feminists and intellectuals alongside scientists, clinicians and biologists, who raised questions in relation to the medicalisation of procreation and women's bodies and the relentlessness of treatments. Debate changed after 1992, in the run-up to the legislation of 1994, to concentrate much more on the embryo. This change was instigated by a new right-wing government.[124] The resulting government report, *La vie en questions: pour une éthique biomédicale*, authored by the Roman Catholic clinician and MP Mattei, formed the basis of the bioethics laws of 1994. During debates Mattei assured Roman Catholic members of the National Assembly and Senate that the bioethics laws would seek to protect the embryo by prohibiting research and by ensuring treatment was only given as part of the 'projet parental'.[125] Access was therefore tightened, with the stability of the couple made a part of the law, and doctors made guardians of the suitable motivation of that couple. This meant that treatment, especially that using a donor, could only be used by couples as a last resort. PID was accepted only as a form of diagnosis on embryos. Likewise, they were persuaded to tolerate embryo storage. Embryo donation is theoretically possible but the necessary decrees to implement this remain unpublished. Research meanwhile is prohibited. This restrictiveness echoes the arguments of religious groups heard during debates in the UK in 1990 and shows a pervasive religious influence in France.

With re-examination due in 2002/3 these same people will be influential as to whether embryo status is further enhanced by the questioning of abortion rights in France. The government appears to have prepared for such a debate in advance through the preparation during 1999 by the Minister of Health, Israel Nisand, of the report of abortion practice in France. (*See* Chapter 5.)

The OPECST Report of 1999 repeatedly criticises the lack of clarity in the bioethics laws on issues relating to the embryo alongside many medical practitioners, and necessarily, religious groups. Decrees implementing the 1994 regulations on embryo storage, donation and research, and PID have never been published. Gamete donor facilities are licensed and strictly monitored, but embryo storage is not. Only the Ministry of Health is aware of the number of stored embryos in France, and this information must be made public, argues OPECST.[126] Additionally, the Report criticises the clinical discretion governing the amount of embryos to be transferred, and the lack of regulation of selective reduction as this might need amendments to abortion law, as it did in the UK in 1990.[127] OPECST points out the contradiction between researched embryos having to be implanted, and the destruction of surplus embryos after five years. Again, the lack of clarity has led to headaches for the CNMBRDP faced with licensing requests. This body had to presume that the decree of 1997 permitting studies beneficial to that particular embryo referred to non-invasive research, embryos which were dead or which had stopped developing: of the six requests for research licenses by the end of 1998 they therefore only refused one on a triploid embryo which was still developing.[128]

As a solution to the embryo question in France, the OPECST Report of 1999 suggested that legislators need to limit the number of embryos fertilised in order to limit the problem of surplus embryos; have a conscience clause for practitioners; store frozen ova as soon as that becomes possible; not create embryos for research (as is possible in the UK) but carry out research either upon seven day old pre-embryos which have been abandoned by a couple and with their informed consent, or upon pluripotent stem cells that are not embryonic.[129] Government bodies the CCNE (in March 1997), the CNMBRDP and the vast majority of the medical professionals consulted by OPECST also advocated these possibilities for embryo research.[130] This was a development in the thinking of the CCNE and the one member who abstained from this opinion was Roman Catholic priest, Father de Denichin, who felt rather that embryos should be left to die naturally and not be researched upon.[131]

One issue which the CCNE remains relatively conservative about, however, is cloning, which it has pointed to as an attack on human dignity, singularity and autonomy involving fantasies of immortality. The CCNE advocated banning cloning outright but argued that the 1994 laws already proscribed any treatment which modified genetic inheritance and non-reproductive.[132] The HFEA and Human Genetics and Advisory Commission in the UK advocated the prohibition of reproductive cloning in 1998 due to, among other things, its lack of safety for the child so produced and its social unacceptability. By contrast with France, however, therapeutic and non-commercial cloning using stem cells was condoned.[133] Again, then, the interests of the child or embryo are being emphasised in such arguments.

It is highly likely that these are rehearsals for the French parliamentary debates on the embryo during re-examination of the 1994 laws. The clash between 'progressive' clinicians and conservative religious groups that took place in France in 1994 (and in the UK in 1990) look set to be repeated. The influence of medical thinking on parliamentary bodies such as OPECST, the CCNE and the CNMBRDP may well also be repeated. The influence of religious groups on issues such as embryo research and abortion may well threaten women's reproductive rights. The persuasive powers of the French government will once more be in the spotlight.

Conclusions

There appears to be a similar moral code underlying policy and legislation in both countries. Established groups such as the medical profession and the

Churches have been invited to play a part in creating guidelines and the status of the embryo has been more important in debates involving the government and health policy network than women's rights. Pronatalists in France were more favourable to assisted conception than on the former two issues as they encouraged couples to have children. They have therefore been successful in so far as assisted conception continues to be reimbursed. The Roman Catholic Church in both countries has played an important part. The restrictiveness of the French law in relation to access and embryo research shows a much greater Roman Catholic influence there. This was condoned by the right-wing government in power when the 1994 bioethics laws were passed and meant that Roman Catholics were much more likely to be members of the policy network at that time, and certainly much more than their British counterparts.

As to the influence of the medical professions, as with other issues in the health policy sector, the French and British governments were, from the beginning of debates on assisted conception, disposed towards the involvement of the most important members of the network, the medical professions, who predetermined government preconceptions of the issues involved and were consulted much more than any other group. The bills that were presented to Parliament by the government in both countries thus reflected this partiality, largely due to the fact that they were the result of consultations organised by the governments themselves.

In the UK, parliamentarians appear to have been particularly influenced by the lobbying of groups such as PROGRESS, who indeed found itself 'satisfied with the passage of those clauses relating to controlled research under licence on the human embryo', in the final Act.[134] The British government was also impressed with the success of the VLA structure. Indeed the fact that self-regulation was sanctioned by the government from the inception of the VLA made approval of its methods almost a foregone conclusion. Moreover, another useful resource for the VLA must have been that, unlike in France, no prominent doctor came out against assisted conception while it was generally presumed that the VLA was set up by the State. Religious groups in the UK were, by contrast, left dissatisfied in 1990 with an Act which licensed embryo research and left the way open for treatment to be offered to homosexual and single, infertile patients. This is despite the fact that religious and medical lobbying groups were equally well organised and funded.

Similarly in France, the medical organisation, CECOS, escaped much criticism and indeed was warmly received by the government when they lobbied to base legislation on their own structure. Indeed, when, in 1988, they were excluded from a list of seventy-nine licensed insemination centres, because of their 1901 status, the furore that this created showed the extent of their status.[135] CECOS were also closely involved in consultations with the government. In

July 1990, Jean Michaud, president of the assisted-conception section of the 'commission nationale de médecine et de biologie de la reproduction' (CNMBR) (which preceded the CNMBRDP by some four years) reported to Jean-François Girard, director general of health, of a meeting between themselves and CECOS on the issue of testing sperm for the AIDS virus.[136] It was also CECOS who complained to the government about sperm banks that were not operating legally.[137] This led to the investigation of two private sperm banks (*see* Chapter 6). The rules were ostensibly laid down by CECOS and the banks were investigated at their instigation. Nor was CECOS the only medical organisation in France to be directly influential. The Braibant Report stated that gamete donation should be retained. This was on the advice of the medical group, the Conseil de l'Ordre, '(c)onformément à l'avis de différentes instances telle que le Conseil de l'Ordre des médecins, la PMA fondée sur des dons de sperme ou d'ovocytes a donc été retenue'.[138]

The influence of feminists on assisted conception is much less tangible than that of other groups involved in the debate. It is more a question of what they did not do, and what other groups did, than what was done by feminists themselves. British feminists did ally with the medical professions and spoke out in favour of research, so that abortion rights would not be jeopardised. These campaigns were successful. This illustrates the usefulness of allying with a prominent member of the policy network if you are an outsider to that network. However, there were aspects of the 1990 Act that would also point to a certain amount of feminist influence *per se*. For example, in the Code of Practice doctors have got to obtain consents (Schedule 3) and there are guidelines for standards in laboratories and licensed centres.[139] Also, more women than men were members of the original HFEA.[140] However, during the passage of the Bill, the only significant amendment was that on the welfare of the child and after the Act feminists were still worried that single, lesbian or virgin women would be denied access to artificial insemination.[141] What is worse, the government introduced an abortion amendment despite the feminist-supported backbench bill by Lord Houghton. Ultimately, feminists were left dissatisfied that there was no formal structure for ensuring the representation of the interests of women or of any other group, such as infertile women, despite the existence of some female members of the HFEA.

In France, feminists did not lobby and ally with the medical professions to the same extent as their British counterparts due to their more radical nature and the fact that abortion was not re-examined in France. However, the radical feminist cause may well have been assisted by the support of Jacques Testart and prominent sociologists such as Marcus Steiff. Feminists were invited to sit on the CCNE in 1992. The OPECST Committee, also in 1992, interviewed, among others, Mme André, Secretary of State for Women's

Rights; M. Kourilsky, the director of the sociological research body, the CNRS; Jacques Testart; psychologists; psychoanalysts; lawyers; sociologists and philosophers.[142] In 1999 the OPECST Committee invited interviewees from similar walks of life to express their opinions. Nonetheless, the meagre input from those echoing the fears expressed by reproductive rights campaigners in 1992 was not repeated. Moreover, during the public and parliamentary debate and bioethics laws which followed these discussions, parliamentarians showed their overwhelming support for the arguments of medical professionals and religious groups. Uppermost in their mind was the protection of the embryo and the limiting of access.

In both countries the dangers to and rights of women patients took a backseat to such issues. That backseat was shared by those groups who campaigned for women's rights, who attempted to ensure that access was guaranteed, and that abortion rights were not affected by assisted conception regulation on embryo status. It cannot be denied that driving this new vehicle were the medical professions.

Conclusion: whose victory? Whose law? The medicalisation of reproduction

This book set out to consider the development of reproductive policy and law in Britain and France over the course of the twentieth century. In particular it set out to assess how effective women's rights campaigners were in influencing the development of women's reproductive rights. This involved an instructive comparative examination of reproductive law, which revealed the legal catalysts for campaigns and the extent of the legal reform enacted as a result.

The study highlighted the conflicts behind regulation on reproduction, and the political contexts in which struggles between interest groups took place. Comparison also usefully underlined the similarities and differences between countries which share the credentials of a West European liberal democracy.

For campaigners in the reproductive policy debate, it has been apparent that the French legal system, with its strict written Codes and constitutional rights, has been more difficult to amend than English law to suit new arising nuances of practice. This has been particularly evident in relation to technological developments in the medical field. Conversely, law in the UK has been more easily modified by statutory amendment.

Equally, it could be argued that this has much to do with the parliamentary systems of each country. Essentially, the political culture and policy style norms of both countries fit with the model of policy communities and policy networks. This political environment, alongside the legal environment, was a factor in determining the regulation of reproduction and the influence of campaigners on reproductive laws for women.

Comparison between the two countries illustrates not only differences in the political and legal systems, and in the relative strength of interest groups in debates, it also shows how the reproductive policy debate has changed over time. In the first decades of the twentieth century it was evident that religious morals and beliefs held sway in both Britain and France. In addition pronatalists were also powerful in French society. As the century wore on, however, each reproductive issue was superseded by another, medically and technologically more advanced – from contraception, to abortion, to assisted conception. Political debates and reproductive laws illustrate how the medical professions began to wrest control and influence over reproductive policy and the government policy network from these groups.

Influence was also determined by the resources women's rights campaigners brought to the policy arena: their expertise, membership, structure and financial resources. These in turn determined both their alliance-building capacity with those supporters available to them in the prevailing legal and political environment, and the strength of those interest groups who were in opposition to those objectives. The presence of a left-wing government has often determined the likelihood of women's rights campaigners being at least involved in policy community consultation.

In relation to all three reproductive issues under consideration, membership of the policy sector or area included feminist campaigners, and that of the policy community included interested parliamentarians, whom feminists relied upon as allies. Those groups on the inside of the policy network who enjoyed the correct resources, who were thus invited to play an important role in policy elaboration, and whose opinions appear to have had a direct influence on the substantive content of the law, were essentially religious groups, French pronatalists and, most importantly, the medical professions.

All these groups campaigned in opposition to each other and conflict and disagreement was a feature of debate on reproduction throughout the century. Conflict between 'outsiders' and 'insiders', or between women's rights campaigners and their opponents within the policy network, is clearly evident.

The influence of women's rights campaigners

To what extent did the campaigns of women's rights groups affect the position of women and their reproductive rights? Did their many efforts have any effect at all on reform?

It was only possible for campaigners to influence a limited number of reforms. Nevertheless, their contribution was invaluable and extensive. It is due to their efforts that legal reform came at all.

In relation to contraception, campaigners such as the MFPF and FPA changed public attitudes and improved services. More recently, the MFPF has played an important role in the liberalising of emergency contraception (*see* Chapter 3). Opinions and attitudes to abortion were also altered, with support for new feminist ideas being marshalled from important left-wing and medical individuals. This support was important for the liberalisation of abortion through statutory reform, and in preventing amendment by religious forces.

Both contraception and abortion have become accepted as medical treatments and are now reimbursed or freely available as part of the health services. Moroever, contraception and abortion in France were both not only reformed but *decriminalised*.

In relation to assisted conception and the issues on which women's rights groups actually campaigned, the importance of counselling to patients is now on a statutory footing in both Britain and France. Access to treatments for single women and lesbians is assured in Britain, and is funded by the French state for heterosexual couples. (Although this access is subject ultimately to clinical discretion.)

To what do feminists owe this influence? Coole [1] has suggested that, behind the fragments, women's groups can participate in the full spectrum of political issues in a feminist way and so mainstream practices can be moved in a more feminist direction. Lovenduski has also talked of the 'agenda-setting' role played by radical feminists in policy debate. In campaigns for legal reform on reproduction, those campaigning for an improvement in women's rights included liberal feminists. These appear to have been prepared to campaign and to attempt to form alliances with those closer to government consultation, such as parliamentarians, left-wing individuals or radical clinicians, who had a place in the policy community. (Though not in the real locus of decision-making: the policy network.) Radical feminists after 1968 radicalised the agenda and tactics of liberals, which in turn radicalised the agenda of their allies in campaigns – particularly in relation to the idea of abortion on demand in France, and the prevention of abortion amendment in the UK.

Why was feminist influence limited? The strength of the feminist movement was generally constrained by the effects of disunity brought about by post-1968 radicalism. This reduced their strength as an interest group attempting to achieve recognition for their demands from the government when that government was operating a policy network system. Disunity therefore compounded their position as outsiders, as radical feminists were not prepared to compromise their aims and tactics in order to be considered for insider status. (Fortunately, this was assuaged by the usefulness of radicalism in radicalising the agenda of campaigners and their allies, as noted above.) In relation particularly to the assisted conception debate, feminists were also operating in a legal vacuum with no law to direct campaigns against, and with less time before the passing of statute in which to formulate aims and demands and to set the agenda of the policy community. This was compounded by the disunity and disagreement among feminists on the issues around assisted conception, which further reduced their success as an interest group in the policy arena of the time.

Those groups on the inside of the policy network had much more influence over reforms made to reproductive regulation. French pronatalists managed to delay reform until late in the century, and ensured that education and information on sexual matters, contraception or abortion were strictly controlled by the State. Essentially, this determined the availability of provision. Religious groups also ensured that contraception and abortion were prohibited early in the century (indeed criminalised in France); and that their reform (particularly to make them a part of the health service) was delayed. Their potential to shape reform is also evidenced by the extent to which the moral status of the embryo is recognised by statute: thus abortion is only available on grounds and at clinical discretion in the UK, and on demand only for a limited period in France; while assisted conception is restricted in provision due to the issue of the 'welfare of the child'. Clinicians also ensured that any necessary reforms were delayed and that reproductive rights overall are subject to clinical discretion.

Why has this been the case? Pronatalists, religious groups and clinicians have played important parts in the policy network on reproduction. They have thus been accorded a privileged postion by governments during consultations on policy being devised (though the relative strengths of these members and the importance of the network to government has varied over the course of the century). Their position contrasts with that of those in the policy community who have struggled to gain recognition for their objectives, and those on the outside even of this who have barely scraped a position of recognition in the policy arena (such as radical feminists).

Clinicians, particularly, were key players in the health policy network. They were thus close to the heart of political decision making in the area of health policy. Why were doctors accorded such a privileged position? Because they had, and still have, professional expertise which the government respects and does not itself have. Medical organisations are also largely well-structured and financed with a large membership of people whose agreement to policy the government feels it needs. This ensures the smooth implementation of that policy. Moreover, this respected expertise as to what is good for women's health is accorded to the medical professionals by the government, because the vast majority of both institutions are male which ensures a mutual recognition of each other's norms. The recognition of the views of the medical professions was likely to have been of particular importance during voting on conscience issues such as abortion and embryo research, when no government whip is given to parliamentarians who then look for expert advice as to how they should vote.

Recognition of the medical professions was also assured by the increasing involvement of technology in reproductive treatment and the subsequent need, particularly in the eyes of the government, for medical assistance. Thus it was felt that safety would be ensured through medical assistance with surgical abortion in the 1960s and infertility treatment in the 1990s. This has led in turn to medical control of discourse: during debate on assisted conception, the importance of research on the embyro was therefore stressed to the detriment of research into the non-medical causes of infertility (thus placing the embryo firmly at the centre of discussions). Consequently, clinicians have been accorded control of access to reproductive treatment.[2] The influence of physicians has also been compounded by the need for women's rights campaigners to form alliances with policy community and policy network members who are from the medical professions.

As evidenced in this book, women's rights groups never enjoyed policy network resources and were therefore never accorded recognition by the government in the build-up to legislation when consultation of interest groups takes place. Nor were they accorded recognition during parliamentary debates when certain MPs supported medical arguments. The number of MPs who advocated medical, or indeed religious, arguments far outweighed the number who spoke up for the campaigns of women's rights groups.

Reproductive rights at the beginning of the twenty-first century

Can women be satisfied with the reproductive rights they now have in France and Britain? We have seen the decriminalisation, reform and liberalisation of reproductive treatment services. These are now provided to a large extent as part of the national health services of both countries. These services are also available in a safe environment.

Yet gaps remain. In the UK, abortion is not yet available at the request of the woman concerned, and emergency contraception has only just become available to women without prescription. Access to contraception, abortion and assisted conception is still only available at clinical discretion, and the equal availability of reproductive services nationwide is lacking. French women appear to have marginally more autonomy in relation to their access to abortion, but the access of homosexuals or single people to assisted conception in France is prohibited by the 1994 bioethics laws.

Are further reforms to women's reproductive rights likely in the future? The future of reproductive reform remains hopeful. In the UK, for example, beneficial developments have come recently from those controlling access to infertility services – the RCOG. In January 2000 they published a report entitled, *The Management of Infertility in Tertiary Care*. The Report sought to ensure equitable service provision on a nationwide basis. This would be achieved primarily through a reduction in the potential cost of individual treatments, thus making more treatment available on the NHS. They also talked of the unacceptably high rate of multiple births, advocating a reduction from three to two in embryos transferred to women during treatment, and the need for counselling to become even more widely available.[3] In France, there have also been positive developments in terms of the reforms of legislation on contraception and abortion, to allow for emergency contraception to become available to minors without adult consent, and for the extension from ten to twelve weeks of pregnancy of the time limit for abortion on demand (*see* Chapter 5).

In both countries, however, the embryo remains a focus for debate on reproduction. Since the beginning of the twentieth century, women have struggled to varying degrees against the central position of the foetus. At the end of the twentieth century and the beginning of the twenty first, the embryo now also features prominently in that struggle.

Indeed, bioethical discussions underline the importance given to the human embryo. This is amply illustrated by debates on embryo status in the European Convention on Biomedicine. At a meeting to discuss the status of the embryo at the Council of Europe in December 1996, for example, differences in opinion between the assembled representatives were so vast that many feared that consensus on such matters as embryo research could never possibly be reached.[4] The embryo is likely to become even more central in ethical and political debate about the status of the embryo, as new technologies such as gene therapy, embryo splitting and cloning become medically safer and more widely available as treatments. This is borne out by the difficulties experienced by the French in resolving the legal status of the embryo during their preliminary re-examination of the 1994 bioethics laws. The UK chose to licence embryo research up to a time limit of fourteen days under the 1990 Act, whereas the French still have not yet decided whether to permit such research (*see* Chapter 7). France is not alone in finding problems in resolving the position of the embryo. Many West European countries, and the vast majority of states in the USA, have piecemeal regulation or no regulation at all.[5] Despite the arguments of Dworkin[6] and others advocating moving the debate away from this war of attrition, the debate on the embryo remains unresolved and as fierce as ever.

The increase in the power over reproduction of medical professionals has coincided with a reassessment of the status of the human embryo. Combined, these two have serious implications for women's rights and reproductive freedom. Foetal rights have, of course, existed for many years, as illustrated by legal restrictions on contraception and abortion. But such rights may increase in the future in new areas such as foetal surgery. As Cynthia Daniels has amply illustrated, case law during the 1980s and 1990s in the USA limited the freedom of pregnant drug addicts (a)s the fetus gained ideological, legal and political independence from the woman, it came also to be seen as public property, to be treated independently by doctors, protected *in utero* by the courts, and retrieved by the state, if necessary after birth. The alienation of the woman's body from the fetus thus provided the grounds for the subordination of women's legal rights and the control of women's behaviour during pregnancy by a whole range of social actors, from medical practitioners, lawyers, and bartenders, to husbands, employers, and agents of the state.[7]

Such rights continue to be affirmed by religious groups in society. In the UK a new threat may be on the horizon: that of pro-life groups attempting to amend provision on abortion and assisted conception by invoking the right to life (Article 2) or the right to respect for private life (Article 8) under the Human Rights Act 1998. In her examination of the shortcomings of human rights legislation for women, McColgan points out the very real dangers coming from this direction. However, she also underlines the obstacles in the 1998 Act to such an action. Requirements for standing under the 1998 Act, for example, exclude intercession by interest groups, though they may be able to file *amicus* briefs. Individuals must establish that they are victims rather than merely having a substantial interest. McColgan sees this as a grave shortcoming, as, alongside future restrictions on state-funded legal assistance and the lack of a human rights commission, this 'will have the effect of restricting access to its benefits for those of small and moderate means, while paving the way for its use by the powerful and wealthy'.[8] Hewson has argued that, 'emotive cases may be used to shock the courts into ruling that a late term or viable foetus is a person, or has legal standing'.[9] This might then be used to work backwards to earlier points in gestation.

But the strength of pro-life campaigners themselves, like French pronatalists, has been weakened in recent times, and the evidence points rather to the increasing importance of clinicians in the policy network and the resulting medicalisation of women's reproductive rights.

Does medicalisation matter?

To what extent has medicalisation affected women's health provision in the area of reproduction? When power and control over health decisions are in the hands of clinicians, women suffer as patients and as women in society from a lack of autonomy over their reproduction. During the twentieth century, women were at the mercy of others making decisions on women's health provision. Such decisions have a far-reaching effect on women's lives. Whether a woman has to bear a child influences fundamentally many other areas in her life. The decision will have consequences for her education, career, health and, indeed, her entire life. Surely she is in the best position to assess such a situation? Is it not time that the ideas of informed consent and autonomy were fully extended to women's reproductive decision-making and recognised by the law?

Feminism and legal reform

But what of feminists now? How far are they resisting the pressures of medicalisation? How far are they likely to campaign on legal reform in the future?

At the beginning of the twenty-first century, the urgency for legal reform has diminished. No longer is abortion criminalised or contraception difficult to obtain. Without legislation to battle against, campaigns are less likely.

With the onset of postmodernism, feminism has taken on a more theoretical and intellectual hue, with emphasis on culture and identity. Those adhering to such a feminist theory are less likely to go into battle over single-issue campaigns such as abortion.

Is there now any ground to be gained in legal reform? Sheldon[10] argues that legal reform can be limited in its impact, particularly when it is likely to be implemented by those less sympathetic to the ideals of the women's movement. Smart has challenged the usefulness of law, and called for non-legal strategies to be used to gain improvements in women's condition.[11] Individual campaigners could thus continue their useful contributions by working to improve medical services on the inside of the profession, or by establishing 'radical' alternative treatment centres.

An essential part of women's campaigns for contraception, particularly from the late 1960s, were demands for women's autonomy and control over their own bodies and reproductive health. Throughout the Western world in more recent years this demand for patient autonomy and demedicalisation has been heard from women *and* men in relation to all aspects of their health. Increasingly, patients are demanding more of a say in their own diagnosis and treatment. This can be seen not only in the doctor's surgery but also in encounters between pharmacists and their 'customers'. Contraceptives becoming available 'over the counter' from pharmacists rather than only on prescription from a doctor, family planning clinic or hospital, and the deregulation of medicines of which this forms a part, is another step in this development.[12]

But Sheldon[13] and Smart[14] both acknowledge the importance of law as a definer of truth and 'authorised discourse'. 'Engagement with the law is thus important as a process of the public formulation of claims and alternative visions.'[15] Sheldon argues that the feminist movement must take a pro-active stance towards the law, challenging its basic assumptions, and the medicalisation and constructions of women which underpin it.[16] Sheldon is referring here to abortion, but these arguments could usefully be extended to legislation on contraception, assisted conception and a myriad of reproductive issues whose regulation and practice affect women's lives. Indeed, I would argue that the current lack of political action may well be disempowering for those women whose reproductive autonomy remains compromised. Should they choose, pro-choice campaigners in the UK may avail themselves of rights provided under the Human Rights Act 1998.

Any threat of amendment by pro-life groups would in all likelihood rekindle pro-choice campaigning. This has happened in the past, and was recently apparent in France in the aftermath of the Nisand Report on abortion and the decision of the Conseil d'Etat on the prohibition of emergency contraception (*see* Chapters 3 and 5). There remains an underlying awareness of abortion rights and the need for these to be protected, whether from French women politicians or British pro-choice organisations such as the BPAS or Pro-Choice Forum.

Marie Fox also suggests moving the debate forward – and away from questions of choice which can lead to the countervailing rights of fathers and foetuses, and can make women appear selfish. She advocates, along with others, focusing rather on women's health in campaigns for abortion rights, also 'focusing on needs may help us to frame a vision of justice founded in the needs and realities of women's lives as a building block towards a meaningful vision of reality'. Fox refers to the much-needed government resources which such an emphasis might pressurise the State to provide.[17]

Feminist debates on reproduction have demonstrated difference and even disunity. This has contributed to their weakness as an interest group. But there can be benefits to disunity.

> The acknowledgement of differentiated feminist interest does not weaken but strengthen feminism. Diversity might facilitate the formation of specialised coalitions of feminist perspectives. The condition to present a unified feminist standpoint with regard to the new technologies is in fact untenable, since such a viewpoint presumes the prevalence of gender differences over other categories such as race and class ... Defining a public debate as an open ended area of meaning construction permits the possibility of continuous contestation.[18]

Such contestation might profitably be combined with legal reform. The arguments of Lovenduski [19] on the usefulness of the different types of feminist campaigners should not be forgotten. Any type of feminist resistance to the law can be usefully harnessed, as long as women are aware of the political context of policy debate and their position within it. Campaigners achieved many things in the twentieth century, but the threat from opponents remains. Too many women are still at the mercy of the law, the State and, most particularly, the medical professions, in their quest for reproductive autonomy in both Britain and in France.

Notes

Chapter 1

1 There are obvious similarities between the three different reproductive issues of contraception, abortion and assisted conception. Failed contraception can lead to a necessity for abortion. The 1920 statute criminalising contraception in France also criminalised abortion (*see* Chapter 2). Women's desires for a right to choose were extended from contraception and abortion to assisted conception in the latter years of the twentieth century (*see* Chapter 7). Genetic diagnosis of the embryo may now lead to a request for abortion on grounds of foetal abnormality.

    Some overlap is also evident from an examination of the campaigns behind the liberalisation of these three issues. This is particularly evident in relation to the most significant interest groups who played a part in these: women's rights groups, the medical professions, pronatalists and religious groups. Nevertheless, these campaigns did take place separately, sometimes as a result of time differences, sometimes as a result of political expediency and political resources.

2 The ideology of pronatalism, or 'natalisme', is a political, ideological, phenomenon peculiar particularly to the French which has played an important role in the debate surrounding reproduction since the late nineteenth century. Its proponents have sought to increase the French birth rate in the face of the rival supremacy of other nations, particularly Germany, and this has had cross-party support.

3 English law, or the law of the United Kingdom, pertains to England and Wales. Scotland has its own legal system and, along with Northern Ireland, its own interpretations of statutes, though these are similar if not identical to the English law they are founded upon. One notable exception is the Abortion Act 1967 which does not apply to Northern Ireland. The interest groups involved in the lack of reproductive rights in Northern Ireland are not examined in this book, though would no doubt make an interesting study.

4 Décision du 15 janvier 1975, J. O. 16 janvier 1975.

5 For an informative discussion of women's rights and the Human Rights Act 1998, see A. McColgan, *Women Under the Law: the False Promise of Human Rights* (Longman, 2000).

6 For a recent discussion of some of these differences in the major areas of the discipline, see the special issue of *Political Studies*, 37 (3), 1989.

7 J. Richardson *et al.*, eds, 'The concept of policy styles', Chapter 1 in J. Richardson *et al.* eds, *Policy Styles in Western Europe* (Allen & Unwin, 1982), p. 2.

8 R. J. Harrison, *Pluralism and Corporatism* (Allen & Unwin, 1980), p. 13.

9 J. Hayward, 'Mobilising private interests in the service of public ambitions: the

salient element in the dual French policy style?', Chapter 5 in Richardson *et al.*, eds, *Policy Styles*, p. 137.

10 Parliamentary sessions are limited to six months annually (art. 28). The government controls the parliamentary agenda (art. 48): in the Fourth Republic, 30 per cent of bills were Private Members' Bills; in the Fifth Republic, it has been 10 per cent. The number of standing committees is limited to six (art. 43) (each being chaired in the 1960s by a government representative); most questions are written and rarely oral. There is no equivalent to Supply Days, which allow opponents to debate an issue of their choice, such deputies only being able to put down a censure motion. An equivalent to Question Time was introduced on Fridays with very low attendance. Bills are debated in the original government form (as in the UK), not as amended in committee. (J. Hayward, *The One and Indivisible French Republic* (Weidenfeld & Nicholson, 1973/1987), pp. 73–75.)

The reduction in the power of select committees in the UK is equally important as they can be a target for interest groups. They often have powers to amend bills before they are debated in Parliament, and can decide whether to refer a bill to that House. In the UK, Standing Orders provide more opportunities to challenge the government, but there has been a preference for more general standing committees rather than select committees. In both countries, resolutions cannot be accepted that would put a charge on the revenue (Harrison, *Pluralism*, p. 151).

11 E. Suleiman, *Politics, Power and Bureaucracy in France* (Princeton University Press, 1974), p. 300. Moreover, parliamentary power is limited by the fetish for secrecy of French political institutions. Some civil servant members of the Conseil d'Etat, serve in the 'cabinets' of certain ministers at the same time. They are then able to argue on behalf of the Minister on his policies in a forum that should be impartial. This potential for partiality has not been questioned as it was believed that administrators were impartial and above politics. *Ibid.*, p. 269.

12 P. Grémion, 'La concertation', in M. Crozier, ed., *Ou va l'administration française?* (Editions d'organisation, 1974).

13 'POS and political protest: anti-nuclear movements in four democracies', *B. J. Pol. S.* 16: 57–85, 66.

14 M. Wright, 'Policy community, policy network and comparative industrial policies', *Political Studies* 36 (4): 593–612, 1988. G. Wistow in 'The health service policy community: professionals pre-eminent or under challenge?', in D. Marsh and R. A. W. Rhodes, *Policy Networks in British Government* (Clarendon Press, 1992), essentially distinguishes between policy communities, policy networks and the professional network which obtain in relation to the medical professions and the NHS in the UK. However, in a comparative study of the UK and France it has been found more useful to use the term 'policy network' to describe the consultative relationship between the government and the medical professions during policy-making.

15 Wright, 'Policy community' p. 605.

16 Y. Mény, 'The national and international context of French policy communities', *Political Studies* 37: 387–399, 389, 1989. The terminology used by Mény differs from that used by Wright. The term 'policy network', in addition to 'policy community', used by Wright, to differentiate between community and network, is not used by Mény. Here, it is proposed to use Wright's terminology.

17 *Ibid.*, p. 394.

18 J. Lovecy, 'An end to French exceptionalism?', *West European Politics*, 22:4 October 1999.

19 D. Colas, *L'Etat et les corporatismes* (PUF, 1988).

20 Wistow in Marsh and Rhodes, eds, *Policy Networks* talks of the health policy community in the UK enjoying a particular type of professionalisation because of the membership of the health professions.

21 C. Kohler Riessman, 'Women and Medicalisation: a new perspective', in R. Weitz (ed.), *The Politics of Women's Bodies: Sexuality, Appearance and Behaviour* (Oxford University Press, 1998), p. 48.

22 *Ibid.*, p. 47.

23 *Ibid.*, p. 48. Is it a result of medical imperialism in an effort by clinicians to improve their power (see I. Illich, *Medical Nemisis: The Expropriation of Healthy*, (Pantheon, 1976))? Is an increasingly complex technical and bureaucratic society resulting in an inadvertent dependence on scientific experts (see I. K. Zola, 'Medicine as an institution of social control', *Sociological Review*, 20: 487–504, 1972; 'In the name of health and illness: on some socio-political consequences of medical influence', *Social Science and Medicine*, 9: 83–87, 1975)? Or is medicalisation alternatively the result of attempts to professionalise in order to create and control markets (see M. S. Larson, *The Rise of Professionalism: A Sociological Analysis* (University of California Press, 1977))?

24 *Ibid.*, p. 57.

25 *Ibid.*

26 Ibid. p. 48.

27 S. Sheldon, *Beyond Control: Medical Power and Abortion* (Pluto, 1997), p. 157.

28 *Ibid.*, p. 168.

29 Kohler Riessman, 'Women and medicalisation', p. 49.

30 Sheldon, *Beyond Control*, p. 169.

31 Kohler Riessman, 'Women and medicalisation', p. 52.

32 *Ibid.*, p. 47.

33 *Ibid.*, p. 54.

34 M. Foucault, *Discipline and Punish: the Birth of the Prison* (Penguin, 1991).

35 Sheldon, *Beyond Control*, p. 154.

36 On health services in France and the UK, see: N. Bosanquet, 'Social policy' in H. Drucker and P. Dunleavy, eds, *Developments in British Politics* (Macmillan, 1984); L. Hantrais, *Contemporary French Society* (Macmillan, 1982); and A. Maynard, *Health Care in the EC* (Croom Helm, 1975). On the power of the medical professions in the UK see P. Jones, 'The British Medical Association: public good or private interest?' in D. Marsh, ed. *Pressure Politics*, (Junction Books, 1983); H. Eckstein, *Pressure Group Politics: the Case of the BMA* (Allen & Unwin, 1960); H. Eckstein, *The English Health Service* (Harvard University Press, 1958/1970).

37 H. Barnett, *Sourcebook on Feminist Jurisprudence* (Cavendish, 1997), p. 202.

38 For further on first-wave feminism in both the UK and France, see P. Levine, *Victorian Feminism* (Hutchinson, 1987); P. Branca, *Women in Europe since 1750* (Croom Helm, 1978); F. Mort, *Dangerous Sexualities: Medico-moral Politics in Britain since 1830* (RKP, 1987); C. G. Moses, *French Feminism in the Late Nineteenth Century* (Suny, 1984); J. Rendall, *The Origins of Modern Feminism: Women in Britain, France and the USA 1780–1860* (Macmillan, 1985).

39 The provisional government after the liberation issued the 'ordonnance du 21 avril

portant organisation des pouvoirs publics en France après la Libération' (Gaz. Pal. 44, II, 290). This was confirmed in the Preamble to the 1946 Constitution. Thus adult women were given the vote in France. Many other rights, such as those relating to divorce, were not accorded to women until the late 1960s: women were not accorded equal authority over their children until 1970. A husband's authority over the family finances did not end officially until 1985 ('loi du 23 décembre 1985'). For an interesting feminist critique of French women and the law, see O. Dhavernas, *Droits des femmes, pouvoir des hommes* (Seuil, 1978).

40 'As a question that raises attitudes that defy logic and reason, it affects women on different levels and resists attempts to apply a simple political solution to its problems; as the first concerted campaign by feminists in France, the fight for voluntary maternity was a hugely successful but equally problem-laden mobilising issue, which highlights the different political positions and preoccupations of different feminist approaches, and shows the way in which the various groups, and the MLF as a whole, evolved over a decade' C. Duchen, *Feminism in France* (RKP, 1986), p. 49.

41 Kohler Riessman, 'Women and medicalisation', p. 57.

42 Artificial insemination, for example, entails long-standing and fairly simple technology.

43 Kohler Riessman, 'Women and medicalization', p. 57.

44 Cf. Sheldon, *Beyond Control* and C. Smart, 'Disruptive bodies and unruly sex: the regulation of reproduction and sexuality in the nineteenth century', in C. Smart, ed., *Regulating Womanhood: Historical Essays on Marriage, Motherhood and Sexuality* (Routledge, 1992), p. 7.

45 J. Lovenduski, *Women and European Politics* (Wheatsheaf 1986), p. 70.

46 Previous attempts by political parties and governments at changing women's status had been unsatisfactory, including the creation in June 1974 of the Secretary of State for the Status of Women, held by Françoise Giroud, which lasted only two years; Giroud's proposals were never implemented.

47 Duchen *Feminism*, p. 129, points out that many in the MLF were unhappy with the Ministry, however, as it had 'meant the ghettoisation (of women's rights) ... (and was) only a skin-deep gesture of appeasement to feminism rather than a real attempt to change male–female relations' socially and politically. Nor did the Minister for Women, Yvette Roudy, subscribe to MLF arguments for non-hierarchical structures, and she was accused of taking personal credit for MLF actions and ideas, acting as if she were its personal spokesman, and that most of the women who were employed in government office benefited from nepotism rather than a meritocracy or community such as theirs.

48 D. Bouchier, *The Feminist Challenge* (Macmillan Press, 1983), p. 83.

49 This group has also been referred to as 'Po et Psych'. Here I am using the original French moniker for this group, a shortened version of, 'Psychanalyse et Politique'.

50 Duchen, *Feminism in France*, p. 17.

51 *Ibid.*, p. 46.

52 Lovenduski, *Women and European Politics*, p. 72.

53 *Ibid.*, p. 115.

Chapter 2

1 Audrey Leathard, *The Fight for Family Planning* (Macmillan Press, 1980), p. 121.

2 M. Brazier, *Medicine, Patients and the Law* (Pelican, 1987), p. 259 and (Penguin, 1992) p. 373. The conviction was ultimately overturned on technical grounds.

3 Leathard, *Family Planning*, p. 21.

4 *Ibid.*, p. 26.

5 *Sutherland* v. *Stopes* [1924] AC 47. The jury found that though 'defamatory of the plaintiff' the words complained of were true in substance and in fact but were not fair comment, and that therefore Sutherland should pay damages. But the Lord Chief Justice gave judgment in favour of the defendant because he himself could find no evidence that the comment was unfair. Stopes appealed to the Court of Appeal and was successful – the jury had followed the instructions of the judge who had wrongly allowed them to distinguish between fact and opinion but who had nevertheless come out in favour of the plaintiff.

6 Leathard, *Family Planning*, p. 68.

7 The Penal Code provision outlawing abortion is now Art 223–10 to 223–12 (not 317).

8 The law of '16 mars 1898 concernant la pornographie' prohibited the giving of information on pornography.

9 Mouvement Français pour le Planning Familial, *D'une revolte à une lutte: 25 ans d'histoire du planning familial* (Editions Tiercé, 1983), p. 24.

10 *Ibid.*, p. 453.

11 This was under 'la loi de 31 juillet 1920', D. P. 21, IV, 162, 'Loi réprimant la provocation à l'avortement et à la propagande anticonceptionnelle'.

12 MFPF, *25 ans*, p. 26.

13 O. Dhavernas, *Droits des femmes* (Seuil, 1978), p. 145.

14 *Ibid.*, pp. 144–146.

15 MFPF, *25 ans*, p. 62.

16 L. Trifirino, medical doctoral thesis, Université Paris VII, 1971, p. 14.

17 She was defended by neo-Malthusians, the feminist press, democrats, Communists and anarchists who took the opportunity to denounce the 1920 law especially where it pertained to propaganda on contraception (MFPF, *25 ans*, p. 29.)

18 *Ibid.*, p. 28.

19 Trifirino, thesis, p. 37.

20 Dhavernas, *Droits des femmes*, p. 147.

21 MFPF, *25 ans*, p. 46.

22 *Ibid.*

23 In 1926, a Labour-sponsored Private Member's Bill was defeated due to union pressure to the annoyance of Labour and Liberal women.

24 Leathard, *Family Planning*, pp. 30–41.

25 *Ibid.*, p. 41.

26 *See* Leathard, *Family Planning*.

27 *Ibid.*, p. 49.

28 *Ibid.*, p. 49.

29 *R.* v. *Bourne* [1939] 1 KB 687.

30 Leathard, *Family Planning*, p. 91.

31 MFPF, *25 ans*, pp. 61–63.

32 *Baxter* v. *Baxter* [1948] AC 274, p. 290.

33 Interestingly, in contrasting vein to the majority speeches in *Sutherland* v. *Stopes*, Viscount Jowitt L. C. in *Baxter* v. *Baxter* also stated that 'reputable clinics had come into existence for the purpose of advising spouses on what is popularly called birth control'.

34 S. Atkins and B. Hoggett, *Women and the Law* (Blackwell, 1984), p. 84. *Forbes* v. *Forbes* [1956], p. 16.

35 T. G. I., Cherbourg, 8 févr. 1899, D.,1900.2.206.

36 F. Dekeuwer-Defossé, *Dictionnaire juridique: droits des femmes* (Dalloz, 1985), p. 365.

37 *Ibid.*

38 Interview with Maitre Michel Grimaldi, academic lawyer, Paris, 10 September 1990.

39 Dekeuwer-Defossé, *Dictionnaire juridique*, p. 333.

40 Leathard, *Family Planning*, p. 136.

41 'to arrange, to such extent as he considers necessary to meet all reasonable requirements in England and Wales, for the giving of advice on contraception, the medical examination of persons seeking advice on contraception, the treatment of such persons and the supply of contraceptive substances and appliances.'

42 Leathard, *Family Planning*, p. 204.

43 *Ibid.*, p. 205.

44 *Sutton* v. *Population Services Family Planning Ltd*, *The Times*, 7 November 1981.

45 *Guardian*, 23 July, 1983.

46 *The Times*, 24 May 1985.

47 *Sidaway* v. *Board of Governors of the Bethlem Royal and the Maudsley Hospital* [1985] 1 All ER 643.

48 For more on this issue see I. Kennedy, *Treat Me Right* (OUP, 1988).

49 MFPF, *25 ans*, p. 150.

50 *Ibid.*, p. 151.

51 'Loi relative à la regulation des naissances et abrogeant les articles L. 648 et L. 649 du Code de la santé publique', Gaz. Pal. 68, I, 103. The 'loi du 28 décembre 1967' introduced the idea of records being kept of prescriptions given by a doctor for contraceptives (which were then to be obtained from a pharmacy). Minors needed the written consent of one parent. Contraceptives were only available from the pharmacy. An IUD had to be fitted by a doctor.

52 B. Pingaud *et al.*, *L'Avortement: histoire d'un débat* (Flammarion, 1975), p. 36.

53 These 'carnets' may not have been used in practice according to Dekeuwer-Deffosez, *Dictionnaire juridique.*, p. 365, but this did not stop groups campaigning for the eradication of something which in principle was very detrimental to women's rights.

54 Dhavernas, *Droits des femmes*, p. 153.

55 The law of '26 mars 1803' put the legal age of majority at 21. The law of '3 janvier 1968' changed the age of majority to 18 (c. civ art. 488).

56 Dhavernas, *Droits des femmes*, p. 153.

57 'Loi portant diverses dispositions relatives à la régulation des naissances', Gaz. Pal. 74, II, 368. After the 1974 amendments ('loi du 4 décembre 1974') no records were kept by the doctor, minors did not need consent, and contraceptives were reimbursed by the French health service. They were also available free of charge

from centres for family planning and education to people without health insurance, and even to minors who wanted this kept confidential.

58 MFPF, *25 ans*, p. 463.

59 Crim. 16 juin 1981, J. C. P., 1982. II. 19707.

60 MFPF document, undated, though perhaps dating from 1983–4 (Bibliothèque Marguerite Durand, Paris).

61 Leathard, *Family Planning*, p. 146.

62 *The Times*, 6 and 8 March 1971.

63 Leathard, *Family Planning*, p. 146.

64 *Gillick v. West Norfolk and Wisbech Area Health Authority* [1984] 1 All ER 465, pp. 593–595.

65 *Ibid.*, p. 596.

66 *Ibid.*, p. 598.

67 [1985] 1 All ER 533, CA.

68 [1985] 3 All ER 402, HL.

69 At p. 432.

70 *Ibid*, p. 413.

71 I. Kennedy, *Treat Me Right*, p. 113.

72 *See Re P (A Minor)* (1981) 80 LGR 301.

73 This translates as, 'nulle intégrité corporelle n'est menacée et une idée de liberté individuelle prévaut sur le caractère médical de la prescription.' (Gérard Mémeteau, 'Le Droit Médical de la Famille', in Jean Carbonnier ed. *Le droit non-civil de la famille* (PUF, 1983), p. 236.)

74 Code de Déontologie art. 43 al2 and Code civil art. 389–3 and 450; Mémeteau, *Droit Médical*, pp. 231–238.

75 *Brock Report*, Cmd. 4485 (HMSO, 1934).

76 *Bravery v. Bravery* [1954] 3 All ER 59. Brazier, *Medicine, Patients and the* Law (2nd edn, 1992), p. 261. Today a wife would probably only have to establish unreasonable behaviour without having to show evidence of damage to her health.

77 He continued, p. 68, '(t)ake a case where a sterilisation operation is done so as to enable a man to have the pleasure of sexual intercourse without shouldering the responsibilities attaching to it. The operation is plainly injurious to the public interest. It is degrading to the man himself. It is injurious to his wife ... to say nothing of the way it opens to licentiousness.'

78 S. A. M. McLean ed., *Legal Issues in Medicine*, (Gower, 1981), p. 177.

79 D. Meyers, *The Human Body and the Law* (Edinburgh University Press, 1970), p. 13.

80 *Ibid.*, p. 14.

81 *Sullivan v. Sullivan* [1970] 2 All ER 168 CA.

82 At p. 64.

83 *Ibid.*, p. 16. See also McLean *Legal Issues*, p. 177.

84 Atkins and Hoggett, *Women and Law*, pp. 84–86.

85 Leathard, *Family Planning*, p. 190.

86 *Devi v. West Midlands AHA* [1980] 7 Current Law S. 44. Unless the woman in question is mentally handicapped and the operation being considered is therapeutic.

87 *Wells v. Surrey AHA*, *The Times*, 29 July 1978; *Udale v. Bloomsbury AHA* (1983) [1983] 2 All ER 522; *Emeh v. Kensington, Chelsea and Fulham AHA* (1983) [1983] 3 All ER 1044.

88   *Allen* v. *Bloomsbury AHA* [1993] 1 All ER 65.

89   *Fish* v. *Wilcox* [1993] 13 BMLR 134.

90   The criminality of sterilisation is also referred to in Soutoul, *La responsabilité médicale*, p. 262. Castration is a felony under the French Penal Code. The state may arrest or compulsorily vaccinate individuals in France, but compulsory sterilisation is unlikely in a Roman Catholic country where contraception and abortion were outlawed for so long.

91   A.-M. Dourlen-Rollier, in Raôul Palmer *et al.* eds, *La sterilisation volontaire en France et dans le monde* (Masson, 1981), pp. 254–256.

92   Dekeuwer-Deffosez, *Dictionnaire Juridique*, p. 366.

93   In 1954 the Académie Nationale de Médicine (ANM) stipulated that it should only be carried out in the event of serious medical indications or threat to life, but that it was something to be left up to the conscience of the individual doctor. In April 1955 and April 1964 the Conseil National de l'Ordre (the regulatory body for the medical profession) concurred, maintaining that therapeutic sterilisation remained a matter for the individual doctor who should act on his own criteria. Non-therapeutic sterilisation was still illegal and 'rigoreusement interdite'. (Dourlen-Rollier, *La sterilisation volontaire*, pp. 254–256.)

94   At the 1975 Congress on Urology (thus concerned mainly with male sterilisation) the President of the Conseil de l'Ordre des Médecins reaffirmed their position stating that sterilisation was still mostly irreversible; could lead to psychological and moral problems in families; and was moreover illegal. (Dourlen-Rollier, *La sterilisation volontaire*, p. 250.) In 1978 the ANM, referring to both male and female requests for sterilisation, still forbade non-therapeutic sterilisation, which they saw as 'une atteinte à l'intégrité du corps' (*Ibid*, p. 251.) For women it could be performed if another pregnancy could worsen an illness or threaten life. Or, with the consent of the patient and with the opinion of a second doctor, if the women concerned had had very difficult births; were over 50, had children and could not take oral contraceptives; or in exceptional cases for eugenic (genetic) reasons. They also stated that they did not wish to see legislation on the subject, and that each doctor should take into account the demographic situation in France when agreeing to the operation. This text was adopted by a majority of the Academy. (*Ibid.*)

95   *Ibid.*, p. 249.

96   Dekeuwer-Defossez, *Dictionnaire juridique*, p. 366.

97   With duels society was seen as guarantor of its members' lives, which precluded the freedom to dispose of one's own life. With sterilisation this was extended from the idea of protecting people from taking their lives to protecting people from damaging their own health.

98   They proposed that sterilisation should be reimbursed like other forms of contraception; that the European standard of allowing voluntary sterilisation after the age of 30 with three children and 35 with two should be applied in France; and that social as well as medical indications should be allowed for voluntary sterilisation. (Dourlen-Rollier, *La sterilisation volontaire*, pp. 256–258.) Doctors themselves surveyed in 1977 were shown to be more conservative in their ideas about criteria for voluntary sterilisation – only a quarter or less agreed with the new criteria of ANESV and even then with a signed consent form and the opinions of a psychologist and second doctor. However, they did think it should

be reimbursed by the state. Moreover, these were provincial doctors whose views could be considered to be rather conservative in comparison to urban doctors. (*Ibid.*, pp. 259–260.)

99 'Doctors should have more leeway, to prevent clandestine operations and the class-bias toward the middle-classes,' he believed. 'It was often less dangerous than contraceptives and abortion. The moral reasoning behind the Academy's statement was outdated and too general' (*Ibid.*, p. 252).

100 *Ibid.*, pp. 254–256.

101 *Ibid.*, p. 250.

102 Mémeteau, *Le Droit Médical*, p. 247.

103 15 per cent of the patients at one CECOS decided not to have the operation after counselling. (MFPF document, Bibliothèque Margeurite Durand, Paris.)

104 *Ibid.*

105 Cass. Civ. 1er, 9 mai 1983, D., 1984; *Ibid.*

106 D. Paintin, *Twenty Questions about Emergency Contraception – Answered*, Birth Control Trust, March 1998. In the UK from July 1999 emergency contraception became available from doctors at local branches of the British Pregnancy Advisory Service (BPAS). Women would be able to pay £10 and immediately receive a packet of emergency contraceptives for them to take home and use whenever they thought it necessary, rather than having to face the difficulty of seeking a prescription from a doctor having already had unprotected sex and facing the prospect of an un-wanted pregnancy. In November 1999 Brook Advisory Centres, providers in the UK of contraceptive advice to younger women, were advising them to stock up on emergency contraceptives before the millennium (Maxine Lattimer, *Pro-Choice Forum Update*, 11 November 1999). In December 1998 Boots chemists in Glasgow, Scotland, began providing emergency contraception to teenagers with the aim of reducing their pregnancy rate (http://news. bbc, 1 December 1998). Trials also took place in Manchester, England, of the provision of emergency contraception in pharmacies in districts with a high teenage-pregnancy rate (*Guardian*, 8 January 2000; *Manchester Evening News*, 15 September 2000).

107 Early Day Motion on Emergency Contraception, *Hansard*, Thursday 11 June 1998.

108 *Le Monde*, 30 November 1999.

109 *Le Monde*, 27 and 28 July 2000.

110 Early Day Motion 1138, *Hansard*, November 30 1999.

111 In the UK, the morning-after pill that has been usually prescribed (at least before November 1999) has been PC4, which is made up of progesterone and oestrogen. PC4 is said to prevent 75 per cent of pregnancies. This is similar to one type of morning-after pill available in France, Tetragynon. Its safer alternative is Norvelon or levonorgestrel, which is made up of progesterone only. This more expensive alternative is 99 per cent efficient if taken during the first 24 hours, and 85 per cent efficient if taken during the first 72 hours. Norvelon also causes less side effects. A study by the World Health Organisation (http://news. bbc, 7 August 1999) has provided evidence of its effectiveness and may have helped to persuade authorities in the UK to initiate the consultation on the drug announced in May 2000. This has been available on prescription since November 1999, which does not mean to say, however, that less enlightened GPs would readily prescribe it. In France, however, it has been available even across the counter in pharmacies since June 1999.

112   '"Overdose" pills curb sought', *Guardian*, November 23 1996, p. 9.
113   *Chatterton* v. *Gerson* [1981] QB 432, though see *Bolitho* v. *City & Hackney Health Authority* [1992] 2 All ER 771.
114   *Whitehouse* v. *Jordan* [1981] 1 All ER 267.
115   *Sidaway* v. *Board of Governors of the Bethlem Royal and the Maudsley Hospital* [1985] 1All ER 643.
116   *Bolitho* v. *City and Hackney Health Authority* [1992] 2 All ER 771.
117   *See* fn. 51 above.
118   *Le Monde*, 30 November 1999.
119   K. Mullan, 'Implications of refusal to sell post-coital contraception', *The Pharmaceutical Journal*, 252, 6 August 1994.

Chapter 3

1   The centre severed ties with the League in September 1922.
2   See Leathard, *Family Planning*, Chapter 2.
3   Leathard, *Family Planning*, p. 14.
4   Stopes' clinics supplied the small check pessary and suppositories, while the Walworth clinic supplied the Dutch cap, a soluble pessary and sheaths, which they considered to be more modern.
5   Malthusianism was propounded from the early nineteenth century in support of the economic necessity of family planning. Eugenicism was seen particularly from later in the same century and argued for the improvement of the human race through the prevention of procreation by 'undesirables'.
6   *Sutherland* v. *Stopes* [1924] AC 47.
7   Leathard, *Family Planning*, Chapter 23.
8   *Ibid.*, Chapter 10.
9   *Ibid.*, pp. 217–219.
10   Interview with N. Pfeffer, London, 27 September 1991.
11   Leathard, *Family Planning*, p. 226.
12   *Ibid.*, Chapter 14.
13   *Ibid.*, Chapter 13.
14   MFPF, *25 ans*, p. 69.
15   *Ibid.*, p. 72.
16   *Ibid.*, p. 75.
17   Derogy was a fellow Communist of Dr. Weill-Hallé's husband. Critics of the article were in the main husbands who believed their wives could become unfaithful; men who feared that women would be taken advantage of if there were no danger of their becoming pregnant; and demographers who felt that it was economically necessary for women to have more children than they wanted, even though the 1920 law perhaps needed to be reformed. (MFPF, *25 ans*, p. 76.) The appearance in January 1956 of *Des Enfants Malgré Nous*, a book on birth control by Jacques Derogy, rekindled the debate in the press and among the public.
18   Such as Françoise Giroud at *L'Express*, who demanded government action on the issue.
19   J. Jenson, 'Struggling for identity: the women's movement and the state in Western Europe', *West European Politics*, 8 (4): 11 October 1985.
20   Dhavernas, *Droits des femmes*, p. 150.

21 MFPF, *25 ans*, p. 276.

22 Under the law of '1 juillet 1901 relative au contrat d'association' associations had to have an AGM and publish statutes, objectives, lists of leading members, and annual reports. (*Ibid.*, p. 273.)

23 Ronsin, *La grève des ventres: propagande néomalthusienne et baisse de la natalité en France XIXe-XXe siècles* (Aubier-Montaigne, 1980), p. 216.

24 Leathard, *Family Planning*, Chapters 7–9.

25 V. Walsh, 'Contraception: the growth of a technology', in J. Hanmer and P. Allen eds, *Alice Through the Microscope* (Virago, 1980), p. 195. In 1926 a Labour-sponsored Private Member's Bill was defeated by Labour Members of Parliament due to trade union pressure, and the fear of working-class voters who were often conservative on social issues. The vote actually showed that Conservatives were more in favour of birth control, especially in the Lords, which angered the women members of the Liberal and Labour parties. (Leathard, *Family Planning*, p. 30.)

26 M. J. Field, in *The Comparative Politics of Birth Control* (Praeger, 1983), p. 235, points out that Roman Catholics are often found supporting liberal parties as they benefit from egalitarian social welfare programmes as immigrants. They are also concentrated in cities and regions, thus having an influence on the election of candidates. However, 'fear of the monolithic Catholic vote persisted long after it ceased to have reality'. (K. Hindell and M. Simms, *Abortion Law Reformed* (Peter Owen, 1971), p. 81.)

27 Field, *Comparative Politics of Birth Control*, p. 21.

28 Leathard, *Family Planning*, p. 47.

29 *Ibid.*, p. 95.

30 MFPF, *25 ans*, p. 132.

31 Dhavernas, *Droits des femmes*, p. 150.

32 MFPF, *25 ans*, p. 144.

33 J. Gouazé *et al.*, *La loi de 1920 et l'avortement: stratégies de la presse et du droit au procès de Bobigny* (Presses Universitaires Lyon, 1979), pp. 56–57.

34 Interview with N. Pfeffer, 1991.

35 C. Francome, *Abortion Freedom* (Allen & Unwin, 1984), p. 57.

36 *Ibid.*, p. 57.

37 Hindell and Simms, *Abortion Law Reformed*, p. 88.

38 Leathard, *Family Planning*, pp. 116–117.

39 MFPF, *25 ans*, p. 90.

40 Leathard, *Family Planning*, p. 113.

41 M. Segalen, *Sociologie de la famille* (Armand Colin, 1987). An INED study of Roman Catholics in 1956 found that 43 per cent were in favour of the liberalisation of contraception, 45 per cent against. A survey in 1966 showed that 62 per cent of practising Roman Catholics were opposed to liberalisation, 24 per cent in favour. (Henri Leridon *et al.*, *La Seconde Révolution Contraceptive* (INED PUF, 1987), p. 24.)

42 Leathard, *Family Planning*, p. 46.

43 Only a third of medical schools gave such courses in 1957. (Walsh, 'Growth of a technology', p. 185.)

44 *Ibid.*, p. 189.

45 Leathard, *Family Planning*, Chapter 13.

46 MFPF, *25 ans*, p. 127.

47 *Ibid.*, p. 146.

48 In 1924 Dr J. Campbell, the Senior Medical Officer for Maternity and Child Welfare, published an extremely important government report which concluded that 3,000 women died in childbirth annually; that pregnancy was more harmful in large families; that induced abortion was prevalent. The question of birth control was not, however, included in its remit. (Leathard, *Family Planning*, p. 30.)

49 *Ibid.*, p. 219.

50 *Ibid.*, p. 43.

51 *Ibid.*, p. 55.

52 *Ibid.*, p. 72.

53 *Ibid.*, Chapters 10 and 11.

54 *Ibid*, p. 83.

55 *Ibid.*, p. 134.

56 *Ibid.*

57 *Ibid.*

58 *Ibid.*, p. 132.

59 *Ibid.*, p. 135.

60 *Ibid.*, p. 133.

61 The Communists, in particular, feared that if contraception were introduced the working classes would lose their hard-earned family state benefits in the short term. The leader of the French Communist Party (PCF), Maurice Thorez, accused the MFPF of Malthusianism and attempting to weaken the working classes by reducing their numbers. It has been argued that the PCF were using the debate on contraception to divert attention from the accusations being brought against Stalin in the USSR at the time and their difficulties in alliance with the Socialist Party. In addition it can be seen as an example of their innate Stalinist puritanism. (MFPF, *25 ans*, pp. 87–89.) Ronsin, *La grève des ventres*, p. 216, argues that birth control in post-war France was seen as modern and 'Western'. Lines between East and West, and birth control or not, were firmly drawn. The Communist Party equated family planning with American Imperialism. It would take until 1965 for them to come out openly in favour of liberalisation.

62 *Ibid.*, p. 92.

63 *Ibid.*, p. 142.

64 *Ibid.*, p. 149.

65 *Ibid.*, p. 151.

66 *Ibid.*, p. 149.

67 *Ibid.*, p. 412.

68 *Ibid.*, p. 151.

69 Pingaud, *L'Avortement*, p. 35.

70 Leathard, *Family Planning*, p. 192.

71 *Ibid.*, p. 186.

72 Under this principle, the government has control over congress decisions on statutes, and dissolutions; the Minister of the Interior controls internal rules; he and the Minister of Health can send delegates to the organisation's headquarters. (MFPF, *25 ans*, p. 273.)

73 *Ibid.*, p. 210.

74 Leathard, *Family Planning*, p. 116.

75 Ronsin, *La grève des ventres*, p. 218.

76 *Ibid.*
77 Leathard, *Family Planning*, p. 193.
78 *Ibid.*
79 *Ibid.*, p. 199.
80 *Ibid.*, p. 194.
81 *Ibid.*, p. 200.
82 Dhavernas, *Droits des femmes*, p. 154.
83 Pingaud, *L'Avortement*, p. 36.
84 *Guardian*, 3 July 1999; *Le Monde*, 25 June 1999.
85 *Le Monde*, 1 July 2000.
86 M. Woolf, 'Curbs on morning after pill for girls under 16', Electronic Telegraph, 1 December 1999, www.telegraph.co.uk.
87 BMA news release, 'BMA supports emergency contraception through pharmacist', 28 February 2000.
88 Early Day Motion on Emergency Contraception, *Hansard*, Thursday 11 June 1998; Early Day Motion 1138, *Hansard*, 30 November 1999.
89 Dhavernas, *Droits des femmes*, p. 152.
90 Leathard, *Family Planning*, p. 232.
91 Despite their liberal rather than radical attitudes to women's rights, Leathard, *Family Planning*, points out, the FPA was not necessarily out of step with women, who, into the late 1970s, were in favour of childrearing and family limitation rather than avoidance. (*Ibid.*, p. 232.) Therefore, 'as an agent of social change (the FPA) essentially provided the means to fertility regulation; wider social and economic factors led individuals to change their fertility desires'. (*Ibid.*, p. 233.) Leathard therefore argues that in the 1920s and 1970s, which were two periods of social change, pressure group lobbying had the most influence on the content of law (rather than inclusion in the policy community), as it led to the first government sanction of State provision in 1930, and the acceptance of its medical nature and full public provision in 1974.
92 Dhavernas, *Droits des femmes*, p. 155.

Chapter 4

1 See discussion of medicalisation in Chapter 1.
2 J. Keown, *Abortion, Doctors and the Law* (Cambridge University Press, 1988), p. 11. Penalties diminished over time and were generally dealt with by the ecclesiastical courts.
3 *Ibid.*, p. 27 and p. 48. Abortion remains criminalised in the Republic of Ireland under the Offences Against the Person Act 1861. After a referendum in 1983 abortion was prohibited by the Constitution. The Abortion Act 1967 does not apply to Northern Ireland. Here case law applies as it did in the rest of the UK before 1967. Many Irish women thus travel to the UK to have their pregnancies terminated – approximately 7,000 in 1997. (*Abortion Statistics 1997*, Series AB no. 24, p. xi.)
4 Ney Bensedon, *Que sais-je?: Les droits de la femmes* (PUF, 1980), p. 117.
5 *Ibid.*
6 MFPF, *25 ans*, p. 453.

7 R.-H. Guerrand and F. Ronsin, *Le Sexe apprivoisé: Jeanne Humbert et la lutte pour le contrôle des naissances* (Découverte, 1990), p. 384.

8 *Le Matin*, 4 September 1917.

9 *See* Chapter 1, fn. 1.

10 M. Ferrand *et al.*, *Que sais-je?: L'Interruption Volontaire de Grossesse* (PUF, 1987), p. 11.

11 Dhavernas, *Droits des femmes*, p. 145; MFPF, *25 ans*, pp. 455–456.

12 *Le Matin*, 4 September 1917.

13 Guerrand, *Le Sexe*, p. 385. Infanticides were more common in rural areas, abortion in urban areas, among all social classes.

14 Ferrand *et al.*, *L'IVG*, p. 12.

15 *Ibid.*

16 MFPF, *25 ans*, p. 457.

17 Chapter III entitled 'Protection de la race' increased penalties for immoral practices such as drug trafficking and alcoholism. Finally, schools had to begin teaching pupils about the declining birth rate. (Dhavernas, *Droits des femmes*, p. 147.)

18 *Ibid.*, pp. 147–148.

19 Ferrand *et al.*, *L'IVG*, p. 14.

20 Knibiehler, *La Femme*, p. 275.

21 *Ibid.*

22 Trifirino, thesis, p. 39.

23 Keown, *Abortion, Doctors and the Law*, Chapter 3.

24 Soutoul, *La responsabilité médicale*, p. 290.

25 As early as 1852 the 'Académie de Médecine' accepted that doctors could perform abortion to save the mother's life. (Guerrand, *Le Sexe*, p. 385.)

26 MFPF, *25 ans*, p. 458.

27 Y. Knibiehler, *La Femme et les médecins* (Hachette, 1983), p. 274.

28 *Ibid.*, p. 275.

29 Francome, *Abortion Freedom*, p. 66.

30 *R v. Bourne* (1938) 3 All ER 61. McNaghten, J. has been criticised by Keown, *Abortion, Doctors and the Law*, p. 58, for ignoring the fact that at common law it had already been established that a mother's life could be saved and that the 1929 Act was more concerned with infanticide.

31 p. 694.

32 p. 693.

33 p. 615.

34 Keown, *Abortion, Doctors and the Law*, p. 79.

35 *R v. Bergmann and Ferguson* [1948] 1 BMJ 1008; R. F. R. Gardner, *Abortion: the Personal Dilemma* (Paternoster Press, 1972), p. 32.

36 *Ibid.*

37 *R v. Newton and Stungo* [1958] CLR 469; [1958] 1 BMJ 1242.

38 D. Marsh and J. Chambers, *Abortion Politics*, (Junction Books, 1981), p. 15.

39 Potts *et al.* eds, 'Natural human fertility: social and biological determinants', *Proceedings of the 23rd annual symposium of the Eugenics Society* (Macmillan/Eugenics Society, 1988), p. 163.

40 *Gillick v. West Norfolk and Wisbech AHA* [1985] 3 All ER 402.

41 In *Rance v. Mid Downs HA* [1991] 1 All E. R. 801, for example, a couple claimed damages for not having their child's spina bifida diagnosed which prevented them

from having the chance to terminate the twenty-six week pregnancy. Their action failed. Brooke J. held that a twenty-six week old foetus was capable of being born alive and could not be lawfully terminated. (Cf. John Murphy, 'Grey areas and green lights: judicial activism in the regulation of doctors' 4 *Northern Ireland Legal Quarterly* (1991) 260.)

42 *C v. S* [1987] 1 All ER 1230.

43 *Abortion Statistics 1997*, Series AB no. 24.

44 D. Morgan, and R. G. Lee, *Blackstone's Guide to the Human Fertilisation and Embryology Act 1990* (Blackstone, 1991), p. 59.

45 *Ibid.*

46 The Communist Party, for example, was more favourable to abortion than to contraception.

47 Dossier collated by M. Sineau. Interview, Paris, 11 September 1990.

48 Dhavernas, *Droits des femmes*, p. 163.

49 *Ibid.*, pp. 163–164.

50 *Ibid.*, pp. 158–162.

51 'Loi du 17 janvier 1975 relative a l'intérruption volontaire de grossesse', Gaz. Pal. 75, I, 8. As a last resort in 1975, in the face of the liberalisation of abortion, eighty-one opponents of abortion used a newly founded right to seize the Constitutional Court. This was in order to have the law declared unconstitutional on the grounds that it was contrary to the preamble of the 1946 Constitution, which declared the sacred and inalienable rights of all human beings (including therefore the unborn child); and to Article 2 of the European Convention on Human Rights which stated that all persons have a right to life protected by the law which could not be ended intentionally unless via capital punishment. The Court decided that it was incompetent to decide on the conformity of a national law with an international treaty (by art. 61 and 55 of the Constitution) but that the law was not unconstitutional as it did not force people to abort, but, rather, respected individual liberties when these people were distressed or in therapeutic need.

52 Case law after the promulgation of the 1975 law in France underlines that opponents and the state felt most strongly about the letter of the law not being followed especially as regards premises not being licensed (JCP 1978, 32, 18831; D. 1978, 16); the giving out of information (*Actes* 70 (1990), p. 26); and not being medically qualified (*L'Unité*, 18–24 (1977), p. 17). On 20 July 1988, the government allowed an amnesty for all illegal abortions. Soutoul, *La responsabilité médicale*, p. 280.

53 Dhavernas, *Droits des femmes*, p. 169.

54 Soutoul, *La responsabilité médicale*, p. 291.

55 However, the law does not specify what medical conditions 'péril' covers. A survey carried out in 1988 in Paris discovered that doctors believed that renal or coronary illnesses counted, but not psychoses or toxaemia ('toxicomanie'). X-ray exposure, and the taking of contraindicated medicines were not included, but AIDS medications were. Some doctors include rape or incestual rape in cases concerning very young minors. (*Actes* 70 (1990), p. 27.) This suggests that rape and incest are not normally included. It should be noted that doctors in France are not criminally liable for infanticide should a viable baby survive an abortion, as doctors in the UK are under the 1929 Act.

56 *Health Statistics Quarterly* 2 (Summer 1999).

57 Keown, 'Miscarriage: A Medico-Legal Analysis', *CLR* (October 1984), 581–604.

58 Rivera, R. *et al.*, The mechanism of action of hormonal contraceptives and intra uterine contraceptive devices, *Am J Obstet Gynecol*, 1999, 181, 1263–1269.

59 Soutoul, *La responsabilité médicale*, pp. 272–275.

60 *Le Monde*, 17 October 1987.

61 C. Bataille, '*RU 486*', *Cahiers du féminisme*, 47, hiver 1988, p. 24.

62 Soutoul, *La responsabilité médicale*, pp. 272–275.

63 *Le Monde*, 21 June 1989.

64 Bataille, *RU 486*, p. 24.

65 *Le Monde*, 17 October 1987.

66 *Le Monde*, 21 June 1989.

67 *Guardian*, 23 April 1991.

68 Bataille, *RU 486*, p. 24.

69 *Le Monde*, 21 June 1989.

70 *Ibid.*

71 Clinics can accept women for daycare surgical abortion if they live within two hours travelling distance, but for medical abortion the travelling time is limited to one hour. If the drug is used, their GP must be informed (which some women may wish to avoid). The cost has also been prohibitive. In February 1992 the BPAS were offering early surgical abortion for £195, but medical abortion for £240 as this cost included the cost of the RU 486 itself plus the prostaglandin, plus the necessary extra visits to the clinic. (*Women's Health*, 15: 18 July 1992.)

72 *Le Monde*, 21 June 1989.

73 *Abortion Statistics 1997*, Series AB No. 24, p. xii.

74 http:// news.bbc.co.uk, 11 March 2000.

75 RCOG Guidelines, *The Care of Women Requesting Abortion* (2000); *Independent on Sunday*, 12 March 2000.

76 This was endorsed in *South Glamorgan CC* v. *W and B [1993] 1 FLR 5574* and *Re W (A Minor) (Medical Treatment: Court's Jurisdiction) [1992] 4 All ER 627*. English law on the autonomy of minors in relation to medical treatment has been criticised as unclear despite the apparent intentions of the Children Act to grant such autonomy. (Cf. M. Brazier and C. Bridge, 'Coercion or caring: analysing adolescent autonomy' (1996) 16 *Legal Studies* 84 and C. Lyon, 'What's happened to the child's right to refuse?' 6 *Journal of Child Law* 6: 84 (1994).)

77 *Re B (a minor)*, *Guardian*, 21 May 1991.

78 *Paton* v. *British Pregnancy Advisory Service* [1978] 2 All ER 987; *Paton* v. *UK* 3 EHRR 410 (1980).

79 M. Fox, 'Abortion Decision-Making: taking men's needs seriously', in E. Lee ed. *Abortion Law and Politics Today* (Macmillan, 1998).

80 *C* v. *S* [1987] All ER 1230.

81 [1996] 2 All ER 10.

82 Soc. 8 juin 1983, G. P., 1984. IR. 8.

83 C. E. 31 oct 1980 J. C. P., 1982. II. 1973.

84 Soutoul, *La responsabilité médicale*, p. 285; G. Mémeteau, 'Le Droit Médical de la Famille', in J. Carbonnier ed., *Le droit non-civil de la famille* (PUF, 1983), p. 247.

85 Rennes, 10 févr. 1983, Doc Juris-Data, no. 040229.

86 *R* v. *Smith (John)* [1974] 1 All ER 376.

87 In *Royal College of Nursing of the United Kingdom* v. *Department of Social Security*, [1981] AC 800 the House of Lords held by 3:2, despite nurses' objections

that they and not doctors were terminating pregnancies after 1972 (when the procedure changed to drug induced abortion); and that according to the Act the medical termination should be a team effort and was lawful if the procedure were initiated by the doctor, 'who remained in charge of it throughout, and was carried out in accordance with his directions ... in accordance with accepted medical practice' (p. 801.). In addition, other members of staff apart from doctors and nurses are not covered by the Act. In *Janaway* v. *Salford AHA* [1988] 3 All ER 1051 it was held in the House of Lords that typing a letter referring a patient to a consultant for an opinion on a possible abortion did not amount to participation 'in any treatment authorised' and could not be conscientiously objected to by the secretary concerned. Participation involves being personally involved in the termination itself.

88 C. Daniels, *At Women's Expense: State Power and the Politics of Fetal Rights* (Harvard University Press, 1993).

89 *Re MB* [1997] 2 FLR 426. Cf. S. Fovargue, and J. Miola, 'Policing pregnancy: implications of the Attorney-General's Reference' (No. 3 of 1994) (1998) 6 *Medical Law Review* 265.

90 In 'wrongful disability' cases parents can be awarded damages if it can be proved that as a result of medical negligence during pregnancy their child was born disabled, and he would not have been born disabled otherwise. Such damages if awarded are for the cost of rearing a disabled child. There is now a statutory duty on a doctor to offer abortion in these circumstances, up to term (with conscientious objection). The Congenital Disabilities Act 1976 dealt *inter alia* with pre-conception damage which resulted in the birth of a living, yet disabled child. (For a discussion of the legal definition of 'viability', see Brazier, *Medicine, Patients and the Law* (2nd edn, Penguin, 1992), pp. 244–245.) In France if a claim is made that the baby has been damaged by the failed abortion, causation must be proven beyond doubt, as in the UK. (Soutoul, *La responsabilité médicale*, p. 261.) 'Wrongful birth' cases relate to the rights of the parent in relation to the cost of upbringing not the rights of the child, where abortion has failed, the woman has remained pregnant, and a child has gone on to be born (*Scuriaga* v. *Powell* (1979) 123 SJ 486). In France, women in such cases have claimed damages for the continuation of their situation of 'détresse' necessary for legal IVG, charges for the original operation and any subsequent one, and expenses for the cost of rearing the child. However, legally the doctor is only under a duty to care and be medically competent, and judges themselves have not expected doctors to complete an abortion: T. G. I., Bobigny, 15 déc. 1976, D., 1977.245; 9 févr. 1983, J. C. P., 1984. II. 20149; 2 juin 1983, G. P., 1983.193; T. G. I., Evreux, 21 déc. 1979, D., 1981.185; 5 juillet 1984 G. P., 1984, Som. 290; Civ. Ie, 9 mai 1983., 1984.121. (Soutoul, *La responsabilité médicale*, pp. 255, 259 and 264.)

Claims for negligence by the child for 'wrongful life' are not available following *McKay* v. *Essex AHA* [1982] 2 All ER 771 where the Court ruled out any claim by the child that she should never have been born at all, for three reasons: because it was impossible to put a price on the difference between disabled existence and non-existence; doctors should not be under a duty to carry out an abortion; a duty to abort would be an infringement of the right to life and demean the value of the lives of the disabled. In France there do not appear to have been cases where children have sought damages for 'wrongful life'. Perhaps this is because there are less links between American and French law in structure and language, and cases for 'wrongful life' in the UK have probably been influenced by similar claims in the United States.

Chapter 5

1 It should be noted that campaigns of this nature did not take place in Northern Ireland.
2 Francome, *Abortion Freedom*, p. 65.
3 L. J. F. Smith, 'The abortion controversy 1936–77: a case study in "emergence of law"', Ph.D. dissertation, University of Edinburgh, 1979, p. 65.
4 D. Marsh and J. Chambers, 'The abortion lobby: pluralism at work?', in Marsh ed., *Pressure Politics*, p. 146.
5 By 1966 their membership had increased to 1,000, perhaps due to the Thalidomide tragedy. (Leathard, *Family Planning*, p. 128.)
6 More than half of ALRA's income came from the Californian Hopkins Donations Fund; between 1961 and 1967, £8,500 with which the organisation funded its more important strategies, such as the commissioning of opinion polls. (Hindell and Simms, *Abortion Law Reformed*, p. 124.)
7 Francome, *Abortion Freedom*, p. 69. Bourne replied that he had performed a curette before and was willing to take the girl on as his patient. The girl was so physically traumatised by the rape that she had to be kept in hospital, and when Bourne performed 'a minimal pelvic examination' on her she mentally broke down. (Gardner, *Abortion*, p. 29.) He saw this as evidence that '(i)n her there was nothing of the cold indifference of the prostitute'. (Hindell and Simms, *Abortion Law Reformed*, p. 70.) Had there been, he would not have considered the therapeutic abortion, illustrating his own and perhaps the general medical attitude of the period. After a week, he performed the operation, informed the police and was arrested at the hospital (the guardsmen who had raped the girl were also arrested). He was subsequently acquitted.
8 *See* fn. 59.
9 Francome, *Abortion Freedom*, p. 66.
10 Smith, 'The abortion controversy', p. 65.
11 Francome, *Abortion Freedom*, p. 90.
12 Leathard, *Family Planning*, p. 128. To prove that their aims did enjoy widespread support, they concentrated on making use of surveys and interviews. In 1962, 72 per cent of the population agreed with abortion for foetal deformity in the wake of the Thalidomide tragedy; in 1965, 70 per cent agreed where the woman's health would be seriously affected (including 60 per cent of Roman Catholics). In 1966, 89 per cent of the non-Catholic clergy interviewed were in favour of legal reform; and in 1967, 65 per cent of doctors interviewed were in favour of ALRA's reform proposals or thought they were too restrictive. (Marsh and Chambers, *Abortion Politics*, p. 20.)
13 Leathard, *Family Planning*, p. 63.
14 Smith, 'The abortion controversy', p. 71.
15 Francome, *Abortion Freedom*, p. 84.
16 Leathard, *Family Planning*, p. 128.
17 Ferrand *et al.*, *L'IVG*, p. 20.

18 *Ibid.*

19 J. Jenson, 'Struggling for identity: the women's movement and the state in Western Europe', *West European Politics* 8 (4): 13 October 1985.

20 F. Isambert *et al.*, *Contraception et avortement: 10 ans de débat dans la presse, 1965–1974* (CNRS, 1979), pp. 102–103.

21 '(It) had precise and limited goals when it was founded, and wanted to concentrate on abortion law reform without placing it in the context of women's liberation.' (Duchen, *Feminism in France*, p. 53.) *see* fn. 25.

22 Gisèle Halimi, one of its founding members and originally the group's defence lawyer criticised left-wing hangers-on who valued socialist revolution over women's oppression. She was criticised in turn for being reformist rather than revolutionary. (G. Halimi, *La Cause des femmes* (Edns Grasset et Fasquelle, 1973), pp. 71–73.)

23 Duchen, *Feminism in France*, p. 53.

24 Halimi, *La Cause des femmes*, p. 83.

25 The manifesto read 'Un million de femmes se font avorter chaque année en France. Elles le font dans des conditions dangereuses en raison de la clandestinité à laquelle elles sont condamnées, alors que cette opération, pratiquée sous contrôle médicale, est des plus simples. On fait le silence sur ces millions de femmes. Je déclare que je suis l'une d'elles. Je déclare avoir avorté'. (Isambert, *Contraception et Avortement*, p. 118.)

26 *Ibid.*, p. 99

27 'This illegal action was more outrageous than all the demonstrations, articles, meetings, debates and so on ... The whole of France knew that women could go into MLAC centres and have an abortion. They could not arrest all the women and doctors at MLAC ... MLAC was more important than Choisir as its actions were constant, daily, "réelles".' (Translation of interview with Janine Mossuz-Lavau, Paris, 7 September 1990.)

28 Francome, *Abortion Freedom*, p. 65.

29 *Ibid*, p. 87.

30 'Proposition de loi no. 469 relative à la diffusion des méthodes de contraception et à l'IVG.'

31 Dhavernas, *Droits des femmes*, p. 159.

32 MLAC suffered the consequences of many new social movements with left-wing members – initially, the PCF refused to join as long as the trotskyite Ligue Communiste Révolutionnaire (LCR) were members and internal disputes restricted their campaigning.

33 *See Le Monde*, 19 November 1974.

34 Hindell and Simms, *Abortion Law Reformed*, p. 79.

35 Francome, *Abortion Freedom*, pp. 57–58.

36 The Roman Catholic Church was thus 'caught off guard ... and talked of "the appalling weight of the abortion lobby"'. (Francome, *Abortion Freedom*, p. 91.) There are several examples of the inefficiency of the Roman Catholic lobby at this time. The Catholic Union did attempt to lobby Roman Catholic MPs during the passage of the Steel Bill, but less than half turned up to vote at the Second Reading. Most of the Roman Catholic MPs' speeches were also discredited by their being anti-contraception, which put women in an impossible position. (Francome, *Abortion Freedom*, p. 91.) In July 1999, mass resignations of SPUC's

leadership indicated a split within the organisation over its future direction. The SPUC's national director, John Smeaton, was criticised for taking a conservative line on abortion. This may indicate a more extreme position among such organisations generally. (*Guardian*, 19 July 1999.)

37 N. Pfeffer, *The Stork and the Syringe* (Polity Press, 1993), p. 93.

38 A. Batiot, 'Radical democracy and feminist discourse: the case of France', in D. Dahlerup ed., *The New Women's Movement: Feminism and Political Power in Europe and the USA* (Sage Publications, 1986), p. 133.

39 Leridon, *Révolution Contraceptive*, p. 125. Roman Catholic support for abortion at this time was also evident in the UK. In a 1966 national opinion poll, 57 per cent of Roman Catholics (in comparison to 75 per cent of the general population) were in favour of making it easier to obtain a legal abortion. (Hindell and Simms, *Abortion Law Reformed*, pp. 88–107.)

40 *La Croix*, November 1974, in 'Supplément aux cahiers français' no. 171, 1975, notice 9.

41 Leridon, *Révolution Contraceptive*, p. 125.

42 H. Eckstein, *The English Health Service* (Harvard University Press, 1970).

43 Cf. Keown, *Abortion, Doctors and the Law*, p. 78.

44 Francome, *Abortion Freedom*, p. 70.

45 Hindell and Simms, *Abortion Law Reformed*, p. 69.

46 For most doctors, however, the medical debates on abortion resulted in the opinion that things should stay as they were with doctors deciding on the merits of individual patients following their own clinical judgement. (J. Lovenduski and J. Outshoorn, *New Politics of Abortion*, Sage 1986, p. 52.)

47 Smith, 'The abortion controversy', p. 55.

48 Francome, *Abortion Freedom*, p. 94.

49 Gardner, *Abortion*, p. 60.

50 The Royal Medico-Psychological Association came out in favour of reform in July 1966, emphasising the social need for abortion as refusal could have a damaging effect on the mental health of mothers and their children. (Keown, *Abortion, Doctors and the Law*, p. 88.) The Medical Women's Federation approved reform in October 1966 and supported, not grounds for abortion, which were hard to define, but one general legal clause that permitted termination by two medical practitioners 'in the interests of physical and mental health of the mother, taking into account her whole family situation and circumstances past, present and future', and the inclusion of a conscience clause. (*Ibid.*, p. 95.)

51 Ferrand *et al.*, *L'IVG*, p. 16.

52 *Ibid.*, p. 20.

53 In a survey in 1972, 40 to 50 per cent of doctors were against abortion even in cases of rape, incest or malformed foetuses. (J. Ardagh, *The New France* Penguin, 1977, p. 397.)

54 Dr M-T G-D (Médecin, gynécologue, mère de 5 enfants) 'C'est un défi à la pudeur, c'est un défi à la morale ... à la famille (qui est, quioque en pensent certaines signataires du Manifeste, la cellule vivante de toute société)'. (F. d'Eaubonne, *Le Féminisme ou la Mort: Femmes en Mouvement* Pierre Horay, 1974, p. 104.)

55 Francome, *Abortion Freedom*, p. 94.

56 Hindell and Simms, *Abortion Law Reformed*, p. 73.

57 Smith, 'The abortion lobby', p. 53.

58 Francome, *Abortion Freedom*, p. 71.

59 Kenneth Robinson, future Labour Health Minister, and an ally of ALRA, introduced a Private Member's Bill in 1961 for abortion on the grounds of social circumstance, foetal abnormality or rape; with the concurrence of two registered medical practitioners (this was practice at the time); and before 16 weeks (allowing for conscientious objection). This was talked out by Roman Catholic MPs (who talked of abuse of the law and the contribution that abnormal children made to society). A similar fate was received by the Private Members' Bills of: Joseph Reeve in 1953; Renee Short in June 1965; and Simon Wingfield Digby in February 1966. The most successful bill was one backed by ALRA, which contained a social clause, was presented by Lord Silkin (Labour), and passed its Third Reading in the HL in March 1966, but ran out of time.

60 This phrase was originally proposed by the Church of England Board of Social Responsibility, the Law Society and the Academy of Forensic Sciences. (Keown, *Abortion, Doctors and the Law*, p. 96.)

61 He widened clause 1 (1) (a) and withdrew clauses 1 (1)(c) and (d) as he felt the old clauses would be necessarily included in the new one. The social clause and rape clause were thus taken out.

62 Hindell and Simms, *Abortion Law Reformed*, p. 176.

63 *Ibid.*, p. 178.

64 Hindell and Simms, *Abortion Law Reformed*, p. 176.

65 The RCOG (with Roman Catholic support in the person of Bernard Braine MP) failed with the consultant clause, mainly due to Steel's objection that the BMA were opposed to differentiation between consultants and other medical professionals, and that two opinions and the safeguards of ministerial powers and the necessity of notification, was restrictive enough. Cf. Keown, *Abortion, Doctors and the Law*, pp. 99–103.

66 Marsh and Chambers, *Abortion Politics*, p. 21.

67 Francome, *Abortion Freedom*, p. 98.

68 *Ibid.*, p. 99.

69 *Le Monde*, 15 December 1973.

70 Ferrand *et al.*, *L'IVG*, p. 24.

71 Pingaud, *L'Avortement*, pp. 124–137.

72 *Ibid.*, pp. 107–123.

73 *Ibid.*, pp. 56–60.

74 Peyret proposed a more radical bill in October 1974, based on the Socialist backbench bill, permitting abortion up to the tenth week for all women who made a written request to a committee.

75 Pingaud, *L'Avortement*, p. 165.

76 *Ibid.*

77 Ferrand *et al.*, L'IVG, p. 35.

78 *Ibid.*, pp. 25, 27 and 31.

79 Despite public opinion polls showing majority support for the Act (63 per cent in 1969 (Leathard, *Family Planning*, p. 175), the fact that the majority of abortions were being carried out privately fuelled press reports of 'abortion rackets' and illegality. In fact, three times as many abortions were carried out in 1971 by the NHS (60,000) as the charitable sector (22,000) or the private sector (20,000) though the private sector's share increased over time. (Leathard, *Family Planning*, p. 174.)

80 Smith, 'The abortion lobby', p. 258.
81 Pro-life backbench bills came for example from Norman St. John Stevas in July 1969, who, with BMA and RCOG support, aimed to make one of the registered medical practitioners a consultant and check racketeering through regulation; Mr Godman Irvine in 1970, who failed, however, to gain support from GPs for his 'consultant clause'; Mr Michael Grylls in 1973 and 1974, who wanted to prevent abortion information being given for profit except by doctors; James White (Labour) February 1975, who sought regulation of referral agencies, a reduction in the time limit to twenty weeks normally, to twenty-four weeks for foetal disability, risk to life having to be 'grave' and risk to health 'serious', and restrictions on foreigners; William Benyon in February 1977, who proposed a similar bill, but with a strengthening of the conscientious objection clause; Sir Bernard Braine in February 1978 and John Corrie in July 1979, who proposed bills similar to White's Bill and to the report of an ineffectual 1975 Select Committee.
82 A separate, less-radical group was set up by them to this end, the Campaign against the Corrie Bill (CAC) in 1979, who practised the same strategies. (Marsh and Chambers, 'The abortion lobby', p. 149.)
83 *Ibid.*
84 *Ibid.*, p. 153.
85 *Ibid*, p. 151.
86 SPUC had a large membership (10,000 in 1972; 26,000 in 1980) and a democratic structure with autonomous local branches, but with policy made by an elected council. It was not a Roman Catholic organisation, but drew much support and funding from the Roman Catholic Church and only supported abortion to save the mother's life in line with Roman Catholic doctrine. SPUC's strength lay at the local level, but in Parliament in the 1970s it was not as strong as Co-ord. (*Ibid.*, pp. 157–158.) LIFE members (20,000 in 1980) were in autonomous local groups and, in contrast to SPUC, worked ostensibly at the local level to educate against abortion among the young and provide alternatives to abortion for pregnant women. SPUC made use of the grass-roots support stirred up by LIFE, but benefited from being seen as less radical. (*Ibid.*)
87 *Ibid.*, p. 159.
88 In the 1970s, the pro-life lobby, despite containing fewer groups and having more of a consensus of opinion, was not as well organised as the pro-Choice lobby, due to their differing strategies and the bulk of their actions being at the local rather than at the national level. The concomitant lack of coordination and disunity played a large part in their ineffectuality as lobbyists. Also, as the government did not want to initiate debate on abortion, Private Members' Bills had to be used '[a]s only the Labour Party appears willing to give time to Private Members' Bills, then groups promoting "conservative" policies have to be circumspect in their aims'. (*Ibid.*, p. 163.)
89 R. Cunningham, 'Legislating on human fertilization and embryology in the United Kingdom', *Statute Law Review*, 1991, pp. 214–227.
90 Morgan and Lee, *HFEA Act*, p. 40.
91 J. Challoner, *The Baby Makers* (Channel Four Books, 1999), p. 100.
92 *Guardian*, 19 July 2000.
93 Written answer, House of Commons, 12 April 2000 (Parliamentary References on Reproductive Health, BPAS).

94 I. Nisand, *LIVG en France* (Report, February 1999).

95 *Le Monde*, 28 July 1999.

96 'French abortionists march in Paris', *BMJ*, 310, 28 January 1995.

97 Some of these points are also made in M. Latham, 'Reform and revolution: the campaigns for abortion in Britain and France', in E. Lee, ed., *Abortion Law and Politics Today* (Macmillan, 1998).

98 Francome, *Abortion Freedom*, p. 130.

99 Leathard, *Family Planning*, pp. 129–130.

100 Francome, *Abortion Freedom*, p. 97.

101 Gardner, *Abortion*, p. 61.

102 Keown, *Abortion, Doctors and the Law*, p. 109.

103 P. Byrne and J. Lovenduski, 'Two new protest groups: the peace and women's movements', in Drucker and Dunleavy *et al.* eds, *Developments in British Politics* (Macmillan, 1984), p. 53.

104 Gardner, *Abortion*, p. 68.

105 Interest group influence can also be gauged through media reports, in the press and legal journals, which, throughout the campaign did not give space to feminist arguments, apart from during the *Bobigny* case, or see abortion as an issue involving freedom for women. Rather, abortion evolved in articles from a criminal act to a social problem, and it was advocated that the Welfare State should take over the role of judges in deciding whether or not women should have abortions. Also legal and medical interest groups were given precedence over campaigners in articles (Isambert, *Contraception et Avortement*).

106 As to the involvement of the MLF, Lovenduski and Outshoorn, *New Politics of Abortion*, p. 272, argue that, although Choisir played an agenda-setting role, no other MLF-affiliated groups played a part. Rather, it was the presence of feminists in governing élites and as professionals that led to the development of policies for women through policy networks. I would dispute this as do many other French commentators, such as Mossuz-Lavau (Interview, Paris, 7 September 1990) Dhavernas (Interview, Paris, 11 September 1990), and members of the MFPF and Choisir themselves.

107 'There's no doubt that pressure from feminists and other groups plus women's courage in openly flounting the law and speaking out against the abortion law, were crucial to the eventual passing of the "loi Veil".' (Duchen, *Feminism in France*, p. 58.)

108 'Although of primary personal relevance to women, it was not the sole concern of women alone, since many men took sides either in defence or in opposition to it. Nor did all women support a liberalising reform which could only give them more control over their own lives ... women as a readily identifiable social group do not form a unified political group and whereas (some groups) may well be ideally committed to eradicating sexism in our society, this commitment does not make them feminist.' (*Ibid.*)

109 MFPF, *25 ans*, p. 235.

110 *Ibid*, pp. 383–396.

111 This helped to ensure that half of all public hospitals did no abortions in 1976. (Ardagh, *The New France*, p. 397.) French feminists have been more active at the local level on this issue than their British counterparts, as it is local policy community members such as doctors and religious groups that have been more hostile.

Many from MLAC and MFPF continued to be cited for crimes under the Veil law into the late 1980s such as giving information to women who were over 10 weeks' pregnant on where to obtain an illegal abortion. The fight of feminists against the medical profession has been particularly ardent. In many parts of France, abortion is difficult to obtain. This is often because the chef de service is hostile to abortion – it is rare for doctors to be forced into carrying out their legal duty. Feminists in both countries continue to campaign on the issue of abortion however, recently to ensure the continued provision of the abortion pill RU 486. The acceptance of feminist rights by the French state was emphasised when the Roman Catholic Church pressurised the pharmaceutical company Roussel to withdraw RU 486.

Chapter 6

1 Some of the material in this Chapter appears in M. Latham, 'Regulating the new reproductive technologies: a cross-Channel comparison', *Medical Law International*, 1998 3: 89–115 and M. Latham, 'The French parliamentary guidelines of May 1997: clarification or fudge?', *Medical Law International*, 1998 3: 235–241.

2 The fee charged for licensing to cover the running costs of the Authority may in turn increase treatment costs and reduce access for infertile patients.

3 *Droit Administratif*, 'Commentary', pp. 469–473; H. Oberdorff, 'L'Administration publique face au progrès médical', pp. 411–419, *L'Actualité Juridique*, 20/6/1991; texts published in *Bulletin Officiel du Ministère de la Santé*, Fascicule No. 88 (35 bis).

4 These were based on 'Projet de loi (No. 2599, Sapin Bill) relatif au corps humain et modifiant le code civil, 25 mars 1992'; 'Projet de loi (No. 2600, Bianco Bill) relatif au don et à l'utilisation des éléments et produits du corps humain et à la procréation médicalement assistée, et modifiant le code de la santé publique'; 'Projet de loi (No. 2601, Curien Bill) relatif au traitement de données nominatives ayant pour fin la recherche en vue de la protection ou l'amélioration de la santé et modifiant la loi no. 78–17 du 6 janvier 1978 relative à l'informatique, aux fichiers et aux libertés'. It is unclear why from 1991 bioethics law was changed from being one whole law covering all aspects of assisted-conception law and related laws into three separate draft bills, but see *Liberation*, 9 September 1992.

5 'Loi no. 94–548 relative au traitement des données nominatives ayant pour fin la recherche dans le domaine de la santé et modifiant la loi no. 78–17 relative à l'informatique, aux fichiers et aux libertés.'

6 'Loi no. 94–653 relative au respect du corps humain.'

7 'Loi no. 94–564 relative au don et à l'utilisation des éléments et produits du corps humain, à l'assistance médicale à la procréation et au diagnostic prénatal.'

8 *Maclennan* v. *Maclennan* [1958] SLT 12. In 1982 the Law Commission did rule that a DI child should be considered the child of the commissioning husband.

9 Schedule 3, paragraph 3(1)(b); Code of Practice 4.4.

10 Cass. Civ. 1ere. 4 mai 1970; D. 1970, Som. 22; G. Memeteau, *Le Droit Médical* (litec, 1985). Consent in medical practice is governed by the Code de Déontologie 1995, art. 36.

11 On 21 July 1989 the Conseil d'Etat published a judgment against the Catholic 'Association des médecins pour le respect de la vie' on whether the content of this decree was legal. The Association contended that under Article 34 of the

Constitution, only Parliament, not government, could pass any law that dealt with civil liberties and procreation. The Conseil argued that the decrees of 8 April 1988 were not new law, but an extension of the 'loi du 31 décembre 1970' on hospital reforms on the provision of expensive technological equipment. By Articles 34, 38 and 45 of the 1970 law the government could regulate all Procréation Médicalement Assistée (PMA) equipment in public and private hospitals. Second, because PMA was a medical cure for sterility, the decree could deal with the technical aspects of such treatment, without Parliament having beforehand to deal with conditions or limits of the treatment, or its consequences for family status. Third, Article L. 753 of the 'Code de la Santé Publique' and the 'loi du 11 juillet 1975' were not breached because they did not include assisted-conception techniques. Fourth, Article L. 761 of the same Code did allow for extension by the Minister of Health to include PMA. (*OPECST Rapport*, 28 February 1992, Tome II, *Textes et Documents*, p. 51.)

12 *OPECST Rapport*, 28 February 1992, Tome II, *Textes et Documents*, p. 50. Donor insemination was included in the 1991 law at the behest of Bruno Durieux, Junior Health Minister, who wanted compulsory testing of sperm donors for AIDS enshrined into law due to a public scandal over blood transfusion. Sperm banks which did not comply with the decrees of 1988 were investigated, and one prosecuted, by the French government in 1991 (*Le Monde* 23 November 1991). As another example of the disputes prevalent in debates in France on the 1991 law, in the National Assembly critics saw it as allowing assisted-conception procedures to be legitimised through the back door in the guise of a simple non-controversial law. It was also argued that it created a confusing legal situation as it skimmed over the ethical issues of assisted conception at the same time as such questions were being discussed in their entirety in a forthcoming report by M. Bernard Bioulac, President of the 'mission parlementaire sur la bioéthique'. (This report was later published as the 'Rapport fait au nom de la commission spéciale sur les projets de loi' No. 2871 Assemblée Nationale, 30 June 1992, also known as the 'Rapport Bioulac'.) Nor had consultation been made with medical experts such as the CNMBR. The Ministry of Social Affairs and Integration argued that civil law problems and ethical issues of assisted conception were not the aim of the Bill in question. It would be a temporary measure, to be completed by the ensuing principal texts on biomedicine. Getting such legislation through was the main thing and this could best be achieved in small stages. (*Le Monde* 23 November 1991.)

13 Article 9 replaces the 'loi du 22 décembre 1976' on organ donation and clause 13 of the 'loi du 31 décembre 1991' (91–1406).

14 Statute on donation and assisted conception, Articles 10 and 8.

15 Code of Practice 5.15.

16 Two clinics were investigated under the 'loi du 31 décembre 1991', clause 13, and were subsequently refused licences for donor insemination. (*Le Monde*, 11 February 1992.)

17 This was also suggested by the BMA Panel of the Law Commission and by the Warnock Commission.

18 For thirty years after the birth, if the father has never recognised the child as his own, he, his wife, his inheritors and the child itself can exclude the child from any inheritance from the father (art. 311–1). All of the above also applies to the unmarried couple except that only the mother and child retain their right to

challenge for ten years (art. 339). The 'loi du 3 janvier 1972' on illegitimacy left the way open for the contesting of paternity (*OPECST Rapport*, 28 February 1992 Tome II), but it provided legally equal status for illegitimate children accepted by their father and mother. Since 1972, the biological father has had superior rights to the social father, although in the context of DI, if the donor is anonymous, tracing the father to prove his identity would be difficult.

19 In 1988 alone there were 5,000 cases contesting paternity in French courts (D. Rousset, 'Témoignage', in 'Mouvement français pour le planning familial', *L'Ovaire-dose?: les nouvelles méthodes de procréation*, Syros/Alternatives, 1989). From the late 1980s, courts began to accept the increased use of DI and social fatherhood as being equivalent to biological fatherhood and indeed superior to it in the context of a firmly established couple and where the social father has consented to the use of DI. At the cour d'appel at Toulouse (1e. Ch. 21 septembre 1987, JCP 1988 II 21036, note ES de la Marnière; *Receuil Dalloz Sirey* 1988, 184, note D. Huet-Weiller), an unmarried father was allowed to contest his paternity of his partner's DI child, and the judgment referred to the fundamental illegality of all sperm and ova insemination. In 'T. G. I. Bobigny 18 janvier 1990', however, a father was not allowed to contest paternity of a DI child whose conception he had consented to and in 'Cour d'Appel de Paris 29 mars 1991' it was found that the court would only consider the contesting of paternity if it could be proved that the child was conceived using DI. (*OPECST Rapport*, 23 February 1992, Tome II: *Textes et Documents*, pp. 132–3.)

20 This might happen where a surrogate mother was being used, for example.

21 C. Bonnet, 'Nouvelles méthodes de procréation et adoption: une chance pour les enfants?', in 'Mouvement français pour le planning familial, *L'Ovaire-dose?*, p. 237.

22 [1990] 1 FLR 167. See Morgan and Lee, *Human Fertilization and Embryology Act 1990*, p. 157.

23 J. L. Baudouin, C. Labrusse-Riou, *Produire l'homme: de quel droit?* (PUF, 1987), p. 55, for example, were in favour of anonymity as the donor did not want a relationship with the child, but if information was given to the child for psychological reasons it should not lead to legal rights.

24 The Constitutional Court, however, held that the 1912 law was not relevant to medically assisted procreation and that no constitutional principle prohibited legislation from proscribing the establishment of 'filiation' between a father and his child.

25 Adoption Act 1976, s. 51.

26 Section 28 (6)(b). In August 2000 (*Guardian*, 26 August 2000), it was announced by Yvette Cooper, Minister for Public Health that new rights would be given to babies conceived after their fathers' deaths. This made it possible for mothers of a child, as a result of using the father's sperm posthumously, to register the name of the child's dead father on the birth certificate. The new rules would apply retrospectively so that mothers would now be able to have the fathers' names re-recorded on their birth register, though followed by the term, 'deceased'. Children in this situation would not be able to inherit from their fathers, or succeed to any titles. Cooper spoke of this being, 'exactly the right thing to do'.

27 Para. 2(2)(b).

28 Schedule 3, para. 4 (1).

29 R v. *Human Fertilisation and Embryology Authority ex p.Blood* (QBD) [1997] 1 FCR.

30 Under Articles 59 and 60 of Treaty of Rome 1957. The use of European Community law, alongside the European Convention on Bioethics, has implications for the possible harmonisation of the legal regulation of assisted conception in Europe. In the *Blood* case, for example, the fact that Belgium currently has no assisted-conception statute and no prohibition on the use of gametes without donor consent, combined with Articles 59 and 60, prevented the HFEA from implementing English law on this matter.

31 The fears of the HFEA that this would set a precedent for posthumous treatment without the gamete donor's consent were assuaged by a further ruling in the Court of Appeal that the removal of sperm from a comatose man without his consent was unlawful under the terms of the 1990 Act. In the instant case this removal could not be criticised as the legal situation had been unclear at that time. After the *Blood* decision, it is now unlawful to use sperm without written consent, unless fresh sperm is used.

32 *Consorts Parpalaix c/ le CECOS et autre*, 1 août 1984, *Gazette du Palais*, 16–18 September 1984, p. 11.

33 Civil Code, Article 6.

34 C. Neirinck, 'Le droit de la filiation et la procréation médicalement assistée' (1994) 149 *Les Petites Affiches*, p. 54.

35 TGI Toulouse, 11 mai 1993.

36 The *Pires* case and the 1994 regulation overrule the judgment in 'TGI Angers 10 novembre 1992' which approved postmortem transfer of an embryo following a husband's death due to his wish to have a third child and the fact that the fertilisation of the embryo had taken place while the parents were still a legal couple and before the death of the husband, only the gestation of the child having been delayed. (L'Abbée, X., 'Sommaires Commentés: Droits de l'enfant' (1994) 4 *Recueil Dalloz Sirey* 30–32.) They also overrule a statement published by the CCNE on 17 December 1993 that postmortem transfer of embryos should be permitted and differed from postmortem insemination. The embryo had a greater right to be transferred than the gamete had to be fertilised, and the parent had a right to gestate the embryo as both parents had agreed to the creation of a child when the embryo had been created. (*Le Monde*, 13 May 1994.)

37 Sheila McLean, professor of law and ethics in medicine at Glasgow University, has argued, for example, that it is unacceptable to discriminate on grounds of marital status when a child could be at risk in a standard two-parent heterosexual family. This was especially true when it was not a question of public resources, when women were paying privately for their treatment. Then clinicians had no business deciding fitness for parenthood. (*Guardian*, 13 March 1991.)

38 In debates in Parliament the original intention by interest groups to outlaw all single and lesbian mothers from DI failed. An amendment by Lady Saltoun to restrict access to DI to married couples and to prevent access to single women and lesbians was defeated by only one vote on 6 February 1990 and ensured government notice of the issue. Clause 13 was then strengthened at the Report Stage in the House of Commons by an amendment which defined the welfare of the child as the need of that child for a father. (R. Cunningham, 'Legislating on human fertilization and embryology in the United Kingdom', *Statute Law Review*, 1991, pp. 214–227.)

39   *HFEA Code of Practice 1995*, 3.19. a.

40   *Ibid.*, 3.26.

41   *Ibid.*, 3.43.

42   *Ibid.*, 3.28.

43   In January 1985 those on the waiting list were told that 'the Unit reserves the right to remove a couple's names from the waiting list and to decline treatment at any subsequent stage should any further information (of a medical or social nature) indicate the need to do so'. Entry on to the list now necessitated a three-year history of infertility, childlessness was defined as having no children by the present relationship or by adoption, and patients accepted onto the waiting list had to satisfy the general criteria established by adoption societies in assessing suitability for adoption. (*Report of the Health Service Commissioner*, case no. W. 376/86–87, *Administration of a Waiting List for Infertility Treatment*, HMSO, London, 1988.)

44   J. K. Mason, and R. A. McCall Smith, *Law and Medical Ethics*, 5 edn, Butterworths, London, 1999, p. 72.

45   *R. v. Secretary of State for Social Services, ex parte Hincks (1980)* 1 BLMR; *R v. Central Birmingham H. A., ex parte Walker (1987)* 3 BLMR 32.

46   1 FLR 512.

47   HFEA Code of Practice para. 3.17 (d).

48   1994, unreported. Another unreported case was that of Mrs Briody in January 2000. Here, Mrs Justice Ebsworth in the High Court accepted that Mrs Briody had been made infertile because of medical negligence for which she was compensated with £80,000. Mrs Briody was refused the cost of surrogacy treatment in the USA, however, as it was held that the costs of private treatment necessary due to her low chances of pregnancy, were unacceptably high. This does seem unfortunate for women like Mrs Briody who have been made infertile through no fault of their own, especially as they cannot be many in number. It is another example, nonetheless, of how far the British government is not prepared to fund the high cost of much infertility treatment.

49   'IVF bar on woman who wed divorcé', *The Times*, 29 June 1994, p. 5.

50   *Le Monde* 13 December 1989.

51   See *OPECST Rapport* 28/2/92, Tome II and the 'Rapport Bioulac' 30/6/92.

52   OPECST, *Rapport sur les sciences de la vie et les droits de l'homme: bouleversements sans contrôle ou législation à la française*, No. 2588 (Assemblée Nationale)/No. 262 (Sénat), 28 fev. 1992; Tome I: 'Questions-clefs et réponses contradictoires', Fascicule No. 2, p. 29.

53   J. Harris, *The Value of Life* (Routledge & Kegan Paul, 1985), p. 143.

54   Baudouin *et al.*, *Produire l'Homme*, p. 167, criticised surrogacy for treating the child as a product and undermining the fundamental right of a mother to keep her child. They recommended that any law regulating surrogacy should advocate that the birth mother be anonymous; that the commissioning couple accept the child once born; that the surrogate hand over the child; that licensed centres be used; that solutions be based on existing adoption laws. Criminalisation was too severe, especially on the child, and could drive surrogacy underground. Their arguments are similar to feminist arguments on the instrumentalisation of women's bodies and children. 'C'est le corps "fonction" et le corps "produit"'. (*Ibid.*, p. 199.)

55   D. Cusine, *New Reproductive Techniques: A Legal Perspective* (Dartmouth Publishing Co., 1990), p. 179.

56 J. K. Mason and R. A. McCall Smith, *Law and Medical Ethics* (Butterworth, London 3rd edn, 1991), p. 70.

57 Interview with Guy Braibant, Paris, 11 September 1990.

58 Conseil d'Etat, Assemblée, 22 janv. 1988; Cour de Cassation, 13 déc. 1989.

59 *A v. C* (1978) 8 Fam Law 170. *Re P.(Minors) (Wardship: Surrogacy)* [1987] 2 FLR 421.

60 Dekeuwer-Defossé, *Dictionnaire juridique*, p. 186.

61 *In re a Baby, The Times*, 15 January 1985. *Re an Adoption Application (surrogacy)* [1987] 2 All ER 826. The English judiciary has been sympathetic to the surrogate mother in cases they have been faced with, 'even in the face of an economic anomaly in that the commissioning couple are inherently likely to be able to provide a better financial environment'. Courts would probably be more likely to favour maternal bonding over genetic incompatibility, and if the child was rejected by both parties it would be placed in local authority care. (Mason and McCall Smith, 5 edn, 1999, p. 81.)

62 2 All ER 826.

63 Art. 345 C. Pén.; T. G. I Marseille, 26 janv. 1982, J. C. P., 83. II. 20028.

64 Dekeuwer-Deffossé, *Dictionnaire juridique*, p. 185. In 'T. G. I. Paris, 5 déc. 1984' a husband had inseminated his wife's sister, and on giving birth the sister gave the child to the couple. The judge decided that this would be allowed to constitute 'adoption simple' rather than the more irrevocable 'adoption ordinaire' as he did not want to break the ties between the child and its mother, the sister. This could be problematic if the correct process of adoption procedures were not followed – the birth mother should therefore protect her rights by not consenting to adoption until after the baby was born as that would enable her to retract her consent to abandoning the child. (P. Malaurie et L. Aynès, *Droit Civil. La Famille* (Cujas, 2nd edn 1989).

65 The 'tribunal de grande instance' had rejected the application on the grounds that it was a surrogate birth and that the contract went against the principles of public order and of the 'indisponibilité' of a person.

66 Art. 3–1 of 26/11/90; decree no. 90–917 of 8/10/90.

67 *OPECST Rapport*, 28/2/92, Tome II, pp. 96–97.

68 In this case the T. G. I. had rejected (28/6/89) and the Cour d'Appel allowed (15/6/90) adoption by the commissioning mother of a child born through the agency Alma Mater. The T. G. I. had argued that surrogacy did not threaten public order as long as it was not commercial and that other abandonments of children and organ donations were legal. They too referred to United Nations Conventions and the child's interest. (*Ibid.*, pp. 97–99.)

69 *Ibid.*, pp. 99–100.

70 Section 44.

71 [1989] 3 All ER 613.

72 See A. Grubb, 'Unborn child (pre-natal injury): homicide and abortion' (1995) (spring 1995), *Medical Law Review* 3(1): 302–310; *Attorney-General's Reference (No. 3 of 1994)*.

73 Morgan and Lee, *HFEA Act*, p. 174.

74 See J. L. Baudouin, Labrusse-Riou, *Produire l'homme*, pp. 84–85. For a discussion of French law on 'brain-life', see *Le Monde*, 8 November 1988, p. 32.

75 Section 14(3) and Section 14(4), respectively.

76 *HFEA (Statutory Storage Period) Regulations 1991* (S. I. 1991 No. 1540).

77 Section 14(1)(c).

78 A. Grubb, 'Statutory Storage Period for Embryos' (1996) *Medical Law Review* 4: 211–215.

79 *HFEA (Statutory Storage Period for Embryos) Regulations 1996* (S. I. 1996 No. 375), reg. 2(2).

80 *Ibid.* reg. 2(1).

81 Sched. 3, paras. 2(4) and 4(1).

82 Regs. 2(4)(b)(i), 2(4)(b)(ii), and 2(2)(c), respectively.

83 CCNE, *Ethique et recherche biomédicale*, Rapport 1986; *Avis relatif aux recherches sur les embryons humains in vitro et à leur utilisation à des fins médicales et scientifiques* (Actes Sud, 1988).

84 Cf. Guy Braibant, *Avant-projet de loi sur les sciences de la vie et les droits de l'homme*, 1989.

85 *Le Monde*, 18 April 2001.

86 Section 14(1)(c).

87 In 1986 the CCNE came out firmly against donation, and favoured the destruction of spare embryos until such time as there were clear legal guidelines, for example relating to 'filiation' and to commercialisation. This could be reviewed in three years. It feared the possibility of a black market in embryos. However, for the Conseil d'Etat in 1988, donation was seen as a preferable option to destruction in order to fulfil the potential of the embryo. It advocated that if a parent died or a couple separated, the embryos must be destroyed or donated after the five years' storage time, during which time the written consent of either could be retracted. The Braibant Report in 1989 ruled that the donation must take place in a licensed centre, the donating couple must have attempted implantation and must consent, and the recipient couple must be infertile or genetically abnormal. A CCNE Avis of December 1989 stated that the donation should be anonymous, non profit-making and only available in a small number of public centres. (*L'Humanité*, 16 December 1989.)

88 Sched. 3, para. 4(1).

89 G. Memeteau (1994), 'L'embryon legislatif' (1994) 44 *Receuil Dalloz Sirey* p. 357.

90 D. Vigneau, 'Dessine-moi un embryon' (1994) 149 *Les Petites Affiches*, p. 68.

91 French government bodies have continually shown a greater reticence toward embryo research than has been shown in the UK. In December 1986 the CCNE published a largely ineffectual moratorium on research until such time as assisted conception was regulated by statute. The Sapin Bill of 1992 (Projet de loi no. 2599 relatif au corps humain et modifiant le code civil, 25 mars 1992) concentrated on the limitations imposed on research on humans by their genetic integrity which ethically should not be interfered with unless it was for their own medical benefit and must therefore have consent.

92 Conseil constitutionnel, Décision no. 94–343 DC, 27 juillet 1994. Cf. Duprat, J.-P., 'A la recherche d'une protection constitutionnelle du corps humain: la décision 94–343–344 d. c. du 27 juillet 1994' (1994) 149 *Les Petites Affiches*, pp. 34–40.

93 The French Parliament distinguished selective reduction from a normal abortion. This means that a clinician carrying out infertility treatment would not have to adhere to the abortion law of 1975 because the pregnancy was not ended by selective reduction. The mother would not therefore have to consider herself to

be in a situation of distress before the tenth week of pregnancy, nor be suffering from a threat to her life, or physical or mental health after this time. (See Memeteau, 'L'embryon legislatif', p. 357.)

94 'Décret 97–613 du 27 mai 1997' regarding research on human *in vitro* embryos and modifying the Public Health Code.

95 Schedule 2, s. 3(2).

96 Schedule 2, s. 3(3).

97 'Décret 97–578 du 28 mai 1997' regarding to multidisciplinary centres for prenatal diagnosis and modifying the Public Health Code, and 'Décret 97–579 du 28 mai 1997' regarding prenatal diagnosis *in utero* modifying the Public Health Code.

98 See Memeteau 'L'embryon legislatif'; Vigneau, 'Dessine-moi un embryon'.

Chapter 7

1 Interview with Françoise Laborie, Paris, 8 July 1999; Anne-Marie de Vilaine, 'Femmes: une autre culture?', in A. –M. de Vilaine, L. Gavarini, M. Le Coadic eds, *Maternité en Mouvement* (Edns Saint-Martin/Presses Universitaires Grenoble, 1986); O. Blaizot, 'Femmes-médecins/médecins-femmes. Pouvoir médical', in MFPF, *L'Ovaire-dose?*, p. 292.

2 M. Stanworth, 'Reproductive technologies and the deconstruction of motherhood' in Stanworth, ed., *Reproductive Techniques: Gender, Motherhood and Medicine* (Polity Press, 1987); Josyane Moutet, 'Technologie, familles et droit', pp. 84–87, *Pénélope*, Cahier no. 9, automne 1983.

3 R. P. Petchesky, 'Foetal images: the power of visual culture in the politics of reproduction', in Stanworth, *Reproductive Techniques*.

4 M. Pelletier, 'PMA: l'opposition enfin dans le débat', spécial colloque, *Dialogue*, mai-juin 1985, p. 6; F. Vinteuil, *Cahiers du féminisme*, printemps 1987, pp. 32–33.

5 L. Birke *et al.*, *Tomorrow's Child* (Virago, 1990); H. Rose 'Victorian values in the test-tube: the politics of reproductive science and technology', in Stanworth, *Reproductive Techniques*.

6 O. Thibault, *Des Enfants Comment?* (Edns Chronique sociale, 1984), pp. 15–16.

7 N. Pfeffer, 'AI, IVF and the stigma of infertility', in Stanworth, *Reproductive Techniques*.

8 M. Stanworth, 'Defining reproductive technology as a feminist issue', paper given at Political Studies Association/British Sociological Association Conference on Rights, Politics and Reproductive Technology, London School of Economics, London, 24 February 1990.

9 F. Collin, 'Les maternités et leurs interprétations', in MFPF, *L'Ovaire-dose?*, p. 41.

10 Also consulted were representatives of the Roman Catholic, Protestant and Jewish faiths. (*OPECST Rapport*, 28 February 1992, Tome II, *Textes et Documents*, p. 311.)

11 M. Stanworth paper, 'Defining reproductive technology'.

12 N. Pfeffer and A. Quick, *Infertility Services: A Desperate Case* (Greater London Association of Community Health Councils, 1988), p. 5.

13 See for example, 'Temoignage', in MFPF, *L'Ovaire-dose?*, pp. 63–65.

14 Y. Roudy, *Citoyennes à part entière*, mai/juin 1985.

15 M.-J. Dhavernas, in MFPF, *L'Ovaire-dose?*, p. 70.

16 O. Blaizot, in *Ibid.*, p. 71.

17 C. Bonnet, 'Nouvelles méthodes de procréation et adoption: une chance pour les enfants?', in MFPF 1989, *L'Ovaire-dose?*, p. 199.

18 A.-M. de Vilaine, 'La révolution procréatique, est-elle démocratique?', in MFPF, *L'Ovaire-dose?*, p. 281.

19 L. Doyal, 'Infertility: a life sentence? Women and the NHS,' in Stanworth, *Reproductive Techniques*.

20 S. Gibson, 'A feminist perspective', Paper given at University of Manchester Centre for Social Ethics and Policy conference on the Human Fertilisation and Embryology Bill, St Mary's Hospital, Manchester, 9 May 1990.

21 M.-M. Chatel, *Malaise dans la procréation: les femmes et la médecine de l'enfantement* (Albin Michel, 1993), pp. 174–177. See also Y. Knibiehler, 'Femmes et médecins: regards sur l'histoire', in MFPF, *L'Ovaire-dose*, p. 297; A.-M. de Vilaine, *Citoyennes à part entière*, 44, juin–août 1985, p. 16.

22 N. Pfeffer and A. Quick, *Infertility Services*, p. 37; M. Warnock, 'The artificial family' in M. Lockwood ed., *Moral Dilemmas in Modern Medicine* (Oxford University Press, 1986), p. 146.

23 See various articles which appeared in *Le Monde* in 1988 written by such sociologists and feminists as Geneviève Delaisi de Parseval, Anne-Marie de Vilaine, Laurence Gavarini, Françoise Laborie and the IVF doctor Jacques Testart.

24 C. Donovan, 'Donor Insemination and the mechanics of reproduction', Department of Social Policy and Social Work, Edinburgh University, May 1991, unpublished paper.

25 A. Oakley, 'From walking wombs to test-tube babies', in Stanworth, *Reproductive Techniques*.

26 H. Rose, 'Wanting babies', Nursing Times, September 1984, pp. 12–14; L. Horne, 'Comments on the Warnock Report', in *Critical Social Policy*, April 1984, pp. 112–114; S. McLean, 'Women, rights and reproduction', in S. A. M. McLean ed., *Legal Issues in Human Reproduction* (Gower, 1989), pp. 213–233.

27 J. Moutet, 'La bioéthique au microscope du droit naturel', *Actes 1990*, pp. 19–25. Vandelac presents some interesting statistics to support her argument: full sterility only affects 3 to 5 per cent of people; 42 per cent of IVF women in 1987 already had a child; between 25 per cent and 60 per cent of 'infertile' women will fall pregnant naturally during IVF treatment; in all societies, 20 per cent of women on average remain childless after two years; women were being treated with IVF not DI when it was their husbands who were infertile; and in 1982 8 per cent of married women under 45 were sterilised and 0 per cent of men, even though vasectomy was less dangerous – such women were a permanent source of new IVF patients. Medical technology was contributing to, stimulating and exaggerating infertility, not curing it as doctors claimed. (L. Vandelac, 'Technologies de procréation; les mots de la stérilité et les effets iatrogènes des anovulants et du stérilet', in MFPF, *L'Ovaire-dose?*., p. 152.)

28 F. Laborie, 'De quelques faces cachées des nouvelles techniques de procréation', in *L'Ovaire-dose?*

29 (What pressure group is operating, brushing aside decisions, ignoring the results of our investigations before the full stakes and implications of these choices have been clearly thought through?) L. Gavarini, in MFPF *L'Ovaire-dose?*, p. 147.

30 *Ibid.*, p. 193; A.-M. de Vilaine, in MFPF, *L'Ovaire-dose?*, p. 117.

31 Moutet, *Actes*; Pelletier, 'PMA: l'opposition enfin dans le débat', spécial colloque, *Dialogue*, mai–juin 1985, p. 12.

32 A. Lifshitz-Krams, 'Techniques nouvelles et éthique de la reproduction', in MFPF, *L'Ovaire-dose?*, p. 177.

33 F. Laborie, 'Peut-on penser les différences?', in MFPF, *L'Ovaire-dose?*, p. 24; 'Collectif de femmes pour la réflexion et l'action sur la reproduction médicalement programmée', 'Appel aux femmes pour débattre de la reproduction médicalement assistée', Décembre 1988, in *Ibid.*, p. 319.

34 V. Marange, 'Droits subjectifs et biomédecine: le contrat illusoire', in *L'Ovaire-dose?*, p. 241; de Vilaine, in *Ibid.*, p. 125. Women were being selectively bred like livestock, excluding the lower classes or radicals, and taking control of women's bodies. To resist this, women must infiltrate and take over control of science and technology from men to change the course of research. (J. Hanmer and P. Allen, 'Reproductive engineering: the final solution?', in *Alice Through the Microscope* (Virago, 1980), p. 227.

35 Mason and McCall Smith, *Law and Medical Ethics* (5 edn, 1999), p. 156.

36 Moutet, *Actes*.

37 J. Gallagher, 'Eggs, embryos and foetuses: anxiety and the law', in Stanworth, *Reproductive Techniques*.

38 Pelletier, 'PMA: l'opposition enfin dans le débat', spécial colloque, Dialogue, mai–juin 1985, p. 6.

39 M.-J. Dhavernas, 'Peut mieux faire', in *Les Temps Modernes*, 1986–7, no. 482, p. 156.

40 Marange, *L'Ovaire-dose?*, p. 249.

41 'Persons are beings with the capacity for valuing their own existence. In the case of human beings, they become persons when the capacity to value their own lives develops and will cease to be persons when they have lost that capacity.' This would mean that personhood and rights would not exist until sometime after birth. Harris, *The Value of Life*, p. 25.

42 S. Franklin, 'The changing cultural construction of reproduction in the context of new reproductive technology: redefining reproductive choice', paper given at PSA/BSA conference on Rights, Politics and Reproductive Technology, LSE, London, 24 February 1990.

43 *L'Ovaire-dose*, p. 143.

44 *L'Ovaire-dose*, p. 233.

45 These echo later arguments put forward by Petchesky in Stanworth, ed., *Reproductive Techniques*.

46 Naomi Pfeffer believed (interview, London, 26 September 1991) that outside these circles FINRRAGE were relatively unknown, among, for example, groups that lobbied in favour of infertile services such as the National Association for the Childless.

47 Its name changed in 1991 to Women's Health.

48 *Women's Health*, March 1992.

49 Interview with Naomi Pfeffer, London, 26 September 1991.

50 See S. Roseblade, 'IVF: debate and activity at the local level', University of Manchester MSc. thesis, 1988.

51 As increasing numbers of people rang in for advice, National Association for the Childless arranged funding from the infertility drugs company Serona to set up a

phone line. The Association was also invited to be a member of the medical interest group PAGICS which campaigned for embryo research.

52 Moutet, *Actes*; interview with Françoise Laborie, Paris, 10 September 1990.

53 D. Decluze, 'N. T. R.', *Paris Féministes*, 38: 13–14 (1987).

54 See OPECST Report 1999.

55 This was confirmed in an interview with Dr Phillippe Granet, a practising fertility specialist, on 8 July 1999.

56 This type of body was also advocated in the Warnock Report.

57 Correspondence between Keith Gibson (MRC) and Marge Berer (WHRRIC), 25/7/85; WHRRIC file on assisted conception.

58 *Unborn Children (Protection) Bill: A new clause 1 to set up a Licensing Body*, p. 3, accompaniment to above correspondence, WHRRIC file on assisted conception.

59 *Ibid.*, p. 2.

60 The VLA berated the services available in the UK, and the 'wide variation of funding, standards, patient selection criteria and treatment protocols between IVF centres … Access to IVF treatment … continues to be determined largely by a couple's financial resources, a matter of continuing concern to the Authority'. (*The Third Report of the VLA for Human IVF and Embryology* (Medical Research Council, 1988), p. 14.)

61 J. Challoner, *The Baby Makers*.

62 Interview with Frédérique Dreifuss-Netter, academic lawyer, member of CNMBRDP, July 1999.

63 Interview with Simone Novaes, 10 September 1990.

64 This groups together, among others, Biologistes et laboratoires d'études de la fécondation et de la conservation des oeufs (BLEFCO); Groupe d'Etude de la FIV Française (GEFF); Société de Médecine de la Reproduction (SMR); Société Française d'Etudes de Fertilité (SFEF); Société d'Andrologie de la Langue Française (SALF); Groupe d'Etudes de Don D'Ovocytes (GEDO). (Interview with Dr Phillippe Granet, 8 July 1999.)

65 This criticism of infertile patients was shared by radical feminists and some doctors, for example by IVF doctor Jean-Yves Diquelou, a militant member of MFPF.

66 *OPECST Rapport*, 28 February 1992, Tome II, p. 51.

67 Roseblade, 'Debate and activity', p. 18.

68 Interim Licensing Authority, *Guideline no. 15*, 1990.

69 Warnock Legislation Group minutes from 1985, WHRRIC file on assisted conception.

70 They have a private tie with the Birth Control Trust (BCT). Dilys Cossey is a link between BCT, Population and Coord. (Phone interview with LARC, 13 March 1992.)

71 Correspondence between Keith Gibson and Marge Berer, 25 July 1985.

72 *L'oeuf transparent* (Flammarion, 1986); *Le désir du gène* (eds F. Bourin, 1992). Among those given publicity by the French media at this time were Athea, gynaecologist; Delaisi, psychoanalyst; Gavarini, sociologist; Laborie, sociologist; Marcus-Steiff, sociologist; de Vilaine, feminist.

73 *Le Monde*, 17 December 1986; *Le Monde*, 10 September 1986; *Le Matin*, 11 September 1986; *Libération*, 11 September 1986; *Le Monde*, 2 February 1987.

74 Testart, *L'oeuf transparent*, p. 11.

75 'Même si les institutions, lentes et inertes, interdisent d'abord, puis redoutent, tolèrent, pratiquent, demandent et finissent par exiger tel ou tel progrès bio-médical' (*Ibid.*); *Libération*, 11 September 1986.

76 *Le Monde des Débats*, June 1999, p. 16.

77 *OPECST Rapport*, 28 February 1992, Tome II, 1992, p. 149.

78 Interview with Frédérique Dreifuss Netter, academic lawyer, member of CNMBRDP, July 1999.

79 *Le Figaro*, 22 April 1986; see 'Instruction "Donum Vitae" de la Congrégation pour la Doctrine de la Foi du 22/2/87', *OPECST Rapport*, 28 February 1992, Tome II., p. 294; 'Discours de S. S. Jean-Paul II au Conseil de l'Europe (8/10/88)', *Ibid.*, p. 293.

80 *OPECST Rapport*, 28 February 1992, Tome II, p. 307.

81 HL Official Report 7 December 1989, p. 1018; *Sunday Times*, 11 March 1990.

82 The media also played an important role in influencing a more diffuse public opinion and, thereby, the votes of MPs.

83 Pfeffer, *The Stork and the Syringe*.

84 *HFEA Fifth Annual Report*, July 1996, p. 48.

85 *Le Monde des Débats*, June 1999, p. 10; *La Croix L'Evènement*, 24/6/89; OPECST *Rapport sur les sciences de la vie et les droits de l'homme*, No. 2588 (Assemblée Nationale)/ No. 262 (Sénat), 28/2/92, Tome I: 'Questions-clefs et réponses contra-dictoires' Fascicule No. 2: 'Les Procréations Médicalement Assistées', p. 48.

86 For example, C. Dyer, 'Baby Cotton and the birth of a moral panic', *Guardian*, 15 January 1985; A. Hutchinson and D. Morgan, 'A Bill born from panic', *Guardian*, 12 July 1985; M. D. A. Freeman, 'After Warnock – whither the law?' *Current Legal Problems* 33: 5; K. Cotton, and D. Winn, *Baby Cotton for love and money* (Dorling Kindersley, 1985); M. Freeman, 'Does surrogacy have a future after Brazier?', *Modern Law Review* 7: 12, spring.

87 *Legislation on Human Infertility Services and Embryology* Cm 46 HMSO; *Human Fertilisation and Embryology: A Framework for Legislation* Cm 259 HMSO. The Green Paper suggested three legislative alternatives for control of research (and IVF): a statutory authority as recommended by Warnock; licences issued from the Secretary of State, as advocated by the pro-life lobby; self-regulation along the lines of the VLA. Following consultation, the White Paper later that year put forward two proposals regarding research. Option A would have made it a criminal offence to carry out any procedures on a human embryo other than those aimed at or preparing the embryo for transfer to the uterus of a woman; though it would not have prevented storage of embryos or destruction of unsuitable or 'surplus' ones. Option B would have liked to have seen the same proposal licensed by the SLA, with prohibitions on genetic manipulation, cloning, trans-species transfer and fertilisation. Research would be limited to a period of fourteen days. Option B won the day, fortunately.

88 Information about informal medical consultation from personal correspondence with British Civil Servant Roy Cunningham, 9 March 1992.

89 Ethics committees have existed in France since the 1970s on genetics, though not until 1982/3 did they contain lay members. Their power was extremely limited, however, nor did they function with any formal recognition. It was with the development of assisted conception and public concern that they gained a higher profile and became more widespread. With thirty-six members, half of which are

renewed every two years, and all of which are renewed every four years, the CCNE was intended to represent all sections of society involved in the debate: the President chose some members from 'principales familles philosophiques et culturelles' (which included Communism), and the government and leading institutions in the field chose the others from leading researchers, doctors, lawyers and sociologists who were interested in ethical issues. The majority of the members were from a medical background, especially as representatives of other social groups were chosen by their group for their medical expertise. The working groups were usually made up of doctors and lawyers.

90 Between 1984 and 1988 Avis were published on controlling the growth of genetic and medical information held on computer (1984); human experimentation (1984, 1986 and 1988); the use of human tissue (1984 and 1987); artificial reproduction (1984); local ethical committees (1984 and 1988); prenatal diagnosis (1985); embryo research (1986) and the abortion pill (1987).

91 C. Ambroselli, *Actes*, été 1985, p. 16.

92 CCNE, *Sciences de la vie*, 1988.

93 The members of the group were chosen by Claude Evin, Minister of Health and Pierre Arpaillanage, Minister of Justice and included lawyers from the Conseil d'Etat, the Cour de Cassation, professors of law and of medicine and members of the Treasury. Rocard wanted the law to be put before Parliament by spring 1989.

94 The Office Parlementaire d'Evaluation des Choix Scientifiques et Technologiques (OPECST) was created by a specific law in 1983. It represents both houses and is made up of 8 Deputies and 8 senators representative of groups in chambers, assisted by a scientific council made up in the main of scientific doctors. Here, it was headed by M. Serusclat, a PS senator. (H.-M. Crucis, 'Le Parlement face aux sciences et technologies', in *L'Actualité juridique – droit administratif*, 20 June 1991, p. 450.) The 'special commission charged with examining the bioethics Bills', headed by M. Bioulac, PS Deputy, was created originally in October 1990 by the commissions of law and of culture, family and society. It held forty auditions and seven round tables. (*Le Monde*, 27 February 1993.)

95 The Sapin Bill on human status, genetic testing and filiation was voted in by 451:44. The Curien Bill on data banks was voted in by 363:31. The National Assembly adopted in theory the setting up of a consultative committee on databanks. The Bianco Bill on organ donation and clinic regulation was voted in by 349:78. The National Assembly originally hoped to adopt the framework of the three Bills before the end of the session in March 1993. The Assembly also enshrined into law the existence and authority of the CCNE and that the law would be looked at every five years to keep pace with medical progress. (*Le Monde*, 27 February 1992.)

96 Interview with Françoise Laborie and Simone Novaes Bateman, Paris, July 1999.

97 Conseil d'Etat, *Les lois bioéthiques: cinq ans après*, May 2000.

98 The Braibant Report coincided from 1988 with a minority government which did not want to risk failure by putting a bill before Parliament. This led in 1989 and 1990 to disagreement between the Ministries affected by the Braibant Report. M. Evin (Minister of Health) believed the sections on organ donation and epidemiological data rights should be enacted but wanted more debate on commercialisation and the eugenics of research, while M. Curien (Research Minister) wanted further public debate on all issues as he believed a consensus on assisted conception and embryo status had not been reached. Both the Conseil

d'Etat and the CCNE President were against having one wide-ranging law. Some feared a repeat of the 1988 law on therapeutic research that had been passed with the support of only five Deputies. The medical profession lobbied for delays and further discussions (*Le Monde*, 13 December 1989). The Prime Minister also wanted further debate. The only Minister to promote the Braibant Report was M. Arpaillanage, the Justice Minister (*Le Monde*, 17 December 1989).

99 *Sunday Express*, 22 April 1990.
100 Interview with Dreifuss-Netter, Paris, 7 July 1999.
101 *Ibid.*
102 *OPECST*, 1999, p. 97 and p. 100.
103 *Rapport Bioulac*, Tome I, p. 90.
104 *Ibid.*, p. 91.
105 *OPECST Rapport*, 28 February 1992, Tome II, p. 145.
106 *OPECST*, 1999, p. 110.
107 *Ibid.*, p. 193.
108 *Ibid.*, p. 111.
109 HL Official Report, 6 March 1989.
110 Morgan and Lee, *HFEA Act*, pp. 125–135.
111 A. Coote, H. Harman and P. Hewitt, 'The family way', *Social Policy Paper No. 1* (IPPR, 1990).
112 *Observer* 25 March 1990.
113 S. Roseblade, *Debate and Activity*, p. 4.
114 *OPECST Rapport*, 28 February 1992, Tome II, p. 150.
115 *OPECST*, 1999, p. 89.
116 M. Brazier, 'The strengths and weaknesses of British law on reproductive medicine', paper to SPTL King's College London, 23 March 1999.
117 M. Freeman, 'Does surrogacy have a future after Brazier?', *Modern Law Review* 7: 2 spring 1999.
118 M. Brazier, A. Campbell and S. Golombok, *Surrogacy: Review for Health Ministers of Current Arrangements for Payments and Regulation*', October 1998, Cm. 4068.
119 For example deputy Gisèle Halimi in 1983 who publicly spoke in favour of NRTs and adoption (*Choisir* 66, fev/mars/avril 1985), Yvette Roudy, Minister for Women, in May 1985 (A.-M. de Vilaine, 'Citoyennes à part entière' 44, juin–août 1985, pp. 14–21) and Health Minister, Mme Barzach in 1987 when commercial surrogacy was outlawed by case law (*Le Monde*, 1 November 1987).
120 Cunningham, *Statute Law Review*, p. 227.
121 *Human Fertilisation and Embryology: A Framework for Legislation*, Cm 259 HMSO, p. 11.
122 Cusine, *New Reproductive Techniques*, p. 185.
123 Challoner, *The Baby Makers*, p. 104.
124 D. Mehl in Espaces-Ethique AP-HP, *Pratiques hospitalieres et lois de bioéthique*, (June 1999), pp. 48–49.
125 Interview with Françoise Laborie and Simone Novaes, Paris, July 1999.
126 *OPECST*, 1999, p. 103.
127 *Ibid.*, p. 101.
128 *Ibid.*, p. 126
129 *Ibid.*, p. 139.
130 *Ibid.*, pp. 131–133.

131 *Le Monde*, 7 May 1997.

132 *Réponse au Président de la République au sujet du clonage reproductif*, 22 April 1997.

133 *Cloning Issues in Reproduction, Science and Medicine*, HGAC and HFEA (1998).

134 Personal correspondence with Anna Humphrey for PROGRESS, 4 March 1992.

135 *Le Monde*, 19 May 1990.

136 *Le Monde*, 26 November 1991 and 11 February 1992.

137 *Ibid.*

138 *Avant-projet de loi sur les sciences de la vie et les droits de l'homme*, 1989, p. 23.

139 Morgan and Lee, *HFEA Act*, p. 113.

140 *Ibid.*, pp. 90–91.

141 *Guardian*, 13 March 1991.

142 OPECST *Rapport*, 28 February 1992, Tome II, pp. 364–367.

Chapter 8

1   D. Coole, *Women in Political Theory* (Harvester Wheatsheaf, 1988) p. 255.

2   See discussion of medicalisation in Chapter 1 of this book.

3   RCOG, *The Management of Infertility in Tertiary Care* (January 2000).

4   Council of Europe Third Symposium on Bioethics 'Medically assisted procreation and the protection of the human embryo', Strasbourg, 15–18 December 1996.

5   Countries such as Italy, Ireland and Belgium (L. Nielsen, 'Procreative tourism, genetic testing and the law', in N. Lowe, and G. Douglas eds, *Families across Frontiers* (Kluwer, 1996).

6   R. Dworkin, *Life's Dominion: an Argument about Abortion and Euthanasia* (Harper-Collins, 1993).

7   C. Daniels, *At Women's Expense: State Power and the Politics of Fetal Rights* (Harvard University Press, 1993), p. 29.

8   McColgan, *Women under the Law*, p. 269.

9   B. Hewson, 'The Human Rights Act 1988 and "fetal rights" – a new threat to women's autonomy?', in Pro-Choice Forum, 'Abortion, ethics and the law: issues for the new millennium' (October 2000).

10 Sheldon, *Beyond Control*, p. 163.

11 C. Smart, *Feminism and the Power of the Law* (Routledge, 1989).

12 For an examination of changing patient behaviour see Vuckovic, N. and Nichter, M., 'Changing patterns of pharmaceutical practice in the United States', *Social Science and Medicine*, 44, 9, 1285–1302, 1997, p. 1285.

13 Sheldon, *Beyond Control*, p. 166.

14 Smart, *Feminism and the Power of the Law*, p. 164.

15 Sheldon, *Beyond Control*, p. 166.

16 *Ibid*, p. 169.

17 M. Fox, 'A woman's right to choose?', in *The Future of Human Reproduction* (Oxford University Press, 1998).

18 J. Van Dyk, *Manufacturing Babies and Public Consent: Debating the New Reproductive Technologies* (Macmillan, 1995), p. 203.

19 Lovenduski, *Women and European Politics*.

Select bibliography

British government publications

Circular 517, April 1924.

Circular 1622, May 1937.

Circular (H. N. (80)46), December 1980.

Circular (H. S. C. (I. S.)32), 1974.

Early Day Motion no. 1324, Hansard Order Paper No. 165, 1 November 1989, Ref: H 5309, 'Impregnation of lesbian women'.

'Human fertilisation and embryology: a framework for legislation', November 1987, Cm 259.

Lane Report, Cmnd 5579.

'Legislation on Human Infertility Services and Embryology', December 1986, Cm 46.

Memorandum 153/MCW, July 1930.

Report of the Health Service Commissioner, case number W. 376/86–87, 'Administration of a waiting list for infertility treatment', 1988.

French government publications

'Avant-projet de loi sur les sciences de la vie et les droits de l'homme', 1989 (Loi Braibant).

Conseil d'Etat, 'Rapport sur la Protection et le Statut de l'Enfant', mai 1990.

Conseil d'Etat, *Sciences de la vie, de l'éthique au droit* (Documentation Française, 1988).

Journal Officiel, Réponses Ministérielles, 26 mars 1987.

Lettres d'information published by the CCNE: octobre 1985, mars 1988, juin 1990.

Ministère des affaires sociales et de la solidarité nationale, dossier guide, août 1984.

OPECST *Rapport sur les sciences de la vie et les droits de l'homme: Bouleversements sans contrôle ou législation à la française*, No. 2588 (Assemblée Nationale)/ No. 262 (Sénat), 28 fev. 1992; Tome I: *Questions-clefs et réponses contradictoires*; Tome II: *Textes et Documents* (Economica, 1992).

OPECST Rapport Claeys/Huriet, *L'application de la loi no. 94–654 du 29 juillet 1994* (No. 1407 Assemblé Nationale/ No. 232 Sénat), 18 février 1999.

'Projet de loi' (No. 2599) relatif au corps humain et modifiant le code civil, 25 mars 1992; 'Projet de loi' (No. 2600) relatif au don et à l'utilisation des éléments et produits du corps humain et à la procréation médicalement assistée, et modifiant le code de la santé publique; 'Projet de loi' relatif au traitement de données nominatives ayant pour fin la recherche en vue de la protection ou l'amélioration de la santé et modifiant la loi no. 78–17 du 6 janvier 1978 relative à l'informatique, aux fichiers et aux libertés.

Proposition Caillavet, no. 47, J. O. Sénat, 1978.

Proposition de loi Serusclat, 'relative à la procréation humaine médicalement assistée' (proposition L. 677–13), July 1989.

Proposition de loi Boutin, 'tendant à assurer le respect de l'integrité de la personne', December 1989.

Rapport fait au nom de la commission sur les projets de loi, No. 2871 (Assemblée Nationale), 30 juin 1992 (also known as the Rapport Bioulac); Tome I: *Exposé Général, Auditions et Discussion Générale, Examen des Articles et Tableau Comparatif du Projet no. 2599*; Tome II: *Examen des Articles et Tableaux Comparatifs des Projets nos. 2600 et 2601*.

Rapport Mézard, no. 450, J. O. Senat débats, 6 juin 1980.

Vivre au féminin, Cahiers Français no. 171 (mai–août 1975).

Archives

ALRA, 'Breaking Chains' 55, spring 1992.

Association La Harpe – Enfant de Droit, 'La Revolution des petits pas', undated.

Bibliotheque Marguerite Durand, Paris, file on pre-Second World War newspaper cuttings on abortion, dossiers on contraception, abortion and on NRTs.

CERES newsletters, May 1989 to spring 1993.

CNIDF, 'La Stérilité: Les mots justes', undated.

ICNY (New York Surrogacy Agency), 'Alternatives for Childless Couples', July 1990.

INSERM, 'Ethique – revue de presse', octobre–décembre 1989.

Laborie, Françoise, 'Draft plan for a research project on: "Europe and human reproductive technologies: new reproductive techniques, the factors and issues involved in their development"', 1990.

Mariette Sineau, Paris, dossier on abortion law and cases, September 1990.

MFPF dossier de presse, 'Parentalités nouvelles', April 1987.

MFPF file on their structure and organisation, September 1990.

MFPF, '"La puce a l'oreille"' numero spécial: sterilisation feminine et masculine, ligature des trompes, vasectomie', undated.

Oxford Women's Health Action Group, 'Whose choice? What women have to say about contraception' (Trojan Press, undated).

SPUC, *Human Concern*, Winter 1991.

WHRRIC file on NRTs.

Women's Health (formerly WRRIC/WHRRIC) newsletters nos. 12–15.

Interviews

In Paris

Janine-Mossuz Lavau, 'Fondation nationale des sciences Politiques', 7 September 1990.

Mariette Sineau, 'Fondation nationale des sciences politiques', 8 September 1990.

Simone Novaes, Françoise Laborie, Michèle Fellous, CNRS researchers, 10 September 1990 and 8 July 1999.

Michel Grimaldi, academic lawyer, 10 September 1990.

Guy Braibant, Conseiller d'Etat, 11 September 1990.

Cécile Dauphin, historian, 11 September 1990.

Odile Dhavernas, lawyer, 12 September 1990.

Dominique Francoise Dreifus-Netter, 9 July 1999.

Philippe Granet, 8 July 1999.

In London

Naomi Pfeffer, 28 September 1991.

Books and articles

Adorno, R., *La Bioéthique et la dignité de la personne* (PUF, 1997).

Albistur, M., and Armogathe, D., *Histoire de féminisme français du moyen age à nos jours* (Des Femmes, 1978).

Ambroselli, C., *Actes* (été 1985), 16.

Ardagh, J., *The New France* (Penguin, 1977), 370–399.

Aron, J. P., *Misérable et glorieuse: La femme de XIXe siècle* (Fayard, 1980).

Atkins, S. and Hoggett, B., *Women and the Law* (Basil and Blackwell, 1984).

Badinter E., 'Ces hommes qui veulent enfanter', *Le Nouvel Observateur* (2–8 mai 1986), 38–40.

Banks, O., *Faces of Feminism: A Study of Feminism as a Social Movement* (Robertson, 1981).

Barnett, H., *Sourcebook on Feminist Jurisprudence* (Cavendish, 1997).

Bataille, C., 'RU 486: C'est aux femmes de faire la loi!', *Cahiers du Féminisme* 47 (1988), 4–7.

Batiot, A., 'The political construction of sexuality: the contraception and abortion issues in France, 1965–75', in Cerny, P., ed., *Social Movement and Protest in France* (Frances Pinter, 1982).

Batiot, A., 'Radical democracy and feminist discourse: the case of France', in Drude Dahlerup ed., *The New Women's Movement: Feminism and Political Power in Europe and the USA* (Sage Publications Ltd, 1986).

Baudouin, J.-L., and Labrusse-Riou, C., *Produire l'homme: De quel droit?* (PUF, 1987).

Baxter, A., *Time Out* (21–28 February 1990), 9.

Bellegarde-Phan, F., 'Les Déclarations de grossesse (en France) ou les déclarations de grossesse dans l'ancienne France', in *Contraception, Fertility, Sterility*, 8(4): 357–361, (1980).

Bensedon, N., *Que sais-je? Les droits de la femme* (PUF, 1980).

Birke, L., Himmelweit, S., and Vines, G., *Tomorrow's Child: Reproductive Technologies in the 1990s* (Virago, 1990).

Bonnet, C., 'Nouvelles méthodes de procréation et adoption: une chance pour les enfants?', in MFPF, *L'Ovaire-dose?:Les nouvelles méthodes de procréation* (Syros/Alternatives, 1989).

Bouchier, D., *The Feminist Challenge* (Macmillan Press, 1983).

Branca, P., *Women in Europe Since 1750* (Croom Helm, 1978).

Brazier, M., 'Embryos' "rights": abortion and research', in Freeman, M. D. A., ed., *Medicine, Patients and the Law* (Stevens, 1988).

Brazier, M., *Medicine, Patients and the Law* (Pelican, 1987; 2nd edn, Penguin, 1992).

Brazier, M., Campbell, A., Golombok, S., 'Surrogacy: review for health ministers of current arrangements for payments and regulation', Cm 4068 (October 1998).

Brazier, M., 'The strengths and weaknesses of British law on reproductive medicine', Society of Public Teachers of Law, King's College London, 23 March 1999.

Bridenthal R., ed., *Becoming Visible: Women in European History* (Houghton Mifflin, 1977).

'Bronwyn', 'La preuve par l'œuf? Les nouvelles technologies de la reproduction', *Paris Féministes*, 2: 8–12, (1985).

Brown, N., and Garner, J. F., *French Administrative Law* (3rd edn, Butterworths, 1983)

Brun, A., 'Qui crée quoi?', *Paris Féministes*, 2 (1985), 10–12.

Byk, C., ed., *Procreation artificielle ou en sont l'ethique et le droit?* (Masson, 1989).

Byrne, P., and Lovenduski, J., 'Two new protest groups: the peace and women's movements', in Drucker and Dunleavy *et al.* eds *Developments in British Politics* (Macmillan, 1984).

Campana J., ed., *L'Insemination artificielle* (Labor et Fides, 1982).

Carbonnier, J., *Introduction. Les Personnes* (14e édn, 1982).

Casalis, F., 'Le droit à l'avortement', *Actes*, 70 (1990), 24–27.

Challoner, J., *The Baby Makers: The History of Artificial Conception* (Channel 4 Books, 1999).

Chatel, M.-M., *Malaise dans la procreation* (Albin Michel, 1993).

CNIDF-INSEE, *Femmes en chiffres* (1986).

Colas, D., *L'Etat et les corporatismes* (PUF, 1988).

Colomer, J., *Droit Civil: Régimes matrimoniaux* (Dalloz, 1988).

'Comments arising from Court of Appeal decision on baby with Down's Syndrome', *British Medical Journal*, 283 (22): 513–568, (1981).

Coole, D., *Women in Political Theory* (Wheatsheaf, 1988).

Coote A., Harman, H., Hewitt, P., 'The family way', *Social Policy Paper No. 1* (IPPR, 1990).

Corea, G., *Mother Machine* (Women's Press, 1988).

Cornu, G., *Droit Civil: La Famille* (Editions Montchrestien, 1984).

Crucis, H., 'Le Parlement face aux sciences et technologies', *L'Actualité Juridique – Droit Administratif* (20 juin 1991), 448–455.

Cunningham, R., 'Legislating on human fertilization and embryology in the United Kingdom', *Statute Law Review* (1991), 214–227.

Cusine, D., *New Reproductive Techniques: A Legal Perspective* (Dartmouth Publishing Co., 1990).

Custos, J., 'Jurisprudence', *L'Actualité Juridique – Droit Administratif* (20 juin 1991), 469–473.

Dalton, R. J., and Kuechler, M.,, *Challenging the Political Order. New Social and Political Movements in Western Democracies* (Oxford University Press, 1990).

Daniels, C., *At Women's Expense: State Power and the Politics of Fetal Rights* (Harvard University Press, 1993).

Decluze, D., 'N. T. R.', *Paris Féministes*, 38: 13–14, (1987).

Dekeuwer-Defossé, F., *Dictionnaire juridique: droits des femmes* (Dalloz, 1985).

Delmas-Marty, M., *Que sais-je? Le mariage et le divorce* (PUF, 1988).

Devreux, A.-M., and Ferrand-Picard, M., 'Médicalisation et contrôle social de l'avortement' in P. Ladrière *et al.*, 'La libéralisation de l'avortement', *Revue Française de Sociologie*, 23: 383–396 (numéro spécial) (1982).

Dhavernas, M.-J., 'Peut mieux faire', *Les Temps Modernes*, 482: 154–156, (1986).

Dhavernas, O., *Droits des femmes, pouvoir des hommes* (Seuil, 1978).

Donegan, J. B., *Women and Men Midwives* (Greenwood, 1978).

Donovan, C., 'Donor insemination and the mechanics of reproduction', Department of Social Policy and Social Work, University of Edinburgh, May 1991.

Dourlen-Rollier, A.-M., in Palmer, R., ed., *La stérilisation volontaire en France et dans le monde* (Masson, 1981).

Dreifus, C., *Seizing Our Bodies: The Politics of Women's Health* (Vintage Books, 1978).

Dreifuss-Netter, F., 'Le désir d'enfant face au droit penal', *Revue de Science Criminelle et Droit Pénal Comparé* (1986), 276–296.

Duchen, C., *Feminism in France* (RKP, 1986).

Dworkin, R., *Life's Dominion: An Argument about Abortion and Euthanasia* (Harper Collins, 1993).

Eaubonne d', *Le Féminisme ou la mort: Femmes en mouvement* (Pierre Horay, 1974).

Eckstein, H., *Pressure Group Politics: The Case of the BMA* (Allen & Unwin, 1960).

Eckstein, H., *The English Health Service* (Harvard University Press, 1970).

Ehrenreich, B., *For Her Own Good: 150 Years' Expert Advice to Women* (Pluto Press, 1979).

Erhel, J., 'Parents separés, embryons ballottés', *Libération*, 23–24 septembre 1989, 29.

Faculté de Médecine et Pharmacie de Nantes, Septièmes journées nationales d'études sur l'interruption de grossesse, 30–31 janvier 1988.

Fagot-Largeault, A., and Delaisi de Parseval, G., 'Les Droits de l'embryon (foetus) humain, et la notion de personne humaine potentielle', *Revue de Metaphysique et de Morale*, 3: 361–385 (1987).

Fee E., ed., *Women and Health: The Politics of Sex in Medicine* (Baywood Publishing Co. Inc., 1975/1983).

Ferrand, M. *et al.*, *Que sais-je? L'Interruption Volontaire de Grossesse* (PUF, 1987).

Field, M., *The Comparative Politics of Birth Control: determinants of policy variation and change in developed countries* (Praeger, 1983).

Figuet, F., 'A l'origine des lois sur "IVG"', *Contraception, Fertilité, Sexualité, numéro spécial supplémentaire au Vol. II*, 3: 30–36, (1983).

Finch, J. D., *Health Services Law* (Sweet & Maxwell, 1980).

Folloni, J., 'Avortement: Un procès d'un autre âge', *Cahiers du Féminisme*, 43: 5, (1987).

Ford, N. M., *When Did I Begin?* (Cambridge University Press, 1988).

Foucault, M., *Discipline and Punish: The Birth of the Prison* (Penguin, 1991).

Fox, M., 'A woman's right to choose? A feminist critique', in J. Harris and S. Holm, eds, *The Future of Human Reproduction* (Oxford University Press, 1998).

Fox, M., 'Abortion decision-making: taking men's needs seriously', in Ellie Lee ed., *Abortion Law and Politics Today* (Macmillan, 1998).

Francome, C., *Abortion Freedom* (Allen & Unwin, 1984).

Franklin, S., 'The changing cultural construction of reproduction in the context of new reproductive technology: redefining reproductive choice', Political Studies Association/British Sociological Association Conference on Rights, Politics and Reproductive Technology, London School of Economics, London, 24 February 1990.

Frears, J. R., *France in the Giscard Presidency* (Allen & Unwin, 1981).

Freeman, M., ed., *Women: A Feminist Perspective* (2nd edn, Mayfield Publishing Company USA, 1979).

Freeman, M., 'Does surrogacy have a future after Brazier?, *Modern Law Review*, 7 (1999), 2.

Gardner, R. F. R., *Abortion: The Personal Dilemma* (Paternoster Press, 1972).

Gelb, J., 'Feminism in Britain: politics without power?', in Dahlerup, D., ed., *The New Women's Movement: Feminism and Political Power in Europe and the USA* (Sage Publications Ltd, 1986).

Gibson, S., 'A feminist perspective', University of Manchester Centre for Social Ethics and Policy conference on the Human Fertilisation and Embryology Bill, St Mary's Hospital, Manchester, 9 May 1990.

Gouazé, J., et al., La Loi de 1920 et l'avortement: stratégies de la presse et du droit au procès de Bobigny (Presses Universitaires Lyon, 1979).

Grémion, P., 'La Concertation', in M. Crozier ed., Ou Va l'Administration Française? (Editions d'organisation, 1974).

Grimal, P., ed., Histoire mondiale de la femme (Nouvelle Librairie de France, 1966).

Grubb, A., 'Unborn child (pre-natal injury): homicide and abortion', Medical Law Review, 3 (1): 302–310 (Spring 1995).

Grubb, A., 'Statutory storage period for embryos', Medical Law Review, 4: 211–215 (1996).

Guerrand, R. H., and Ronsin, F., Le Sexe apprivoisé: Jeanne Humbert et la lutte pour le contrôle des naissances (Découverte, 1990).

Halimi, G., La Cause des femmes (Edns. Grasset et Fasquelle, 1973).

Halimi, G., 'Mères porteuses: une question de G. Halimi au Gouvernement', Choisir, 66: 10–12 (1985).

Hanmer, J., and Allen, P., 'Reproductive Engineering: The Final Solution?' in Hanmer, J., and Allen, P., eds, Alice Through the Microscope (Virago, 1980).

Hantrais, L., Contemporary French Society (Macmillan, 1982).

Harris, J., The Value of Life (RKP, 1985).

Harris, J., and Holm, S. (eds), The Future of Human Reproduction (Oxford University Press, 1998).

Harrison, R. J., Pluralism and Corporatism (Allen & Unwin, 1980).

Hayward, J., The One and Indivisible French Republic (Weidenfeld & Nicholson, 1973/1987).

Hayward J., State and Society in Contemporary Europe (Robertson, 1979).

Hayward, J., The State and the Market Economy (Wheatsheaf, 1986).

Heritier-Augé F., 'La Cuisse de Jupiter: réflexions sur les nouveaux modes de procréation', L'Homme, 94: 5–22, (1985).

Heuni, B., Criminal Justice Systems in Europe (Helsinki, 1985).

Hewson, B., 'The Human Rights Act 1988 and "fetal rights" – a new threat to women's autonomy?', in Pro-Choice Forum, Abortion, Ethics and the Law: Issues for the New Millennium (October, 2000).

Hindell, K., and Simms, M., Abortion Law Reformed (Peter Owen, 1971).

Horne, L., 'Comments on the Warnock Report', Critical Social Policy (April 1984), 112–114.

Iglitzin Ross, F., ed., Women in the World: A Comparative Study (Clio Press, 1976).

Illich, I., Medical Nemesis: The Expropriation of Health (Pantheon, 1976)

International Planned Parenthood Federation, The Human Right to Family Planning (IPPF, 1983).

Isambert F., et al., Contraception et avortement: Dix ans de Débat dans la Presse, 1965–1974 (CNRS, 1979).

Jacquinot, F., 'Le Rapport du comité d'ethique sur la personne humaine', Gazette du Palais (1988), 723.

Jacquinot, F., 'La Première Loi relative a l'experimentation humaine', Gazette du Palais, 4 (1989), 107–108.

Jenson, J., 'Struggling for identity: the women's movement and the state in Western Europe', West European Politics, 8(4): 5–18 (1985).

Jones, P., 'The British Medical Association: public good or private interest?' in Marsh, D., ed., *Pressure Politics* (Junction Books, 1983).

Jordan, A. G., and Richardson, J. J., *British Politics and the Policy Process: An Arena Approach* (Allen & Unwin, 1987).

Jordan, A. G., 'Policy Community versus "new" institutionalist ambiguity', *Political Studies*, 37: 470–484 (1990).

Kandel, F., '10 ans de féminisme – dossier', *Politique d'Aujourd'hui*, 3–4: 98 (1981).

Kanter, H., *Sweeping Statements: Writings from the Women's Liberation Movement 1981–83* (Women's Press, 1984)

Kay, E., 'Equality and difference: the case of pregnancy', *Berkeley Women's Law Journal*, 1: 21–35, (1985).

Kayser, P., 'Les Limites morales et juridiques de la procréation artificielle' (1987) *Dalloz*, 189.

Kennedy, I., *Treat Me Right* (Clarendon Press, 1988).

Keown, J., 'Miscarriage: a medico-legal analysis', *Cambridge Law Review* (October 1984), 581–604.

Keown, J., *Abortion, Doctors and the Law* (Cambridge University Press, 1988).

Kitschelt, H., 'Political opportunity structures and political protest: anti-nuclear movements in four democracies', *British Journal of Political Studies*, 16: 57–85.

Klein, R., talk given on NRTs from a feminist perspective, Lyceum Club, Melbourne, Meeting of the Australian Federation of University Women, 9 April 1987.

Knibiehler, Y., *La Femme et les médecins* (Hachette, 1983).

Knight, B., *Legal Aspects of Medical Practice* (Churchill Livingstone, 1976).

L'Abbée, X., 'Sommaires commentés: droits de l'enfant', 4 (1994) *Dalloz*, 30–32

'La famille: une idée moderne', *L'Express* (13 June 1986).

Laborie, F., 'Ceci est une éthique', *Les Temps Modernes*, 462: 1214–1253, (1985); 463: 1518–1543, (1985).

Langlois, H., 'Les Comités d'éthiques locaux', *Etudes* (February 1988), 177–187.

Larson, M. S., *The Rise of Professionalism: A Sociological Analysis* (University of California Press, 1977).

Latham, M., 'Reform and revolution: the campaigns for abortion in Britain and France', in Lee, E. ed., *Abortion Law and Politics Today* (Macmillan, 1998).

Latham, M., 'Regulating the new reproductive technologies: a cross-Channel comparison', *Medical Law International*, 3: 89–115, (1998).

Latham, M.,'The French parliamentary guidelines of May 1997: clarification or fudge?', *Medical Law International*, 3: 235–241, (1998).

Lattimer, M., *Pro-Choice Forum Update*, 11 November 1999.

Laubier, C., ed., *The Condition of Women in France* (RKP, 1990).

Leathard A., *The Fight for Family Planning: The Development of Family Planning Services in Britain 1921–1974* (Macmillan Press, 1980).

Leclerc, L., 'Le Bébé-eprouvette boum', *Quotidien de Paris* (21 janvier 1988), 19.

Lee, E. ed., *Abortion Law and Politics Today* (Macmillan Press, 1998).

Leeson J., and Gray, *Women and Medicine* (Tavistock, 1978).

Legrand, J., 'L'Occasion manquée de la gauche', *F Magazine*, 23 (January 1980), 10–12.

Leridon, H., *et al.*, *La Seconde Révolution contraceptive* (INED/PUF, 1987).

Lernout, F., 'Procréation médicalement assistée: non aux progrès à hauts risques', *La Croix* (17 February 1988).

Levine, V., *Victorian Feminism* (Hutchinson, 1987).

Leys, C., *Politics in Britain* (Heinemann 1983).

Lockwood, M., 'When does a life begin?', in Lockwood, M., ed., *Moral Dilemmas in Modern Medicine* (Oxford University Press, 1986).

Lorber, J., *Women Physicians* (Tavistock, 1984).

Lovecy, J., 'An end to French exceptionalism?', *West European Politics*, 22:4 (October 1999).

Lovenduski J., *Politics of the Second Electorate* (RKP, 1981).

Lovenduski, J., *Women and European Politics* (Wheatsheaf, 1986).

Lovenduski, J., and Ootshoorn, J., *The New Politics of Abortion* (Sage, 1986).

Lucas, F., 'Les Droits de la vie; biologie, ethique et droit', *L'Homme et la Société*, 85: 164–171 (1987).

Malaurie, P., et Aynès, L., *Droit Civil. La Famille* (Cujas, 1989).

Marks E., and de Courtivron, I., *New French Feminisms* (Harvester Press, 1980).

Maroteaux, F., *et al.*, 'Réflexions sur les problèmes éthiques du diagnosic anténatal', *Archives Françaises de Pédiatrie*, 4: 445–8 (1984).

Marsh, D., and Chambers, J., *Abortion Politics* (Junction Books, 1981).

Marsh, D., and Chambers, J., 'The abortion lobby: pluralism at work?' in Marsh, D., ed., *Pressure Politics* (Junction Books, 1983).

Marsh, D., and Rhodes, R. A. W., eds, *Policy Networks in British Government* (Clarendon Press, 1992).

Mason, J. K., and McCall Smith, R. A., *Law and Medical Ethics*, 5th edn (Butterworths, 1999).

Maynard, A., *Health Care in the EC* (Croom Helm, 1975).

McColgan, A., *Women under the Law: The False Promise of Human Rights* (Longman, 2000).

McLean, S., *Legal Issues in Medicine* (Gower, 1981).

McLean, S., ed., *Legal Issues in Human Reproduction* (Gower, 1989).

Mémeteau, G., 'Le Droit médical de la famille', in Jean Carbonnier ed., *Le Droit non-civil de la famille* (PUF, 1983)

Mény, Y., 'The national and international context of French Policy Communities', *Political Studies* 37: (1989), 387–399.

Méricourt, A., 'Bio-éthique: faut-il une loi?', *Cahiers du feminisme*, 52: 10–11, (1990).

Meulders-Klein, T., 'Le Droit de l'enfant face au droit à l'enfant et les procréations médicalement assistées', *Revue Trimestrielle de Droit Civil*, 87:4 (1988).

Meyers, D., *The Human Body and the Law* (Edinburgh University Press, 1970).

MFPF, *D'une Revolte à une lutte: 25 ans d'histoire du planning familial* (Editions Tiercé, 1983).

MFPF, 'Inculpation de deux militantes du MFPF pour 'publicité et provocation à l'avortement', *Livre PFU*, 58: 23–4 (1986).

MFPF, *L'Ovaire-dose?:Les nouvelles méthodes de procréation* (Syros/Alternatives, 1989).

MFPF, 'Dix ans plus tard', *Paris Féministes* (1–15 October 1989), 18–19.

Michaud, M., 'Situation juridique du comité national d'éthique', *Etudes* (1988), 37–44.

Moran, M., *Politics and Society in Britain* (Macmillan, 1985).

Morgan, D., and Lee, R. G., *Blackstone's Guide to the Human Fertilisation and Embryology Act 1990* (Blackstone, 1991),

Mort, F., *Dangerous Sexualities: Medico-moral Politics in England since 1830* (RKP, 1987).

Moses, C. G., *French Feminism in the Late Nineteenth Century* (Suny, 1984).

Moutet, J., 'Technologie, familles et droit', *Pénélope*, 9 (automne 1983), 84–87.

Moutet, J., 'La Bioéthique au microscope du droit naturel', *Actes* (1990), 19–25.

Naudin, C., 'Ethique: les propositions du Conseil d'Etat', *La Croix* (24 mars 1988).

Neirinck, C., *De la bioéthique au bio-droit* (Librairie générale de droit et de juris-prudence, 1994).

Neirinck, C., 'Le droit de la filiation et la procréation médicalement assistée', *Les Petites Affiches*, 149: 54 (1994).

Nielsen, L., 'Procreative tourism, genetic testing and the law', in Lowe, N., Douglas, G. (eds) *Families across Frontiers* (Kluwer, 1996).

Novaes, S., 'Social integration of technical innovation: sperm banking and AID in France and in the United States', *Social Science Information* 24(3): 569–584 (1985).

Novaes, S., 'Vide juridique: notion-écran en l'absence de repères sociaux? L'encadrement législatif de la procréation artificielle', in *Sociologie du Droit, Sociologie et Droit: Journées Annuelles de la Société de Sociologie* (Bordeaux, 20–21 November 1987), 1–13.

Novaes, S., 'Giving, receiving, paying', *International Journal of Technology Assessment in Health Care*, 5(4): 639–657 (1989).

Novaes, S., 'Circulation extra-corporelle de gamètes: pratiques institutionnelles et refer-ences ethiques', in *Rapport de fin de contrat no. 212/86, Mission Interministérielle Recherche et Expérimentation*, Paris, June 1990, 7–172.

Novaes, S., 'Shaping guidelines for genetic screening in reproductive medicine: decision-making by the Genetics Advisory Board of the French Federation of CECOS Semen Banks', Sixth Annual Meeting of the International Society for Technology Assessment in Health Care, Houston, Texas, 20–23 May 1990.

Oberdorff, H., 'L'Administration publique face au progrés médical', *L'Actualité Juri-dique – Droit Administratif* (20 June 1991), 411–419.

Okin, S. M., *Women in Contemporary Political Thought* (Princeton University Press, 1979).

Outshoorn, J., 'Abortion law reform: A woman's right to choose?', in Buckley, M., and Anderson, M., eds, *Women, Equality and Europe* (Macmillan, 1988).

Paintin, D., *Twenty Questions about Emergency Contraception – Answered* (Birth Control Trust, March 1998).

Pateman C., and Gross, *Feminist Challenges: Social and Political Theory* (Allen & Unwin, 1986).

Pelletier, M., 'PMA: l'opposition enfin dans le débat': spécial colloque', *Dialogue* (May–June 1985), 6.

Petchesky, R. P., 'Foetal images: the power of visual culture in the politics of reproduc-tion', in M. Stanworth ed., *The Sexual Politics of Reproduction* (Polity, 1987).

Pfeffer, N., and Quick, A., *Infertility Services: A Desperate Case* (Greater London Association of Community Health Councils, 1988).

Pfeffer, N., *The Stork and the Syringe: A Political History of Reproductive Medicine* (Polity Press, 1993).

Pickles, D., *The Government and Politics of France* (Methuen, 1973).

Pingaud, B., *et al.*, *L'Avortement: Histoire d'un Débat* (Flammarion, 1975).

Potts, M., *et al.* eds, 'Natural human fertility: social and biological determinants', *Proceedings of the 23rd annual symposium of the Eugenics Society* (Macmillan/ Eugenics Society, 1988).

Purdy, L., 'Surrogate mothering: exploitation or empowerment?', *Bioethics*, 3(1): 19–44, (1989).

Rendall, J., *The Origins of Modern Feminism: Women in Britain, France and the USA 1780–1860* (Macmillan, 1985).

Rhodes, R. A. W, *Beyond Westminster and Whitehall* (Unwin Hyman, 1988).

Rich, A., 'Anger and tenderness: the experience of motherhood', in Elizabeth Whitelegg, *The Changing Experience of Women* (Robertson/Open University, 1982).

Richardson, J., *et al.* eds, *Policy Styles in Western Europe* (Allen & Unwin, 1982).

Rivera, R., *et al.*, 'The mechanism of action of hormonal contraceptives and intra-uterine contraceptive devices', *American Journal of Obstetrics and Gynecology*, 181: 1263–1269, (1999).

Roberts G., and Lovecy, J., *West European Politics Today* (Manchester University Press, 1983).

Ronsin, F., *La Grève des ventres: Propagande néomalthusienne et baisse de la natalité en France XIXe-XXe siècles* (Aubier-Montaigne, 1980).

Rose, H., 'Wanting babies', *Nursing Times* (September 1984), 12–14.

Roseblade, S., 'IVF: debate and activity at the local level', University of Manchester MSc. Thesis, 1988.

Roudy, Y., *Citoyennes à Part Entière*, 43 (mai/juin 1985), 18–21.

Rousset, D., 'Témoignage', in 'Mouvement français pour le planning familial', *L'Ovaire-dose?: les nouvelles méthodes de procréation* (Syros/Alternatives, 1989).

Rover, C., *Love, Morals and the Feminists* (RKP, 1970).

Rowbotham, S., *Hidden from History* (Pluto Press, 1974).

Rubellin-Devichi, C., 'Le Droit, la bioéthique et les nouvelles méthodes de procréation', *Neuropsychiatre de l'Enfance*, 35: 106, (1987).

Rubellin-Devichi, C., 'Personnes et droits de famille', *Revue Trimestrielle de Droit Civil*, 87:2 (1988).

Ruedig, A., 'Peace and ecology movements in Western Europe', *West European Politics*, 11(1) 27–39, (1988).

Salat-Baroux, F., *Les Lois de bioéthique* (Dalloz, 1998).

Sarde, M., *Regards sur les françaises (Xe–XXe siècles)* (Seuil, 1985).

Saulnier, P., *et al.*, 'Dix ans de féminisme en France', *Politique d'Aujourd'hui*, 3–4: 87–102, (1981).

Scales, A., 'Towards a feminist jurisprudence', *Indiana Law Journal*, 56(3): 375–444, (1980–81).

Segalen, M., '"Généreuse et raisonnable": L'église et le contrôle de la fécondité dans les années 1950', in *Populations et Cultures* (AFL, 1989).

Segalen, M., *Sociologie de la Famille* (Armand Colin, 1988).

Serault, J., 'Les Transformations de mdèle familial et de ses fonctions socio-economiques', in Carbonnier, J., ed., *Le Droit non-civil de la famille* (PUF, 1983).

Sériaux, A., 'Droit naturel et procréation artificielle: Quelle jurisprudence?', *Dalloz* (1985), 53.

Serusclat, J., 'Irruption des techniques de procreation médicalement assistée et leurs incidences', in 'La Protection Sociale et ses Maux', *L'Evenement Européen*, 5: 28–40, (1989).

Shapiro, W., 'Whatever happened to Warnock?', *Nursing Times* (29 October 1986), 31–32.

Sheldon, S., *Beyond Control: Medical Power and Abortion* (Pluto Press, 1997).

Sheldon, S., and Thomson, M., *Feminist Perspectives on Health Care Law* (Cavendish, 1998).

Shorter, E., *A History of Women's Bodies* (Allen Lane 1982).

Sims, P., 'Test tube babies in debate', *Ethics and Medicine: A Christian Perspective*, 4: 3, (1988).

Skegg, P. D. G., *Law, Ethics and Medicine* (Clarendon Press, 1988).

Smart, C., *Feminism and the Power of the Law* (Routledge, 1989).

Smart, C., 'Sexual subjects and unlawful bodies: law, sexuality and reproduction', Political Studies Association/British Sociological Association Conference on Rights, Politics and Reproductive Technology, London School of Economics, London, 24 February 1990.

Smart, C. ed., *Regulating Womanhood: Historical Essays on Marriage, Motherhood and Sexuality* (Routledge, 1992).

Smith, L. J. F., 'The abortion controversy 1936–77: a case study in "emergence of law"', Ph.D. dissertation, University of Edinburgh, 1979.

Soutoul, P., *La Responsabilité médicale et les problèmes médico-légaux en gynécologie et reproduction* (Maloine, 1989).

Stanworth M. ed., *Reproductive Techniques: Gender, Motherhood and Medicine* (Polity Press, 1987).

Stanworth, M., 'Defining reproductive technology as a feminist issue', Political Studies Association/British Sociological Association Conference on Rights, Politics and Reproductive Technology, London School of Economics, London, 24 February 1990.

Steinberg, D. L., *Bodies in Glass: Genetics, Eugenics, Embryo Ethics* (Manchester University Press, 1997).

Suleiman, E., *Politics, Power and Bureaucracy in France* (Princeton University Press, 1974).

Terré F., *L'Enfant de l'esclave* (Flammarion, 1987).

Terré F., and Simler P., *Droit Civil. Régimes Matrimoniaux* (Dalloz, 1989).

Testart J., and Frydman, R., 'Human IVF: actual problems and prospects', INSERM Symposium 24, 19/22 September 1984 (Elsevier Science, 1985).

Testart, J., *L'Oeuf transparent* (Flammarion, 1986).

Testart, J., *Le Désir du gène* (Edns. F. Bourin, 1992).

Thébaud, P., *et al.*, *Histoire des femmes* (Plon, 1990).

Thibault, O., *Des enfants comment?* (Edns. Chronique sociale, 1984).

Thibault, O., 'Ne tirez pas sur le biologiste!', *Citoyennes à Part Entière*, 44: 14–15 (1985).

Thomson, J. J., 'A Defence of Abortion', in R. M. Dworkin ed., *The Philosophy of Law* (Oxford University Press, 1977).

Thouvenin, D., 'La Disponibilité du corps humain: corps sujet ou corps objet?', *Actes* (1985), 35–41.

Touraine, A., ed., *Mouvements sociaux d'aujourd'hui* (Les Editions ouvrières, 1982).

Tournier, D., 'Le Meilleur des mondes', *Elle*, 2199 (1988), 10–23.

Trifirino, L., Thèse doctorale médicale, Université de Paris VII, 1971.

Tristan, A., et De Pisan, A., *Histoires du MLF* (Calmann-Levy, 1977).

Ungerson, C., ed., *Women and Social Policy* (Macmillan, 1985).

Valance, F., and Lhaiik, H., 'Les Françaises se rebiffent', *Le Nouvel Observateur* (29 November 1985), 39–45.

Van Dyk, J., *Manufacturing Babies and Public Consent: Debating the New Reproductive Technologies* (Macmillan, 1995).

Verret, P., 'La Valse-surprise: histoire du mariage d'ouvrier', *Autrements série Mutations* 78, 105 Mariage/Mariages (1989), 78–83.

Vesale, C., *La Fabrique du corps humain: Ethique médicale et droits de l'homme* (Actes Sud, 1987).

Vicinus, M., *Suffer and Be Still: Women in the Victorian Age* (Indiana University Press, 1972).

Vilaine, A.-M., de, 'Nouvelles méthodes de procreation: Pour qui, pourquoi?', *Citoyennes à Part Entière* 44: 16 (1985).

Vilaine, A.-M. de, 'Femmes: Une autre culture?', in A. – M. de Vilaine, L. Gavarini, M. Le Coadic eds, *Maternité en Mouvement* (Edns. Saint-Martin/Presses Universitaires Grenoble, 1986)

Vincent, M., *Femmes: Quelle libération?* (Editions Sociales, 1976).

Vinteuil, F., *Cahiers du Féminisme*, 39: 32–33 (1987).

Voluntary Licensing Authority, *The Third Report of the Voluntary Licensing Authority for Human IVF and Embryology* (Medical Research Council, 1988).

Vuckovic, N., and Nichter, M., 'Changing patterns of pharmaceutical practice in the United States', *Social Science and Medicine*, 44(9): 1285–1302 (1997).

Walsh, V., 'Contraception: the growth of a technology' in Hanmer, J., and Allen, P., eds, *Alice Through the Microscope* (Virago, 1980).

Warnock, M.,'The artificial family' in Lockwood, M., ed. *Moral Dilemmas in Modern Medicine* (OUP, 1986).

Webb, C., *Feminist Practice in Women's Health Care* (John Wiley and Sons Ltd, 1986).

Weeks, J., *Sex, Politics and Society: The Regulation of Sexuality since 1800* (Longman, 1981).

World Health Organisation, *Health for All 2000: Fertility Awareness Methods*, report on a WHO Workshop, Poland, 26–29 August 1986 (EUR/HFA, target 15).

WHRRIC, 'Warnock Report: oppose scientists' control over women's bodies', *Outwrite*, August 1989 (WHRRIC file on NRTs).

Wollstonecroft, M., *A Vindication of the Rights of Woman with Strictures on Political and Moral Subjects* (1792; reprint Garland, 1974).

Wright, V., *The Government and Politics of France* (Hutchinson, 1983).

Wright, M., 'Policy Community, Policy Network and comparative industrial policies', *Political Studies*, 36(4): 593–612 (1988).

Zeldin, T., *The French* (Flamingo, 1983).

Zola, I. K., 'Medicine as an institution of social control', *Sociological Review*, 20: 487–504 (1972).

Zola, I. K., 'In the name of health and illness: on some socio-political consequences of medical influence', *Social Science and Medicine*, 9: 83–87 (1975).

Index